T0291367

Institutional Change and China Capitalism
Frontier of Cliometrics and its Application to China

Transformations in Banking, Finance and Regulation

Print ISSN: 2752-5821
Online ISSN: 2752-583X

Series Editors: Sabri Boubaker
(*EM Normandie Business School, France*)
Duc Khuong Nguyen
(*IPAG Business School, France*)

Presently, the banking and finance sectors evolve within a globalized and highly uncertain environment. Each business and financial decision requires careful consideration of country-specific and international factors due to high levels of shock transmission and volatility spillovers. Furthermore, it would be remiss to omit the COVID-19 health crisis, which caused harmful effects to all areas of the real economy and made profound changes in the way our firms, economies, and markets used to function.

Many other already well-known aspects, including the repercussions of quantitative easing policies, disruptive technologies in finance (e.g., FinTech, Big Data, Data Analytics, Artificial Intelligence, and Blockchains), as well as innovative financing instruments for startups (e.g., ICOs and crowdfunding) are currently revolutionizing banking and finance and posing numerous challenges to regulatory bodies and policymakers. Climate change emergencies also put pressure on governments and firms worldwide to improve policy on governance, corporate social responsibility, and sustainability practices.

This book series "Transformations in Banking, Finance, and Regulation" attempts to address these issues by focusing on transformative perspectives in banking and finance. Accordingly, it provides evidence-based guidance, recommendations, and pathways to assist businesses and policy decision-makers through an interdisciplinary and in-depth understanding of ongoing changes in the behavior of economic agents.

Published

Vol. 2   *Institutional Change and China Capitalism: Frontier of Cliometrics
          and its Application to China*
          edited by Antoine Le Riche, Antoine Parent and Lei Zhang

Vol. 1   *Financial Transformations Beyond the COVID-19 Health Crisis*
          edited by Sabri Boubaker and Duc Khuong Nguyen

Institutional Change and China Capitalism

Frontier of Cliometrics and its Application to China

Editors

Antoine Le Riche
Sichuan University, China

Antoine Parent
University of Paris 8, France

Lei Zhang
Sichuan University, China

 **World Scientific**

NEW JERSEY · LONDON · SINGAPORE · BEIJING · SHANGHAI · HONG KONG · TAIPEI · CHENNAI · TOKYO

Published by

World Scientific Publishing Europe Ltd.

57 Shelton Street, Covent Garden, London WC2H 9HE

Head office: 5 Toh Tuck Link, Singapore 596224

USA office: 27 Warren Street, Suite 401-402, Hackensack, NJ 07601

Library of Congress Cataloging-in-Publication Data

Names: Riche, Antoine Le, editor. | Parent, Antoine, editor. | Zhang, Lei, editor.
Title: Institutional change and China capitalism : frontier of cliometrics and its application
    to China / editors, Antoine Le Riche, Sichuan University, China,
    Antoine Parent, University of Paris 8, France, Lei Zhang, Sichuan University, China.
Description: Hackensack, NJ : World Scientific, 2022. | Series: Transformations in banking,
    finance and regulation, 2752-5821 ; 2 | Includes bibliographical references and index.
Identifiers: LCCN 2021035002 | ISBN 9781800611221 (hardcover) |
    ISBN 9781800611238 (ebook) | ISBN 9781800611245 (ebook other)
Subjects: LCSH: Organizational change--China. | China--Economic policy--21st century. |
    China--Economic conditions--21st century. | Economic development--China. |
    Capital market--Psychological aspects. | Econometrics.
Classification: LCC HD58.8 .I5777 2022 | DDC 658.4/060951--dcundefined
LC record available at https://lccn.loc.gov/2021035002

British Library Cataloguing-in-Publication Data
A catalogue record for this book is available from the British Library.

For any available supplementary material, please visit
https://www.worldscientific.com/worldscibooks/10.1142/Q0331#t=suppl

Desk Editors: Nimal Koliyat/Michael Beale/Shi Ying Koe

Typeset by Stallion Press
Email: enquiries@stallionpress.com

Preface

The idea of this book was conceived during the two terms as Visiting Professor at the School of Economics, Sichuan University in December 2018 and May 2019. The research has benefited from two French grants, "Hubert Curien Research Fellowship" (Program Campus France 2019: "Discovery of China" 942060f) and program PHC XU GUANGQI, project n°45599rf, 2020, and one Chinese Grant ("教育部直属高校特色项目：宏观经济与金融经济创新人才培养体系建设聘请外教特色项目"). Some of the original essays in this book were first presented at seminars in complexity economics, Sichuan University, China, in November 2018 and May 2019, and at the *12th International Conference on the Chinese Economy*, "A New Era for China: Growth Sustainability and Broaden International Development," CERDI, IDREC, University of Clermont Auvergne, France and CCES, Fudan University, Shanghai, China, held in Clermont-Ferrand, 24–25 October, 2019. The papers have been contributed by scholars from China, France, Germany, Italy, and the United States. They address a wide range of topics that highlight China's move to capitalism and, in each case, help us understand that China's transition to capitalism has been foremost a matter of institutional revolution.

The book aims to provide a radically new view of the rise of Chinese capitalism by drawing on recent developments in complexity economics, macroeconomic dynamics, network analysis, and behavioral finance to illustrate the various facets of China's transition to capitalism. Each of the developments described is placed in a short

historical time frame (mid-20th century), i.e. each chapter constitutes a historical depth which is usually lacking in the analyzes of
Chinese take-off. We wanted to innovate in this book by addressing
in China's take-off questions at the frontier of research in cliometrics
and complexity economics. The book, structured in three parts, seeks
to account for the profound institutional change that led China to
progressively adopt capitalism, using empirical and theoretical techniques as well as in terms of network structure.

Together these papers attest to the vitality of current research in
cliometrics and complexity economics.

About the Editors

Antoine Le Riche is Associate Professor at the School of Economics, Sichuan University and Associate Researcher at CAC Cliometrics and Complexity—IXXI Complex Systems Institute, Ecole Normale Supérieure de Lyon. He got his PhD in Economics at Aix-Marseille University in 2014. His research areas are in macroeconomics and international trade.

Antoine Parent is Professor of Economics at the University of Paris 8, Founding Director of the Team CAC Cliometrics and Complexity—IXXI Complex Systems Institute, Ecole Normale Supérieure de Lyon, (www.ixx i.fr/recherche/cliometrie-et-complexite), Affiliate Researcher at OFCE—Sciences Po (Observatoire Français des Conjonctures Economiques). He is Chair of the Committee on Research in Economic History of the EHA in 2022. His research areas are in cliometrics and complexity, monetary and financial cliometrics, and institutional economics.

 **Lei Zhang** is Professor of Economics at the School of Economics, Sichuan University. He was educated at Peking University (BSc) and University of Warwick (PhD). His previous academic career includes positions at University of Warwick, with visiting positions at Peking University, University of Iowa, Southwest University of Finance and Economics in China and Rome University at Tor Vergata. He has also worked at the Bank of England as a Houblon-Norman and George fellow. His current main research interest includes endogenous financial crises and macroeconomic implications of imperfect credit markets.

Contents

Part II: The Theoretical and Institutional Approach to China's Transition to Capitalism   109

5. The "Take-off" of Chinese Economy: An Evolutionary Model of Reform and Open-up   111

Zhiming Fu, Antoine Le Riche, Antoine Parent, and Lei Zhang

6. New Evidence on the Impact of Institutions on Economic Development in China   137

Linda Glawe and Helmut Wagner

7.   Rise of Capitalism and Chinese Women's Internal and Cross-Border Migrations 1980–2020: A Gender Study   163

Beatrice Zani

Part III: China's Financial Institutions and Financial Integration   215

8.   Chinese Presence in Africa: A Panel Smooth Threshold Regression Approach   217

Ibrahim Nana

List of Contributors

Cécile Bastidon
LEAD, Université de Toulon, PL Pompidou, 83000 Toulon, France; and CAC-IXXI, ENS Lyon, France, bastidon@univ-tln.fr

Jean-Louis Combes
Université Clermont Auvergne Ecole d'Economie - Pôle tertiaire - La Rotonde, 26 Avenue Léon Blum 63000 Clermont-Ferrand, France, j-louis.combes@uca.fr

Chuantao Cui
School of Economics, Sichuan University, No. 24, South Section 1, Yihuan Road, Chengdu, China 610065, chuantaocui@scu.edu.cn

Marie-Eliette Dury
Université Clermont Auvergne, CNRS, CERDI, - Pôle tertiaire - La Rotonde, 26 Avenue Léon Blum 63000 Clermont-Ferrand, France, m-eliette.dury@uca.fr

Zhiming Fu
School of Economics, Sichuan University, No. 24, South Section 1, Yihuan Road, Chengdu, China 610065, zhimingfu@scu.edu.cn

Linda Glawe
Faculty of Economics, University of Hagen, 58084 Hagen, Germany, linda.glawe@fernuni-hagen.de

Fengming Li
School of Economics, Sichuan University, No. 24, South Section 1, Yihuan Road, Chengdu, China 610065, lifengmingscu@foxmail.com

Ibrahim Nana
Université Clermont Auvergne Ecole d'Economie - Pôle tertiaire -
La Rotonde, 26 Avenue Léon Blum 63000 Clermont-Ferrand,
France, ibrahim.nana@etu.uca.fr

Mary-Françoise Renard
Université Clermont Auvergne Ecole d'Economie - Pôle tertiaire -
La Rotonde, 26 Avenue Léon Blum 63000 Clermont-Ferrand,
France, m-francoise.renard@uca.fr

Shuo Shi
Fudan University, China Center for Economic Studies, 600 Guoquan
Rd, Shanghai, China 200433, shishuostone@foxmail.com

Kiril Tochkov
Texas Christian University, TCU Box 298510 Fort Worth, Texas
76129, USA, k.tochkov@tcu.edu

Helmut Wagner
Chair of Macroeconomics, Faculty of Economics, University of
Hagen, 58084 Hagen, Germany, helmut.wagner@fernuni-hagen.de

Chunlin Wan
School of Economics, Sichuan University, No. 24, South Section 1,
Yihuan Road, Chengdu, China 610065, chunlinwan@scu.edu.cn

Bing Xiao
Université Clermont Auvergne, IUT Aurillac, CLERMA EA 38 49,
100 rue de l'Egalité, 15000 Aurillac, France, bing.xiao@uca.fr

Hui Xiong
School of Finance, Zhejiang University of Finance and Economics,
18 Xueyuan Street, Xiasha Higher Education Park, Hangzhou,
Zhejiang, China 31001, h.xiong@zufe.edu.cn

Xiao Yang
School of Public Finance and Taxation, Central University of
Finance and Economics, 39 South College Road, Haidan District,
Beijing, China 100081, 2020210004@email.cufe.edu.cn

Beatrice Zani
Department of East Asian Studies, McGill University, 688
Sherbrooke W., Montreal, QC, Canada, beatrice.zani92@gmail.com

© 2022 World Scientific Publishing Europe Ltd.
https://doi.org/10.1142/9781800611238_fmatter

List of Figures

List of Tables

Introduction

Antoine Le Riche[*,†,§], **Antoine Parent**[†,‡,¶], **and Lei Zhang**[*,‖]

School of Economics, Sichuan University, China
†*CAC-IXXI, Complex Systems Institute, France*
‡*Paris 8 University, OFCE-Sciences Po, France*
§*antoineleriche@scu.edu.cn*
¶*antoine.parent02@univ-paris8.fr*
‖*zlei@scu.edu.cn*

The economic development of China has been the subject of a considerable body of work. From a historical perspective, the most striking element to analyze is how Chinese development since 1978 placed China at a dominant position in the world today. Two factors combine to explain the Chinese singularity in a long-term perspective: (1) the take-off cannot be assimilated with a mere catch-up effect characteristic of an emerging economy; (2) the institutional factors behind the Chinese take-off have been present for centuries without activating economic growth. It is this peculiarity which constitutes the main object of analysis within this book: Institutions were already present in the past, but the take-off only took place at the end of the 20th century.

The book therefore encompasses a major institutional dimension because only an analysis of institutional arrangements can explain this late take-off. It is a question of understanding how the latent institutional factors (present but inactive in the past), under the effect of specific institutional reforms, provoked the take-off. In the Chinese case, the economic growth is actually the manifestation of an institutional rearrangement and North's categories of institutional analysis should be kept in mind by the reader to highlight the Chinese take-off. As it was the case for western countries (US and European), we contend that the changes in the Chinese economy are of institutional origin and essence: It is clear that this book is in line with North's approach, and in a way, a continuation of it. We will shed light on these institutional changes in the rest of the book using categories and tools borrowed from new institutional economics, complexity economics, macro-dynamics, network analysis, and behavioral finance.

Thus, the ultimate aim of this book is to propose a "New Institutional Complexity Economics" to China's economic development. The structure of the book will adopt three levels of institutional analysis: Part I is dedicated to an empirical institutional approach to market integration and regional policy in China; Part II provides a theoretical and institutional framework to model and explain China's take-off; Part III assesses China's institutional reforms of financial markets on the road to financial integration with the rest of the world. In the remainder of the introduction, we develop the main topic of the book, review the literature, and finally, present the different subjects covered.

Aim of the Book: Using the North's Institutional Categories to Explain China's Take-off

The scientific objective of the book is to produce an explanation of Chinese economic changes based on a complex institutional analysis. The analysis of the regimes, systems, and structures that led to the recent take-off of the Chinese economy will be driven by tools of complexity economics, most notably, new institutional economics, macro-dynamics, network analysis, and behavioral finance. The focus of the analysis here is on the nature of the interactions between actors that stimulate the transformation of the Chinese economy. The methodological exchanges between these different academic fields will be fruitful for a renewed understanding of the underlying dynamics of Chinese economic and social systems and their transformation. Such a multidisciplinary approach aims to extend North's scientific project to China.

The role of institutional change in Chinese economic development is the main topic of the book. The question of the "Great Divergence" has been debated at length in the literature. The sustainability over time of certain institutions in China is a striking feature. We assume that the Chinese economic boom in the short historical time (since 1978) is linked to these institutions inherited from the past. The role of these institutions in the recent take-off is revisited in light of the tools of complexity economics. The objective of the book is to understand the effects of the different institutional shocks due to the 1978 reforms, with the idea that the Chinese economic miracle can only be understood in light of its institutional past: If the institutions had been present for a very long time, only the institutional arrangements resulting from the 1978 reforms triggered the take-off; but the take-off would not have been possible without the presence (sometimes millennia) of certain key institutions.

The approach is therefore as follows: We analyze how the institutional reforms undertaken since 1978 (heir of a long history) have enabled the effective liberalization of the Chinese market economy. But the originality of the work also consists in proposing a theoretical modeling which reproduces and explains the take-off of China and its present dominant position in the world, using the tools of macroeconomic dynamics, to better characterize the dynamic trajectories of the Chinese economy. An evolutionary model borrowed from biology (a modified "prey–predator" model) is proposed in the theoretical part of the book to describe this process of transition from the planned economy to the market economy and analyze what remains the original mechanism of a historic transformation unmatched to date in the world.

Transposing North's categories of analysis of the origins of US's growth to China seems particularly relevant. Of course, the two countries differ in many senses (China, an old Empire, vs. USA, a small colonial settlement at the origin), but both of them reached at a point of their history the position of the dominant economy in the world. North's explanation of US take-off relies on two major factors: the rise of export trade and the strengthening of the economic integration among US states (note that three chapters of the book are devoted to these specific topics). The theme of integration refers to the law of one price through two channels, scale economies and reductions in transaction costs (North, 1968). In his explanation, North (1971) departs from initial growth theories à la Solow and pinpoints that technological progress, along with factors of production capital and labor and total productivity factors, cannot be the only source of the economic development. Instead, they are a consequence rather than a cause of economic development. North (1971) downplays the role of technological progress alone as a factor of growth and defends an explanation in terms of market-prone institutions. He forwards the idea that the rising of western economies during the first industrial revolution is mainly a matter of *efficient market organization.* The first two chapters of our book will demonstrate that the economic integration of grain markets in China (an indicator for efficient market organization) was not achieved at the provincial level from the 18th century to the beginning of the 20th century, which explains why the institutional conditions were not in place to allow for the take-off. The first chapter demonstrates that the legacy of the Empire to the young Republic in 1912 was actually the fragmentation of grain markets. The second chapter provides evidence that, at the turn of the Great Divergence, market integration even diminished in China between the end of the 18th century and the beginning of the 19th century. In his explanation of the rise of Western European countries, North generalized the view that economic development is a matter of market factors efficiency: "Efficient economic organization is the key to growth.... Efficient organization entails the establishment of institutional arrangements and property rights that create an incentive to channel individual economic effort into activities that bring the private rate of return close to the social rate of return" (North and Thomas, 1973: 1). A relevant question comes naturally: Is the same explanation valid for China's take-off?

As mentioned above, an extraordinary peculiarity of the Chinese society is the existence of long-lasting institutions favorable to economic growth, but these did not play this role for centuries. This evokes the issue of endurance of inefficient organizations in China in the long run. North (1981: 12) provides explanations for this kind of situation: "... because of deep-seated ideological convictions that the system is unjust. Individuals may also obey customs, rules and laws because of an equally deep-seated conviction that they are legitimate. Change and stability in history require a theory of ideology to account for these deviations from the individualistic rational calculus of neoclassical theory." This passage seems particularly relevant if we refer to the Maoist episode from 1949 to 1977. To understand the institutional persistence or change, ideology matters, and an adequate theory of institutions should include the "ideological factor." North (1981: 58) examines the role of "evolving ideology," which is obviously a key element to understand and analyze the transformations of the Chinese world since 1978.

As noted by Hodgson (2017), from his book *Institutions, Institutional Change, and Economic Performance*, North (1990) *"argued that institutional change occurs when economic or political 'entrepreneurs,' who have the bargaining strength to change institutions, perceive some advantage in doing so."* Here again, these categories of analysis are essential for understanding the transition to Chinese capitalism, and this vein of analysis will be developed in the theoretical and institutional sections of the book (most notably in Chapters 5 and 6) as playing a core role in the adoption of capitalism by China.

When we continue reading North's work, and the progression of his thought, we can only be struck that he offers us a "toolbox" which actually can be applied to China: "Dormant" institutions which under the effect of an adapted institutional change (the 1978 reforms) will give birth to a top world capitalist economy. What is striking in the case of China is that her recent trajectory (from 1978 reforms) does not seem to be limited by its previous evolution in time. In the words of North, it seems that in the very long run (historically), China remained on the same developmental path due to the absence of competitive markets and the existence of inefficient institutions. During the Maoist episode, one may mobilize North's argument of difficulties to move ideologies deeply integrated into the existing organizational structures inherited from the past. Up to the process of 1978 reforms, China offers the example of a society doomed to stay in an inefficient developmental path. In a way, China would illustrate that institutional change is path-dependent. Indeed, this is what the reading of North (1994) and North (2005) applied to the understanding of China suggests.

As quoted by Hodgson (2017), North (1994: 364) wrote: "It is culture that provides the key to path dependence... Societies that get 'stuck' embody belief systems and institutions that fail to confront and solve new problems of societal complexity." Indeed, in the case of China, path dependence refers to the millennium importance of bureaucratic and centralized system, and this is probably the main legacy of the past in which the communist institutions of 1949 have managed to mold themselves perfectly. Then, how the communist party succeeded in adapting pro-market reforms in 1978 China? Here again, the reading of North (2005) could be enlightening, especially his idea of "embedded cognition": The book *Understanding the Process of Economic Change* is devoted to how cognition in a society is endogenously shaped by the social environment. The pressure of the environment (for instance, conquer world markets in the case of China) can change the mind and trigger the objectives assigned to the institutions. Greif and Mokyr (2017) extend the North approach to cognitive rules, institutions, and economic growth: They defend the view that "Belief in progress, the scientific method, and science-based technology provided the cognitive foundations of modern growth. When the states were growth-oriented, the cognitive foundation of the European legal systems rendered them effective in the emergence of modern growth."

We decisively adopt this framework to characterize the Chinese take-off. What is the institutional innovation that rendered this take-off feasible in the case of 1978 China? What has been the incentive to introduce transition-enhancing legal changes that triggered economic growth in China? How has the high cost of changing the law (i.e. becoming pro-market) disappeared? According to Greif and Mokyr (2017), the transition to the modern economy required more than formal legal reforms; it required changing the cognitive rules of society and embedding these changes in the legal code. According to Greif and Mokyr (2017), it should require "forming different cognitive rules regarding the nature of the economy, the practice of business and commerce, the mechanisms of conflict resolution and contract enforcement, and the precise role of government in managing human affairs." This analytical grid will be ours to understand what triggered the take-off of China. More anecdotally, Greif and Mokyr (2017) also mention another important driver of changes in cognitive rules, namely "the needed decline in fatalism and of the belief that human life's outcomes were the result of God's will and hence were inevitable destiny."

The project of our book is therefore clearly in line with a perspective à la North, Hodgson (2017) and Greif and Mokyr (2017). To recapitulate, the guideline and the novelty of our book on China can be expressed as follows: It aims at explicating the role of institutional and organizational change in China's take-off, institutions being conceived as "systems of established, socially embedded rules." Ultimately, the goal of this book is to explain, in the case of China, what McCloskey, referring to 18th century Europe, has termed the "Great Enrichment." Three centuries later, the challenge is to explain "China's Great Enrichment."

Existing Approaches to China's Long-Run Economic Development

The most debated topic in Chinese economic history is certainly that of the Great Divergence with respect to western countries (for an exhaustive review of the state of the art about the Great Divergence, refer to Brandt *et al.* (2014)). Roughly speaking, the issue is to know whether the Great Divergence started before the Industrial Revolution. On this debate, the reference book is that of Pomeranz's *The Great Divergence* (2000), in which the author defends the view of a late divergence beginning not prior to the 19th century. In the literature, the cons are much more numerous, including (notably) Broadberry *et al.* (2018) who study in comparative perspective the standards of living of Chinese population over a millennium ("China, Europe and the Great Divergence: a study in historical national accounting, 980–1850"). They contend that the Great Divergence did not begin in the 19th century but much earlier, the decline of Chinese GDP per capita starting in the mid-18th century if not in the end of the 17th century. Their main thesis relies on a Malthusian explanation, in a kind of Solow growth model representation: The population grew faster than the agricultural output. To support their thesis, the authors rely on numerous quantitative works upon a wide range of indicators that go in this direction. They quote the following works:

1. Allen *et al.* (2010: 28) who find falling real wages in China,
   with welfare ratios declining from 1.7 to 0.8 in Suzhou/Shanghai
   between 1738 and 1818 and from 1.7 to 1.0 in Beijing over the
   same period, and continuing to decline further until the 1850s;
2. Bernhofen *et al.* (2016) who show growing grain price divergence
   in Chinese regions from the 1740s, while European grain prices
   continued to converge, so that a large gap opened up between
   Western Europe and even the most advanced regions of China,
   the Lower and Middle Yangzi;
3. The comparative study by Li and van Zanden (2012) who showed
   GDP per capita in the Lower Yangzi to be only around half the
   level of the Netherlands already by the 1820s;
4. Estimates of Chinese national income produced by Shi *et al.*
   (2014) for the period 1661–1933 which show a similar percentage decline in GDP per capita during the Qing Dynasty as in
   Broadberry *et al.* (2018).

In this way, Broadberry *et al.* (2018) depart from the outcomes
of Maddison (1998), which found an increase in China GDP per
capita during the Northern Song Dynasty; their outcomes of falling
living standards over the Qing Dynasty also calls into question
the picture drawn by Pomeranz (2000) who characterizes China's
18th century as a flourishing period. The back-to-back referral of
Maddison (1998) and Pomeranz (2000) is made in Broadberry *et al.*
(2018) from a strictly Malthusian approach: "The most important
result in this study is the finding of a substantial decline in Chinese
GDP per capita during the Qing dynasty, largely as a result of a
widely accepted large increase in population, without an equivalent
expansion of the cultivated area or crop yields."

The authors also deal with the issue of regional market integration, which is a perennial in the analysis of Chinese economic take-
off, whatever the epoch. They contend that "Chinese GDP per capita
declined sharply during the Qing dynasty, so that by the middle of
the eighteenth century, the gap between China and the most developed parts of Europe was too large to be bridged by regional variation
within China." In the first chapter of our book, we resume the issue of
regional market integration, but from a cliometric perspective, which
means that market integration is assessed "forward-looking," i.e. in

terms of the legacy of past regional market integration for the mid-20th century. The outcomes presented in Chapter 1 corroborate to a fragmentation of the Chinese economy, prior to China's republican period (1912–1949). Going back further in the history of grain market integration should be seen as a kind of laboratory experiment for our institutionalist explanation of the recent Chinese take-off. The first two chapters provide econometric evidence that the grain markets in China from 1738 to 1911 are not integrated and thus inefficient. At that time, the institutional conditions for market efficiency were not in place to allow the Chinese economy to take off, unlike the institutional market-prone revolution that took place in 1978 (see Chapters 5 and 6).

In an open conclusion, Broadberry *et al.* (2018) point out that China's pronounced delay with regard to western countries until at least the mid-18th century is certainly due to institutional factors, suggesting that "the Great Divergence had deep institutional roots." In a way, Broadberry *et al.* (2018) rediscover North's institutionalist thesis but do not develop it, which is the subject of our book. In fact, the issue we deal with is very different from that of Broadberry *et al.* (2018) and the perspective differs too, since the problem we deal with in our work is not that of the institutional causes of the Great Divergence but that of the institutional causes of the "Chinese Great Enrichment." The research question that runs through the book is how institutions that persisted for centuries and are mentioned as the possible cause for the Great Divergence and the economic delay of China from the 18th century to the 20th century by Broadberry *et al.* (2018) have, in reality, fostered the take-off from 1978. Actually, the notion of institutional change, or even institutional revolution, is the driving force of our book to explain China's take-off.

Additionally, Mitchener and Ma (2014) mention the profusion of new databases covering long-run macroeconomic data:

1. new wages and GDP series at the national and regional levels (Li and van Zanden, 2012; Xu *et al.*, 2016; Xu *et al.*, 2018; Ma *et al.*, 2014);
2. new population series (Cao, 2001);
3. new measures of human capital using age heaping and anthropometrics in 18th–20th centuries China (Baten *et al.*, 2010; Gao, 2015);

4. new urbanization rates (Xu *et al.*, 2018);
5. new price indices (Peng, 2006; Allen *et al.*, 2010; Liu, 2015);
6. new regional grain price statistics to test grain market integration (Shiue, 2002; Keller and Shiue, 2007 and Peng *et al.*, 2009, 2016);
7. unprecedented exploitation covering databases on natural disasters, climate changes, and warfare in a millennium perspective (Bai and Kung, 2011);
8. new money supply and public finances data (Liu, 2015);
9. long-term interest rates (Peng *et al.*, 2009; Tang, 2016; Keller *et al.*, 2016).

In their special issue, Mitchener and Ma (2014) aim at furthering and diversifying this vein of research; they present five new topics and we invite the reader to refer to this special issue.

In a more institutional perspective, the study of the formation of the bureaucratic state in China in historical perspective has led to many writings including the forerunner works of Ko *et al.* (2018), Moriguchi and Sng (2014), Rosenthal and Wong (2011), Sng (2014). Additionally, Greif and Tabelinni (2017) studied the comparative role of cultural values on the formation of economic institutions in Western Europe and China.

Our objective is not to pursue in the path of diversification of the illustrative subjects of Chinese economic history but to refocus on explanatory elements of what makes the uniqueness of China's trajectory in world economy: The high level of human capital in China through centuries stands out as an observation shared by many studies. Some articles emphasize "the intriguing combination of relatively low living standards with high human capital in traditional China" (Baten *et al.*, 2010). This will be a key element of our reflection. Indeed, the argument of "intriguing combination" needs further development: It remains an observation but has not, to our knowledge, been the subject of an explanatory model. The combination of high human capital and low income level, acted in the cliometric literature for past Centuries China, also applies today (see international statistics for the current period). Baten *et al.* (2010) conclude as follows: "Further research should explore the possible historical root of this relatively high level of human capital accumulation, in particular its linkage with long-lasting institutions in traditional China, such as a relatively open Civil-Service Examination, a unified written character and a precocious government bureaucracy" (p. 357). This is in fact the major topic of our book: the role of long-lasting institutions and institutional change in the Chinese take-off. Predominantly in the literature, the institutions associated with the bureaucracy are supposed to play a negative role on the economy and are put forward to explain the Great Divergence. The bureaucracy acted as a binding system that would have been the cause of the structural delay with regard to western countries (see for instance, the conclusion of Broadberry *et al.*, 2018). However, the Chinese institutions have been sustainable over the ages, and today, it is necessary to understand how these long-lasting institutions triggered the Chinese economic development. Thus, the aim of the book is to explain the institutional mechanism of China's take-off, which is a historic transformation. How have Chinese institutions made it possible to foster the structural transformations of the Chinese planned economy toward a market economy? To address this issue, the book adopts an original methodological framework that combines institutional economics, macroeconomic dynamics, and complexity economics.

Novelty of the Book: Revisiting China's Take-off in Terms of Cliometrics and Complexity Economics

The book is composed of three parts: (I) Market Integration as an Institution, Convergence and Frontier in China; (II) The Theoretical and Institutional Approach to China's Transition to Capitalism; (III) China's Financial Institutions and Financial Integration.

The rationality and progression of the book are then as follows. Part I focuses on the reality of the integration of grain markets in the modern history of China, a measure for the efficient organization of markets, and about the regional convergence across China. Chapter 1 provides econometric evidence that the legacy of the late imperial China to China's Republican period (1912–1949) was actually characterized by a fragmentation of market and not an integration. Based on the exploitation of original sources on grain prices, Chapter 2 gives additional support to the view that integration was not achieved by the end of the Qing Dynasty. Chapter 3 stresses that

it is necessary to wait for the institutional reforms of regional planning in the post-1978 era to speak of a true regional convergence in
China. Chapter 4 reintroduces the notion of borders into the regional
economic analysis of China's take-off.

Part II deals with a theoretical and institutional explanation
of the Chinese take-off. Chapter 5 explains, through a macroeconomic dynamic model, the Chinese take-off by the transition from a
planned economy to a market economy with particular emphasizes on
the external effect of market liberalization. A Prey–Predator model
identifies the equilibrium states of the two regimes and replicates
the dynamic trajectory of China adopting capitalism (i.e. market
institutions). Chapter 6 studies the role of the quality of institutions on China's economic development. Chapter 7 proposes, to
the best of our knowledge, one of the very first gender studies of
the changes in internal and cross-border migration flows over two
generations of women induced by Chinese capitalism over the past
40 years.

Part III broadens the issue of economic integration to the question
of the integration of Chinese financial markets and proposes a novel
nonlinear econometric analysis of Chinese FDI in Africa (Chapter 8),
a behavioral finance approach to Shanghai and Shenzhen stock market performance in order to test whether anomalies, that would
reveal a still incomplete stage of financial development, persist today
(Chapter 9). The final chapter (Chapter 10) develops a network
analysis of Chinese equity markets in the world and concludes that
Chinese financial development, however late it has been, as compared
to the rapid integration of goods markets since 1978, shows many
similarities with the trends observed in the past in developed countries. This outcome suggests that the institutional revolution that set
China on the take-off path is now progressively affecting even Chinese
financial institutions after the traditional market institutions.

Ultimately, these outcomes reveal that the various facets in institutional complexity economics undertaken in this book (regional science, macroeconomic dynamics, nonlinear econometrics, behavioral
finance, network analysis) provide a relevant analytical framework
to understand the profound transformations that have led China to
become a major capitalist economy in such a short period of time.
This book gives evidence that the profound changes that occurred

and triggered the transition to China capitalism are, by essence, institutionalist.

In Chapter 1, the authors study the relationship between international trade openness and domestic market integration in late imperial China. More specifically, they focus on a natural experiment namely the Unequal Treaties of the second half of the 19th century that lifted the long-existing international trade restriction system. The integration of domestic markets is analyzed while looking at the existence of a long-term common movement in the grain prices between provinces. The econometric results show that trade openness did not lead to better integration of the Chinese domestic grain markets. Their results support the hypothesis according to which long-distance trade has not generated efficiency gains in domestic markets. They evidence a strong segmentation between domestic and international grain markets owing to different traded products and operators.

Chapter 2 analyzes the market integration across province in China from 1644 to 1912. The authors reinvestigate the question of the Great Divergence from the study of China intraregional divergence in market integration. Cui and Xiong provide a unified framework that explains the concept of market integration and analyze it with prefecture-level rice price data. Their analysis shows that the rice market integration was on the decline during the Qing Dynasty, which proves that the institutional conditions for an efficient market were not in place at the time.

Chapter 3 adopts a regional science perspective to deal with the economic policies implemented at the provincial level in order to study the comparative economic development within China and its regions. The authors present distinct stages of economic development policies. Prior to the Chinese take-off, the different provinces had unequal levels of development. The economic development goal was to reduce the level of inequality between these regions. After the Chinese take-off, there was still inequality between regions and the aim of the economic development policy was to improve the comparative advantage of few regions by implementing priority development area, e.g. Eastern Coastal Areas. After that, economic policies aimed at harmonizing the level of economic development between provinces in China (e.g. Heilongjiang province).

Chapter 4 investigates the trade relationship between the Northeast region in China with the rest of the world. The analysis of such a relationship is motivated by the fact that China's Northeast has struggled to modernize its economy during the market transition. Moreover, this region was isolated from the world for decades, and by the time China opened up, the Northeast proved to be unprepared for the new economic challenges. This analysis is a unique opportunity to study the response of an emerging economy to an outdated industrial model that carries a financial, social, and environmental burden. This chapter explores the trade patterns of Heilongjiang, a border province in the Northeast, and uses a gravity model to estimate the trade costs associated to the province's major trading partners over the period 1978–2017. This chapter also studies the evolution of trade barriers between Heilongjiang province and its main trading partners. The results show that, prior to late 1990s, Heilongjiang's overall trade flows were very low. The empirical analysis shows that Heilongjiang exhibits a home bias, trading more with the rest of China than with any other country. The border effects with Russia are substantial. The other trading partners of Heilongjiang in Northeast Asia record lower trade costs than Russia overall, but the barriers seem to have been on the rise since the early 2000s. The discussion of the potential factors contributing to the high border effects of the province points to the lacking infrastructure, especially the cross-border infrastructure with Russia and the costly access to seaports, as the main culprit. The author concludes that there exists possibility for improvement that could allow Heilongjiang to take advantage of its potential for trade and regional integration within Northeast Asia with the One Belt One Road initiative.

Chapter 5 argues that this evolution is mainly explained by the reforms implemented. Two interesting features of aversion to pre-existing ideology because of the historical lessons associated with the "Great Leap Forward" and the "Cultural Revolution" and to uncertainty of outcomes associated with institutional innovations are put forward. Indeed, this makes the reform process to resemble that of evolution with biased local mutations. The chapter uses a simple evolutionary model, based on biology, to explain how reforms allow an economy to move from a planned to a market economy. The authors present the case where no reforms are implemented and show that there exist two stable stationary equilibria: (i) a full market economy and (ii) a full planned economy. After the introduction of reforms, the authors provide evidence that there is only one stable stationary solution that corresponds to a full market economy.

Chapter 6 investigates the role of the quality of institutions in the economic performance of provinces in China. They perform OLS and TSLS estimations over 31 provinces, autonomous regions, and municipalities. Their main results show that institutional quality has a strong positive impact on provincial per capita income; meanwhile, integration and geography have only an indirect impact by influencing institutions.

In Chapter 7, Beatrice Zani draws the contours of a gender approach to migrations in China. In China, women's labor migrations from the countryside to the city and marriage migrations to Taiwan have been complexifying and pluralizing over the last 40 years. A crossed analysis of two generations of migrant women's mobility experiences, professional paths, and economic practices helps to identify lines of continuity and of discontinuity in rural-to-urban and cross-border migratory patterns and to pinpoint broader social and economic transformations characterizing contemporary Chinese capitalism. This chapter provides with an innovative gender approach to apprehend how internal and cross-border migrations of women are framed into the large-scale historical restructuring of Chinese capitalism, society, and labor market. It combines a micro-sociological analysis of migrants' biographical, professional, social, and economic careers with a gender perspective to project mobility experiences and practices into the larger scale of macro-social and macro-economic transformation. Both first and second generation of Mainland Chinese rural women have been engaged into a double-step migration: from the countryside to the city in Mainland China, and from the Mainland to Taiwan. By focusing of the changes in terms of marriage practices, as well as social and economic experiences in the Chinese and the Taiwanese societies and labor markets, the author looks at the extent to which globalization and modernity contributed to the transformation of migratory paths as well as of actors' biographical and professional careers. These are nowadays increasingly oriented toward the achievement of urbanity, economic independence, and social mobility by young migrants. These prove their ability to mobilize innovative and inventive tools to achieve their projects, which digital labor and e-commerce are illustrative of.

In Chapter 8, Ibrahim Nana assesses an important aspect and consequence of China's take-off, namely the impact of the presence of China in Africa over the past 20 years. The relationship between China and African countries are first placed in a historical perspective. From this, the author investigates the effect of these trade flows with a panel threshold regression approach to apprehend whether there exists technology transfer between China and Africa. The dataset refers to the period 1995–2015 for 49 African countries and takes into account technological sophistication index, intermediate goods, and Chinese foreign direct investments. The statistical results show that there exists a threshold of absorptive capacity above which an effective direct technology transfer through global value chain exists. From this derives a policy recommendation that Africa should improve its absorptive capacity.

Chapter 9 provides in-depth analysis of Chinese financial markets in terms of behavioral finance. The authors aim to study financial market anomalies using daily data from the Shenzhen share market and the Shanghai share market over the 1995–2019 period to understand how financial reforms have affected those markets. Chinese stock markets separate foreign investors from domestic investors through dual classes of stocks. During this period, the Chinese equity market has changed in different directions: (i) an increase in both listed companies and the size of the market; (ii) the institutional and individual investors have become more mature. The authors present the reforms made to build a modern financial system, to accelerate the move toward deregulation, and reduce the role of the state in the economy. They categorize the financial reforms as follows: (1) initialization, (2) reforms against the speculators, (3) reforms of governance, and (4) reforms of information disclosure. The authors conclude that globally this sequence of regulations improved the efficiency of both the Shenzhen and Shanghai markets.

Nevertheless, based on a behavioral approach, the authors provide evidence that the Chinese stock markets display daily and monthly calendar effects. Indeed, they find a strong February effect (identified as a Chinese New Year effect) and a negative Thursday effect in Shenzhen and Shanghai stock markets. The persistence of these anomalies in Chinese financial markets would reveal, in terms of financial development, a slower process of convergence toward a financial market economy than for goods.

In Chapter 10, Cécile Bastidon and Antoine Parent present the integration of Chinese equity markets to world equity markets over the last 60 years. The authors use a monthly frequency database from OECD, which entails 32 countries over the period 1960–2018 allowing for historical dynamics analysis. They compare the Chinese dynamics of financial integration with the dynamics of more mature economies. Such a goal is reached using a topological analysis of assets' networks derived from the common component of price time series. In particular, they apply the methodology of the minimal spanning tree to long-run financial data. While the usual financial integration indicators in the literature are measured either country by country or at a global level, these network representations take into account the interaction effects between country and world integration dynamics and its intensity. Their results show a low financial integration of Chinese equity markets converging only very recently toward international contemporary standards.

References

Allen, R., J.-P. Bassino, D. Ma, C. Mool-Murata, and J. L. van Zanden (2010). "Wages, Prices, and Living Standards in China, Japan, and Europe," *Economic History Review*, 64, 8–38.

Bai, Y. and J. Kung (2011). "Climate Shocks and Sino-nomadic Conflict," *Review of Economics and Statistics*, 93, 970–998.

Baten, J., D. Ma, S. Morgan, and Q. Wang (2010). "Evolution of Living Standards and Human Capital in the 18–20th," *Explorations in Economic History*, 47, 347–359.

Bernhofen, D., M. Eberhardt, J. Li, and S. Morgan (2016). "Assessing market (dis)integration in early modern China and Europe," *CEPR Discussion Paper 11288*.

Brandt, L., D. Ma, and T. Rawski (2014). "From Divergence to Convergence: Re-evaluating the History Behind China's Economic Boom," *Journal of Economic Literature*, 52, 45–123.

Broadberry, S., H. Guan, and D. D. Li (2018). "China, Europe and the Great Divergence: A Study in Historical National Account, 980–1850," *Journal of Economic History*, 78, 955–1000.

Cao, S. (2001). *History of China's Population: Qing Era*, (in Chinese) Shanghai: Fudan University Press.

Gao, P. (2015). "Rise from chaos? The development of modern education in 20th century China," *Ph.D. thesis submitted to the Economic History Department at London School of Economics*.

Greif, A. and J. Mokyr (2017). "Cognitive Rules, Institutions and Economic Growth: Douglas North and Beyond," *Journal of Institutional Economics*, 13, 25–52.

Greif, A. and J. Tabelinni (2017). "The Clan and the Corporation: Sustaining Cooperation in China and Europe," *Journal of Comparative Economics*, 45, 1–35.

Hodgson, G. M. (2017). "Introduction to the Douglass C. North Memorial Issue," *Journal of Institutional Economics*, 13, 1–23.

Keller, W. and C. Shiue (2007). "Markets in China and Europe on the Eve of the Industrial Revolution," *American Economic Review*, 97, 1189–1216.

Keller, W., C. Shiue, and X. Wang (2016). "Capital Markets in China and England in the 18th and 19th centuries: Evidence from Grain Prices," *NBER Working Paper 21349*.

Ko, C. Y., M. Koyama, and T.-H. Sng (2018). "Unified China and Divided Europe," *International Economic Review*, 59, 285–327.

Li, B. and J. L. van Zanden (2012). "Before the Great Divergence? Comparing the Yangzi Delta and the Netherlands at the Beginning of the Nineteenth Century," *Journal of Economic History*, 72, 956–989.

Liu, G. (2015). *The Chinese Market Economy, 1000–1500*, Albany: The State University of New York Press.

Ma, Y., H. de Jong, and T. Chu (2014). "Living Standards in China between 1840 and 1912: A New Estimate of Gross Domestic Product per capita," *GGDC Research Memorandum no.147*.

Maddison, A. (1998). *Chinese Economic Performance in the Long-Run*, Paris: OECD Development Centre.

Mitchener, K. J. and D. Ma (2014). "Introduction to the Special Issue: A New Economic History of China," *Explorations in Economic History*, 63, 1–7.

Moriguchi, C. and T. H. Sng (2014). "Asia's Little Divergence: State Capacity in China and Japan Before 1850," *Journal of Economic Growth*, 19, 439–470.

North, D. C. (1968). "Sources of Productivity Change in Ocean Shipping, 1600–1850," *Journal of Political Economy*, 76, 953–970.

North, D. C. (1971). "Institutional Change and Economic Growth," *Journal of Economic History*, 31, 118–125.

North, D. C. (1981). *Structure and Change in Economic History*, New York: Norton.

North, D. C. (1990). *Institutions, Institutional Change and Economic Performance*, Cambridge and New York: Cambridge University Press.

North, D. C. (1994). "Economic Performance Through Time," *American Economic Review*, 84, 359–367.

North, D. C. (2005). *Understanding the Process of Economic Change*, Princeton: Princeton University Press.

North, D. C. and R. P. Thomas (1973). *The Rise of the Western World: A New Economic History*, Cambridge and New York: Cambridge University Press.

Peng, X. (2006). *Grain Prices since Qing: Historical Interpretation and Reinterpretation*, (in Chinese) Shanghai: Shanghai People's Press.

Peng, X. (2016). *From Exchange to Markets: A Research on Traditional Private Market Economy*, (in Chinese) Zhejiang University Press.

Peng, X., Z. Chen, W. Yuan, and H. C. (2009). "Shallow water and heavy boat: Market mechanism in modern Chinese rural credit," (in Chinese). In Qiugen Liu and Debin Ma (eds.) *The Evolution of Chinese Industry, Commerce and Finance, an International Symposium*. Shijiazhuang, China: Hebei University Press, 117–146.

Pomeranz, K. (2000). *The Great Divergence: China, Europe, and the Making of the Modern World Economy*, Princeton, NJ: Princeton University Press.

Rosenthal, J.-L. and B. Wong (2011). *Before and Beyond Divergence: The Politics of Economic Change in China and Europe*, Cambridge, MA: Harvard University Press.

Shi, Z., Y. Xu., Y. Ni, and B. van Leeuwen (2014). "Chinese National Income, ca. 1661–1933," *November CGEH Working Paper Series 62*.

Shiue, C. (2002). "Transport Costs and the Geography of Arbitrage in Eighteenth Century China," *American Economic Review*, 92, 1406–1419.

Sng, T.-H. (2014). "Size and dynastic decline: The principal-agent problem in late imperial China, 1700–1850," *Explorations in Economic History*, Elsevier, vol. 54(C), 107–127.

Tang, J. (2016). "Interest Rates and Financial Market Integration in China in the Long Run," *Ph.D. thesis submitted to Economic History Department of London School of Economics*.

Xu, Y., Y. Ni, and J. L. van Zanden (2016). "Calculation China's Historical Economic Aggregate: A GDP-centered Overview," *Social Sciences in China*, 37, 56–75.

Xu, Y., B. van Leeuwen, and J. L. van Zanden (2018). "Urbanization in China, ca. 1100–1900," *Frontiers of Economics in China*, 13, 322–368.

Part I

Market Integration as an Institution, Convergence, and Frontier in China

Chapter 1

Have Unequal Treaties Fostered Domestic Market Integration in Late Imperial China?

Jean-Louis Combes[*,‡], Mary-Françoise Renard[*,§,||],
and Shuo Shi[†,¶]

*Université Clermont Auvergne, CNRS
IRD, CERDI, F-63000, Clermont-Ferrand, France
†Fudan University, CCES, 200433, Shanghai, China
‡j-louis.combes@uca.fr
§m-francoise.renard@uca.fr
¶shishuostone@foxmail.com

Abstract

The objective of this chapter is to study the relationship between international trade openness and domestic market integration in Late Imperial China. More specifically, we focus on a natural experiment, namely the unequal treaties of the second half of the 19th century that lifted the long-existing international trade restriction system. The integration of domestic markets is analyzed while looking at the existence of a long-term common movement in the grain prices between provinces. The econometric results show that trade openness did not lead to better integration of the Chinese domestic grain markets. Our results support the hypothesis according to which long-distance trade has not generated efficiency gains in domestic markets. We evidence a strong segmentation between domestic and international grain markets owing to different traded products and operators.

||Corresponding author.

1.1. Introduction

One of the main characteristics of China's development is the mixing of political centralization and economic decentralization. It may result in fragmentation and inequalities across China's provinces. This situation has expanded since the reform and open-up strategy was adopted in 1978, with trade and investment policies being concentrated in coastal provinces for the first time. More generally, the Chinese case raises a more general question concerning the relationship between trade openness and domestic market integration. Are the two dynamics independent or complementary? Does trade openness generate positive spillovers between external and domestic trade?

In a country as large and geographically diverse as China, the topic of provincial market integration is crucial for understanding the movements of production factors and their impact on economic growth. This chapter investigates the historical integration of China's domestic markets. In contrast to the existing literature, we examine this market integration from the perspective of international trade environment. Specifically, we study the impact of the unequal treaties signed during the 19th century and at the beginning of the 20th century between the Qing Dynasty (1644–1912) and foreign powers on the domestic market integration. These unequal treaties have led, among other things, to trade openness. Thus, they can be seen as a natural experiment highlighting the impact of trade openness on domestic market integration.

More precisely, this chapter econometrically evaluates domestic grain market integration before and after the unequal treaties. The law of one price (LOP) in late imperial China (1736–1911) using the maximum likelihood (ML) method of cointegration developed by Johansen (1988) and Johansen and Juselius (1990) is thus tested. In addition, a robustness test based on price sigma convergence is implemented. It appears mainly that the unequal treaties have not led to a better integration of domestic cereal markets. They remain fundamentally fragmented in late imperial China. In Section 1.2, we explain the potential links between unequal treaties and the domestic market integration. In Section 1.3, we present the methodology and the data, while in Section 1.4, we discuss the results. Section 1.5 concludes the chapter.

1.2. Unequal Treaties and Domestic Market Integration

Economic development has often been linked to market integration. This means there are strong relationships between different regions in a country that lead to convergence of prices, the so-called "law of one price" (hereinafter referred to as LOP). The consequence is that one region depends on the situation of the other ones more than its own history (Marshall, 1920). There are no or few economic restrictions on the mobility of goods and services, production factors, and people between them (Tinbergen, 1965).

This relationship has been used to understand why China did not face an industrial revolution as in Europe, with the hypothesis that market integration is an indicator of economic efficiency and more generally of development. For a long time, the underdevelopment in China, despite the unified political system, was supposed to induce less integrated markets than in Europe and was used to explain the lag between both. This idea has been weakened mainly by Pomeranz (2010), who suggested that China's markets during the 18th century were closer to the markets described in the neo-classical model than the European ones. Shiue and Keller (2007) provided empirical support by studying 121 prefectural markets. However, these results have been challenged by other studies concluding on a disintegration of markets in Northern as well as Southern Chinese regions (Bernhofen *et al.*, 2015, 2017, Gu and Kung, 2019).

China's situation under the Qing Dynasty (1644–1912) was very unique. At the beginning of the period we are interested in, the Qing Dynasty had good economic results, a territorial expansion, and a growing population (from 138 million in 1700 to 381 million in 1820 and 430 million in 1850), and an economic growth stronger than the Japanese one (Maddison, 2007). Political centralization was strong with a multi-level bureaucratic hierarchy. Nevertheless, with an increasing population and without substantial improvement in agricultural productivity, market integration decreased after 1776 (Gu, 2013). Several rebellions weakened the government, the most important being the Taiping Rebellion (1850–1864). At its peak, the Taiping Heavenly Kingdom controlled 16 provinces most of which were the major tax revenue sources of the central government. To fight against this rebellion, the central government created a new type of army, which involved a strong delegation of power to the provincial authorities (Maddison, 2007). It was very costly. With authorities unable to pay anymore for hydraulic structures, the banks of the Yellow River had been abandoned, and it was impossible to use it to send grains to Beijing (Maddison, 2007). Then, to increase its income, the government implemented a new tax, *Lixin Tax*, at the provincial level. "Political boundaries determine market size when commodity circulation is restricted by taxation, trade policies, and currency" (Gu, 2013, p. 73). Brandt *et al.* (2014) consider economic failure is due to an imperial institutional system that protected vested interests, such as the local gentry. The revolts that happened during this period induced a decrease in the level of standard of the population, and the whole economic system has been weakened or collapsed during the treaties period.

Before the Qing Dynasty, China has been engaging in foreign trade for a long time, mainly with proximate countries mostly in Asia (Keller *et al.*, 2011). In the Ming Dynasty (1368–1644), tributary trade was accepted but controlled by the central government, or *Chaoting*, with stringent restrictions. Although the Qing Dynasty adopted restrictive trade policy, several provinces were still allowed to maintain authorized coastal ports to international trade. In 1685, four customs were set up in the cities of Canton (Guangdong Province), Xiamen (Fujian Province), Ningbo (Zhejiang Province), and Songjiang (Jiangsu Province) to regulate trade with foreign merchants. In the second half of the reign of Emperor Kangxi (1662–1722), foreign merchant ships were allowed to trade with China at all the ports specified. Trade regulation evolved into the Canton System (1757–1842) under which all the trade with the West was only allowed on the southern port of Canton (now Guangzhou) (Van Dyke, 2005). Foreign trade was restricted, and rice exports were prohibited.

Since the mid-19th century, however, the Canton System gradually vanished: The unequal treaties between the Qing government and the West knocked off the long-term trade restrictions in China. As the result of military failure in the Opium War (1840–1842), China was forced to sign the Treaty of Nanjing (1842). It abolished the traditional tributary system, liberalized the highly regulated trading system, legalizing the opium trade, and opened additional ports to foreign trade. In addition to Guangzhou and the four treaty ports[1] opened to foreign trade and residence by the Treaty of Nanjing, more provinces in China were opened to foreign merchants by the following treaties. Based on the Treaty of Tianjin (1858), China opened Tainan, Haikou, Shantou, Haicheng, Nanjing, Penglai, Tamsui, Yantai, and Yingkou. The Convention of Beijing (1860) legalized Tianjing as a trade port. By the Traité de Paix (1885), Baosheng and Liangshan were opened. By the Treaty of Shimonoseki (1895), Shashi, Chongqing, Suzhou, and Hangzhou were opened to Japan. Therefore, most of the Chinese provinces succumbed and opened trading ports to major industrial countries. Less regulated trade environment often improves, theoretically, market integration, though it takes a rather long historical process.

With new industrial enterprises in the ports, we could consider they need to increase the demand and then facilitate transportation. Several studies have been devoted to the relationships between transport costs and trade (Anderson and van Wincoop, 2004). With the invention of railways at the beginning of the 19th century, the transport costs which are one of the main obstacle to trade, decreased a lot in Europe, e.g. 36% in France between 1841 and 1851 (Caron, 1997). This resulted in an integration of markets and a spatial concentration of activities. This integration is very dependent on the quality of infrastructure and its deterioration has a strong impact on trade (Limao and Venables, 2001). In the case of China, the openness arising from the treaties gave the opportunity for foreigners to produce in China and to trade with the mainland. Therefore, it should be an opportunity to invest in infrastructure, which could decrease transaction costs and fuel domestic market integration. Profit opportunities in international trade could have encouraged both private agents and the Chinese state to promote domestic trade (improvement of transport and communication infrastructure, payment system, commercial law, etc.).

However, this virtuous dynamic may not manifest for two reasons: if people involved in domestic trade and in international trade are

---

[1]The four treaty ports were Amoy in Xiamen, Foochowfoo in Fuzhou, Ningpo, and Shanghai.

not the same and if the goods traded internationally are different from those traded in domestic markets. The first reason rests on the opposition between, on the one hand, merchants, who are active in the ports and would be more interested in international trade and, on the other hand, officials, who would be more concerned about domestic trade. Their main objective could be to ensure a regular supply of necessities (such as grains) to urban markets to avoid social and political unrests. There is a traditional opposition between government and the administration, interested in the inland country and some merchants, interested in trade and technological progress. The ports affected by the treaties are usually considered as "enclaves of modernity," and it has little relevance for the other cities, and even less so for the rest of the country; China's agriculture has not been significantly concerned by the openness of the country (Maddison, 2006). China's firms were family owned, and domestic trade was not based on legal contracts but was part of the social relationships, which determined the social life: relationships between individuals, bonds of friendship, family commitments, and so on (Fairbank and Goldman, 2010). Then, "the insertion of a treaty port economy in the traditional Chinese empire represented initially what seemed like a small rupture to a giant closed political system" (Brandt *et al.*, 2014, p. 81). Without any modern constitution or commercial law, a small number of Western-style enterprises could hardly overthrew one ounce of the dominant traditional mentality. An example reflects the institutional barriers that existed at that time. When the British firm Jardine Matheson established a steam-powered silk filature in Shanghai during the 1860s, they prepare for "their inability to obtain prompt and efficient delivery and storage of cocoons in the immediate rural hinterland outside treaty port" (Brandt *et al.*, 2014, p. 83). The frontier between the modern institutions in the treaty ports and the traditional ones (including informal monopolies and the guild system) was quite strong. Until the mid-20th century, China had an ethnocentric vision of the world because of its ideology, mentalities, and educational system (Maddison, 2006). It seems that local markets were vibrant, but trade was cut off between regions (Rawski, 1972).

The second reason for the lack of virtuous cycle between openness and market integration may be due to the opposition between internationally tradable goods and domestically tradable goods. First, we must notice that China's trade openness was less important than in some similar countries. In 1870, China's exports accounted for 5.6% of Asian and western Exports, and 3.9% in 1913. For the same years, India's trade accounted for 13.9% and 8.8%, respectively (Maddison, 2006). Large countries are often less open than small ones, but it may not explain the difference between these two large countries. China's foreign trade policy has often been restrictive, allowing limited exchange between domestic and foreign traders in specific areas (Keller *et al.*, 2011). The tradition of a lack of interest for foreign products from the government is well known. It reflects the nationalism and the wish for self-sufficiency, but also a kind of reality. It is reported than in the 1830s, the Chinese native nankeen cotton cloth was superior in quality and cost compared to Manchester cotton goods (Greenberg, cited by Keller *et al.*, 2011). In 1890, agriculture represented 68.5% of GDP and handicraft, 7.7% (Maddison, 2007). Exports are mainly composed of tea and silk. Imports are mainly devoted to opium (37% in 1870), and cotton later in the 20th century. Then, China's imports became more diversified after 1911. China did virtually import no equipment or modern means of production, which could have been traded domestically. Traditionally, it also imports luxury goods from Europe. These types of products are dedicated to very few people in the population and may not be a vector for market integration.

In either case, domestic markets in late imperial China would be more isolated than integrated. Even though the unequal treaties forced China to open some ports, introducing a friendly environment for price convergence, China's rigid social system and autarkic economy might still impede domestic market integration. If so, the LOP is unlikely to hold.

1.3. Data and Methodology

As shown by Fackler and Goodwin (2001), market integration occurs when supply or demand shocks in one region is partially or fully transmitted to another region. Market integration is the subject of major studies insofar as it leads to efficiency gains and ensures the interregional smoothing of shocks (e.g. Shiue, 2002). For markets to be fully integrated, the LOP must hold. The LOP is a stronger assumption than market integration. It indicates that price changes in a given location net of transaction costs are perfectly transmitted to prices in other locations through trade. Arbitrage clears the spatial price differences. Although the literature has highlighted the limitations of an approach that relies exclusively on price data (e.g. Barett and Li, 2002), owing to the lack of sufficiently reliable data on quantities traded, the usual method for testing market integration is to consider the long-term price co-movements between different locations (Federico, 2012). Specifically, it is assumed that if prices diverge permanently, then arbitrage opportunities are not fully exploited, and markets are not integrated.

To examine the market integration in late imperial China, we focus on grain prices that were more marketized than other important staple commodities, such as maize, potato, and sweet potato. In the 18th century, accounting for roughly 40% of the gross national product, 20% of China's total grain output was traded between the provinces of which the Yangzi region was the logistics center (Peng, 2006; Xu and Wu, 2000). Grain was used by Shiue and Keller (2007), Li (2000), and Gu (2013) among others in their work on market integration in historical China.

In the cointegration tests, we specifically use data on grain prices in 13 provinces in late imperial China with a maximum period spanning from 1738 to 1911. The data are obtained from Chen and Kung (2016).[2] The Qing government originally kept those grain prices. Local officials reported grain prices to the central government each month. Given that cropping patterns were different across regions in the Qing Dynasty, to ensure comparability, we follow Chen and Kung (2016) and convert one "dan" of grain (of various kinds) into the standardized kilocalories.[3] This conversion based upon sources compiled by the Institute of Nutrition and Food Safety, Chinese Center for Disease Control and Prevention (2002).[4] We then calculated the yearly average price and adjusted the price according to purchasing

---

[2]Their data on grain price is based on "Qing Dynasty's Price of Food Database," Institute of Modern History, the Academia Sinica, Taiwan (http://mhdb.mh.sinica.edu.tw/foodprice/about.php), and "Grain Prices Data during Daoguang to Xuantong of the Qing Dynasty," Institute of Economics, Chinese Academy of Social Science (2010).

[3]The *dan* is the unit of weight employed at the time. Each dan equals 83.5 kg.

[4]The standard calories of various crops were obtained from Yang (1996).

power parity, which was USD 1,900. The deflator was obtained from Peng (2006).

Our utilization of grain prices from a nationally representative sample departs from the seminal work by Shiue and Keller (2007), who select the southern and central regions of China. Our sample is on province-level that deviates from the county-level sample used by Gu (2013). Therefore, our focus is on market integration between provinces and not within provinces. Indeed, long-distance trade is likely more affected by international trade treaties than short-distance trade.

1.3.1. *Province classification*

In our sample, the 13 provinces are Fujian, Guangdong, Guangxi, Henan, Hubei, Hunan, Jiangsu, Jiangxi, Shandong, Shanxi, Sichuan, Zhejiang, and Zhili. The sample is constrained by the availability of consistent data for the period.[5] We classified the provinces according to two rules: geographic location and overseas trade policy.

The geographic location was probably decisive in connecting domestic markets to international trade in late imperial China. Coastal provinces with ports received price information more conveniently through international trade activities and could be more integrated. By contrast, markets in inland provinces would be less likely to be integrated because grain prices in landlocked markets were determined by regional transactions rather than their international counterparts. Therefore, we classify 12 provinces into coastal and inland groups (see Table 1.1). Hubei is dropped in this classification because its data is inconsistent with that of other inland provinces in study periods.

Based on the opening timeline of each provincial trade port, we classify 13 provinces into three groups, namely opened group, less-opened group, and closed group (see Table 1.2). A province is classified as opened if the ports there were opened by China, as less opened if the ports there were forced to open by the unequal treaties. It is noteworthy that the provinces in the closed group had no ports

---

[5]In Chen and Kung (2016)'s dataset, there are 18 provinces. Among them, 13 provinces are used in our sample. The five provinces that are not used in our sample are Anhui, Gansu, Guizhou, Shaanxi, and Yunnan.

Table 1.1.   Province classification based on geographic locations.

Group	Provinces
Coastal	Fujian, Guangdong, Guangxi, Jiangsu, Shandong, Zhejiang, Zhili,
Inland	Henan, Hunan, Jiangxi, Shanxi, Sichuan

Table 1.2.   Province classification based on opening policies.

Group	Provinces
Opened	Fujian, Guangdong, Jiangsu, Zhejiang
Less opened	Hubei, Jiangxi, Shandong, Sichuan, Zhili
Closed	Guangxi, Henan, Hunan, Shanxi

opened by China or according to the unequal treaties in our study period.

1.3.2.   *Cointegration test*

We consider two local markets of a homogeneous good: grains. When trade happens, the price in the importing market P_t^i is the sum of the price in the exporting market P_t^e and transaction costs T_t^{ei}. The arbitrage condition would thus hold as $P_t^i = P_t^e + T_t^{ei}$. The market integration relationship to be investigated is given as the following equation under the assumption of stationary transaction costs:

$$\ln P_t^i = a + b \ln P_t^e + \varepsilon_t. \tag{1.1}$$

If $b = 1$, the LOP holds and the markets are fully integrated. If $0 < b < 1$, the prices tend to move in the same direction, but the markets are not fully integrated. However, when the price series are non-stationary, the LOP cannot be tested by estimating this regression (Engle and Granger, 1987). In this situation, cointegration tests are the appropriate tool. The multivariate Johansen test (Johansen and Juselius, 1990) will be used here since it allows for hypothesis testing on the parameters in the cointegration vector and exogeneity tests. The Johansen test is based on a vector autoregressive error correction model (VECM). If P_t denotes an $(n \times 1)$ vector of $I(1)$ prices, then the kth-order VECM is given by

$$\Delta P_t = \sum_{i=1}^{k-1} \Gamma_i \Delta P_{t-i} + \Pi P_{t-k} + \mu + \beta t + \varepsilon_t, \qquad (1.2)$$

where $\Gamma_i = -(I - \Pi_1 - \cdots - \Pi_i)$; $i = 1, 2 \dots, k-1$; $\Pi = -(I - \Pi_1 - \cdots \Pi_k)$; each of Π_i is an $n \times n$ matrix of parameters; ε_t is an identically and independently distributed n-dimensional vector of residuals with zero mean and variance matrix Ω_t; μ is a constant term; and t is trend. Since P_{t-k} is $I(1)$ but ΔP_t and ΔP_{t-i} variables are $I(0)$, Eq. (1.2) will be balanced if ΠP_{t-k} is $I(0)$. So, it is the Π matrix that conveys information about the long-run relationship among the variables in P_t. The rank of Π, r, determines the number of cointegration vectors, as it determines how many linear combinations of P_t are stationary. According to Stock and Watson (0000), there will be $n - r$ different stochastic trends between the provincial prices series. Consequently, r could be interpreted as a proxy of the strength of market integration. When $r = 0$, each provincial price follows its own trend and the degree of market fragmentation is maximum. When $0 < r < n - 1$, provincial markets are integrated, but the LOP does not hold in the presence of at least two common stochastic trends. When $r = n - 1$, there exists a unique common stochastic trend between all prices (and all the pairwise prices are cointegrated). The empirical question is therefore the extent to which unequal treaties impact r.

To examine the strength of market integration r, we propose two likelihood ratio test statistics. The null hypothesis of at most r cointegrating vectors against a general alternative hypothesis of more than r cointegrating vectors is tested by

$$\text{Trace statistic}(\lambda - \text{trace}) = -T \sum_{i=r+1}^{n} \ln\left(1 - \hat{\lambda}_i\right). \qquad (1.3)$$

The null of r cointegrating vector against the alternative of $r + 1$ is tested by

$$\text{Maximum eigenvalue statistic}(\lambda - \text{max}) = -T \sum_{i=r+1}^{n} \ln\left(1 - \hat{\lambda}_{r+1}\right).$$

$$(1.4)$$

$\hat{\lambda}_i$s are the estimated eigenvalues (characteristic roots) obtained from the Π matrix and T is the number of usable observations.[6]

1.3.3. *Robustness check: Sigma price convergence*

We check the robustness of the results of the cointegration tests by examining time evolution of price convergences. Following Wolszczak-Derlacz (2008) who derives the concept from the literature of real convergence, we define sigma convergence as the evolution over time of the spatial dispersion of provincial prices. Sigma convergence occurs when the price dispersion declines over time. Specifically, for each year, the standard deviation of the grain price distribution between provinces is calculated and presented in a graph. It must be checked whether unequal treaties lead to a break in the price dispersion trend.

1.4. Results

The search for a common stochastic trend implies that all the price series are non-stationary and integrated of the same order. For most province groups in our sample, however, the price series are often found to be stationary by the results of unit root tests for each group.[7] This limits our application of the cointegration tests to the geographic location groups and opening policy groups with at least two price series integrated of order one or $I(1)$.

1.4.1. *Geographic location group*

Table 1.3 presents the cointegration results of the geographic location groups. Both the trace and λ-max tests show one cointegrating vector for Jiangsu and Shandong in the coastal group, 1741–1806. This implies that the grain prices in Jiangsu and Shandong contain the same stochastic trend and so are cointegrated. Since there are only two provinces in this group, the finding of cointegration suggests that the LOP holds for grain markets in Jiangsu and Shandong

---

[6]For details, see Johansen and Juselius (1990).

[7]The results of unit root tests are reported in the appendix.

Table 1.3.   Cointegration results of the geographic location groups.

Eigen value	Trace test		Maximum eigen value test			
	Null	λ−trace	Null	λ−max	Cointegration	LOP
		Coastal group, 1741–1806 (lag = 1)				
		Guangdong and Zhejiang				
0.324	$r = 0^{**}$	30.390	$r = 0^{***}$	24.678	Yes	Yes
0.087	$r \leq 1$	5.712	$r = 1$	5.712		
		Coastal group, 1871–1909 (lag = 1)				
		Fujian, Guangxi, and Zhili				
0.373	$r = 0$	36.011	$r = 0$	18.200	No	No
0.265	$r \leq 1$	17.812	$r = 1$	12.016		
0.138	$r \leq 2$	5.796	$r = 2$	5.796		
		Inland group, 1743–1814 (lag = 1)				
		Jiangxi and Sichuan				
0.179	$r = 0$	17.661	$r = 0$	14.098	No	No
0.048	$r \leq 1$	3.563	$r = 1$	3.563		
		Inland group, 1871–1911 (lag = 2)				
		Jiangxi, Shanxi, and Sichuan				
0.306	$r = 0$	23.804	$r = 0$	14.960	No	No
0.134	$r \leq 1$	8.843	$r = 1$	5.886		
0.070	$r \leq 2$	2.957	$r = 2$	2.957		

Note: *Significant at the 10% level. **Significant at the 5% level. ***Significant at the 1% level. The optimal lag specification of the coastal group (1871–1909) is selected by the Schwarz information criterion (SIC). For other groups, the optimal lag specification is selected by the AIC.

before the 1860s. The cointegration results for the remaining three groups indicate that the grain markets in the coastal group after the 1860s, as well as in the inland group, are unintegrated: there is no common stochastic trend.

1.4.2.   *Opening policy groups*

Table 1.4 presents the cointegration results of the opening policy groups. For Guangxi, Hunan, and Shanxi in the closed group, 1871–1908, both the trace and λ-max tests reject the null hypothesis of none cointegrated vectors, revealing at least two vectors with common stochastic trends. This suggests that the LOP does not hold because the common stochastic trend is not unique. By contrast,

Table 1.4. Cointegration results of the opening policy groups.

Eigen value	Trace test		Maximum eigen value test		Cointegration	LOP
	Null	λ-trace	Null	λ-max		
		Opened group, 1816–1860 (lag = 1)				
		Guangdong and Zhejiang				
0.320	$r = 0$	23.408	$r = 0$	16.580	No	No
0.147	$r \leq 1$	6.828	$r = 1$	6.827		
		Less-opened group, 1871–1910 (lag = 1)				
		Jiangxi and Sichuan				
0.185	$r = 0$	13.027	$r = 0$	8.193	No	No
0.114	$r \leq 1$	4.834	$r = 1$	4.834		
		Closed group, 1871–1908 (lag = 1)				
		Guangxi, Hunan, and Shanxi				
0.465	$r = 0^{**}$	42.992	$r = 0^{**}$	23.775	Yes	No
0.281	$r \leq 1$	19.217	$r = 1$	12.531		
0.161	$r \leq 2$	6.685	$r = 2$	6.685		

Note: *Significant at the 10% level. **Significant at the 5% level. ***Significant at the 1% level. The optimal lag specification of the closed group (1871–1908) is selected by the Schwarz information criterion (SIC). For other groups, the optimal lag specification is selected by the AIC.

for the opened and less-opened groups where trading port were opened by China or according to the unequal treaties, little evidence is found for the existence of market integration in both the pre- and post-1860 periods.

1.4.3. *Robustness check: Sigma price convergence*

Figure 1.1 shows the evolution of the grain price standard deviation between provinces in the coastal and the inland group for each year. Besides, Figure 1.2 shows the evolution in the opened, less-opened, and closed groups. These two figures reveal that the dispersion in grain prices between Chinese provinces is not characterized by a downward trend. This provides another evidence that there was little systematic market integration in later imperial China, either before the unequal treaties or after.

The fragmentation of China's territory seems to be an old story because of several phenomena: the growing size of the population as previously mentioned, the provincial-based administrative

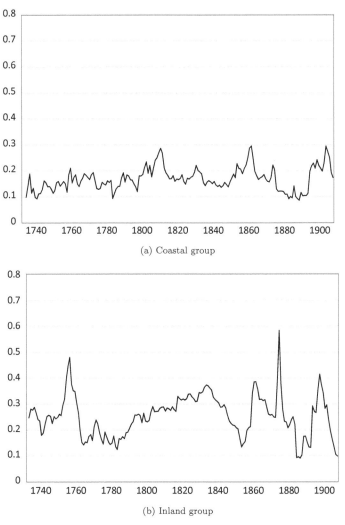

Fig. 1.1.   Sigma convergence of the grain prices in the geographic location groups, 1737–1911: (a) coastal group; (b) inland group.

organization, the technology and may be mainly, the poor level of transportation infrastructure. Several studies have been devoted to the link between population and grains. For instance, Chen and Kung (2016) found that, like potato in Europe, maize can be at the origin of population growth during 1776–1910 but unlike the potato, it had no significant effect on economic growth because of the lack of new

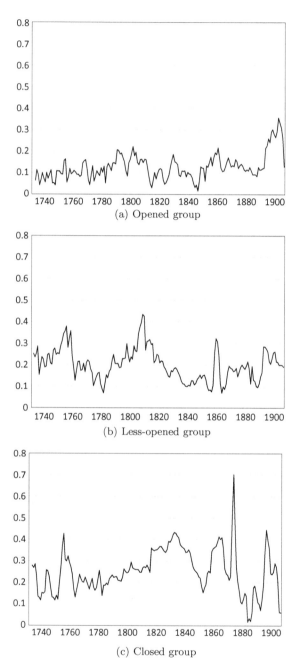

Fig. 1.2. Sigma convergence of the grain prices in the opening policy groups, 1737–1911: (a) opened group; (b) less-opened group; (c) closed group.

technology. It seems to be the same with grains and the absence of industrial revolution in China. It did not allow a better efficiency of the markets, which may explain the lack of integration. Transportation is another condition to market integration. Most of the interregional trade relied on natural waterways (Shiue, 2002). Transports were, and stayed, for years one of the most serious problems of the Chinese economy (Domenach and Richer, 1987). In 1890, manufacturing industries and modern mode of transport amounted to 0.5% of GDP, and the railways was practically non-existent. China's exports amounted to 0.6% of GDP, which is low compared with that of other Asian countries (Maddison, 2007). It was probably not sufficient to influence the market integration. The new trade flows and the new ideas arriving at the opened ports did not concern the rest of the country, at least in the short term, and it seems that the improvements in transport were mainly on the sea between them.

1.5. Conclusion

Since 1978, China gradually opened its market to the rest of the world and became a major powerhouse of the global economy. China's economic miracle is greatly due to the improvement of resource allocation efficiency through domestic and international market integration. The initiation of China's market integration, however, should be revisited from a long-term perspective.

This chapter focuses on China's domestic market integration in the 18th and 19th centuries. During this period, the increased market integration in Western Europe finally triggered the Industrial Revolution. By contrast, China's domestic markets seemed more isolated than integrated. It was likely the result of the trade restriction by the Chinese government. The unequal treaties between the Qing government and western powers, however, might affect the trade restriction and invigorate market integration.

We thus evaluate domestic market integration in late imperial China. Specifically, the objective of the chapter is to study the consequences of unequal treaties that lift the long-existing international trade restriction system on domestic grain market integration. The degree of market integration is assessed by focusing on both long-term co-movements and sigma convergence in grain prices between provinces. The hypothesis tested is that of complementarity between international and domestic trade integration: Better access to international markets would promote better functioning of domestic markets. It appears that the hypothesis according to which these treaties would have fostered a greater integration of domestic markets between provinces is significantly rejected. We find no evidence for market integration to hold after the 1870s. Our findings are in line with Cheung's (2008) argument that the markets in China were only sporadically integrated in the late imperial era. They are also an illustration of the opposition between the Mandarins, fixed in the past, turned to the continent, not open to progress, and the Compradore, interested in changes and turned to the sea, both of them being sometimes considered as the "double face of Asia" (Bergère, 1998). The name of Compradore has been given to some Chinese merchants working with foreigners and building a little private industrial sector. The treaties have been a shock and induced a strong transformation of the ports, but during the Qing Dynasty, they probably did not affect most of China's economy and people, even though they may have initiated a process of change in the long-term. So, they did not play out as a force of integration for the domestic markets.

Appendix: Unit Root Tests for the Order of Integration

Before proceeding to the cointegration tests, we need to examine the univariate time series properties of the data and to confirm that all the price series are non-stationary and integrated of the same order. To this end, we perform the augmented Dickey–Fuller (ADF) test for each time series. All the price series are transformed in a natural logarithm. Lag lengths are chosen based on the Akaike information criteria (AIC).

Our strategy for the unit root tests is as follows. For each province-period-specific series, we report its ADF test result in natural logarithm level. If the unit-root null is rejected for the level of the series, then the series is stationary or $I(0)$. For the non-stationary series, we then report its ADF test result in logarithm first difference. If the unit-root null is rejected for the first difference of the series but cannot be rejected for the level, then we say that the series contains one unit root and is integrated of order one, $I(1)$. We only perform cointegration tests for the group with at least two $I(1)$ series.

Geographic location groups

Table A.1.1 presents the results of the ADF tests in natural logarithm level for the coastal group. Jiangsu and Shandong (1742–1806), as well as Fujian, Guangxi, and Zhili (1871–1909), show non-stationary grain prices. Other province-period-specific series are found stationary. Table A.1.2 presents the results of the ADF tests in logarithm first differences for the non-stationary series. The null

Table A.1.1.   ADF tests in natural logarithm levels, coastal group.

Province name	Study period	t-statistic	P-value	Lags
Fujian	1742–1806	−4.069**	0.011	0
Guangdong	1742–1806	−4.046**	0.012	1
Guangxi	1742–1806	−3.967**	0.015	0
Jiangsu	1742–1806	−2.859	0.183	1
Shandong	1743–1806	−2.875	0.178	0
Zhejiang	1742–1806	−5.553***	0.000	3
Zhili	1742–1806	−4.411***	0.000	0
Fujian	1816–1860	−4.996***	0.001	2
Guangdong	1816–1860	−2.149***	0.506	9
Guangxi	1816–1860	−3.315*	0.077	0
Jiangsu	1816–1860	−6.167***	0.000	0
Shandong	1818–1860	−4.015**	0.015	1
Zhejiang	1817–1860	2.886	0.177	0
Zhili	1821–1860	−4.386***	0.006	4
Fujian	1871–1909	−2.622	0.273	0
Guangdong	1871–1909	−3.577**	0.045	7
Guangxi	1871–1909	−2.755	0.222	0
Jiangsu	1871–1909	−3.557**	0.047	1
Shandong	1871–1909	−3.983**	0.018	3
Zhejiang	1871–1909	−3.265*	0.087	0
Zhili	1871–1909	−2.784	0.211	4

Note: Trend and intercept are included in the test equation of each province. *Significant at the 10% level. **Significant at the 5% level. ***Significant at the 1% level. The lag length is chosen based on the Akaike Information Criterion (AIC).

Table A.1.2.   ADF tests in logarithm first difference, coastal group.

Province name	Study period	t-statistic	P-value	Lags
Jiangsu	1742–1806	-6.593^{***}	0.000	3
Shandong	1743–1806	-16.607^{***}	0.000	1
Fujian	1871–1909	-6.387^{***}	0.000	0
Guangxi	1871–1909	-6.832^{***}	0.000	1
Zhili	1871–1909	-3.960^{***}	0.000	6

Note: Trend and intercept are included in the test equation of each province. *Significant at the 10% level. **Significant at the 5% level. ***Significant at the 1% level. The lag length is chosen based on the Akaike Information Criterion (AIC).

hypothesis of non-stationarity can be rejected for the five prices in first differences.

Table A.1.3 presents the results of the ADF tests in natural logarithm levels for the inland group. Although Hunan (1816–1870) fails to reject the null hypothesis of non-stationary, the rest series of their group are unlikely to have unit root. Jiangxi and Sichuan (1745–1814), in togetherness with Jiangxi, Shanxi, and Sichuan (1871–1911) cannot reject the null hypothesis of non-stationary. In Table A.1.4, the null hypothesis of non-stationarity can be rejected for the five prices in first differences.

Opening policy groups

Table A.1.5 presents the results of the ADF tests in natural logarithm levels for the opened group. Only Guangdong and Zhejiang (1816–1860) in a pair cannot reject the null hypothesis of non-stationarity. Table A.1.6 presents the results of the ADF tests in logarithm first difference the non-stationary series. The null hypothesis of non-stationarity can be rejected for the two provinces in first differences.

Table A.1.7 presents the results of the ADF tests in natural logarithm levels for the less-opened group. Hubei, Jiangxi, and Sichuan

Table A.1.3. ADF tests in natural logarithm levels, inland group.

Province name	Study period	t-statistic	P-value	Lags
Henan	1745–1814	−4.695***	0.002	1
Hunan	1743–1814	−3.248*	0.084	0
Jiangxi	1743–1814	−1.989	0.597	2
Shanxi	1743–1814	−4.582***	0.002	1
Sichuan	1743–1814	−1.818	0.686	0
Henan	1818–1870	−3.278*	0.081	1
Hunan	1816–1870	−3.010	0.139	0
Jiangxi	1817–1870	−3.762**	0.027	0
Shanxi	1818–1870	−3.301*	0.077	1
Sichuan	1816–1870	−3.318*	0.0740	1
Henan	1871–1911	−3.895**	0.021	0
Hunan	1871–1911	−3.167*	0.105	1
Jiangxi	1871–1911	−1.854	0.660	0
Shanxi	1871–1911	−3.182	0.102	3
Sichuan	1871–1911	−2.582	0.290	0

Note: Trend and intercept are included in the test equation of each province. *Significant at the 10% level. **Significant at the 5% level. ***Significant at the 1% level. The lag length is chosen based on the Akaike Information Criterion (AIC).

Table A.1.4. ADF tests in logarithm first difference, inland group.

Province name	Study period	t-statistic	P-value	Lags
Jiangxi	1743–1814	−69.843***	0.000	1
Sichuan	1743–1814	−8.608***	0.000	0
Jiangxi	1871–1911	−6.498***	0.000	0
Shanxi	1871–1911	−4.459***	0.000	3
Sichuan	1871–1911	−6.258***	0.000	0

Note: Trend and intercept are included in the test equation of each province. *Significant at the 10% level. **Significant at the 5% level. ***Significant at the 1% level. The lag length is chosen based on the Akaike Information Criterion (AIC).

Table A.1.5. ADF tests in natural logarithm levels, opened group.

Province name	Study period	t-statistic	P-value	Lags
Fujian	1738–1806	−4.187***	0.008	0
Guangdong	1738–1806	−4.216***	0.007	1
Jiangsu	1738–1806	−3.093	0.116	1
Zhejiang	1738–1806	−5.633***	0.000	0
Fujian	1816–1860	−4.996***	0.001	2
Guangdong	1816–1860	−2.149	0.506	9
Jiangsu	1816–1860	−6.167***	0.000	0
Zhejiang	1817–1860	−2.886	0.177	0
Fujian	1871–1909	−4.760***	0.003	0
Guangdong	1871–1909	−3.606**	0.041	0
Jiangsu	1871–1909	−4.013**	0.016	1
Zhejiang	1871–1909	−3.642**	0.037	0

Note: Trend and intercept are included in the test equation of each province. *Significant at the 10% level. **Significant at the 5% level. ***Significant at the 1% level. The lag length is chosen based on the Akaike Information Criterion (AIC).

Table A.1.6. ADF tests in logarithm first difference, opened group.

Province name	Study period	t-statistic	P-value	Lags
Guangdong	1816–1860	−7.280***	0.000	0
Zhejiang	1817–1860	−7.466***	0.000	0

Note: Trend and intercept are included in the test equation of each province. *Significant at the 10% level. **Significant at the 5% level. ***Significant at the 1% level. The lag length is chosen based on the Akaike Information Criterion (AIC).

(1871–1910) in a group cannot reject the null hypothesis of non-stationarity. Table A.1.8 shows that the null hypothesis of non-stationarity in first differences can be rejected for Jiangxi and Sichuan other than Hubei.

Table A.1.7.   ADF tests in natural logarithm levels, less-opened group.

Province name	Study period	*t*-statistic	*P*-value	Lags
Hubei	1742–1790	−3.968**	0.016	0
Jiangxi	1742–1790	−3.578**	0.007	0
Shandong	1742–1790	−4.973**	0.001	1
Sichuan	1742–1790	−1.876	0.652	0
Zhili	1742–1790	−4.587***	0.003	1
Hubei	1805–1852	−4.273***	0.008	0
Jiangxi	1805–1852	−3.811**	0.025	0
Shandong	1805–1852	−3.170	0.104	4
Sichuan	1805–1852	−3.656**	0.036	0
Zhili	1805–1852	−3.892**	0.021	1
Hubei	1871–1910	−2.600	0.282	0
Jiangxi	1871–1910	−1.923	0.624	0
Shandong	1871–1910	−3.798**	0.027	3
Sichuan	1871–1910	−2.533	0.312	0
Zhili	1871–1910	−3.510*	0.051	0

Note: Trend and intercept are included in the test equation of each province. *Significant at the 10% level. **Significant at the 5% level. ***Significant at the 1% level. The lag length is chosen based on the Akaike Information Criterion (AIC).

Table A.1.8.   ADF tests in logarithm first difference, less-opened group.

Province name	Study period	*t*-statistic	*P*-value	Lags
Hubei	1871–1910	−2.966	0.156	6
Jiangxi	1871–1910	−6.139***	0.000	0
Sichuan	1871–1910	−6.065***	0.000	1

Note: Trend and intercept are included in the test equation of each province. *Significant at the 10% level. **Significant at the 5% level. ***Significant at the 1% level. The lag length is chosen based on the Akaike Information Criterion (AIC).

Table A.1.9 presents the results of the ADF tests in natural logarithm levels for the closed group. Guangxi, Hunan, and Shanxi (1871–1910) in a group cannot reject the null hypothesis of non-stationarity. Table A.1.10 shows that the null hypothesis of non-stationarity can be rejected for all the three prices in first differences.

Table A.1.9. ADF tests in natural logarithm levels, closed group.

Province name	Study period	t-statistic	P-value	Lags
Guangxi	1743–1860	−3.914**	0.017	0
Henan	1743–1860	−4.692**	0.002	1
Hunan	1743–1860	−3.001	0.140	0
Shanxi	1743–1860	−4.190***	0.008	1
Guangxi	1816–1860	−3.314*	0.077	0
Henan	1816–1860	−3.201*	0.098	1
Hunan	1816–1860	−3.436*	0.059	1
Shanxi	1816–1860	−3.338*	0.074	1
Guangxi	1871–1908	−1.520	0.804	3
Henan	1871–1908	−3.851**	0.024	0
Hunan	1871–1908	−1.566	0.788	7
Shanxi	1871–1908	−3.176	0.105	3

Note: Trend and intercept are included in the test equation of each province. *Significant at the 10% level. **Significant at the 5% level. ***Significant at the 1% level. The lag length is chosen based on the Akaike Information Criterion (AIC).

Table A.1.10. ADF tests in logarithm first difference, closed group.

Province name	Study period	t-statistic	P-value	Lags
Guangxi	1871–1908	−6.848***	0.000	1
Hunan	1871–1908	−5.225***	0.000	9
Shanxi	1871–1908	−4.431***	0.006	3

Note: Trend and intercept are included in the test equation of each province. *Significant at the 10% level. **Significant at the 5% level. ***Significant at the 1% level. The lag length is chosen based on the Akaike Information Criterion (AIC).

Summary

We find that in the 18th and early 19th centuries, grain prices in China's provincial markets are stationary. Then, in most cases, the search for a common stochastic trend is then irrelevant: China's domestic markets were more isolated than integrated. By contrast, after 1870, grain prices began to show a non-stationary pattern in several coastal provinces and most of the inland provinces. For the provinces with less or even without any opened ports, grain prices were in the transition away from stationarity. This tendency toward non-stationarity, however, does not necessarily imply the existence of common stochastic trends.

References

Anderson, J. and E. van Wincoop (2004). "Trade Costs," *Journal of Economic Literature*, 42, 691–751.

Barett, C. and J. Li (2002). "Distinguishing Between Equilibrium and Integration in Spatial Analysis," *American Journal of Agricultural Economics*, 84, 292–307.

Bergère, M. C. (1998). *Le mandarin et le compradore*, Paris: Hachette Litterature.

Bernhofen, D., M. Eberhardt, J. Li, and S. Morgan (2015). "Assessing Market (Dis)Integration in Early Modern China and Europe," *CESifo Working Paper, No. 5580, Center for Economic Studies and Ifo Institute (CESifo)*, Munich.

Bernhofen, D., M. Eberhardt, J. Li, and S. Morgan (2017). "The Evolution of Markets in China and Western Europe on the Eve of Industrialisation," *Research Paper Series, 2017/12*, University of Nottingham.

Brandt, L., D. Ma, and T. Rawski (2014). "From Divergence to Convergence: Reevaluating the History Behind China's Economic Boom," *Journal of Economic Literature*, 52, 45–123.

Caron, F. (1997). *Histoire des chemins de fer en France, Tome 1: 1740–1883*, Paris: Fayard.

Chen, S. and J. K. Kung (2016). "Of Maize and Men: The Effect of a New World Crop on Population and Economic Growth in China," *Journal of Economic Growth*, 21, 71–99.

Cheung, S. (2008). *The Price of Rice: Market Integration in Eighteenth-Century China*, Bellingham: Center for East Asian Studies, Western Washington University.

Domenach, J. L. and P. Richer (1987). *La Chine, Tome 1, 1949–1971*, Seuil, Paris: Points Histoire.

Engle, R. F. and C. W. J. Granger (1987). "Co-integration and Error Correction: Representation, Estimation, and Testing," *Econometrica*, 55, 251–276.

Fackler, P. L. and B. K. Goodwin (2001). *Chapter 17 Spatial Price Analysis Handbook of Agricultural Economic*, Amsterdam: Elsevier, pp. 971–1024.

Fairbank, J. K. and M. Goldman (2010). *Histoire de la Chine, Des origines à nos jours*, Paris: Tallandier.

Federico, G. (2012). "How Much Do We Know About Market Integration in Europe?" *Economic History Review*, 65, 470–497.

Gu, Y. (2013). "Essays on Market Integration: The Dynamics and Its Determinants in Late Imperial China, 1736–1911," *Degree of Doctor of Philosophy a thesis submitted to the Hong Kong University of Science and Technology*, Hong Kong University of Science and Technology.

Gu, Y. and J. K. Kung (2019). "Malthus Goes to China: The Effect of Positive Checks on Grain Market Development, 1736–1910," *Revise and Resubmit, Journal of Economic History*.

Johansen, S. (1988). "Statistical Analysis of Cointegration Vectors," *Journal of Economic Dynamics and Control*, 12, 231–254.

Johansen, S. and K. Juselius (1990). "Maximum Likelihood Estimation and Inference on Cointegration—with Applications to the Demand for Money," *The World Economy*, 52, 169–210.

Keller, W., B. Li, and C. H. Shiue (2011). "China's Foreign Trade: Perspectives from the Past 150 Years," *The World Economy*, 34, 853–892.

Li, L. (2000). "Integration and Disintegration in North China's Grain Markets, 1738–1911," *Journal of Economic History*, 60, 665–966.

Limao, N. and A. J. Venables (2001). "Infrastructure, Geographical Disadvantage, Transport costs and Trade," *World Bank Economic Review*, 15, 451–479.

Maddison, A. (2006). "La Chine Dans l'économie Mondiale de 1300 à 2030," *Outre-terre,* 2(15), 89–104.

Maddison, A. (2007). *Chinese Economic Performance in the Long Run*, Second Edition, Revised and updated: 960–2030 AD.

Marshall, A. (1920). *Principles in Economics*, London: Macmillan Press.

Peng, K. (2006). *Grain Price since the Qing Dynasty*, Shanghai: Shanghai People Press.

Pomeranz, K. (2010). *Une grande divergence*, Paris: Albin Michel.

Rawski, E. (1972). *Agricultural Change and the Peasant*, Cambridge, MA: Harvard University Press.

Shiue, C. H. (2002). "Transports Costs and Geography of Arbitrage in 18th Century China," *American Economic Review*, 92, 1406–1419.

Shiue, C. H. and W. Keller (2007). "Markets in China and Europe on the Eve of the Industrial Revolution," *American Economic Review*, 97, 1189–1216.

Stock, J. H. and M. W. Watson (1988). "Testing for common trends." *Journal of the American Statistical Association*, 83(404), 1097–1107.

Tinbergen, J. (1965). *International Economic Integration*, Amsterdam: Elsevier.

Van Dyke, P. A. (2005). *The Canton Trade: Life and Enterprise on the China Coast, 1700–1845*, Hong Kong: Hong Kong University Press.

Wolszczak-Derlacz, J. (2008). "Price Convergence in the EU-an Aggregate and Disaggregate Approach," *International Economics and Economic Policy*, 5, 25–47.

Xu, D. and C. Wu (2000). *Chinese Capitalism, 1522–184*, London, UK: Palgrave Macmillan.

Yang, Z. (1996). *Statistics and the Relevant Studies on the Historical Population of China*, Beijing: China Reform Publishing House.

https://doi.org/10.1142/9781800611238_0003

Chapter 2

The Decline of China's Intraregional Market Integration in the Qing Dynasty

Chuantao Cui[*,§]**, Xiao Yang**[†,¶]**, and Hui Xiong**[‡,∥,**]

School of Economics, Sichuan University, China
†School of Public Finance and Taxation
Central University of Finance and Economics, China
‡School of Finance
Zhejiang University of Finance and Economics, China
§chuantaocui@scu.edu.cn
¶2020210004@email.cufe.edu.cn
∥h.xiong@zufe.edu.cn

Abstract

This chapter shows that China's intraregional market integration was on the decline during the Industrial Revolution era when Western Europe went through an increasing market integration based upon econometric analysis. We present a unified theoretical framework which can help understand the concept of market integration more clearly. Beyond traditional measures, we propose and apply a new method to estimate the market integration intensity: the arbitrage cost between two prefectures and the associated arbitrage probability. All empirical results are consistent with the conclusion of a decreasing intraregional market integration in Qing China.

**Corresponding author.

2.1.   Introduction

For a long time, the Great Divergence has been one of the most controversial issues in economic history. The debate focuses on when and why the Great Divergence arose, that is, around what time and for what reasons Western Europe economically superseded parts of the world. One influential view, called western centrism, argues that Western Europe's "exceptional" path of economic development is rooted in its unique characteristics which could have been shaped centuries earlier than the Industrial Revolution: scientific culture and Christian tradition that led to technological progress (Landes, 2006), better institutions (North and Thomas, 1973), better structure of class relations, which led to a free labor market (Brenner, 1976) and better demographic patterns (Clark, 2005, 2008). As a result, Western Europe's economic progress outperformed that of the rest of the world.

However, a different view based on the California School's works, represented by Pomeranz's *The Great Divergence* (2000), has received attention in recent years.[1] According to the California School, the rise of Western Europe occurred just before and during the Industrial Revolution and depended very much on a relatively sudden shift out of the traditional Malthus trap. Since then, Western Europe took off and followed a sustained development route which made up the West's current supremacy. In contrast, Asian economies were trapped in the Malthus cycle and were constrained by the negligible productivity growth together with a growing population. They argue that, East Asia—particularly China—is comparable to the Western Europe on the eve of Industrial Revolution in terms of economic performance, measured by various indicators; it was exogenous shocks like coal usage and colonial exploitation rather than endogenous factors that brought luck to the Western Europe.

Both the Western Centrism supporters and the California School scholars attach great importance to the role that market integration plays in the economic growth and social development. In general, market integration facilitates specialization and technology diffusion and helps reduce the production cost. Unger (1983) and Allen and Unger (1990) argue that market integration is helpful in

---

[1]See also Wong (1997) and Frank (1998).

optimizing resource allocation and in promoting economic development. Many works point out that a better-functioning market or
more integrated markets, in association with a set of institutions,
e.g. non-distortionary pricing system, efficient legal framework, and
clear property rights, would lead to more efficient resource utilization and would provide greater incentives for investments, which
are vital for raising income per capita for any economy. It is the
well-functioning markets that distinguish the West from the rest
of the world, inducing the Industrial Revolution and giving rise
to the Great Divergence (North, 1981; North and Thomas, 1973;
North and Weingast, 1989). Moreover, various scholars examine how
the market integration helped different countries or regions develop
during the Industrial Revolution era based on historical data and
archives. For instance, Rothenberg (1992) analyzes the commodity, financial, and labor market integrations in Massachusetts during
1750–1850, Mora-Sitja (2007) investigates the labor market integration in Catalonia during 1772–1816, and Ronsijn (2014) studies the
commodity market integration in Flanders during 1780–1850.

In an influential paper, Shiue and Keller (2007) provide econometric evidence to support California School's revisionist view. They
compare the degree of grain market integration in Western Europe
and China, two of the most advanced regions in the preindustrial
era, but who would start to industrialize about 150 years apart, and
find that the market integrations in China and in Western Europe
were overall comparable in the late 18th century. Their finding has
helped the revisionist view gain popularity in academia significantly.
The above test, however, is static. Bernhofen *et al.* (2017) conduct a
dynamic analysis using Shiue and Keller (2007)'s method and find a
secular decrease in the market integration in China in the late 18th
and early 19th centuries. In contrast, they show that the market integration was stable or improved in Belgium and England at the same
time.

For China's case, there seems to be a consensus, and scholars
generally emphasize the disintegration between regions: They argue
that local markets in China were vibrant, but commercial connections
between regions were weak and hence the diminishing interregional
trade (Pomeranz, 2000; Rawski, 1972). In this chapter, we use rigorous econometric analysis to show that China's market integration
was on the decline even within a region during Western Europe's
Industrial Revolution era. Thus, our research complements the early

argument by showing that both the interregional and the intraregional market integrations were weakened in Qing China, which deepens our understanding of Shiue and Keller (2007) and Bernhofen *et al.* (2017)'s findings.

More generally, our analysis also sheds light on the fundamentals underlying market integration. How do we understand market integration under a theoretical framework? The market, itself a fairly complicated object, is determined by interactions of numerous factors. Market integration, an indicator of economic performance of a set of spatially independent markets, could conceptually be more complex. Current literature basically interprets market integration in pragmatic ways. For instance, Studer (2008), Shiue and Keller (2007), Yan and Liu (2011), and Bernhofen *et al.* (2017) do correlation and cointegration analyzes, which can detect linear relationships between prices of different markets. Although price correlations and cointegration statistics are probably the most widely used measures of market integration, it is difficult to understand, intuitively, the market integration intensity in terms of price correlations and cointegration statistics. We do not know exactly what mechanism induces larger or smaller price correlations or cointegration statistics. In this chapter, we propose a unified theoretical framework which helps us understand the market integration in a clearer way. Specifically, we follow Spiller and Huang (1986) and Sexton *et al.* (1991) and emphasize the efficiency of arbitrage of agricultural products in different locations. Moreover, traditional measures can also find their own positions under our framework and bear clearer economic meanings.

In our framework, the two key elements are the arbitrage cost and the arbitrage probability. For a homogeneous good, two locations are in a consolidated market, or equivalently, markets of these two locations are integrated if the prices in the two markets differ by exactly the arbitrage cost from one location to another. That is, two markets are integrated if the law of one price holds. Applying a method that is widely used in agricultural economics, our research directly estimates the arbitrage cost between two markets and the associated arbitrage probability. Obtaining the arbitrage costs and the corresponding arbitrage probabilities of the pre- and post-Industrial Revolution periods, we can identify the secular trend clearly.

This chapter is organized as follows. Section 2.2 discusses data, time, and the reason we focus on the Yangzi delta. Section 2.3

proposes a unified theoretical framework of market integration. Section 2.4 explains the empirical strategy in detail. Importantly, based on the proposed framework, we introduce a new methodology which can be used to directly estimate the arbitrage cost and the arbitrage probability between two local markets. The conventional measures also become more understandable in our framework. We present the empirical results in Section 2.5. Section 2.6 turns to robustness checks, and Section 2.7 concludes the chapter.

2.2. Data, Yangzi Delta and Time Range

Throughout the chapter we shall focus on China's Yangzi delta, which refers to the area of southern part of Jiangsu province, northern part of Zhejiang province, and the Shanghai city. More specifically, it consists of the following 17 prefectures: Changzhou, Hai, Jiangning, Songjiang, Suzhou, Taicang, Tong, Yangzhou, Zhenjiang, Hangzhou, Huzhou, Jiaxing, Jinhua, Quzhou, Ningbo, Shaoxing, and Taizhou. Yangzi delta was the most prosperous region in China during the Qing Dynasty (1644–1912). And it was a reasonably comparable region in agricultural, commercial, and proto-industrial developments to those in Western Europe on the eve of the Industrial Revolution (Li, 2010; Shiue and Keller, 2007). Therefore, had the Industrial Revolution occurred anywhere in China, Yangzi delta would have been the region that embraced it and would have witnessed a rising intraregional market integration. If on the other hand we observe a declining intraregional market integration in the Yangzi delta, it would not be surprising to see that have happened elsewhere in Qing China.

It should be noted that the Yangzi delta is more meaningful economically than administratively. Skinner (1964) suggests that the traditional Chinese society is a mixed system of a centrally hierarchical structure combined with a host of parallel locally hierarchical subsystems. He also proposes eight macro-regions as the units for analyzing various factors that impact China's dynastic development. The Yangzi delta is one of these eight macro-regions. Skinner stresses the importance of analysis units and argues that they are largely neglected in historical scholarship and that a topic cannot be thoroughly understood unless the proper analysis units are fully analyzed.

We use the prefecture-level rice price data here, which is the monthly average price of mid-quality rice. Rice is the most important product traded in the Qing Dynasty and its market can be regarded as competitive (Wu, 2007). The Qing government established a set of special institutions to document grain prices in the local markets. The local officials were required to report prices of major grains, further categorized by different grades, on a routine basis with the minimum frequency of once per month. The prices recorded were retail prices of grains in each prefecture, in the standard accounting units of taels (silver currency) per bushel. Such documentation comprises the first-hand resources of the database we use.

The database is constructed and maintained by Dr. Yeh-Chien Wang, and it is available for public use since 2008. The data come from the grain price lists in the Palace Archives of the Number One Historical Archives in Beijing (Gongzhong liangjiadan) from 1736 to 1911. The database covers 21 provinces and 331 prefectures. There are 42 grains included and for each kind, a high price and a low price are reported. The time span differs across regions and across grains. This systematic database is the most comprehensive one of its sort. More conveniently, all prices are expressed in the unified units and are thus comparable across time, and the time originally based on the Chinese lunar calendar is also converted according to the Western calendar system.

In this chapter, we focus on two periods: Jan. 1770–Dec. 1779 and Jan. 1810–Dec. 1819, when the data are of the highest quality. Moreover, the Industrial Revolution took place roughly between 1760 and 1830 in the Great Britain. So the time we choose are reasonably good for comparison. Our second period is just before the Daoguang Depression to avoid business cycle complications. Under the reign of Emperor Daoguang (1820–1850), China experienced a depression. The grain price underwent an unusually low level from 1825 to 1850 (Kishimoto, 1997). In doing the robustness check, we also try some other time period and find no significant changes in the result.

2.3.   Theoretical Framework

Based on Skinner (1964) and Shiue and Keller (2007), our research focuses on the Yangzi delta and analyzes the price relationship between two rice markets in pairwise prefectures. Since arbitrage will affect price levels of two prefectures' rice markets, integrated markets tend to be associated with a unique price after arbitrage cost being taken into account. Thus, testing price integration is equivalent to testing whether local prices adhere to the law of one price. If local markets are not integrated, there is no arbitrage between markets, and therefore the local prices are not systematically related. In contrast, if local markets are integrated, arbitrage occurs through trade between prefectures, and arbitrageurs will help prices to achieve their equilibrium levels.

Hypothetically, consider the "autarkic" rice prices of a pair of prefectures i and j at time t, P_t^{iA} and P_t^{jA}.[2] By the quotation marks on autarkic, we stress the idea that prefecture i does not engage in trade with prefecture j *only*. Conceptually, this is not autarkic for prefecture i in a strict sense, which requires prefecture i not to engage in trade with the rest of the world because prefecture i may trade with a third prefecture, say prefecture l, and P_t^{iA} should have been influenced by this factor. A symmetric argument applies to prefecture j as well.[3] Let us denote the prefecture with the higher price j and the one with the lower price i.[4] For $k \in \{i, j\}$, a lot of factors might enter into the determinant set of P_t^{kA}, e.g. consumer preferences, agricultural technology, market power, weather, so on and so forth.

Assume that there is a merchant who seeks the arbitrage opportunity between prefectures i and j. Correspondingly, there is an arbitrage cost C_t^{ij} between the two regions that follows the log-normal distribution,

$$C_t^{ij} = e^{V_t^{ij}}, V_t^{ij} \sim N(b_t^{ij}, \delta_{ijt}^2).$$

The arbitrage cost includes, for instance, the transportation cost, storage expense differential between locations, in-transit loss, etc. Sometimes, even though the geographic distance between two

---

[2]Throughout the chapter, we use prefecture i and market i interchangeably.

[3]Note that "autarkic" prices may not always be observable.

[4]Theoretically, we assume that the rice price is a continuous random variable and the probability of two prices being equal is zero. Empirically, in the rare case of two equal prices, we pick one of them randomly and add to it an arbitrarily small number to make it prefecture j.

markets does not change, C_t^{ij} may decline due to e.g. the improvement of transportation technology.

Now consider the observed rice prices in markets i and j at time t, P_t^i and P_t^j. If market i is not integrated with market j, then the prices in the two separated markets are independent of each other and there should be no systematic relationship between them. We would have $P_t^i = P_t^{iA}, P_t^j = P_t^{jA}$.

However, if the two markets in prefectures i and j are integrated, whenever there exists an arbitrage opportunity between the two regions, arbitrage would make the following equation hold:

$$P_t^j - P_t^i = e^{V_t^{ij}}. \tag{2.1}$$

In other words, P_t^i and P_t^j are systematically related to each other based upon the law of one price. Let us denote the probability for Eq. (2.1) to hold λ_t^{ij}. Many shocks could affect the arbitrage probability λ_t^{ij}. For instance, an increased population in prefecture j would likely lead to an increased demand for rice in market j, which would raise P_t^{jA} and thus λ_t^{ij}. Similarly, improved irrigation system in prefecture i would make the supply of rice go up in market i, which would probably lower P_t^{iA} and make λ_t^{ij} go up.

One point that we want to emphasize is *market integration is not treated as "all or nothing" here.* When one looks at all the prefecture pairs at some point in time, then some are integrated and some are not, or arbitrage is present between some pairs and absent between other pairs. From a probabilistic perspective, for a given prefecture pair at a given time, it follows some distribution of being integrated and not being integrated.

2.4. Empirical Strategy

2.4.1. *Estimating arbitrage cost and arbitrage probability*

Based on the above theoretical framework and following Spiller and Huang (1986) and Sexton *et al.* (1991), we propose a method which can be used to estimate the arbitrage cost and the probability of having an arbitrage opportunity. This method helps overcome a number of lingering problems in the existent models: (a) arbitrage costs can be estimated within the model; (b) market integration is not treated as "all or nothing," and it is assumed that local markets sometimes are linked by arbitrage while at other times are separated, depending upon the relevant factors discussed in the previous section.

Regime 1 (Arbitrage): Since there is arbitrage, Eq. (2.1) holds. We take logs on both sides and get

$$\log(P_t^j - P_t^i) = V_t^{ij}. \tag{2.2}$$

Since $V_t^{ij} \sim N(b_t^{ij}, \delta_{ijt}^2)$, we have $\log(P_t^j - P_t^i) \sim N(b_t^{ij}, \delta_{ijt}^2)$. Recall that the probability of a pair of markets being integrated, or the probability that Eq. (2.1) holds is λ_t^{ij}.

Regime 2 (No Arbitrage): If no arbitrage takes place, then the local markets are separated (not integrated). The probability of this event, or the probability that Eq. (2.1) does not hold is $1 - \lambda_t^{ij}$.

Now, we introduce a new random variable, U_t^{ij}, to capture the barriers to trade between prefectures i and j at time t, such that the following equation holds:

$$\log(P_t^j - P_t^i) = V_t^{ij} + U_t^{ij}. \tag{2.3}$$

We further assume $U_t^{ij} \sim N(a_t^{ij}, \sigma_{ijt}^2)$. No restriction is placed on a_t^{ij}: it could be positive, negative, or zero. Further more, V_t^{ij} and U_t^{ij} are assumed to be independently distributed. Therefore, we have $\log(P_t^j - P_t^i) \sim N(b_t^{ij} + a_t^{ij}, \delta_{ijt}^2 + \sigma_{ijt}^2)$.

Consider a switching regression model with the above two regimes: arbitrage (A), and no arbitrage (NA). To estimate the model, the likelihood function is formulated as follows:

$$L_T^{ij} = \prod_{t \in T} \left[\lambda_T^{ij} f_{ijt}^A + (1 - \lambda_T^{ij}) f_{ijt}^{NA} \right], \tag{2.4}$$

where T can be one of two time sets: the first one is Jan. 1770–Dec. 1779 (denoted as period 1 or T_1) and the second one is Jan. 1810–Dec. 1819 (denoted as period 2 or T_2), that is $T \in \{T_1, T_2\}$; f_{ijt}^A and f_{ijt}^{NA}

are density functions based on Eq. (2.2) and Eq. (2.3), respectively:

$$f_{ijt}^A = \frac{1}{\delta_{ijT}}\phi\left(\frac{\log(P_t^j - P_t^i) - b_T^{ij}}{\delta_{ijT}}\right), \qquad (2.5)$$

$$f_{ijt}^{NA} = \frac{1}{\sqrt{\delta_{ijT}^2 + \sigma_{ijT}^2}}\phi\left(\frac{\log(P_t^j - P_t^i) - (b_T^{ij} + a_T^{ij})}{\sqrt{\delta_{ijT}^2 + \sigma_{ijT}^2}}\right), \qquad (2.6)$$

where $\phi(.)$ denotes the standard normal density function. The maximum likelihood estimates of the parameters $b_T^{ij}, a_T^{ij}, \delta_{ijT}, \sigma_{ijT}$ and λ_T^{ij} can be obtained by maximizing the logarithmic function of Eq. (2.4).

For a given period T and for each pair of prefectures i and j, we focus on the arbitrage probability λ_T^{ij} and the arbitrage cost b_T^{ij}. To get a clear picture, we graph them against the geographic distance d^{ij}. We do this for the periods Jan. 1770–Dec. 1779 and Jan. 1810–Dec. 1819. By comparing and contrasting, we can identify the trend of market integration in Qing China.

2.4.2. *Price correlation and ADF t-statistic*

Price correlation is the basic and probably the most widely used measure of market integration. Correlation coefficient $Corr(P_T^i, P_T^j)$ is estimated for two time series of spot price for rice of prefectures i and j. If the two local markets are integrated, the law of one price prevails and the two time series should move in tandem. Empirically, the larger $Corr(P_T^i, P_T^j)$ is, to the higher degree the markets i and j are integrated.

It is even clearer if we examine the price correlation in our proposed framework. When it is in Regime 1 (with the probability λ_T^{ij}), $Corr(P_t^i, P_t^j)$ is positive.[5] When it is in Regime 2 (with the probability $1 - \lambda_T^{ij}$), $Corr(P_t^i, P_t^j)$ is zero. Intuitively, $Corr(P_T^i, P_T^j)$ can be thought of as a "weighted average" of Regimes 1 and 2.[6] It follows that the greater $Corr(P_T^i, P_T^j)$ is, the higher the probability of

---

[5]The value is between zero and one. More specifically, the magnitude depends on the variances of P_t^i and C_t^{ij}, the total arbitrage cost: the larger is $Var(P_t^i)$ relative to $Var(C_t^{ij})$, the higher is $Corr(P_t^i, P_t^j)$.

[6]Strictly speaking, the correlation coefficient over a whole sample is not a linear function of the correlation coefficients over its constituent subsamples.

Regime 1 is, and therefore there is a higher integration of market i and market j.

Another popular approach to examining market integration is testing for cointegration among time series of prices for market pairs. In our research, generally, P_t^i and P_t^j are individually non-stationary.[7] To test whether there is a long-run equilibrium relationship between P_t^i and P_t^j or whether the two price series are cointegrated, we follow Engle and Granger (1987) and estimate the following equation by OLS:

$$P_t^j = \alpha_T^{ij} + \beta_T^{ij} P_t^i + e_t^{ij}. \tag{2.7}$$

If P_t^i and P_t^j are cointegrated, there will be some parameters α_T^{ij} and β_T^{ij} such that $P_t^j - \alpha_T^{ij} - \beta_T^{ij} P_t^i = 0$ is satisfied in the long run.[8] To test for this, one needs to examine the time series property of e_t^{ij}. Since P_t^i and P_t^j are cointegrated if and only if e_t^{ij} is stationary, an augmented Dickey–Fuller test on $\hat{e}_t^{ij}$, the residual of Eq. (2.7), is employed:

$$\Delta \hat{e}_t^{ij} = \theta_T^{ij} \hat{e}_{t-1}^{ij} + \sum_{k=1}^{n} \psi_{Tk}^{ij} \Delta \hat{e}_{t-k}^{ij} + u_t^{ij}, \tag{2.8}$$

where the lagged $\Delta \hat{e}_t^{ij}$'s are added as regressors to reduce the serial correlation problem. Under the null hypothesis that e_t^{ij} is non-stationary, the parameter θ_T^{ij} is equal to zero. According to Keller and Shiue (2007), the stronger is the evidence that $\theta_T^{ij} < 0$, the more convincing is that P_t^i and P_t^j are cointegrated, or that local markets in prefecture i and in prefecture j are integrated. The measure they use is the t-statistic for θ_T^{ij}. A very negative t-statistic indicates a strong support for the cointegrating relationship between P_t^i and P_t^j.

Like the price correlation, it is very helpful to study the above t-statistic in our proposed framework. When it is in Regime 1

---

[7]The null hypothesis of a unit root cannot be rejected using the augmented Dickey–Fuller test. The average p-value for the null of a unit root is 0.42.

[8]In general, there are three functional forms for Eq. (2.7). Aside from the one presented here, the other two are the following: α_T^{ij} is omitted from the right hand side; a deterministic trend term $\gamma_T^{ij} t$ is added to the right hand side.

(with the probability λ_T^{ij}), P_t^i and P_t^j are cointegrated and thus the t-statistic is very negative. When it is in Regime 2 (with the probability $1 - \lambda_T^{ij}$), P_t^i and P_t^j are not cointegrated and thus the t-statistic is close to zero. Again, the whole-sample t-statistic can be thought of as a "weighted average" of Regimes 1 and 2. Therefore, the more negative the t-statistic is, the higher the probability of Regime 1 is, and consequently there is a higher integration of market i and market j.

2.5.   Empirical Results

Our data cover 17 prefectures in the Yangzi delta, an area of 133,080 square kilometers. The population of this region rose from 44.89 million in 1776 to 55.13 million in 1825. As discussed before, we focus our attention to two periods: Jan. 1770–Dec. 1779 (denoted as period 1) and Jan. 1810–Dec. 1819 (denoted as period 2). For each prefecture k, the monthly rice price data are used. To investigate local market integration, we first estimate the pairwise arbitrage cost and the corresponding arbitrage probability, utilizing the methodology proposed in the previous section, and then we calculate the conventional measures in the literature: the price correlation and the cointegration t-statistic. Through cross-time comparison, a time trend of market integration can be identified.

2.5.1.   *Arbitrage cost and arbitrage probability*

Applying the methodology detailed in Section 2.4.1, we obtain the maximum likelihood estimates (MLE) of interested parameters. In particular, for a given period T and for each pair of prefectures i and j, we focus on the arbitrage probability λ_T^{ij} and the arbitrage cost b_T^{ij}, where T can be period 1 (Jan. 1770–Dec. 1779) or period 2 (Jan. 1810–Dec. 1819).

Figure A.2.1(a) graphs the arbitrage cost b_T^{ij} against the distance between prefectures i and j. In the scatter plot, each point represents a point estimate of b_T^{ij}. To make things clearer, we also draw the lowess (locally weighted scatterplot smoothing) curves for period 1 and period 2. The lowess curves are generally upward sloping, indicating a positive relationship between the arbitrage cost and the physical distance. This is intuitive as the further two markets are lying from each other, the higher the transportation cost and the in-transit loss are. More importantly, period 2's lowess curve clearly lies above period 1's. That is, the arbitrage cost is generally higher in period 2 than in period 1. This pattern is further supported by the summary statistics of b_T^{ij}'s. For instance, its mean rises from 3.17 in period 1 to 3.78 in period 2, and at the same time, its median increases from 3.27 in period 1 to 3.87 in period 2.[9]

Similarly, Figure A.2.1(b) graphs the arbitrage probability λ_T^{ij} against the distance between prefectures i and j. Again, each point represents a point estimate of λ_T^{ij}, and the curves are the lowess functions of periods 1 and 2. Apparently, period 2's lowess curve is beneath period 1's in the graph, which implies that the arbitrage probability is generally lower in period 2 than in period 1. Summary statistics of λ_T^{ij}'s echo this pattern: Its mean drops from 0.76 in period 1 to 0.61 in period 2; and meanwhile, its median declines from 0.80 in period 1 to 0.64 in period 2.

Overall, changes in the arbitrage cost and the arbitrage probability point to a same conclusion here: The market integration in the Yangzi delta was weakened, rather than strengthened, from the period Jan. 1770–Dec. 1779 to the period Jan. 1810–Dec. 1819. Such a Chinese phenomenon is in stark contrast to what had happened in the Western Europe at times before and after the Industrial Revolution.

2.5.2. *Price correlation and ADF t-statistic*

To be complete, we also use the conventional measures of price correlation coefficients and cointegration test statistics to check the local market integrations. Section 2.4.2 spells out the details of the methods, particularly, in the context of our proposed framework.

Figure A.2.1(c) shows the scatter plots and lowess curves of the price correlation, $Corr(P_T^i, P_T^j)$, vs. the geographic distance between a pair of prefectures, d^{ij}. As in Shiue and Keller (2007), the price correlation appears to be negatively related to the physical distance. It seems that distance is an obstacle for the law of one price to

---

[9]Note that in our model, the level of arbitrage cost is $e^{b_T^{ij}}$.

hold. More importantly, the lowess curve in period 2 lies beneath the one in period 1. As our theory suggests that a larger correlation indicates a higher degree of market integration, the graph shows that the market integration became weaker in period 2 than in period 1. It is also verified by changes in price correlation's summary statistics: The mean and the median drop from 0.74 and 0.81 in period 1 to 0.50 and 0.56 in period 2, respectively.

In Figure A.2.1(d), we plot the ADF t-statistic on Eq. (2.7)'s θ_T^{ij} against the distance between prefectures i and j, and the associated lowess functions. From the scatter plot, we see that most ADF t-statistics are very negative, implying that the cointegration relationship exists for P_t^i and P_t^j in a majority of times. More importantly, the lowess curve in period 2 lies above the one in period 1. According to our theory, a more negative ADF t-statistic implies a higher degree of market integration. Figure A.2.1(d) tells us that the market integration became weaker in period 2 than in period 1. The changes in ADF t-statistics also verify the following finding: The mean and the median rise from –3.39 and –3.33 in period 1, to –2.86 and –2.81 in period 2, respectively.

To sum up, both the conventional measures for quantifying market integration, the price correlation between local markets and the ADF t-statistic used to test the cointegrating relationship between local market prices, show that the market integration became weaker in the period of Jan. 1810–Dec. 1819 than in the period of Jan. 1770–Dec. 1779. This result is consistent with our conclusion based on the arbitrage cost and the arbitrage probability.

2.6.   Robustness Check

In this section, we conduct two robustness checks. In particular, alternative time spans and geographical region are specified one at a time. We investigate how sensitive our conclusion in the previous section is to the above changes.

2.6.1.   *Alternative time ranges*

First, we examine whether the time spans we choose are critical for our results. We modify period 1 from Jan. 1770–Dec. 1779 to

Jan. 1760–Dec. 1799, and period 2 from Jan. 1810–Dec. 1819 to Jan. 1800–Dec. 1839. That is, we extend each period from 10 years to 40 years. Figures A.2.2(a)–A.2.2(d) are the counterparts of Figures A.2.1(a)–A.2.1(d), respectively. It is obvious that all the results still hold qualitatively despite the change in time ranges.

2.6.2. *Alternative macro-region: Middle Yangzi region*

Second, we want to see whether the decline of intraregional market integration is a special case occurring only to the Yangzi delta. So we repeat our exercises using the rice price data of a different region, a macro-region called the Middle Yangzi region (Skinner, 1964). This is a relatively prosperous area in then China but less developed than the Yangzi delta. Again, Figures A.2.3(a)–A.2.3(d) are the counterparts of Figures A.2.1(a) to A.2.1(d), respectively. When we compare Figure A.2.3(b) with Figure A.2.1(a) or Figure A.2.3(c) with Figure A.2.1(c), we find that local markets integrated to a lesser degree in the Middle Yangzi region than in the Yangzi delta, in a cross-section sense. Despite this difference between these two macro-regions, the weakening trend of intraregional market integration holds for both regions, no matter whichever measure is used. Therefore, the weakening of intraregional market integration is not specific to only the Yangzi delta; it is rather a general phenomenon taking place in China in the Qing Dynasty.

In summary, our sensitivity analysis based upon different time windows and macro-region indicates that results in the previous section are very robust. The intraregional market integration became weaker as time went by in China in the Qing Dynasty. This is a stylized fact supported by strong empirical evidence.

2.7. Conclusion

In this chapter, through econometric analysis, we demonstrate that the intraregional market integration was on the decline during the Industrial Revolution era when Western European countries saw increasing market integration. Our result echoes the findings of Bernhofen *et al.* (2017), who however, apply a different approach and do not distinguish the intraregional and interregional market integrations.

This chapter also contributes to the literature by presenting a unified theoretical framework in which the notion of market integration can be understood with ease. Essentially, it is based upon the law of one price, with stochastic factors taken into account. The key parameters include the arbitrage cost and the associated arbitrage probability. Our numerical exercises show that China went through a rise in the former and a decline in the latter in the late 18th and early 19th centuries. Finally, the traditional measures of market integration, the price correlation, and the cointegration t-statistic become more intuitive in the context of our framework.

Future research may extend our analysis along two lines. First, one can go one step further and explore the reasons why the arbitrage cost and the corresponding arbitrage probability within a region deteriorated in Qing China during the Industrial Revolution era. It would be helpful if we can pinpoint some major events or socioeconomic developments that underlie the observed changes. Second, our theoretical framework and the associated empirical methodology can be utilized to study the interregional market integration evolution in Qing China to test whether Rawski (1972) and Pomeranz (2000)'s arguments hold, econometrically.

Acknowledgments

We thank the participants of the complexity seminar at Sichuan University for their helpful comments and suggestions. Chuantao Cui acknowledges financial support from Sichuan University's Startup Research Grant.

Appendix

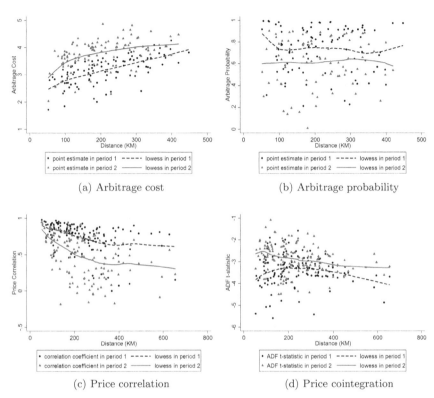

(a) Arbitrage cost   (b) Arbitrage probability

(c) Price correlation   (d) Price cointegration

Fig. A.2.1. Baseline: (a) arbitrage cost; (b) arbitrage probability; (c) price correlation; (d) price cointegration.

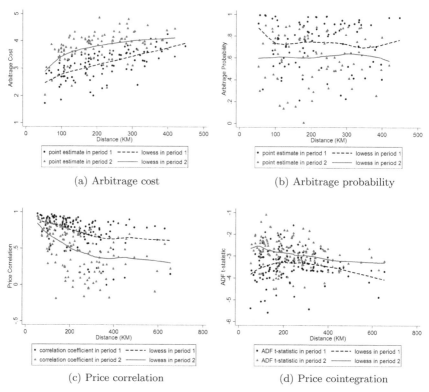

(a) Arbitrage cost

(b) Arbitrage probability

(c) Price correlation

(d) Price cointegration

Fig. A.2.2. Alternative times: (a) arbitrage cost; (b) arbitrage probability; (c) price correlation; (d) price cointegration.

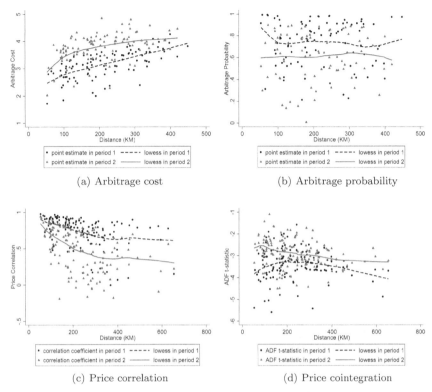

(a) Arbitrage cost   (b) Arbitrage probability

(c) Price correlation   (d) Price cointegration

Fig. A.2.3. Middle Yangzi region: (a) arbitrage cost; (b) arbitrage probability; (c) price correlation; (d) price cointegration.

References

Allen, R. C. and R. Unger (1990). "The depth and breadth of the market for polish grain, 1500–1800," in *Baltic Affairs: Relations between the Netherlands and North-Eastern Europe, 1500–1800*, pp. 1–18.

Bernhofen, D., M. Eberhardt, J. Li, and S. Morgan (2017). "The evolution of markets in China and Western Europe on the eve of industrialisation," *Discussion Papers 2017-12*, University of Nottingham, GEP.

Brenner, R. (1976). "Agrarian Class Structure and Economic Development in Pre-industrial Europe," *Past & Present*, 70, 30–75.

Clark, G. (2005). "Human Capital, Fertility, and the Industrial Revolution," *Journal of the European Economic Association*, 3, 505–515.

Clark, G. (2008). *A Farewell to Alms: A Brief Economic History of the World*, Vol. 25, Princeton, USA: Princeton University Press.

Engle, R. F. and C. W. J. Granger (1987). "Co-integration and Error Correction: Representation, Estimation, and Testing," *Econometrica*, 55, 251–276.

Frank, A. G. (1998). *ReOrient: Global Economy in the Asian Age*, Berkeley: University of California Press.

Keller, W. and C. H. Shiue (2007). "Market Integration and Economic Development: A Long-run Comparison," *Review of Development Economics*, 11, 107–123.

Kishimoto, M. (1997). *Price and Economic Fluctuation of Qing China*, Tokyo: Kenbun Shuppan.

Landes, D. S. (2006). "Why Europe and the West? Why not China?" *Journal of Economic Perspectives*, 20, 3–22.

Li, B. (2010). *China's Early Modern Economy: A Study of GDP of the Huating-Lou Area in the 1820s*, Beijing: Zhonghua Book Company.

Mora-Sitja, N. (2007). "Labour Market Integration in a Pre-Industrial Economy: Catalonia, 1772–1816," *Oxford Economic Papers*, 59, i156–i177.

North, D. C. (1981). *Structure and Change in Economic History*, New York, USA: Norton.

North, D. C. and R. P. Thomas (1973). *The Rise of the Western World: A New Economic History*, Cambridge, UK: Cambridge University Press.

North, D. C. and B. R. Weingast (1989). "Constitutions and commitment: The evolution of institutions governing public choice in seventeenth-century England," *The Journal of Economic History*, 49, 803–832.

Pomeranz, K. (2000). *The Great Divergence: China, Europe, and the Making of the Modern World Economy*, Princeton, USA: Princeton University Press.

Rawski, E. S. (1972). *Agricultural Change and the Peasant*, Cambridge, USA: Harvard University Press.

Ronsijn, W. (2014). "Smallholders, Spinners, Weavers and the 'Scarcity of Markets' in the Flemish Countryside, C. 1780–1850: Motivations Behind the Multiplication of Periodic Markets," *Rural History*, 25, 39–60.

Rothenberg, W. B. (1992). *From Market Places to a Market Economy: The Transformation of rural Massachusetts, 1750–1850*, Chicago, USA: University of Chicago Press.

Sexton, R. J., C. L. Kling, and H. F. Carman (1991). "Market Integration, Efficiency of Arbitrage, and Imperfect Competition: Methodology and Application to US Celery," *American Journal of Agricultural Economics*, 73, 568–580.

Shiue, C. H. and W. Keller (2007). "Markets in China and Europe on the Eve of the Industrial Revolution," *American Economic Review*, 97, 1189–1216.

Skinner, G. W. (1964). "Marketing and Social Structure in Rural China, Part I," *The Journal of Asian Studies*, 24, 3–43.

Spiller, P. T. and C. J. Huang (1986). "On the Extent of the Market: Wholesale Gasoline in the Northeastern United States," *The Journal of Industrial Economics*, 35, 131–145.

Studer, R. (2008). "India and the Great Divergence: Assessing the Efficiency of Grain Markets in Eighteenth-and Nineteenth-century India," *The Journal of Economic History*, 68, 393–437.

Unger, R. W. (1983). "Integration of Baltic and Low Countries Grain Markets, 1400–1800," in *The Interactions of Amsterdam and Antwerp with the Baltic Region, 1400–1800*, New York, USA: Springer, 1–10.

Wong, R. B. (1997). *China Transformed: Historical Change and the Limits of European Experience*, Ithaca, New York: Cornell University Press.

Wu, C. (2007). *Economic History: Historical View and Methodology*, Shanghai: Shanghai University of Finance and Economics Press.

Yan, S. and C. Liu (2011). "Market Integration in Southern and Northern China in the Eighteenth Century: A Study Based on Grain Price Data in Qing Dynasty," *Economic Research Journal*, 12, 124–137.

Chapter 3

China's Regional Convergence and Policy: A View from Regional Science

Chunlin Wan[*,†] and Fengming Li[*,‡,§]

*School of Economics, Sichuan University, China
†chunlinwan@scu.edu.cn
‡lifengmingscu@foxmail.com

Abstract

Since the founding of the People's Republic of China, substantial changes have occurred in China's economic growth and regional development strategies. This study first reviews the four main stages of China's regional economic strategy and then analyzes the transformation of the country's regional development path from unbalanced regional development to coordinated regional development. It then lists the main tools of the regional policies. Lastly, it evaluates the gap in China's regional economic development, discusses its existing problems, and offers solutions. This study promotes an understanding of the development of China's regional policy as well as its regional coordinated development strategies.

3.1. Introduction

Since the founding of the People's Republic of China (PRC), substantial changes in China's economic growth and regional development strategy have resulted in significant impacts on the economic

---

§Corresponding author.

development of different regions in the country. Therefore, a study of the evolution of China's regional policies is beneficial to understand China's economic and regional development.

First, this study reviews the four stages of China's regional economic strategy development since the founding of the PRC. The first stage (1949–1978) was the balanced development stage. To rectify the concentration of industry and transportation in coastal areas, China's central government implemented the "balanced layout" strategy in inland areas in this stage. The main feature of this strategy was to pursue balance in economic development under closed market conditions. The second stage (1979–1998) was the unbalanced development stage. To assess the comparative advantages between the coastal areas, the central government implemented the "unbalanced development strategy." This strategy supported coastal areas, as the superior areas, to take the lead in development and helped it develop under open market conditions. The third stage (1999–2011) was the stage of unbalanced but coordinated regional development. To narrow the regional development gap, the preferential policy in this stage supported less developed areas. It split the overall strategy into four perspectives: "western development," "northeast revitalization," "central rise," and "coastal first." The fourth stage (2012–present) is the coordinated regional development stage (Zhu and Zhang, 2004; Deng *et al.*, 2015; Bo and An, 2016). Regional policies aim at comprehensive and coordinated development by combining economic zones and belts. Thus, through the exploration of regional policy evolution, regional policy tools, and regional development problems, we can understand the development of China's regional policies and their impacts. This is conducive to the construction of a modern regional development system appropriate for the new era.

The remainder of this chapter is organized as follows. Sections 3.2–3.5 review the four development stages of China's regional strategy. Section 3.6 analyzes the evolution of China's regional economic development gap. Section 3.7 presents the conclusions.

3.2. The Stage of Balanced Development (1949–1978)

In the early days, China inherited an extremely unbalanced regional development. The eastern coastal region dominated economic growth.

Table 3.1. Number of industrial enterprises above scale in 1952.

Eastern region	Number	Central region	Number	Western region	Number
Beijing	34,386	Shanxi	3,318	Inner Mongolia	1,353
Tianjin	82	Jilin	3,542	Guangxi	90,090
Hebei	7,553	Heilongjiang	5,769	Chongqing	5,863
Liaoning	10,696	Anhui	4,439	Sichuan	14,340
Shanghai	25,878	Jiangxi	4,225	Guizhou	52
Jiangsu	9,661	Henan	4,246	Yunnan	2,161
Zhejiang	3,269	Hubei	5,028	Shaanxi	5,402
Fujian	6,131	Hunan	290	Gansu	1,447
Shandong	1,41,292			Qinghai	48
Guangdong	12,362			Ningxia	686
Hainan	35			Xinjiang	771
Total	2,51,345		30,857		1,22,213
Percentage	62.15%		7.63%		30.22%

Source: China Statistical Yearbook.

According to the data of 1952, 62.2% of industrial enterprises above designated size were in this region. Other than a few big cities, such as Wuhan and Chongqing, the industrial base of the mainland was extremely weak. This was especially true for the central region, which accounted for only 7.6% (see Table 3.1). Thus, development was extremely uneven and had gaps among the eastern, central, and western regions.

Narrowing the economic development gap between the coastal and inland areas was the Chinese central government's priority at that time. The First Five-Year Plan (1953–1957) indicated that "it is one of the major tasks to properly distribute industrial productive forces in all regions of the country: to locate them near the production and consumption areas of raw materials and fuels, to make the industry distribution suitable for the conditions for consolidating national defense, and to gradually improve the economically backward areas."

Combining the characteristics of Chinese regional distribution and the lessons from the Soviet Union, the first generation of Chinese leadership gradually formed the idea of balanced development, that is, the mainland layout of key industrial. First, the strategy in this stage was aimed at rapidly changing the over-dependence on coastal areas. Second, the strategy aimed at laying the industrial foundation in the central and eastern areas to facilitate new industry growth.

Due to the historical conditions in China, the enterprises built during this period mainly belonged to the heavy and defense industries. During the period of the First Five-Year Plan, 472 of the 694 industrial investment projects were in the inland or mainland areas. Of the 156 key construction projects, aided by the Soviet Union (150 were constructed), 118 were located in the mainland and only 32 were located along the coast. During the same period, with the increasing investment in key national projects, the percentage contribution of mainland industrial output to the national total industrial output rose from 29.2% in 1952 to 32.1% in 1957. Meanwhile, under the guidance of preferential investment policies, the share of capital construction investment in the central and western regions rose from 21.7% and 15.1%, respectively, in 1953 to 28.2% and 23.0%, respectively, in 1957 (see Figure 3.1).

In the mid- to late-1960s, due to the need to be combat ready, the central government decided to distribute industries and move economic activities to third-tier areas. This was done to preserve as much economic strength, that may be otherwise damaged by the war, as possible. At the same time, various regions established relatively independent industrial systems to prevent the possible impact of the war on the overall economy. According to the policy of "putting national defense construction first, speeding up the third-tier construction, and gradually changing the industrial layout," the National

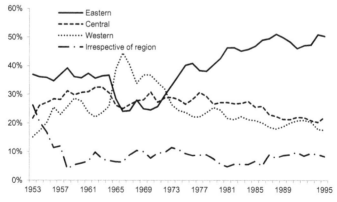

Fig. 3.1.   Capital construction investments in various regions of China (1953–1995).

Source: China's Fixed Assets Investment Statistics (1953–1995).

Planning Conference held in August 1965 decided that the focus of state investment should be on the large mainland third-tier areas. Additionally, the focus of each province's construction should be on its own small third-tier areas (see Table 3.2).

During the period of the Third Five-Year Plan (1966–1970), the infrastructure investment in the mainland accounted for 64.7% of the national total. From this, 52.7% was used in the third-tier areas. From 1969 to 1972, Sichuan province, which had more large projects than other areas, accounted for 12.1% of the national investment. Hubei and Guangdong provinces accounted for 7.4% and 3.3%, respectively. Shanghai accounted for only 2.4% in the same period.

Through large-scale investment in the central and western regions, the inland economy developed rapidly. Hence, the goals of having a balanced distribution of productive forces and laying an industrial foundation for the inland regions within a short period of time were realized. Without the industrial development and infrastructure construction during this period, inland economic and social development may have been delayed for decades. It is the industrial foundation laid during this period that strongly supported the rapid growth of the coastal areas, and by extension, the entire national economy after the introduction of the program of reforms. The program of reforms encouraged opening up the country to foreign investment (henceforth, "Reform and Opening").

Although the balanced development idea focusing on inland areas narrowed the development gap between the coastal areas and the mainland to a certain extent, the ideas copied from the classical theories of Marxism and the experiences of the Soviet Union left several

Table 3.2.   Number of large- and medium-sized capital construction investment projects.

Period	National	Eastern region	Central region	Western region	Irrespective of region
1953–1957	595	241	157	119	78
1958–1962	581	245	130	132	74
1963–1965	355	127	76	62	90
1966–1970	743	162	219	330	32
1971–1975	742	208	241	272	21

Source: China's Fixed Assets Investment Statistics Code (1950–2000).

problems. First, the government overemphasized resource allocation.
The national mandatory plan was regarded as the key method to realize efficient distribution. However, doing so resulted in the role of the
market in resource distribution being neglected. Second, the overemphasis on the importance of politics and national defense, along with
the ignorance of economic importance, resulted in serious location
problems for many large-scale enterprises. It created a large amount
of inefficient investment. From 1953 to 1980, the total value of fixed
assets of China's state-owned industries increased by 20 times and
the working capital increased by 18 times. However, the total value
of output increased by only 7.2 times. Third, the supplements provided to the inland areas made it difficult for the eastern coastal
areas to retain their comparative advantage on location and industrial foundations. This resulted in a slowdown in economic growth
and eventually led to the loss of social fairness and national economic
efficiency (Xiao and An, 2019).

3.3.   Unbalanced Development Stage (1979–1998)

3.3.1.   *Priority development area—Eastern coastal areas (1979–1990)*

In the 1960s and 1970s, China experienced a period of relative chaos
in political and economic development. The national economy was on
the verge of collapse. Low self-development abilities in economically
backward areas, frequent economic fluctuation, structural imbalance,
and declining efficiency were prominent issues. Moreover, the massive investment injecting into the areas after 1949 did not result
in satisfactory economic outcomes. Instead, this balanced development strategy artificially distorted the distribution function of the
market and resulted in low growth of efficiency and the economy
(Liu *et al.*, 2020).

   In 1988, based on the idea of "Two Overall Situations" proposed
by Deng Xiaoping, the central government changed the balanced
development strategy to an unbalanced development strategy, giving priority to improving efficiency. Eastern coastal areas with comparative advantages in capital, location, and development levels were
prioritized for development. Input in such areas could result in higher
efficiency and promote economic growth in other areas.

Improving efficiency was the dominant goal of implementing preferential policies in the coastal region. Policies from within China and from overseas were implemented to facilitate economic development (or economic processes) in coastal areas within a short period of time. Economic development of coastal areas was not the ultimate goal of the Chinese central government. Rather, the goal was to cultivate the coastal areas into a national economic growth focus through the implementation of preferential policies, and then to realize the common prosperity and development of the national economy through diffusion effects (Xiao and An, 2019).

During this period, the central government prioritized coastal areas with better location and economic conditions, shifted the investment layout eastward and implemented "special policies and flexible measures" for Guangdong and Fujian provinces. The main policies, measures, and tools included the following:

1. *Investment policies*: The main policy was to increase infrastructure investment in coastal areas. At the beginning of the Reform and Opening, the central government increased investments in the energy industry, high-tech industries, ports, aviation airports, and urban construction. Increased investments were also focused on the construction of roads and communication systems in special economic zones and coastal cities. From 1979 to 1990, infrastructure investment in coastal areas in the eastern region increased from 43.5% to 53.8%. The investment volume increased from 20.6 billion Yuan to 85.5 billion Yuan, an increase of 314.2% (see Table 3.3).
2. *Preferential policies*: To better absorb the industries and capital transferred by developed countries and establish wider economic ties with the global economy, the central government provided a large number of tax policies for coastal areas to let in foreign capital and expand foreign trade. In addition, some special concessions were given to foreign investors who invested in infrastructure supply, material trade, and entry and exit of personnel in China.
3. *More discretionary power*: Coastal special economic zones, open cities, open areas, and various industrial parks were given greater space in decision-making, including extensive authority on project approval, foreign trade management rights, project construction, land use conveyance, and foreign economic activities.

Table 3.3.   Regional distribution of capital construction investment.

Year	Capital construction investment (Billion Yuan)				Proportion (%)		
	National	Eastern	Central	West	Eastern	Central	West
1979	474.04	206.35	136.33	131.36	43.53	28.76	27.71
1980	514.34	231.74	147.57	135.03	45.06	28.69	26.25
1981	415.62	203.06	117.87	94.69	48.86	28.36	22.78
1982	517.50	253.41	146.87	117.22	48.97	28.38	22.65
1983	536.44	259.69	146.42	130.33	48.41	27.29	24.30
1984	685.68	331.79	198.60	155.29	48.39	28.96	22.65
1985	979.59	488.70	267.95	222.94	49.89	27.35	22.76
1986	1086.00	560.28	294.99	230.73	51.59	27.16	21.25
1987	1253.50	679.31	318.11	256.08	54.19	25.38	20.43
1988	1491.08	835.05	363.94	292.09	56.00	24.41	19.59
1989	1448.25	802.22	340.00	306.03	55.39	23.48	21.13
1990	1589.07	854.71	383.48	350.88	53.79	24.13	22.08

Source: Calculated according to the relevant data of Compilation of Statistical Data for 50 Years of New China (1949–1999), China's Fixed Assets Investment Statistics Code (1950–2000) and China Statistical Yearbook (2000–2004).

4. *Special economic zones and industrial parks*: First, since 1979, the central government has successively established five special economic zones along the coast in Shenzhen, Zhuhai, Shantou, Xiamen, and Hainan. Second, it has supported 14 coastal open cities (including Dalian and Qinhuangdao), of which 12 open cities have set up the first batch of economic and technological development zones. Third, it has opened the Yangtze river delta, Pearl river delta, Xiamen–Zhangzhou–Quanzhou Triangle in southern Fujian, Shandong peninsula, Liaodong peninsula, Bohai Rim, and Pudong New Area. Last, it has taken the lead in setting up bonded areas along the coast.

5. *Institutional innovation*: This is one of the core purposes and components for implementing the opening up and coastal preferential policies. Giving coastal areas more privileges and development space, exploring the coexistence mode of various ownership systems, and gradually establishing a market economy framework that can be extended to other regions of the country are important tools for the coastal preferential policy.

The formation of the regional unbalanced development strategy, which prioritized improving efficiency in the eastern region, was not only the result of introspection on the actual effect of the balanced development strategy, but also an effective response to the changes in the domestic and foreign economic, political, and social environment that China was facing at that time. The unbalanced regional development strategy had a significant driving and promoting effect on both the eastern coastal regions and the overall economic growth of the country. This was achieved by focusing on the development of the eastern coastal areas, which had a better foundation and greater development potential. However, the unbalanced development strategy also plunged the mainland and the coast into a comparative income trap, widening the gap between the two regions. The share of GDP in the eastern region increased from 52.3% in 1978 to 60.1% in 1990, while the central and western regions dropped from 31.2% and 16.5%, respectively, to 26.8% and 13.1%, respectively. This signified potential to mitigate prioritizing the improvement of efficiency in the east by stressing the need to narrow the development gap between the coast and the mainland.

3.3.2. *Regional coordinated development strategy (1991–1998)*

To implement the layout of an unbalanced development strategy, special economic zones were established in the eastern coastal areas. Furthermore, a series of preferential policies were bought into force, such as approval authority for foreign capital construction projects, taxation, foreign exchange retention and use, foreign trade, and credit. In 1979, Shekou and Shenzhen took the lead in establishing a special economic zone. In 1980, Zhuhai, Shantou, and Xiamen also set up special economic zones. In 1984, 14 coastal port cities were opened. In 1985, the Yangtze river delta, Pearl river delta, Xiamen–Zhangzhou–Quanzhou Triangle, Jiaodong peninsula, and Liaodong peninsula economic development zones were established. Since then, the economy in the eastern coastal areas has shown a pattern of vigorous development and has become the driving force for the rapid economic growth of the entire nation.

Meanwhile, to promote the coordinated development of the regional economy and optimize the distribution of regional resources, the central government adopted the following policies during this period:

1. *Implementation of an all-round opening up policy*: In November 1988, the State Council approved the "Minutes of Discussion on Xinjiang's Opening Up," which gave Xinjiang a series of preferential policies in progressing toward the opening of the region's borders. In 1991, the No. 25 document of the State Council defined the guidelines and preferential policies for border trade. Deng Xiaoping's speech in 1992 signified the acceleration of the opening of the central and western regions on the back of achievements of coastal areas. In 1992, the State Council gradually approved the opening of the Heihe, Suifenhe, Manzhouli, Hunchun, Yining, Tacheng, Bole, Pingxiang, Dongxing, Wanding, Ruili, Hekou, and Erenhot regions. Additionally, Chongqing, Yueyang, Wuhan, Jiujiang, Wuhu, Huangshi, Yichang, Wanxian, Fuling along the Yangtze River, and inland provincial capitals were gradually opened up. The Yangtze Gorges economic open zone as well as several state-level economic and technological development zones was formed in the central and western regions. Moreover, the examination and approval authority of local government were extensive in order to encourage foreign direct investment in these regions. As a result, a multi-level, multi-channel, and all-round pattern of opening up had been formed nationwide, combining the capitals of coastal, border, riverside, and inland provinces.

2. *Adjustment of national investment and industrial distribution policies*: To accelerate economic development in the central and western regions, the central government increased the investment percentage in the central and western regions. The government also actively promoted the transfer and diffusion of some coastal processing and manufacturing industries to resource-rich areas in the central and western regions. During the Eighth Five-Year Plan (1991–1995), the central government proposed giving equal priority to the western region in the development and utilization of resources, and the distribution of large- and medium-sized construction projects to increase investment. During the Ninth Five-Year Plan (1996–2000), to speed up the construction of energy and raw material industrial bases in the central and western regions,

the central government further increased investment in key construction projects in these regions. Since the mid-1990s, the investment percentage of the national budget in coastal areas has been declining, while those in the central and western regions have gradually increased. The ratio of investment in coastal areas to inland areas dropped from 0.95 in 1994 to 0.84 in 1998.

In September 1993, the State Council once again decided to increase special loans by 5 billion Yuan per year from 1994 to 2000 to support township enterprises in the central and western regions. In February 1995, the State Council officially approved the implementation of the East–West Cooperation Demonstration Project for Township Enterprises. Furthermore, the Ministry of Agriculture set up a number of demonstration zones for east–west cooperation between township enterprises. To solve the overcapacity issue of cotton and spinning production, and the detachment between processing capacity and raw material base, the central government proposed to guide coastal areas and central cities to gradually transfer the primary processing capacity of cotton spinning to cotton-producing areas that were in the process of a spindle pressing transformation in the central and western regions. The government prioritized supporting some large- and medium-sized cities, such as Beijing, Tianjin, Shanghai, and Guangdong for policies and funds to transfer spindles to Xinjiang.

Based on the different comparative advantages of various regions in China, the unbalanced regional development strategy was in line with China's economic and social development environment at that time. Thus, it changed the low efficiency situation of high input and low output. The unbalanced regional development strategy not only realized the rapid development of eastern coastal areas, but also had a significant driving and promoting effect on the overall economic growth of China. However, the strategy also plunged the inland and the coastal areas into a comparative income trap and widened the gap between regions. This shows that the unbalanced development strategy of giving priority to improving efficiency in the east needs to be further adjusted, and the adjustment should be aimed at narrowing the development gap between the coast and the mainland.

3.4. Regional Coordinated Development Stage with Complementary Advantages (1999–2011)

The development of the western region, the "depression disease" in the old industrial bases, such as the northeast region, the "stagflation disease" in coastal cities, and the "lag disease" in the central region were prominent to varying degrees. After years of development, the old industrial bases in Northeast China and other regions had seen resource depletion, industry aging, and a decline of leading industries. As successive industries were not developed in time, and new leading industries were not labeled, the economy remained in a depressed state. The urban areas of the Yangtze river delta, the Pearl river delta, and the Bohai Rim Beijing–Tianjin–Tangshan urban agglomerations along the eastern coast are highly populated and industry intensive. These regions have a high percentage of traditional industries, heavy traffic, serious environmental pollution, and a lack of room for development of high-tech and tertiary industries. The central region has sluggish development and slow growth, which made it the "economically depressed" region of the entire country (Zhu and Zhang, 2004).

In response to the above problems, a major strategic plan had been proposed to build a harmonious society and coordinate regional development. The central government proposed to "continue to promote the development of the western region, revitalize the old industrial bases in the northeast region, promote the rise of the central region, encourage the eastern region to take the lead in development, form a regional industrial structure with reasonable division of labor, obvious characteristics and complementary advantages, and promote the common development of all regions."

3.4.1. *Western development strategy (1999–)*

The central government had insisted on coordinated development of the regional economy since the 1980s. In the early 1990s, the central government established an all-round policy of opening borders. This involved opening 13 border cities, five cities along the Yangtze River, the capital cities of the four provinces along the border, and the capital cities of 11 inland provinces. However, from the perspective of effectiveness, the substantive differences in the central region's policies were apparent. The regional gap was growing rapidly within the Chinese economy. Therefore, the gap between coastal and inland areas was widening. Critics blame this on the "unequal investment of central government," "unfair policy environment," and "different start lines for competition" (Zhu and Zhang, 2004). However, in this process, the Reform and Opening leading regions established their regional advantages. Under the influence of market forces, the phenomenon of going southeast appeared in capital and manpower.

In this context, to promote the coordinated development of Chinese regions, narrow the regional economic gap, and build an efficient, coordinated, and sustainable pattern of land and space development, the central government put forward the strategic concept of western development at the end of 1999. It began the third regional policy adjustment since the Reform and Opening was introduced. In March 1999, the State Council issued "Several Opinions on Further Promoting the Development of the Western Region" and put forward ten ideas on further promoting the development of the western region. The Central Economic Work Conference, held at the end of the same year, formally put forward a strategy for the development of the western region. In 2000, the central government's "Report on the Work of the Government" formally proposed the implementation of the strategy of developing the western region and formed the office of the leading group for its development. In 2001, the Tenth Five-Year Plan (2001–2005) further emphasized the need to "implement the strategy of developing the western region and promote coordinated regional development." The targets for western development included Shaanxi, Gansu, Ningxia, Qinghai, Xinjiang, Sichuan, Chongqing, Yunnan, Guizhou, Tibet, Inner Mongolia, and Guangxi.

To promote the development of the western region, the following policies were implemented:

1. *Acceleration of the construction of infrastructure*: These policies focused on implementing large-scale trans-regional resource allocation projects, such as West-to-East Gas Transmission and West-to-East Electricity Transmission, and speeding up the construction of trans-regional railway corridors. After 20 years of construction, the mileage of highways in the western region increased from 549,800 km to 2.0265 million km. The mileage of expressways

Table 3.4.   Mileage of infrastructure in western region (10,000 km).

Year	Highway	Expressway	Railway	Inland waterway
1999	54.98	0.25	2.46	2.19
2000	57.13	0.36	2.2	2.19
2001	71.96	0.43	2.58	2.35
2002	74.67	0.57	2.67	2.35
2003	76.03	0.69	2.67	3.09
2004	77.82	0.87	2.71	3.07
2005	80.14	1.05	2.76	3.08
2006	127.85	1.17	2.92	3.09
2007	135.71	1.49	2.95	3.10
2008	143.97	1.65	2.95	3.10
2009	152.46	1.85	3.28	3.11
2010	158.95	2.13	3.58	3.16
2011	164.58	2.53	3.64	3.19
2012	171.00	2.90	3.74	3.20
2013	176.22	3.38	3.95	3.28
2014	181.99	3.82	4.36	3.31
2015	187.45	4.4	4.78	3.35
2016	193.37	4.75	5.02	3.38
2017	197.5	5.09	5.20	3.38
2018	202.65	5.36	5.29	3.38

Source: China Statistical Yearbook.

increased from 25,000 km to 53,600 km, accounting for 37.6% of the whole country (see Table 3.4).

2. *Environmental policies*: In the late 1990s, the central government started natural forest protection, ecological agriculture, sand prevention and control, and other projects in the western region. In 2002, the central government officially started the project of returning farmland to forests and grasslands by publishing the "Regulations on Returning Farmland to Forests."

3. *Policies and measures to improve the level of science and technology education*: Science, technology, and talents were the foundations of the prosperity of the western region. Policies in this regard included encouraging the full use of resources, such as western central cities, old industrial bases, military enterprises, scientific research institutions, and universities, to improve the innovation capabilities. In conjunction with accelerating the popularization of nine-year compulsory education, the focus was on

vigorously developing continuing, vocational, and technical education for professional and technical personnel, actively developing higher education, and improving the education system in the western regions.

4. *Policies and measures to improve the market economy*: These policies focused on improving the investment environment, attracting foreign and domestic investors, promoting the reform of political and economic systems, improving administrative efficiency, perfecting the market economy, and accelerating the adjustment of the layout and structure of the state-owned economy. To further relax the non-public economic investment access, efforts were made to actively encourage social capital to participate in infrastructure and ecological environment construction, the development of advantageous industries, equity participation, mergers, and reorganization of state-owned enterprises. Various policies and measures to support the reform, reorganization, and transformation of state-owned enterprises were inclined toward the western region.

Key policy instruments included the following:

1. *Capital investment*: Since the implementation of the western development policy, the central government continuously increased the proportion of financial construction funds, including central capital construction investment funds and construction treasury bonds, used in the western region. Furthermore, there was an increase in the proportion of construction funds used in railways, other transportation, water conservancy, agriculture, forestry, information industry, and other sectors. The proportion of fixed asset investment rose from 19.9% in 2003 to 26.7% in 2017. Preferential loans from international financial organizations and foreign governments were also used in the western region. Domestic loans for fixed asset investment increased from 116 billion Yuan in 2003 to 712 billion Yuan in 2017. Moreover, since the implementation of the policy, the state has continuously provided financial support for major infrastructure construction projects. On the one hand, the proportion of fixed data investment funds in the western region, from the state budget, has remained at approximately 40.0% since 2003. On the other hand, the proportion of the entire country is just approximately 20% (see Figure 3.2).

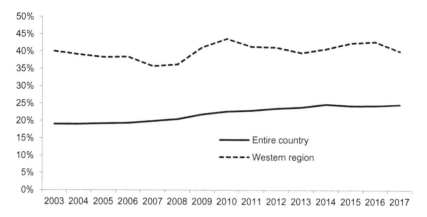

Fig. 3.2.   National budget funds account for total investment in fixed assets.
Source: China Statistical Yearbook.

2. *Preferential policies on tax, land, and mineral resources*: For
   domestic-funded and foreign-funded enterprises in the western
   region, the enterprise income tax was levied at a reduced rate
   of 15% from 2001 to 2010. There was also reduced enterprise
   income tax for newly established enterprises in transportation,
   electricity, water conservancy, postal services, and television. To
   protect the ecological environment, the income from agricultural
   specialties produced by returning farmland to forests and grass-
   land was exempt from the overall tax on agricultural specialties.
   This exemption was applicable within 10 years from the year
   of obtaining the income. Furthermore, the construction land for
   national and provincial highways in the western region was exempt
   from farmland occupation tax.
3. *Financial transfer payments*: Since 2000, the central government
   has allocated financial transfer payments to western regions (see
   Table 3.5). The central government subsidizes the basic living
   expenses of laid-off workers from local state-owned enterprises,
   the basic pension for retirees from enterprises, and the minimum
   living guarantee expenditure for urban residents. The allocation
   of subsidies for special funds, such as education, science and technology, health, politics and law, culture, and cultural relics, should
   also be tilted toward the western region. The central government's
   poverty alleviation funds target relatively low-income areas in the
   western region.

Table 3.5.   Key projects and investment scale of western development.

Commencement year	Number of key projects	Investment scale	Representative project
2000	10	>100 billion Yuan	Airport construction, returning farmland to forest and seedling projects, and infrastructure construction in universities
2001	12	>200 billion Yuan	Qinghai–Tibet railway, west-to-east power transmission project, highway construction, returning farmland to forests, urban infrastructure
2002	14	>330 billion Yuan	West-to-East Gas Transmission, West Airport, Water Pollution Control in Three Gorges Reservoir Area, Returning Farmland to Forest
2003	14	>130 billion Yuan	Urban infrastructure in Tibet and Xinjiang, returning farmland to forests and grass, rural drinking water, rural energy, ecological migration and relocation of poverty alleviation
2004	10	About 80 billion Yuan	Trunk highway, branch airport construction project, key coal mine project, rural infrastructure construction
2005	10	>130 billion Yuan	Zhengzhou–Xi'an Passenger Dedicated Line, Main Branch Airport, Key Coal Mine Project
2006	12	165 billion Yuan	Highway construction, regional airport construction, key coal mine projects and hydropower station construction
2007	10	152 billion Yuan	Regional airport construction, education, health and other social undertakings
2008	10	436 billion Yuan	Expressway construction projects, township oil route reconstruction projects, airport expansion projects, regional airport construction, and the second line of West-East Gas Transmission Project
Total 2000–2008	102	>1723 billion Yuan	

Source: According to the data on the progress of key projects provided by the Chinese government portal website (http://www.gov.cn) and the China Western Development Network (http://www.chinawest.gov.cn) from the Western Development Office of the State Council.

3.4.2.   *Strategy of revitalizing Northeast China (2003–)*

In November 2002, the central government explicitly proposed to support the northeast region and other old industrial bases to accelerate their adjustment and transformation. It also proposed supporting cities and regions that mainly exploited resources to develop incumbent industries. The goal was to strengthen economic exchanges and cooperation among the eastern, central, and western regions to realize complementary advantages, common development, and form economic zones with the region's own characteristics. In March 2003, the government stressed that "effective measures should be taken to support the accelerated adjustment and transformation of old industrial bases in Northeast China and other regions." Focusing on accelerating the realization of the goals and key tasks of the revitalization of the northeast region, the policies and measures included the following:

1. *Economic policy support*: This included increasing policy support for the development of the equipment manufacturing industry in Northeast China and adjusting the preferential import tax policy to exempt key supporting components and raw materials imported by domestic enterprises for the development and manufacturing of major technical equipment and products. These exemptions include import duties or implementing the principle of levying and returning the value-added tax (VAT) on imports after levying.
2. *Acceleration of the strategic adjustment of the state-owned economy*: This included improving the mechanism for the rational flow of state-owned capital and promoting the concentration of state-owned capital in important industries, key areas, and advantageous industries that are vital to the national economy.
3. *Deepening of the reform of the investment system and simplifying the approval procedures for the adjustment and transformation of old industrial bases*: This included, in particular, increasing the support of government bonds or special funds.
4. *Establishment of a regional coordination mechanism*: This included building a public platform and cooperation network across administrative regions.

5. *Treatment of the subsidence area*: This included a 50% increase in the central government subsidies to the three northeastern provinces for the treatment of subsidence areas left over from mining in the former state-owned key coal mines.
6. *Strengthening of infrastructure construction*: This included strengthening of the transportation and power grid links between Northeast China and North China, construct modern ports, construct railway projects running through the eastern part of the northeast region, and form a new sea route in the northeast.

The main policy instruments included the following:

- *Project investment*: To support the economic revitalization of the northeast region, the National Development and Reform Commission implemented special projects to revitalize the old industrial bases, transform national debt funds, and develop high-tech industries.
- *Fiscal instruments*: The central government started giving priority to VAT taxpayers in Northeast China, who produce products in equipment, petrochemical, metallurgical, shipbuilding, and automobile manufacturing, and agricultural product processing industries from 1st July 2004. Input taxes included in the purchase of fixed assets, goods and taxable services used for self-made fixed assets, and transportation expenses paid for fixed assets can be deducted from the newly increased VAT in the current year.
- *Financial instruments*: The central government allowed commercial banks in the Northeast to adopt flexible measures to dispose non-performing assets and independently reduce off-balance-sheet interest arrears of loan enterprises. In 2005, the central government increased small secured loans for laid-off and unemployed people and prioritized the country's rural poverty alleviation loans to the Northeast.

3.4.3. *The rise strategy of Central China (2004–)*

The rise strategy of the central region refers to the regional policy to promote the common rise of Henan, Hubei, Hunan, Jiangxi, Anhui, and Shanxi provinces in the central economic zone. In April 2006, the central government issued "Several Opinions on Promoting the

Rise of the Central Region," proposing to build the central region into an important grain producer, energy and raw material base, a modern equipment manufacturing and high-tech industrial base, and a comprehensive transportation hub. In December 2016, the strategic orientation of the "Plan to Promote the Rise of Central Region (2016–2025)" was further developed into a new orientation of "one centre and four districts." These are the nationally important advanced manufacturing center, the key new urbanization area, the core area of modern agricultural development, the demonstration area of ecological civilization construction, and the all-round opening of important support areas. The policies and measures to promote the strategic orientation can be summarized as follows:

1. *Support to the economic development of major grain-producing areas*: This included measures such as increasing the transfer payments from the central government, supporting major grain-producing areas to improve their financial security, gradually narrowing the gap between local financial revenues and expenditures, giving priority to major grain-producing areas through various state subsidies to support agricultural production, and improving the incentive policy and gradually increase the central government's incentives to major grain-producing areas and counties. From 2004 to 2018, the grain output of the central provinces continued to grow, with Henan province having the highest growth rate of 56.18% in 2018 compared to 2004. In 2018, the grain output in the central region reached 200 million tons, accounting for 30.5% of the national grain output (see Table 3.6).

2. *Implementation of intensive land use policies*: This included implementation of the strictest farmland protection system, strictly observing the red line of farmland, strictly protecting basic farmland, and establishing a compensation and incentive mechanism for farmland protection.

3. *Increasing support for fiscal, taxation, and financial policies*: This included increasing government's balanced transfer payments to the central region with emphasis on supporting the central region to improve peoples' livelihoods and promoting the equalization of basic public services.

4. *Strengthening investment and industrial policy support and guidance*: This included increasing investment in the central budget

Table 3.6.   Grain output in Central China (10,000 tons).

Year	Shanxi	Anhui	Jiangxi	Henan	Hubei	Hunan	Central
2004	1062	2743	1663	4260	2100	2640	14468
2005	978	2605	1757	4582	2177	2679	14778
2006	1025	2854	1897	5112	2099	2654	15640
2007	1009	2974	1912	5253	2139	2698	15986
2008	1034	3141	1975	5406	2145	2822	16524
2009	955	3169	2029	5507	2291	2929	16880
2010	1108	3208	1989	5582	2304	2882	17072
2011	1225	3314	2099	5734	2407	2984	17763
2012	1309	3543	2141	5898	2485	3062	18438
2013	1362	3541	2182	6024	2586	2990	18685
2014	1387	3831	2220	6134	2658	3079	19309
2015	1314	4077	2236	6470	2915	3094	20106
2016	1380	3962	2234	6498	2796	3052	19923
2017	1355	4020	2222	6524	2846	3074	20041
2018	1380	4007	2191	6649	2839	3023	20090

Source: China Statistical Yearbook.

and special construction funds and giving appropriate preferential treatment to the central region for planning, layout, examination, approval, and funding arrangements of major projects.

5. *Improving policies related to ecological compensation*: This included increasing the central government's balanced transfer payments to key ecological functional areas, such as the Three Gorges reservoir area, Danjiangkou reservoir area, and Shennongjia forest region, supporting the development of ecological compensation pilot projects in Danjiangkou reservoir area and upstream areas, Huaihe river source, Dongjiang river source, Poyang lake wetland, etc., and encouraging horizontal ecological environment compensation between ecological protection in the upper and lower reaches of Xin'an River and Dongjiang river basins and other beneficiary areas.

3.5.   The Period of Comprehensive and Coordinated Development Led by the Sub-region (2012–present)

The 18th National Congress of the Communist Party of China was held in 2012, and the 13th Five-Year Plan (2016–2020) proposed a new direction for China's regional economic development strategy. After 2014, the central government implemented a comprehensive and coordinated development strategy led by sub-regions. These efforts included the Belt and Road Initiative, the coordinated development of Beijing, Tianjin, Hebei, and the Yangtze River Economic Belt, the construction of Guangdong, Hong Kong, and Macao, the integration of the Yangtze river delta, the ecological protection of the Yellow river basin, and other high-quality developments. Since then, as a major innovation in the spatial pattern of China's economic development, the top-level design for comprehensive and coordinated development has gradually transformed into concrete actions (Wang and Wei, 2015).

3.5.1.   *Inland opening led by the Belt and Road Initiative*

In September and October 2013, during his visit to Central and Southeast Asian countries, Chinese President Xi Jinping successively put forward major initiatives to jointly build the Silk Road Economic Belt, and the 21st century Maritime Silk Road (henceforth, "the Belt and Road Initiative"). The Belt and Road Initiative received significant attention from the international community. The Belt and Road Initiative, as a bridge, will promote the coordinated economic development of the eastern and western regions. It emphasizes the all-round opening of land and sea. While it geographically runs through the east and west, it also connects the north and the south. However, the main line will run through the east and west directions. Through the major land and sea routes connecting Asia and Europe, the west changed from being the back end of the opening to being the front end. To effectively promote inland areas to fully realize their comparative advantages and implement a more proactive opening strategy, the main policies and objectives included the following:

1. *Northwest and Northeast*: These regions focused on the following important measures: supporting the realization of Xinjiang's unique geographical advantages and the role of opening an important window to the west; deepening exchange and cooperation with Central Asia, South Asia, West Asia, and other countries; forming an important transportation hub, trade and logistics,

cultural, scientific, and educational centers on the Silk Road Economic Belt; given the comprehensive economic and cultural advantages of Shaanxi and Gansu, and the ethnic and cultural advantages of Ningxia and Qinghai, building a new highland for Xi'an's inland reform and opening-up, accelerating the development and opening-up of Lanzhou and Xining, promoting the construction of Ningxia's inland open economic experimental zone, and form a channel, trade and logistics hub, important industries, and cultural exchange bases for Central, South, and West Asian countries; supporting the realization of Inner Mongolia's geographical advantages in connecting Russia and Mongolia, improving Heilongjiang's railway corridor to Russia and the regional railway network, as well as land and sea intermodal transport cooperation between Heilongjiang, Jilin, Liaoning, and Russia's Far East, and promote the construction of the Beijing–Moscow Eurasia high-speed transport corridor.

2. *Southwest*: The southwest regions focused on the following measures: supporting the realization of Guangxi's unique advantage of being adjacent to ASEAN countries via land and sea; accelerating the opening and development of the Beibu Gulf Economic Zone and Pearl river–Xijiang Economic Zone; building an international channel facing the ASEAN region; creating a new strategic fulcrum for the opening and development of Southwest and Central South regions, and forming an important gateway for the organic connection between the 21st century Maritime Silk Road and the Silk Road Economic Belt; supporting the realization of Yunnan's geographical advantages; promoting the construction of international transportation channels with neighboring countries; creating a new high ground for economic cooperation in the Greater Mekong sub-region and becoming the influence center facing South and Southeast Asia.

3. *Inland*: Inland areas must take advantage of the vast inland depth, abundant human resources, and good industrial foundation. They must rely on key regions, such as the urban agglomeration in the middle reaches of the Yangtze River, Chengdu–Chongqing urban agglomeration, Central Plains urban agglomeration, Hohhot–Baotou–Erdos–Yulin urban agglomeration, and Harbin–Changchun megapolis. They should also focus on the following: promoting regional interactive cooperation and industrial

agglomeration development; creating an important support for Chongqing's western development, and opening up inland economic highlands, such as Chengdu, Zhengzhou, Wuhan, Changsha, Nanchang, and Hefei; accelerating cooperation between the middle and upper reaches of the Yangtze river and the Federal District along Russia's Volga river; establishing a coordination mechanism for railway transportation and port customs clearance of the EU–China corridor; supporting inland cities, such as Zhengzhou and Xi'an, in building airports and land ports; strengthening customs clearance cooperation among inland, coastal, and border ports; optimizing the layout of special customs supervision areas, innovate processing trade modes, and deepen industrial cooperation with countries along the route.

3.5.2. *Coordinated development of Beijing, Tianjin, and Hebei*

Beijing, Tianjin, and Hebei Provinces have a total population of more than 100 million and account for more than one-tenth of the country's total GDP. It is the core region of the Bohai Rim Economic Circle and spreads to Shandong and Liaoning. As the third growth pole of China's economy, the coordinated development of Beijing, Tianjin, and Hebei is of great significance. Through the integration of factors in Beijing, Tianjin, and Hebei, coordinated development can promote industrial upgrading and transfer, build a transportation integration network, expand the ecological space of environmental capacity, realize regional coordinated development, and play an exemplary role in developing regional cooperation with other regions.

The coordinated development strategy of Beijing, Tianjin, and Hebei will relieve Beijing's "non-capital functions" and control the capital's "big city disease" through transportation, ecological, and industrial coordination. It will promote the development of the surrounding areas and solve the long-standing unbalanced development problem in Beijing, Tianjin, and Hebei. The most important goal is to focus on building a city group with world-class competitiveness and forming a new national economic growth pole. The implementation of the Beijing–Tianjin–Hebei coordinated development strategy will not only have a diffusing effect on the revitalization of the northern economy and a positive impact on the four major sectors, but also provide replicable beneficial experiences for the internal coordination of other urban agglomerations.

3.5.3.   *Coordinated development of the Yangtze River Economic Belt*

The Yangtze River Economic Belt is the core economic belt connecting the east with the west. It intersects with the Belt and Road Initiative. The Yangtze River Economic Belt includes 11 provinces and cities, with a population of approximately 600 million and accounts for more than 40% of the country's total GDP.

In 2014, the State Council issued the "Guiding Opinions on Promoting the Development of the Yangtze River Economic Belt by Relying on the Golden Waterway," marking the formal rise of the Yangtze River Economic Belt into a national strategy. The "Development Plan for Urban Agglomeration in the Middle Reaches of the Yangtze River" was approved by the State Council in April 2015. The construction of the Yangtze river's golden waterway, the expansion of the Three Gorges Project's capacity building, and the construction of a global comprehensive three-dimensional transportation corridor are all accelerating. Cooperation in ecological environment protection, customs clearance, water conservancy facilities, and tourism between provinces is also underway. From 1st December 2014, the reform of regional customs clearance integration was expanded from the Yangtze river delta region to the entire Yangtze River Economic Belt. Sichuan, Yunnan, and Guizhou reached a consensus to co-construct and cooperate to build shipping and logistics center in the upper reaches of the Yangtze River. The strategy of the Yangtze River Economic Belt will expand the economic growth space from the coast to the inland area along the river, forming a pattern of industrial gradient transfer, with complementary advantages of upstream, midstream, and downstream, and cooperation and interaction.

On 25th March 2016, the central government adopted the development plan of the Yangtze River Economic Belt. It established a new development pattern of "one axis, two wings, three poles and many points" in the Yangtze River Economic Belt to achieve coordinated development of the upper, middle, and lower reaches of the Yangtze river. "One axis" is to build a green development axis along the Yangtze river based on the golden waterway of the

Yangtze river, fully realizing the core role of Shanghai, Wuhan, and Chongqing, and promoting economic development from the coastal upstream to the upstream. "Two wings" refers to the two major transportation channels of Shanghai–Ruili and Shanghai–Chengdu. Focusing on these can enhance the urban population and industrial agglomeration capacity of the important node cities, on both sides of the north and south, by promoting the connectivity of transportation. "Three poles" refers to the three urban agglomerations in the Yangtze river delta, the middle reaches of the Yangtze river, and Chengdu–Chongqing. This will allow the realization of the role of the central cities and form the three growth poles of the Yangtze River Economic Belt. "Multi points" refers to realizing the supporting role of the prefecture level cities outside the three urban agglomerations and strengthening the central cities' economic contact and interaction with the three urban agglomerations.

3.5.4. *The Great Bay Region of Guangdong,*
Hong Kong, and Macao

The Great Bay Region includes the Hong Kong Special Administrative Region, Macao Special Administrative Region, and the Guangdong province areas of Guangzhou, Shenzhen, Zhuhai, Foshan, Huizhou, Dongguan, Zhongshan, Jiangmen, and Zhaoqing. At the end of 2018, this whole region had an area of 56,000 square km and a total population of approximately 70 million. It is one of the regions with the highest degrees of openness and the strongest economic vitality in China. It has an important strategic position in the overall development of the country. The construction of the Great Bay Region is not only a new attempt at promoting the formation of all-round opening in the new era, but also a new practice at promoting the development of "one country, two systems."

To enhance the supporting and leading role of the Great Bay Region in the country's economic development and opening up to the outside world, the central government supports the integration of Hong Kong and Macao into the overall development of the country, enhances the well-being of compatriots in Hong Kong and Macao, and maintains the long-term prosperity and stability of Hong Kong and Macao. The CPC Central Committee and the State Council issued and implemented the "Outline of the Development Plan for the Great Bay Region" in February 2019. The outline proposes the construction objectives of the Great Bay Region, which are formed by an international first-class bay area and a world-class urban agglomeration framework with abundant vitality, outstanding innovation capability, optimized industrial structure, smooth factor flow, and beautiful ecological environment. The specific measures include in-depth implementation of an innovation-driven development strategy, the strengthening of infrastructure connectivity, and accelerating the development of the advanced manufacturing and modern service industries.

3.5.5. *Regional integration of Yangtze river delta*

The Yangtze river delta is one of the regions with the most active economic development, the highest degree of openness, and the strongest innovation capability in China. It has a pivotal strategic position in the overall situation of the country's modernization and the all-round opening pattern. In November 2018, Xi Jinping announced the first China International Import Expo that he supported for the development of the Yangtze river delta regional integration. It has now become a national strategy. In December 2019, the CPC Central Committee and the State Council issued the "Outline of the Yangtze River Delta Regional Integrated Development Plan." This plan mainly includes the following four policy measures. First, implement a coordinated development plan for the manufacturing industry in the Yangtze river delta to promote high-quality development of the manufacturing industry. Second, take the path of "scientific innovation + industry," promote the deep integration of innovation and industrial chains, lead the construction of scientific innovation centers, and strengthen the construction of comprehensive national science centers in Zhangjiang, Shanghai, Hefei and Anhui. Additionally, improve the open sharing cooperation mechanism to support in-depth implementation of the innovation-driven development strategy. Third, cooperate to build an integrated comprehensive transportation system. Fourth, strengthen inter-provincial coordination, strengthen the protection of forests, rivers, lakes, wetlands, and other important ecosystems, and enhance the functions of ecosystems by building co-protection and joint governance of the ecological environment.

3.5.6.   *Ecological protection and high-quality development in the Yellow river basin*

The Yellow river originates from the Qinghai–Tibet plateau and flows through nine provinces and is 5,464 km in length. It is the second largest river in China after the Yangtze river. The Yellow river basin provinces had a total population of 420 million at the end of 2018, accounting for 30.3% of the country's total population. These nine provinces are important gathering areas for grain, energy, and industry in China, with a GDP accounting for 26.5% of the country's total in 2018.

In September 2019, Xi Jinping presided over a symposium on ecological protection and high-quality development in the Yellow river basin. At the symposium, he put forward a major national strategy of four major goals and tasks to promote ecological protection and high-quality development of the Yellow river basin. The goals are as follows. First, strengthen the protection of the ecological environment. Second, ensure the long-term stability of the Yellow river. Third, promote the economical and intensive use of water resources. And fourth, promote high-quality development of the Yellow river basin.

3.6.   Evaluation of China's Regional Policy

3.6.1.   *The gap of China's regional economic development*

Regarding the problem of imbalanced development in China, many scholars have accurately measured the regional economic gap (e.g. Jian *et al.*, 1996; Cai and Du, 2000; Deng *et al.*, 2015). The research conclusions show that from the time of the Reform and Opening, the regional economic disparity in China showed a narrowing trend before gradually expanding from the 1990s. These studies were mainly aimed at the effects of the Reform and Opening before 2005. We remeasured the regional economic disparity in China using the Theil Index from the introduction of the Reform and Opening, and extended the time span of the survey to 40 years (1978–2018).

Table 3.7 shows the Theil Index from 1978 to 2018. The second to fourth columns are the Theil Index within the regions.

Table 3.7.   Theil index from 1978 to 2018.

Year	East	Northeast	Central	West	Regional	Provincial
1978	0.341	0.027	0.013	0.029	0.090	0.281
1980	0.300	0.029	0.011	0.026	0.087	0.253
1982	0.237	0.020	0.013	0.023	0.077	0.207
1984	0.205	0.017	0.015	0.022	0.074	0.187
1986	0.182	0.023	0.009	0.026	0.072	0.174
1988	0.136	0.016	0.007	0.022	0.077	0.154
1990	0.121	0.017	0.010	0.020	0.066	0.135
1992	0.112	0.022	0.010	0.022	0.088	0.156
1994	0.096	0.022	0.007	0.028	0.109	0.171
1996	0.100	0.013	0.006	0.025	0.112	0.175
1998	0.113	0.018	0.007	0.025	0.117	0.188
2000	0.097	0.017	0.004	0.023	0.109	0.168
2002	0.107	0.016	0.004	0.024	0.116	0.182
2004	0.113	0.015	0.004	0.025	0.117	0.187
2006	0.109	0.009	0.006	0.031	0.069	0.183
2008	0.095	0.011	0.007	0.042	0.107	0.171
2010	0.077	0.014	0.009	0.056	0.079	0.135
2012	0.062	0.018	0.005	0.061	0.064	0.114
2014	0.052	0.018	0.005	0.056	0.048	0.091
2016	0.049	0.021	0.007	0.045	0.044	0.083
2018	0.053	0.007	0.011	0.037	0.051	0.089

Source: The data from 1978 to 1998 comes from the Compilation of Statistical Data of the 50 years of New China, and the data from 1999 to 2018 comes from the China Statistical Yearbook.

The fifth column is the Theil Index between the four regions (eastern, central, western, and northeast regions), and the sixth column is the inter-provincial Theil Index. Figure 3.3 is drawn from the Theil Index between the four regions and provinces.

In terms of changes in the inter-provincial Theil Index (see Figure 3.3), the evolution of interregional disparities in China narrowed before the 1990s and began to expand until 1999. This is consistent with the conclusions of other research results. From 1999 to 2004, interregional disparities showed a steady trend. The disparity showed signs of shrinking after 2004. The value of the Theil Index fell to 0.18 in 2004, to 0.16 in 2009, and to 0.09 in 2018. This suggests that the coordinated regional economic development in China has entered a new phase. The evolution of the Theil Index between the four regions is consistent with the inter-provincial Theil Index. Before

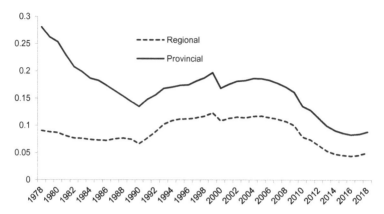

Fig. 3.3.   The regional and provincial Theil Index from 1978 to 2018.
Source: China Statistical Yearbook.

2004, the economic gap between the four major regions declined and then increased. From 1978 to 1990, the economic gap between the four regions gradually narrowed. From 1990 to 1999, the economic gap between the four regions widened. There has been a noticeable trend of a narrowing gap from 2004. Therefore, the gap between regions in the third and fourth stages is currently narrowing.

In terms of regional disparities (see Figure 3.4) from 1978 to 1990, interregional disparities were always greater than the disparities between the four regions. During this period, the average contribution rate of interregional disparities to the Theil Index reached 59.3%, while the average contribution rate of disparities between the four regions was 40.7%, This shows that the main source of the imbalance in regional economic development during this period was the interregional disparities. However, after 1990, the gap between the contribution rate of interregional and between-region disparities to the Theil Index has been expanding. The expansion of the economic gap between the four regions has gradually become an important reason to hinder coordinated development.

3.6.2.   *Problems in China's regional policy*

Conflicts of interest among regional policy groups have led to increased spatial imbalances. The core objective of the central government in formulating regional policies is to solve regional

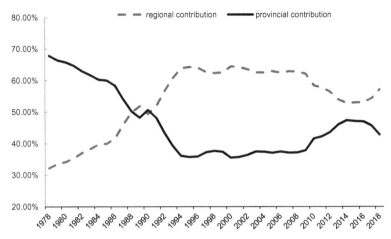

Fig. 3.4.   The regional and provincial contributions to Theil Index from 1978 to 2018.

Source: China Statistical Yearbook.

development problems and coordinate regional development. However, in the process of policy implementation, local governments often pursue their own interests, consequently diluting the core goal of coordinated regional development. The local government's excessive protection of its own interests, caused by administrative division barriers and the vicious competition of repeated construction between regions, has hindered the coordinated development of regional competition and cooperation. This has exacerbated the problem of spatial imbalance (An, 2015).

The numerous regional strategies, plans, and instructions have resulted in insufficient synergy. From the perspective of content, there are comprehensive regional policies (such as the development of the western region, the rise of the central region, and the revitalization of the northeast region) as well as thematic regional policies (such as various types of innovation parks, logistics parks, and urban–rural reform pilot zones). In terms of coverage space, there are cross-administrative regions and large plates (such as the Yangtze River Economic Belt and Beijing–Tianjin–Hebei) as well as specific administrative units and small plates (such as the Shanghai Free Trade Pilot Zone). Too many regional strategies, plans, and instructions have objectively led to the spatial decentralization of policy resources, and the efficiency of policy carried by specific regions has been reduced, making it difficult to promote transcendent development in specific areas (Li, 2020).

Regional policies point to an overemphasis on spatial intervention and a neglect of "human prosperity." The spatial intervention of regional policies emphasizes the development of regional economic development policies, such as establishing economic parks and strengthening infrastructure construction, to promote regional economic growth and achieve "prosperity in the region" (Deng and Gong, 2018). However, insufficient consideration is given to social heterogeneity. Under the guidance of regional heterogeneity, policies have difficulties in targeting specific groups. This makes it difficult for regional policies to play a role in improving the efficiency of resource allocation.

3.6.3. *Suggestions on regional policy*

We have the following suggestions on regional policy:

1. *Improve the effectiveness evaluation mechanism for regional policies*: According to national strategies, policy types, and regional development conditions, objective and scientific identification standards are established for regional spatial orientation. Regulation of the behavior of policy executors should be undertaken. The completion of the core objectives of regional policies should be included in the performance evaluation standards of local governments to avoid the core objectives of regional policies being diluted (Deng and Gong, 2019). The promulgation of the policy should be accompanied by an online application supervision system, which can support local governments in applying and approving policies and provide supervision. Local governments should also report the evaluation indicators of policy effects on the system in a timely manner, track and evaluate them, and establish an effective exit mechanism. When the implementation effect of regional policies makes it difficult to achieve the intended purpose, decision-making departments should focus on addressing the issue of precise policy innovation in the region.
2. *Dynamically adjust the policy content*: The orientation of the regional policy should be based on the characteristics of regional development to achieve spatial heterogeneity and target matching.

For different regional development bottlenecks, policy guidance and support should be carried out more precisely according to the specific historical conditions and endowments. The orientation of regional policy should focus on "people's prosperity." Environmental protection, social harmony, ecological security, and equalization of basic public services are given top priority in the policy objectives and measures, and scientific and comprehensive policy evaluation standards are formulated (Lambooy and Boschma, 2001). Accelerate the reform of the household registration system and establish a unified social security system for the whole country.

3. *Increase the construction of regional coordination mechanisms*: Following measures have to be included: acceleration of the construction of inter-government coordination mechanisms and granting local governments "partial priority" to coordinate the distribution of financial rights between the central and local governments; establishment of a developed regional information network support system to form a unified personnel administration, fiscal expenditure, and information network system; breaking regional barriers to establish open, unified, and transparent capital and factor markets; a cross-regional collaboration organization can be established to achieve development plans for the entire region and coordinate the functional positioning and industrial division of labor among local governments (Iammarino *et al.*, 2018).

3.7. Conclusion

Regulating and optimizing the regional development pattern has always been a national strategy to which China pays close attention at every important stage of development. This study reviews the four main stages of China's regional economic strategy since 1949. We observe that China's regional strategy has gone from a balanced development, to improving efficiency priorities, to a coordinated development of regional policies that continue to be deepened, refined, and implemented. The regional economic structure has evolved toward multi-polarization, multi-level, and openness. From the guiding policy of blindly emphasizing the national "one game of chess" and implementing the "great unification" to the strategic thinking and guiding policy of "four major sectors," from the plate with a relatively wide geographical scope to the plate with a relatively small geographical scope, and on the basis of the "four large plates" strategy, the spatial pattern of regional policy guidance with urban agglomeration as the core is further refined.

Since the Reform and Opening, China's overall economic strength has increased rapidly, and the comparative advantages of economic development in different regions have been brought into play. From 1978 to 2018, China's regional economic gap experienced contracting and expanding cycles. The Theil Index dropped from 0.27 in 1978 to 0.09 in 2018. Under the drive of constantly adjusting regional policies, the gap in regional development levels has gradually narrowed, and the economic development of various regions appears to be converging. However, the factors restricting the coordinated development of the region still exist, and the imbalance of regional development remains prominent. The development strategy of the region needs to be further promoted to build a comprehensive and coordinated development pattern.

References

An, X. (2015). "New Features of China's Regional Economic Development and Future Policy Trends," *Regional Economic Review*, 5, 12–19.

Bo, W. and H. An (2016). "Evolution and Future Prospects of China's Regional Development Thoughts," *Journal of Nankai: Philosophy and Social Science Edition*, 3, 115–124.

Cai, Y. and Y. Du (2000). "The Convergence and Difference of Economic Growth in China: Implications for the Strategy of Western Development," *Economic Research*, 10, 30–37.

Deng, M. and Q. Gong (2018). "The Spatial Attribute and Reconstruction Path of China's Regional Policy," *China Soft Science*, 4, 74–85.

Deng, M. and Q. Gong (2019). "Research on the Optimization of Regional Policy for Regional Policy," *Regional Economic Review*, 39, 39–46.

Deng, X., Z. Lu, and X. Chen (2015). "The evolution and impact of China's regional policy: A study of regional support policy for western China," *The Evolution of Economic and Innovation Systems*. Cham: Springer, pp. 119–141.

Iammarino, S., A. Rodríguez-Pose, and M. Storper (2018). "Regional inequality in Europe: Evidence, theory and policy implications," *CeprEPR Discussion Papers*.

Jian, T., J. D. Sachs, and A. M. Warner (1996). "Trends in Regional Inequality in China," *China Economic Review*, 7, 1–21.

Lambooy, J. G. and R. A. Boschma (2001). "Evolutionary Economics and Regional Policy," *Annals of Regional Science*, 35, 113–131.

Li, L. (2020). "The Logical Framework and Theoretical Explanation of Regional Coordinated Development in China," *Economic Perspectives*, 69–82.

Liu, B., J. Zhu, and Y. Zhou (2020). "The Evolution and Prospect of China's Regional Economic theory," *Management World*, 36, 182–194.

Wang, Y. and H. Wei (2015). "National Regional Development Strategy Adjustment and Response During the "Thirteenth Five-Year Plan" Period," *Management World*, 83–91.

Xiao, J. and S. An (2019). "From Regional Unbalanced Development to Regional Coordinated Development: China's Regional Development for 40 Years," *Regional Economic Review*, 37, 19–20.

Zhu, W. and Y. Zhang (2004). "Four Adjustments and Judgments of China's Regional Policy Since Reform and Opening Up," *Economic Research*, 38–43.

https://doi.org/10.1142/9781800611238_0005

Chapter 4

China's Trade and Opening since 1978: A Regional Perspective from the Northeast*

Kiril Tochkov

*Department of Economics, Texas Christian University,
Fort Worth, TX 76129, USA*
k.tochkov@tcu.edu

Abstract

China's rapid growth has masked the fact that some of its regions have failed to keep up with the modernization and efficiency drive during the market transition. China's Northeast was once the most prosperous part of the country and a model for socialist industrialization efforts. But since the reforms and opening up, the region has struggled to turn its old industrial base into a vibrant economy. Trade represents a possible channel for stimulating economic growth, especially in border regions. Accordingly, this chapter explores the trade patterns of Heilongjiang, a border province in the Northeast, and uses a gravity model to estimate the trade costs vis-à-vis its major trading partners, and Russia in particular, over the period 1978–2017. The results indicate a profound change from a relatively isolated border region into a more open economy over the sample period. Moreover, Heilongjiang exhibits a home

---

*This chapter was first presented at the 12th International Conference on the Chinese Economy organized by Mary-Françoise Renard, "A New Era for China: Growth Sustainability and Broaden International Development," CERDI, IDREC, University of Clermont Auvergne, France and CCES, Fudan University, Shanghai, China, held in Clermont-Ferrand, France, 24–25 October 2019.

bias, trading with the rest of China more intensively than with any other country. The border effects with Russia are substantial, although they have declined somewhat over the past two decades. Other trading partners in Northeast Asia record lower trade costs than Russia overall, but the barriers seem to have been on the rise since the early 2000s. The discussion of the potential factors contributing to the high border effects of Heilongjiang points to the lacking infrastructure, especially the cross-border infrastructure with Russia and the costly access to seaports, as the main culprit.

4.1. Introduction

Over the past 40 years, China has experienced a fundamental economic transformation, turning into one of the largest manufacturing and trading nations in the world. In the process, attention has focused on the highly successful provinces along the coast, where vibrant regional economies and special economic zones have been busy producing export goods and trading them with the world. As the income gap between the coast and interior widened, policy makers and scholars rushed to explore options for a more balanced development strategy. In recent years, China's trade practices and global initiatives have garnered more scrutiny as the country's influence on the world stage grows, bringing it into conflict with other major powers. At the same time, border regions in China, and the Northeast in particular, have remained largely outside the scope of scholarly interest.

The main reason for this lack of attention lies in the fact that China's Northeast has struggled to modernize its economy since the introduction of market reforms in the late 1970s. Once considered the cradle of industrial development and among the wealthiest parts of China, the Northeast has relied on an industrial structure dominated by large state-owned enterprises (SOEs) engaged in mining and heavy industries. Promoted as a model of socialist industrialization since the 1950s, the region's economic structure made it a key target of state planning directives as well as the recipient of generous government subsidies. However, when the focus shifted to efficiency improvements and modernization during the early decades of market transition, SOEs in the Northeast missed the opportunity to restructure and benefit from the opening of the economy to foreign trade and investment.

This study examines the case of a Northeast province and its trade relationship with the world over the past 40 years. In particular, we employ a gravity model to estimate the extent and evolution of trade barriers between Heilongjiang province and its main trading partners over the period 1978–2017. Trade composition and patterns are investigated in detail, and potential hurdles impairing the cross-border exchange of goods are explored and discussed. To the best of our knowledge, this is the first trade-related empirical study of China's Northeast in general, and Heilongjiang province in particular. The relevant literature has focused largely on historical periods of economic development and trade in the 19th and early 20th centuries (Kung and Li, 2011) and the recent revitalization strategies for the Northeast (Huang, 2004; Izotov and Suslov, 2012; Hou *et al.*, 2019).

The trade relations of China's Northeast deserve a closer look for several reasons. The region was isolated from the world for decades, and by the time China opened up, the Northeast proved to be unprepared for the new economic challenges. This is a unique opportunity to study the response of an emerging economy to an outdated industrial model that carries a financial, social, and environmental burden. Trade as a channel for the revitalization of the region has not been the main focus of policy makers, although regional authorities have implemented various measures to stimulate cross-border exchange of goods (i.e. allowing Russian rubles to be accepted as payment in the border city of Suifenhe). As China and Russia have developed closer links over the past decade, trade might play an increasingly important role in the economy of Heilongjiang. However, mistrust, onerous bureaucratic hurdles, lack of cross-border infrastructure, and logistical challenges still create barriers that prevent the region from taking full advantage of its potential for regional integration with Northeast Asia. This study fills the gap in the literature by quantifying these trade costs and investigating their change over four decades of reforms and opening in China.

The chapter is organized as follows. In Section 4.2, the historical development of Heilongjiang's economy is traced. Section 4.3 describes the gravity model and the dataset used in the estimation, while Section 4.4 presents the results of the empirical investigation. Section 4.5 summarizes the findings and discusses their implications for further expansion of trade in China's Northeast.

4.2. Historical Overview

Heilongjiang is nowadays a Chinese province in the Northeast, but historically, it was part of Manchuria, which played a key role in East Asian history. The territory of today's Heilongjiang became a border region after the signing of the Treaty of Aigun in 1859 and the Treaty of Peking in 1860, sealing the annexation by the Russian Empire of the lands north of the Amur River and east of the Ussuri River. Rich in natural resources, sparsely populated, and with a strategic location at the crossroads of Northeast Asia, the region attracted the attention of Russia and Japan, turning into a conflict zone between the two powerful neighbors at a time when the central government in China was too weak to assert sovereignty over its northeastern territories.

Initially, the Qing emperors of China wanted to protect their Manchurian homeland from Chinese migration, but since the late 19th century, the restrictions were gradually lifted, and the region experienced a large influx of ethnic Chinese who took advantage of the fertile black soil of the region, boosting agricultural development. In a period of only 50 years, this process resulted in a net migration of over 8 million people into Manchuria (Gottschang, 1987). Soy emerged as the primary crop for cultivation, mainly because it proved to be a valuable export. At the time, China was producing 80% of the world output of soy, and the majority of it was grown and processed in Manchuria (Perkins, 1969). The exports of soy from the region increased continuously and experienced a major surge after WWI in response to growing world demand (Kung and Li, 2011).

The commercialization and exports of agricultural products were facilitated by two major infrastructure developments. A new treaty port in Niuzhuang (now called Yingkou) opened Manchuria up for foreign trade as a consequence of the Treaty of Tianjin (1859). Moreover, Russia, which was the dominant imperialistic power in the region at the time, built a key network of railroads, providing a straight link between its own Trans-Siberian rail and its seaport in Vladivostok and expanding later a connection to the seaport of Dalian in the south (Urbansky, 2008). The new Chinese Eastern Railway turned Harbin from a small village into a major international transportation hub and the administrative center of Heilongjiang, which it remains to this day. More importantly, it boosted the transportation links and the trade relations of the region with the rest of the world. The railway freight tonnage in Manchuria increased from 2 million tons in 1901 to 36 million in 1931 (Gottschang, 1987).

After the defeat of Russia in the Russo–Japanese War of 1905, Japan expanded its influence in the region, culminating in a Japanese invasion and subsequent creation of a quasi-colonial state in Manchuria in 1932. The economic policies of Japan emphasized a rapid government-led expansion of mining and the industrial sector at the expense of agriculture, leading to a modernization of Manchuria's economy and infrastructure (Murakami, 2012). At the same time, the region continued its strong export orientation, with exports making up around 17% of GDP and imports around 22% in 1934 (Eckstein *et al.*, 1974). More importantly, the population in Manchuria became more prosperous, whereby farmers who were involved in the cultivation of soybeans destined for exports were the major beneficiaries (Kung and Li, 2011). The industrialization drive during the Japanese occupation led to a divergence in economic development between Manchuria and the rest of China, with the former recording rapid economic growth, while the latter stagnated (Eckstein *et al.*, 1974).

The Soviet Union occupied Manchuria after the defeat of Japan in WWII and again took control of the Chinese Eastern Railway, turning it over to China only at the end of 1952 (Urbansky, 2008). The re-integration of Manchuria (now Northeast China) into China proper marked a new phase in the economic development of the region. Helped by the existing industrial infrastructure, the Chinese government invested heavily into developing the Northeast into a model of industrial progress under the newly established Soviet-style planned economy with an emphasis on heavy industries and mining. Oil was discovered around Daqing in the late 1950s, making the town famous around the country and turning it into a model socialist enterprise (Hou, 2018). The GDP per capita of Heilongjiang in 1952 was twice as high as the Chinese average (238 Yuan vs. 119 Yuan), and this gap disappeared only in the mid-2000s (National Bureau of Statistics, 2010).

The market transition in China in the 1980s and 1990s turned the once proud industrial homeland of China into a rust belt. While the coastal areas of East and South China boomed thanks to the rapid emergence of export-oriented manufacturing and an influx of foreign direct investment, China's Northeast with its large SOEs was struggling to respond to the new market signals and efficiency drives. Stagnation, unemployment, and environmental pollution plagued the region. In response, the central government implemented three major drives (in 2003, 2009, and 2016) to revitalize the "Old Industrial Base" of the Northeast, which had a positive effect (Chung *et al.*, 2009; Wang *et al.*, 2014; Hou *et al.*, 2019). A key part of these strategies has been the regional integration and trade cooperation with Russia and other neighboring countries in Northeast Asia. This aspect received a major boost from the One Belt One Road initiative of the Chinese government since the mid-2010s, which has focused on expanding the infrastructure and promoting trade between China and other parts of Eurasia and the world.

4.3. Methodology and Data

4.3.1. *Gravity model*

Investigating trade flows and their determinants requires an empirical model that takes into account the characteristics of both trading partners as well as factors that might facilitate or impair the exchange of goods. The most popular model that has been used in the literature is based on Newton's universal law of gravitation, which, in general terms, states that the gravitational force is directly proportional to the product of their masses and inversely proportional to the square of the distance between their centers. Applied to international economics, this relationship defines the strength of the trade link between two entities (customs unions, countries, regions, firms, etc.) as a function of the product of their size and the physical distance between them. The gravity model was introduced in economics by Tinbergen (1962) and was initially considered as purely empirical until Anderson (1979) developed a formal theoretical foundation.

In line with Anderson and van Wincoop (2003), the basic gravity framework can be expressed as

$$x_{ij} = \frac{y_i y_j}{y^W} \left(\frac{t_{ij}}{P_i P_j} \right)^{1-\sigma}, \qquad (4.1)$$

where the left-hand side variable denotes the exports of country i to country j, y is the country's nominal income, y^W is the world income, t denotes the bilateral trade costs, and σ is the elasticity of substitution. The price levels, P, represent the average trade barriers of a country vis-à-vis all of its trading partners. Once Eq. (4.1) is linearized and trade costs are broken down into various components, the gravity equation transforms into

$$ln x_{ij} = ln(y_i y_j) - ln y^W + (1-\sigma)ln b(1-\delta_{ij}) + (1-\sigma)\rho ln d_{ij}$$
$$+ (1-\sigma)\tau_{ij} - (1-\sigma)ln P_i - (1-\sigma)P_j, \quad (4.2)$$

where b is defined as the border effect, δ_{ij} is a categorical variable that takes the value of one for intranational trade and zero otherwise, d is bilateral distance, and τ_{ij} includes all remaining trade costs. Equation (4.2) is transformed into a stochastic model given by

$$ln\left(\frac{x_{ij}}{y_{it}y_{jt}}\right) = \beta_0 + \alpha_i \lambda_i + \alpha_j \lambda_j + \beta_1 ln d_{ijj} + \beta_2 (RUS)$$
$$+ \beta_3 (NEA) + \beta_4 (ROW) + \varepsilon_{ij}. \quad (4.3)$$

The dependent variable is the log of exports that has been adjusted for the size of the two involved countries. The main focus of the analysis is on the coefficients of the variables for trade with Russia (RUS), Northeast Asia (NEA), and the rest of the world (ROW). These dummy variables take the value of 1 for trade between Heilongjiang and each of the listed countries or regions and zero otherwise. The zero in this case represents the control group, which is defined as the trade between Heilongjiang and the rest of China. Accordingly, the coefficients represent the corresponding bilateral trade costs relative to those involved in intranational trade. Equation (4.3) takes into account factors that vary across countries but not across time via exporter and importer fixed effects. Similarly, factors that vary across time but not across countries are controlled for by including time fixed effects (η_t).

We estimate the border effects for each of the three entities trading with Heilongjiang over the period 1978–2017 and convert the resulting coefficients into *ad valorem* tariff equivalents (expressed in %) to facilitate their interpretation. To gain more detailed insights into the border effects for each country and their changes over time, we employ a different methodology developed by Novy (2013), which allows the calculation (rather than estimation) of bilateral trade costs in a given year. In line with this approach, trade costs between countries i and j can be expressed as

$$\tau_{ij} = \left(\frac{x_{ii}x_{jj}}{x_{ij}x_{ji}}\right)^{1/(2(\sigma-1))} - 1. \qquad (4.4)$$

Equation (4.4) uses a similar logic as the border effect variables in Eq. (4.3), calculating the ratio of intranational trade to cross-border trade. The main advantage is that it allows the calculation of bilateral trade costs for a given year and pair of trading partners. At the same time, it is worth mentioning that the trade costs resulting from Eq. (4.4) are not identical to the ones generated by the regression model in Eq. (4.3).

4.3.2. *Data*

The main variable in the analysis, trade flows, is measured as exports and imports of Heilongjiang expressed in current US dollars (USD). The annual observations were obtained from publications of the Heilongjiang Statistical Office, which in turn relies on data from China's General Administration of Customs. The sample period covering the period 1978–2017 is determined by the availability of data, whereby statistics for 1979 and 1984 are missing. We selected 45 trading partners of Heilongjiang, which represent more than 90% of the province's exports and more than 87% of imports. These include 18 Asian countries (Bangladesh, Hong Kong, India, Indonesia, Japan, Kazakhstan, North Korea, South Korea, Malaysia, Mongolia, Pakistan, Philippines, Singapore, Taiwan, Thailand, Turkey, UAE, and Vietnam) with a share of around 32% of exports and 13% of imports; 11 countries in Europe (Belgium, Denmark, Germany, France, Italy, Netherlands, Poland, Russia, Spain, Sweden, and the UK) with a share of 50% of exports and 67% of imports; six countries in Africa (Algeria, Egypt, Morocco, Nigeria, South Africa, and Sudan) claiming around 4% of exports and 5% of imports; six countries in Latin America (Brazil, Chile, Ecuador, Mexico, Panama, and Peru) with a share of 3% of exports and 5% of imports; and four countries in North America and Oceania (Canada, USA, Australia, and New Zealand) absorbing around 9% of exports and sending 8% of imports.

The data on GDP (in current USD) were obtained from the World Bank's World Development Indicators for all countries and from the

CEIC database for Heilongjiang.[1] The distance between the province and its trading partners was calculated as the great circle distance between Harbin, the provincial capital of Heilongjiang, and the capital of each country.

The benchmark for the border effects estimation requires observations on the intranational trade between Heilongjiang and the rest of China. In the absence of such data, we follow the literature and calculate it as the provincial gross value of industrial and agricultural production net of aggregate consumption and international exports. The resulting number represents the value of the goods produced in Heilongjiang that are "exported" to other parts of China. The trading partner in this case is defined as China as a whole and the corresponding national GDP of China is used.

4.4. Results

4.4.1. *Descriptive statistics*

First, we explore the trade patterns of Heilongjiang based on descriptive statistics. Over the entire sample period, the province exported mostly to Europe (50%) and Asia (32%). Imports were predominantly from Europe (67%) and to a lesser extent from Asia (13%). As Table 4.1 indicates, the large share of Europe is due to Russia, which has an international border with Heilongjiang. In 1978, when the Sino-Soviet relations were still frosty, there was barely any trade between China's Northeast and Russia, making North Korea a key trading partner. As the diplomatic ties improved over the 1980s, Russia quickly emerged as the main destination for Heilongjiang's production, absorbing more than a third of its exports. This share surged in the 2000s, reaching a peak of 67% in 2007, before gradually declining again to around 30% in recent years. Hong Kong (as an entrepôt) and Japan used to play a prominent role but were replaced by the US and India over the past two decades. In terms of imports, the dynamics are similar, although Russia has grown in importance as the source of purchased foreign goods, reaching a share of almost

---

[1]Taiwan's GDP was obtained from the Statistical Office of Taiwan, while North Korea's GDP is an estimate by South Korea's Central Bank (Bank of Korea).

Table 4.1.   Top trade partners of Heilongjiang (% of exports/imports).

	Exports			Imports		
	#1	#2	#3	#1	#2	#3
1978	N Korea (58.9)	Hong Kong (34.4)	Russia (1.6)			
1985	Russia (36.5)	Hong Kong (18.8)	Japan (16.1)			
1990	Russia (33.0)	Hong Kong (16.1)	Japan (15.8)			
1995	Russia (18.4)	Japan (16.0)	Hong Kong (14.0)	Russia (40.4)	S. Korea (11.1)	Japan (9.4)
2000	Russia (31.9)	Japan (14.7)	S. Korea (14.0)	Russia (59.2)	S. Korea (8.3)	USA (5.1)
2005	Russia (63.2)	S. Korea (5.8)	Japan (4.4)	Russia (52.6)	USA (9.2)	Japan (9.1)
2010	Russia (26.3)	USA (8.2)	India (4.9)	Russia (34.6)	USA (9.9)	Brazil (6.0)
2015	Russia (29.3)	USA (6.2)	India (5.1)	Russia (65.6)	USA (7.7)	Brazil (5.5)
2017	Russia (30.6)	USA (14.9)	Belgium (6.8)	Russia (68.6)	Brazil (5.4)	USA (4.6)

70% in 2017. Brazil and the US have replaced Japan and South Korea as the main importers in Heilongjiang after Russia.

As with China, the foreign trade of Heilongjiang developed slowly. As can be seen from the first panel of Figure 4.1, the province had very low levels of cross-border exchange until the late 1990s, when it began to intensify, reaching a peak of roughly $15 billion worth of exports per year between 2007 and 2014. Imports increased with a delay, recording their highest level of $23 billion in 2012. Since 2011, Heilongjiang has been running a trade deficit, averaging $6 billion per year and exceeding $8 billion in 2017. Given the dominant role of Russia in the province's trade, the patterns in the second panel of Figure 4.1 are similar. In 2011, the imports from Russia quintupled from the previous year, pushing Heilongjiang into a trade deficit. The surge was caused by the completion of the Eastern Siberia–Pacific Ocean oil pipeline, which linked the Siberian oilfields with the oil town of Daqing in Heilongjiang.

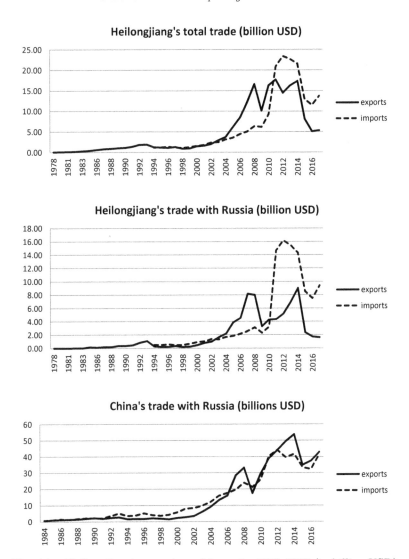

Fig. 4.1. Heilongjiang's exports and imports, 1978–2017 (in billion USD).

In contrast, China has been running trade surpluses vis-à-vis Russia since the mid-2000s, as the third panel in Figure 4.1 illustrates. Furthermore, China's trade with Russia does not seem to pass through the Northeast provinces. Figure 4.2 shows that Heilongjiang's exports to Russia represented less than a third of total Chinese exports to Russia, and this share has been declining rapidly

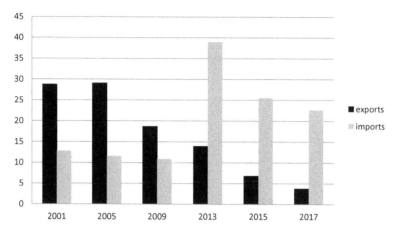

Fig. 4.2.   Heilongjiang's share in China's trade with Russia (%).

to reach a low of 4% in 2017. Imports from Russia have been lingering at around 10% of the national level before surging in early 2010s thanks to the oil imports through the Northeast. But the share has been declining as well. This pattern is explained by the fact that China prefers to ship its exports to the larger market of Western Russia via the maritime route rather than via the Northeast, which would require the use of the relatively costly and logistically inefficient Trans-Siberian Railway.

4.4.2. *Border effects*

The empirical analysis begins with the estimation of the border effects between Heilongjiang and its main trading partners. The results from the gravity model are displayed in Table 4.2. The benchmark for evaluating the trade costs is Heilongjiang's intranational trade. The negative signs of all coefficients suggest that the province has a home bias because exports and imports are lower than with the rest of China. For the entire sample period, the province's Northeast-Asian neighbors exhibit the lowest border costs amounting to a tariff equivalent of 145%. We split the sample into two subperiods of equal length, which, by chance, correspond to the years of relatively low levels of foreign interaction and the surge since the late 1990s, respectively (see Figure 4.1). The border effects with Northeast Asia appear to decline in the second subperiod, indicating the increasing

Table 4.2. Border effects of Heilongjiang, 1978–2017.

	1978–2017		1978–1998		1999–2017	
Russia	−4.527***	**210.11**	−0.542	**14.51**	−3.360***	**131.64**
	(0.509)		(2.545)		(0.603)	
NE Asia	−3.581***	**144.79**	−4.850***	**236.19**	−2.643***	**93.62**
	(0.359)		(0.423)		(0.442)	
ROW	−7.026***	**479.21**	−3.403***	**134.14**	−6.193***	**370.32**
	(0.445)		(0.321)		(0.528)	
ln(*Distance*)	−1.273***		−2.580*		−0.564***	
	(0.084)		(1.459)		(0.096)	
Constant	−33.698***		−9.514		−37.371***	
	(1.786)		(10.180)		(1.758)	
Obs.	2,289		708		1,581	
R^2	0.56		0.79		0.48	

Note: Robust standard errors are in parentheses. Exporter/Importer and year fixed effects included. The tariff equivalent of the border effects (in %) is shown in bold assuming an elasticity of substitution $\sigma = 5$. *$p < 0.10$; ***$p < 0.01$.

intensity of cross-border exchange of goods with countries like Japan and South Korea.

In contrast, Heilongjiang faces higher trade costs vis-à-vis Russia, which have increased over time. In the years before 1998, the border effect is negative but not significantly different from intranational trade. In the recent decade, the average tariff equivalent reaches 132%, suggesting that despite the closer links between China and Russia, Heilongjiang still faces major trade hurdles with its northern neighbor. The rest of the world has the highest border effects, which have almost tripled between the first and second subperiods.

For robustness purposes, we also conduct the estimation using PPML, an alternative methodology, which allows us to include zero trade flows. The estimates, presented in Table 4.3, are somewhat lower in magnitude than in the OLS estimation, but the ranking is similar, with Northeast Asia having the lowest trade costs followed by Russia. However, a comparison between the first and second subperiods reveals a major difference. Russia's border effects drop from 195% to 43%, which is the opposite of the pattern observed in Table 4.2. This confirms that omitting zero trade flows might introduce a bias in the model.

Table 4.3.   Results of the PPML estimation.

	1978–2017		1978–1998		1999–2017	
Russia	−3.592***	**145.47**	−4.340***	**195.94**	−1.439***	**43.30**
	(0.256)		(3.335)		(0.342)	
NE Asia	−2.735***	**98.13**	−5.668***	**312.47**	−2.403***	**82.35**
	(0.208)		(0.821)		(0.284)	
ROW	−5.795***	**325.78**	−5.683	**314.02**	−4.952***	**244.87**
	(0.245)		(4.343)		(0.328)	
ln(*Distance*)	−0.014		−0.043		0.013	
	(0.088)		(1.927)		(0.113)	
Constant	−26.909***		−26.717		−30.049***	
	(0.651)		(13.418)		(0.824)	
Obs.	2,828		1,099		1,729	
R^2	0.88		0.93		0.69	

Note: Robust standard errors are in parentheses. Exporter/Importer and year fixed effects included. The tariff equivalent of the border effects (in %) is shown in bold assuming an elasticity of substitution $\sigma = 5$. ***$p < 0.01$.

Next, we calculate the border effects for the top 13 trading partners of Heilongjiang in each year between 1994 and 2017 using the approach described by Eq. (4.4).[2] The results in Figure 4.3 are not directly comparable to the ones in Table 4.3 due to the different methodologies and sample periods used, but the patterns and trends are similar. Russia is the trading partner with the lowest trade hurdles, which have decreased since the late 1990s, dipping below the tariff equivalent of 100%, although in recent years the levels have been again on the rise. Northeast Asia has also experienced larger border effects with Heilongjiang, which started increasing in the early 2000s and reached levels above 200%. By contrast, the rest of the trading partners were facing higher but decreasing trade costs with China's Northeast, although this trend seems to have reversed in 2010. Overall, Asian countries have recorded lower border effects than Europe or North America.

---

[2]The trading partners include Australia, Germany, Hong Kong, India, Indonesia, Japan, Malaysia, the Netherlands, Russia, Singapore, South Korea, UK, and the USA. These countries make up more than 70% of Heilongjiang's exports and imports.

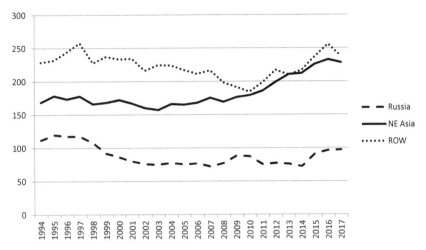

Fig. 4.3: Border effects by trading partner and year (in %).

Note: Annual border effects by year and trading partner calculated using Eq. (4.4) and assuming an elasticity of substitution $\sigma = 8$. Northeast Asia includes Japan and South Korea.

To test the robustness of our results, we conduct a regression analysis with the border effects as the dependent variable and a trade cost variable calculated by the World Bank as the independent variable. The data covers the period 1995–2013 and is reported by country pairs, which in our case means between China and each of the 13 main trading partners of Heilongjiang. The World Bank estimated the trade costs using the gravity framework, and we would expect a positive correlation between our and their measure. The results of the panel estimation with country and year fixed effects, presented in Table 4.4, confirm this prediction, suggesting that Heilongjiang's bilateral border effects and China's bilateral trade costs with the same set of trading partners are significantly correlated, although the magnitude of the coefficient is relatively low.

4.4.3. *Potential determinants of trade hurdles*

After quantifying the trade costs, we identify and discuss potential factors that could have contributed to the border effects between Heilongjiang and its main trade partners. One of the key determinants of trade flows is the geographical location. From a historical

Table 4.4. Panel estimation of relation between border effects and trade costs.

Trade costs	0.006***
	(0.002)
Constant	2.056***
	(0.236)
Obs.	237
R^2	0.83

Note: Robust standard errors are in parentheses. Country and year fixed effects included. Dependent variable is border effects between Heilongjiang and its trading partner. Main independent variable is bilateral trade costs as measured by the World Bank. ***$p < 0.01$.

perspective, Heilongjiang sits at the crossroads of Northeast Asia and could have emerged as a trade hub for neighboring countries like Korea, Japan, Russia, Mongolia, and the rest of China. Traditionally, Heilongjiang had a multi-ethnic population and colonial ties with Russia and Japan. Its infrastructure, especially the Chinese Eastern Railway network, has facilitated the movement of goods across the Northeast. Abundance of natural resources and heavy industrial development have created excellent conditions for the production of export-oriented commodities.

As our analysis shows, despite the potential for trade, relatively high border effects have impaired the cross-border exchange of goods. The Sino–Soviet conflict of the 1960s turned Heilongjiang into a region bordering an enemy state, which isolated the province and placed the emphasis on national security rather than on economic development and international exchange. The legacy of this conflict has repercussions to this day, illustrated by the fact that there is not a single permanent bridge over the Amur River or the Ussuri River connecting Russia and China. Interestingly, the freezing of the rivers for several months over the winter facilitates the transportation of goods because trucks and cars can cross the border driving on the ice. Relaxed visa rules on the Chinese side allow Russians to visit border towns in China, which certainly boosts petty trade across the border. At the same time, the region of the Russian Far East bordering

Heilongjiang is sparsely populated and economically underdeveloped, lowering the potential for major cross-border investment and trade.

Heilongjiang is a landlocked province, and although the border rivers represent key transportation routes, the fact is that the province has no easy access to the sea. The options are the Chinese port of Dalian and the Russian port of Vladivostok, which is less than 100 miles from the border crossing in Heilongjiang. The associated transportation costs are an additional hurdle to the province's trade. The tariffs for using the Russian railway network are considered high and port logistics are not very efficient. For instance, according to data from the World Bank's Logistics Performance Index Database, 50% of surveyed logistics professionals in 2018 ranked Russia's railway cargo tariffs as high or very high (as compared to 33% in the case of China). Similarly, only 9% of respondents opined that the quality of rail infrastructure in China was low or very low vs. 50% for Russia.

Differences in the track gauge also constitute a trade barrier. Russia's track is significantly wider than the one in China, requiring a costly and time-consuming bogie exchange at the border. Besides the spatial distances, time differences also have an adverse effect. China (and thus Heilongjiang) shares the same time zone only with Mongolia and two Russian border regions, which are not adjacent to Heilongjiang. The time difference increases the costs of communication and doing business, which, in turn, affect trade and investment flows (Tomasik, 2013).

4.5. Conclusion

China has achieved a successful transition to a dynamic manufacturing superpower since the start of market reforms four decades ago, but not all regions of the country benefited from the economic boom. The border province of Heilongjiang is a case study of how remote regions of the country have failed to restructure and modernize an economy that for decades served as the model of industrialization in China. This chapter focuses on cross-border exchange of goods between Heilongjiang and its major trade partners to study the potential of trade as a channel for economic growth. In particular, we quantify the trade costs between the province and the rest of the world and discuss the potential factors that might have impaired the integration efforts of the region with the world.

Our results show that Heilongjiang's overall trade flows were very low until the late 1990s when they experienced rapid growth, especially with Russia, which emerged as the most important trade partner by far. Unlike the rest of China, Heilongjiang has been running trade deficits with Russia over the past decade, while the province's share in Chinese exports to Russia has steadily declined. The empirical analysis indicates that Heilongjiang exhibits a home bias, trading more with the rest of China than with any other country. The border effects with Russia are substantial, exceeding an average *ad valorem* tariff equivalent of 140% over the entire sample period, although they have declined somewhat over the past two decades. The other trading partners of Heilongjiang in Northeast Asia record lower trade costs than Russia overall, but the barriers seem to have been on the rise since the early 2000s. The discussion of the potential factors contributing to the high border effects of the province points to the lacking infrastructure, especially the cross-border infrastructure with Russia and the costly access to seaports, as the main culprit.

Our analysis suggests that there is still room for improvement that could allow Heilongjiang to take advantage of its potential for trade and regional integration within Northeast Asia. The One Belt One Road initiative of the Chinese government has focused on upgrading and expanding the existing infrastructure in order to stimulate the exports of Chinese goods. Heilongjiang is well placed to benefit from this strategy. At the same time, the closer ties between Russia and China and the deeper integration of China's economy in the global supply chains in Northeast Asia are likely to create additional incentives for Heilongjiang, and China's Northeast as a whole, to continue opening up to the world.

References

Anderson, J. (1979). "A Theoretical Foundation for the Gravity Equation," *American Economic Review*, 69, 106–116.

Anderson, J. and E. van Wincoop (2003). "Gravity with Gravitas: A Solution to the Border Puzzle," *American Economic Review*, 93, 170–192.

Chung, J., H. Lai, and J. Joo (2009). "Assessing the 'Revive the Northeast' (zhenxing dongbei) Programme: Origins, Policies and Implementation," *The China Quarterly*, 197, 108–125.

Eckstein, A., C. Kang, and J. Chang (1974). "The Economic Development of Manchuria: The Rise of a Frontier Economy," *The Journal of Economic History*, 34, 239–264.

Gottschang, T. (1987). "Economic Change, Disasters, and Migration: The Historical Case of Manchuria," *Economic Development and Cultural Change*, 35, 461–490.

Hou, G., Z. Zou, T. Zhang, and Y. Meng (2019). "Analysis of the Effect of Industrial Transformation of Resource-Based Cities in Northeast China," *Economies*, 7, 1–22.

Hou, L. (2018). *Building for Oil: Daqing and the Formation of the Chinese Socialist State*, Cambridge, MA: Harvard University Asia Center.

Huang, Q. (2004). "Rejuvenation and Modernization of the Northeast China Traditional Industrial Base," *China and World Economy*, 12, 113–126.

Izotov, D. and V. Suslov (2012). "So Far Only Intentions: First Results of the Program for Cooperation between Eastern Regions of Russia and Northeast China (2009–2018)," *Problems of Economic Transition*, 55, 3–21.

Kung, J. and N. Li (2011). "Commercialization as Exogenous Shocks: The Effect of the Soybean Trade and Migration in Manchurian Villages, 1895–1934," *Explorations in Economic History*, 48, 568–589.

Murakami, H. (2012). "Emergence of the Japanese Developmental State: Japanese Management of 'Manchukuo' through Special Corporations," *Asian Journal of Political Science*, 20, 129–153.

National Statistics Bureau of China (2010). *China Compendium of Statistics, 1949–2008*, Beijing: China Statistics Press.

Novy, D. (2013). "Gravity Redux: Measuring International Trade Costs with Panel Data," *Economic Inquiry*, 51, 101–121.

Perkins, D. (1969). *Agricultural Development in China, 1368–1968*, Chicago: Aldine.

Tinbergen, J. (1962). *Shaping the World Economy*, New York: The Twentieth Century Fund.

Tomasik, R. (2013). "Time Zone-Related Continuity and Synchronization Effects on Bilateral Trade Flows," *Review of World Economics*, 149, 321–342.

Urbansky, S. (2008). *Kolonialer Wettstreit: Russland, China, Japan und die Ostchinesische Eisenbahn*, Frankfurt am Main: Campus Verlag.

Wang, M., Z. Cheng, and P. Zhang (2014). *Old Industrial Cities Seeking New Road of Industrialization: Models of Revitalizing Northeast China*, Singapore: World Scientific Publishing.

Part II

The Theoretical and Institutional Approach to China's Transition to Capitalism

Chapter 5

The "Take-off" of Chinese Economy: An Evolutionary Model of Reform and Open-up

Zhiming Fu[*,§], Antoine Le Riche[*,†,¶], Antoine Parent[†,‡,‖], and Lei Zhang[*,]**

[*]*School of Economics, Sichuan University, China*
[†]*CAC-IXXI, Complex Systems Institute, France*
[‡]*Paris 8 University, OFCE-Sciences Po, France*
[§]*zhimingfu@scu.edu.cn*
[¶]*antoineleriche@scu.edu.cn*
[‖]*antoine.parent02@univ-paris8.fr*
[**]*zlei@scu.edu.cn*

Abstract

In this chapter, we analyze how the "take-off" of the Chinese economy is due to a gradual shift from a planned to a market economy. This evolution is mainly explained by reforms implemented which we present chronologically. We use a simple evolutionary model, based on biology, to explain how reforms allow an economy to move from a planned to a market economy. We present the case where no reforms are implemented and show that there exist two stable stationary equilibria: (i) a full market economy and (ii) a full planned economy. After the introduction of reforms, we are able to prove that there is only one stable stationary solution that corresponds to a full market economy.

5.1. Introduction

The last four decades have witnessed a dramatic transformation of the Chinese economy. While this rapid economic development is unprecedented, unwinding causes for such transformation is less straightforward. In this chapter, we emphasize the importance of history in affecting how institutions have been evolving to allow for a major role played by markets in efficiently allocating resources.

The reform process since 1978 exhibits two interesting features of aversion to pre-existing ideology because of the historical lessons associated with the "Great Leap Forward" and the "Cultural Revolution" and of aversion to uncertainty of outcomes associated with institutional innovations. In effect, this makes the reform process resemble that of evolution with biased local mutations. Aversion to pre-existing ideology and uncertainty permits market-friendly measures to be experimented locally. If successful, they are adopted gradually and replicated throughout the country. Although the process of market liberalization was not smooth, the process itself has generated a significant *externality* effect in expanding the increasingly dominant role of markets. Both the biased institutional innovations and the externality effect of market liberalization have undoubtedly been conducive to the "take-off" of the Chinese economy. The presence of such externality effect, which naturally makes market expansion incentive compatible for additional participating agents, indicates that outcomes of this process are locally irreversible.

There is extensive literature, as in Huang (2012), describing how various elements affecting the rapid expansion of the Chinese economy during this period: the initial rural reform in 1978, the emergence and the expansion of township and village enterprises (hereafter, TVEs), population dividend, the price reform in the 1990s, the tournament structure in promoting local and provincial officials, accession to World Trade Organization (hereafter, WTO), the latecomer advantage, and so on. This chapter does not intend to negate these important contributions, rather our approach is complementary in nature and attempts to provide a novel framework to describe the aggregate effect of the reform process. Our model indicates that an *ex post* successful reform does not necessarily require a well designed mechanism *ex ante*, especially in the absence of full information. However, the successful measures tried locally do possess the property of incentive compatibility for local inclusion of new participants, allowing expansion through replication. This makes the process of market liberalization self-sustaining. Both the biased innovations and externality quicken this process. While the reform process is certainly conducive to converging to markets as main mechanisms in resource allocation, we do not argue that such process is *ex ante* optimal.

We present the reform measures associated with market liberalization. During the period from 1979 to 1984, the implementation of reforms has been to provide economic incentive to develop a market economy. In order to achieve such a goal, the government needed to rely market prices on allocating resources implying the implementation of a dual-track price system. The introduction of the dual-track price system in February 1985, allows state owned entrepreneurs' (hereafter, SOEs) products to be sold at two different prices. In particular, outputs under the planned quota were sold at the planned price meanwhile the residual outputs above the quota could be sold at market prices which are determined by the demand and supply. Over the period 1994–2004, the government goal was to establish a full market economy as it was still a combination of planned and market economies by the end of 1993. The two main changes in the Chinese society during this period were the following: (i) privatization reforms, and (ii) joining the WTO. The final stage of reforms are linked to relatively conservative and more associated with social welfare programs aiming at reducing inequalities particularly between urban and rural areas over the period 2005–2012.

The growth "take-off" in western Europe during the Industrial Revolution has generated an important income divergence between the western economies and China. Maddison (1983) provides evidences that per capita income in western Europe rose significantly from only 30% above that of China at the beginning of the Industrial Revolution to about 900% of that of China by 1870. When comparing economic growth, the East Asian countries witnessed take-off only in the late 20th century, starting with Japan just after the Second World War, followed by the East Asian Tigers in the 1960s, the "Tiger cubs" after that, and more recently China. The 6% to 10% sustained economic growth rate during their boom period reduced the disparity between those countries and placed the newly industrialized economies of the past among the advanced economies of today.

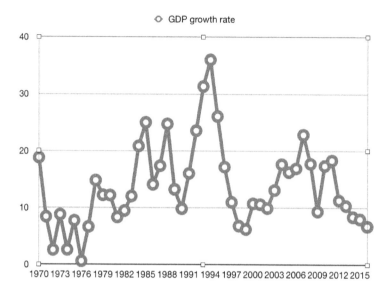

Fig. 5.1.   GDP growth of China since 1970.

Figure 5.1 shows the GDP growth of China from 1970.[1] It shows that starting from 1977, with the introduction of reforms, there does exist a "take-off" of the Chinese economy.

Our chapter is the first to apply biological interactions modeling to economy. In this model we extend the nearly century-old Lotka–Volterra theory, i.e. link species interactions to biodiversity patterns to an interaction between planned economy and private economy. In a first step, we restate the assumptions and results of the Lotka–Volterra model. After that, we translate the model to an economic one in order to disentangle the impact of the external effect of the market economy, the relative efficiency of the market economy, and the local biased reforms on how production process is operating (planned and market operating). In the configuration in which no reform has been implemented, we show that neither the external effect nor the relative efficiency of the market economy have an impact on the stability properties of the stationary solutions. Indeed,

---

[1]Data are from "Trends and Cycles in China's Macroeconomy" by Chang, Chen, Waggoner, and Zha and the manuscript "China's Macroeconomic Time Series: Methods and Implications" by Higgins and Zha.

there exists four stationary solutions: two corner solutions, one interior solution, and one trivial solution. Both corner solutions are stable whatever the external effect or the relative efficiency of the market economy. The economy could converge to any of these two equilibria depending on the initial conditions. Conversely, when the reforms are introduced, we show that the push due to the existence of reforms will decide the final outcome of the production process of the economy. Indeed, we are able to show that in the presence of reforms, the production process will tend to a full market economy whatever the values of the parameters of the model.

The rest of the chapter is organized as follows. In Section 5.2, we discuss how, chronologically, reforms played a key role for the existence of such a "take-off." Section 5.3 presents an "evolutionary" model, based on the works of Lotka (1926) and Volterra (1926), and analyzes its stability with and without the presence of reforms. Section 5.4 concludes the chapter. Proofs are gathered in the Appendix.

5.2.   Reforms

The rapid development of the Chinese economy in the past 40 years has attracted a growing attention in the role of institutional reforms driving its economic "take-off." There is extensive literature, as in Huang (2012), describing how various elements have affected the rapid expansion of the Chinese economy in the end of the 20th century: the initial rural reform in 1978, the emergence and the expansion of township and village enterprises, population dividend, the price reform in the 1990s, the tournament structure in promoting local and provincial officials, accession in 2001 to the World Trade Organization, the latecomer advantage, and so on. In most of the literature, institutional reforms and their corresponding consequences are reviewed and discussed in chronological order. In particular, Chinese reforms which took place during 1979–2012 could be categorized into four stages as described by Qian (2000) and Huang (2012): (i) initialization of reforms in rural China, (ii) reinforcement of the reforms, (iii) establishment of the market economy, and (iv) implementation of reforms promoting equity.

Conversely, these reforms could also be understood as gradualist reform: partial and incremental reforms are implemented at the beginning and reforms are deepened over time. In the following, we present the reforms in a gradualism perspective and further divide the reforms into four stages, with each of them corresponding to a specific focus of the government.

According to Feltenstein and Nsouli (2003) and Liu and Garino (2001), China's reforms implementation follow a more gradual process, which began in the agricultural sectors, allowing markets to develop. Second, industrial growth is coming largely from new firms as state-owned firms were quite inefficient.

5.2.1.   *Initialization of reform in rural China*

The first stage, during the period from 1979 to 1984, is the initialization of the reform which provided economic actors the incentive for developing the economy. After the Third Plenum of the Eleventh Chinese Communist Party Congress in December 1978, the government changed its focus from class struggle to economic development. This attempt was to introduce some market solution to the planned economy. However, such a task was not easy as there exists a close link between planned economy and socialism during this period of time. To maintain stability and avoid unnecessary confrontations, the government strategically started its reform in rural areas and specific economic zones open to international trade, such as Guangdong and Fujian. Since most of the population and capitalism were rural in the 1980s, Huang (2012) pointed out that rural reforms played an important role in explaining the Chinese "take-off," i.e. China's transition to a market economy. In the following, we emphasize our exposition on rural reforms including agricultural reform and the development of commune–brigade enterprises (hereafter, CBEs), also known as TVE in 1984.

The agricultural reform was associated with the introduction of household responsibility system (hereafter, HRS) by "households of Xiaogang production brigade" in Anhui province December 1978. In particular, households in Anhui province had to sign a contract which allowed them to divide the commune's land. Moreover, they could keep their production after paying a quota of grain to the state. By the end of 1984, 98% of households in rural China had adopted this system. This reform greatly promoted farmers' incentive for production and increased farm products significantly as indicated by

Lin (1992) where the decollectivization increased total factor productivity and could have accounted for half of output growth during 1978–1984. This reform leads to additional effects. Riskin (1987) found that poverty in rural area declined sharply after the reform as rural per capita income more than doubled. Meanwhile, consumption of rural residents increased by 51% between 1978 and 1983. Taylor (1993) pointed out that the agricultural reform released labor from rural land and provided a huge number of surplus labor (100 to 150 million workers) to the economy.

The rural reforms through the development of CBE ameliorate the competitiveness of the rural area. The literature points out at least four effects: (i) Riskin (1987) showed that CBEs raise the productivity and promote allocative efficiency which account for four-fifths of gains from income; (ii) Wong (1988) found that several industries, such as food processing, textiles, and coal mining, grew very fast since then; (iii) Naughton (2006) stated that the contribution of rural businesses to gross domestic product increased from 6% in 1978 to 26% in 1996; (iv) Huang (2012) found that rural industry reform lowered rural–urban income gap and promoted competition to SOEs in the 1980s. Contrary to the traditional wisdom, these findings show that public ownership promotes productivity. According to Che and Qian (1998) and Roland (2000), this happened because CBEs can circumvent China's weak legal institutions and thus improve productivity.

5.2.2. *Reinforcement of the reform*

The relative success of rural reforms encouraged the government to expand the reforms to urban areas aiming at establishing a mixed economy, where the planned economy and the market economy have an equal weight. In order to achieve such a goal, the government needed to rely market prices on allocating resources implying the implementation of a dual-track price system, as depicted in Figures 5.2(a)–5.2(c), and contract responsibility system in SOEs.

The introduction of the dual-track price system, officially admitted by the government in May 1984 and was effective in February 1985, allows SOEs' products to be sold at two different prices. In particular, outputs under the planned quota were sold at the planned price; meanwhile, the residual outputs above the quota could be sold at market prices which are determined by the demand and supply.

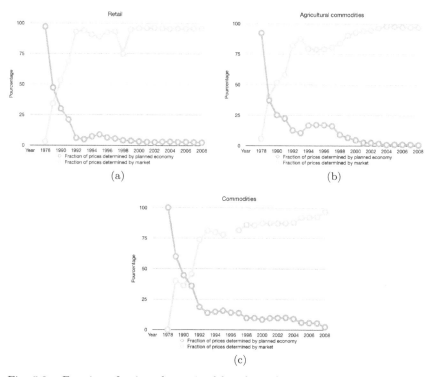

Fig. 5.2. Fraction of prices determined by planned economy and market economy: (a) retail prices; (b) agricultural commodity prices; (c) commodity prices.

Wu and Zhao (1987) argued that disadvantages of dual-track price system, acceptable as a temporary rule, outweigh its advantages. Byrd (1987) stated that the implementation of dual-track price system resulted in a continuously increasing importance of the market in allocating industrial goods. Naughton (1995) found that the dual-track price system greatly increased the incentive for production and thus increased output greatly. Gao *et al.* (1996) showed that government subsidization for urban households increased market demand for food and raised the market prices of staple foods. Liew (1993) found that the removal of price controls over industrial products reduced production costs, raised output, and diminished corruption.

At the same time, the government started the reform of SOEs by introducing contract responsibility system (hereafter, CRS). According to CRS, managers of SOEs signed contracts with government on the retention of their product and profit. Such a system allows important increases in both enterprises' autonomy and their incentive to produce more. By 1987, 80% of SOEs above medium size had joined the CRS. In 1989, this share was close to 100%. It is generally believed that CRS increased the SOEs' incentive for production and helped the transformation to a market economy, as argued by Koo (1990). However, empirical findings show that the impact of CRS on productivity is mixed.[2]

5.2.3. *Establishment of a market economy: 1994–2005*

Over the period 1994–2004, the government goal was to establish a full market economy as it was still a combination of planned and market economies by the end of 1993. In the following, we describe the two main changes in the Chinese society during this period: (i) privatization reforms, and (ii) joining the WTO.

In order for a market economy to perform properly, one necessary condition has to be satisfied: well-defined private property rights. However, all properties are owned by state or collectively before the implementation of the constitutional amendment in 1988 which recognized the importance of private enterprises. In 1999, laws were established to protect private properties. The recognition of private property right led to the emergence of market-oriented firms, which include private firms, collectives, stock holding companies, foreign wholly owned firms, and joint ventures with foreign investment. Conversely, a diversified ownership allows the government to reform the SOEs. In particular, a number of small or medium-sized SOEs were sold to individuals and became private firms. According to Brandt *et al.* (2008), the number of SOEs decreased by 48% during 2001–2004, which forced millions of redundant workers in SOEs to leave their jobs. At the same time, the private sector grew, accounting for as much as 70% of China's gross domestic product by 2005. The recognition and protection of private property rights have vitalized the private sector and the economy, which had been verified by a series of chapters, as in (Liu and Garino, 2001) and (Bolton, 1995).

In December 2001, China joined the WTO. It was important for the development of the Chinese economy since it brought more trade

---

[2]See Choe and Yin (2000) for a review of the literature.

flows, investments, and so on, encouraged more international trade and investment in China, and opened up the world market for China's exports. It obviously promoted gross domestic product growth and brought tremendous changes to China's economic structure. Brandt *et al.* (2012) and Yu and Li (2014) showed that WTO membership brought China higher productivity growth. Zhiming *et al.* (2013) found that joining WTO increased economic growth significantly by raising foreign trade and foreign direct investment but had insignificant influence on technological innovation. However, existing studies (Brandt *et al.*, 2012; Elliott and Zhou, 2013) found that though the share of SOEs to gross domestic product decreased after joining WTO, SOEs enjoyed a higher rise in productivity. In addition to the economic influence, some studies such as Chow (2003) pointed out that WTO membership also affected China's legal and political institutions.

All of these reforms led to more and more price determined in the market, as shown in Figure 5.2.

5.2.4. *Reforms promoting equity: 2005–2012*

A number of economists pointed out that reforms in the fourth stage during 2005–2012 are relatively conservative and mostly associated with social welfare programs aiming at reducing inequalities particularly between urban and rural areas. Compared to urban areas, rural areas have inefficient agricultural productivity and inadequate social welfare system. To improve this, the government abolished agricultural tax and implemented new rural cooperative medical system (hereafter, NCMS) and new rural social pension scheme (hereafter, NRSP).

First, the central government abolished agricultural tax between 2004 and 2005 to relieve the tax burden of farmers. Thereafter, both theoretical and empirical studies examined this reform on farmers income. Theoretical studies such as Heerink *et al.* (2006) and Yu and Jensen (2010) argued that agricultural tax abolition would increase agricultural production and income significantly for a range from 5% to 11%. However, Wang and Shen (2014) stated empirically that the impact of abolishing agricultural tax on production, input, and productivity is not significant. Furthermore, it did not significantly raise the net income of farmers.

Second, NCMS was launched in 2003 and had broad coverage only after 2004. The goal was to provide medical insurance to rural residents and promote equity in health care. Empirical studies show that NCMS helped improve rural residents' access to health services but were not enough for the low-income groups. Specifically, quite a few studies, such as Ran and Jin (2007), Han *et al.* (2010), and Li *et al.* (2015), argue that NCMS is not enough to satisfy the health needs of the lower income groups and more attention is needed for the poor. Zhou *et al.* (2012) find that there exists a wide gap of outpatient services between high-income residents and low-income residents.

Third, before the implementation of NRSP between 2009 and 2012, the rural elderly did not have any social pension because of which they had to work until they could not physically work. After the implementation of that reforms, few studies found that NRSP had a positive effect on retirement of the rural elderly. Specifically, Zhang *et al.* (2014) and Chen *et al.* (2015) found that NRSP recipients increased their retirement probability by 15–25%. An indirect effect of that reforms concerns the children of NRSP recipients. Indeed, Eggleston *et al.* (2018) showed that they migrate out of rural area at a higher probability than prior to the reform.

5.3. An "Evolutionary" Model

5.3.1. *Prey–Predator model as an example*

Mathematical modeling of prey–predator interactions have attracted greater attention since the original work by Lotka and Volterra in the 1920s,[3] and they have been extensively studied for their rich dynamics.[4]

The Lotka–Volterra equations can be written simply as a system of first-order nonlinear ordinary differential equations. Time is continuous. Assumptions of this model are: (i) There is no shortage of food for the prey population; (ii) The amount of food supplied

---

[3]See Lotka (1926) and Volterra (1926).
[4]See for instance Murdoch *et al.* (2003), Seo and DeAngelis (2011), and Turchin (2003).

to the prey is directly related to the size of the prey population; (iii) The rate of change of population is directly proportional to its size; (iv) The environment is constant and genetic adaptation is not assumed to be negligible; (v) Predators will never stop eating.

Let x denote the density of prey and y the density of predator. Then, their evolution is

$$\dot{x} = x(a - by), \dot{y} = y(-c + dx), \tag{5.1}$$

where a, b, c, and d are all positive constants.

When taking a closer look at the prey equation, we can see that the prey are assumed to reproduce exponentially, which is represented by the term ax. Such an equation also shows that the rate at which predators kill prey is proportional to the product of the number of prey and the number of predators, or in other terms, how often the two populations meet. This is represented by the term bxy. Therefore, in the case in which there is no population of prey or predators, the population of prey cannot decrease. It follows that the equation for prey can be summed up as the rate at which new prey is born minus the rate at which prey is killed off.

Looking at the evolution of predator, it is possible to see that the growth of the predator population is proportional to the amount of times the two populations meet. This is similar to the rate at which predators kill prey except that a different constant is used to describe this relationship since the rate at which predators kill and the rate at which they reproduce are not identical. This term is represented by the term dxy. Since prey cannot kill the predators, the decrease in predator population is due to death by natural causes or by emigration. This is assumed to be an exponential decay, which is represented by the term cy. The equation for predators can be summed up as the rate at which they consume prey minus the natural death rate of the population.

We are interested in solutions to these differential equations in the first quadrant $x, y \geq 0$. At steady state, the evolution of prey and predator, x and y, are constant, i.e. $\dot{x} = \dot{y} = 0$, and thus it holds that

$$0 = x(a - by) \text{ and } 0 = y(-d + cx).$$

By direct inspection of the previous expression, this system has two stationary solutions: one corner solution

$$x = 0, \ y = 0$$

and one interior solution

$$x = \frac{c}{d}, \ y = \frac{a}{b}.$$

The Jacobian matrix of system (5.1) is

$$J = \begin{pmatrix} a - by & -bx \\ -cy & -c + dx \end{pmatrix}. \tag{5.2}$$

Consider the Jacobian matrix at $(x, y) = (0, 0)$:

$$J = \begin{pmatrix} a & 0 \\ 0 & -c \end{pmatrix}. \tag{5.3}$$

One eigenvalue is given by a and the other one by $-c$. The stationary solution is thus unstable. The direction of x is unstable, while the direction of y is asymptotically stable.

Consider now the Jacobian matrix at $(x, y) = \left(\frac{d}{c}, \frac{a}{b}\right)$:

$$J = \begin{pmatrix} 0 & -\frac{bc}{d} \\ \frac{ad}{b} & 0 \end{pmatrix}. \tag{5.4}$$

Eigenvalues are $\pm i\sqrt{ac}$: Both eigenvalues are imaginary.

In order to investigate the stability of the stationary solutions we consider an invariant motion $E(x, y)$ satisfying the following equation:

$$\frac{d}{dt}E(x(t), y(t)) = \frac{\partial E}{\partial x}\dot{x} + \frac{\partial E}{\partial y}\dot{y} = 0.$$

Such a variable does not change along a solution curve. Suppose that $y \neq a/b$, it is possible to write the slope of vector field in the phase plane as follows:

$$\frac{dy}{dx} = \frac{y(cx - d)}{x(a - by)}.$$

By using separation of variables, this yields

$$\frac{a - by}{y} dy = \frac{cx - d}{x} dx$$

and

$$\frac{d}{dt} E(x(t), y(t)) = \left(\frac{d}{x} - c\right)(ax - bxy) + \left(\frac{a}{y} - b\right)(cxy - dy).$$

Direct computations show that $\frac{d}{dt} E(x(t), y(t)) = 0$, implying that $E(x, y)$ is an invariant motion of (5.1). Hence, the interior solution is not spiral, but the populations of prey and predator underlie oscillations. In the following, we provide a numerical example when the initial conditions (x_0, y_0) are set to $(10, 100)$ and the parameters equal $a = 12, b = 1, c = 0.3$, and $d = 0.01$.

The population fluctuations can also be represented in the evolution of the preys and predators over time. Figure 5.3 shows how the populations of the predator and prey typically oscillate. Note that the oscillations are dependent on the initial conditions.

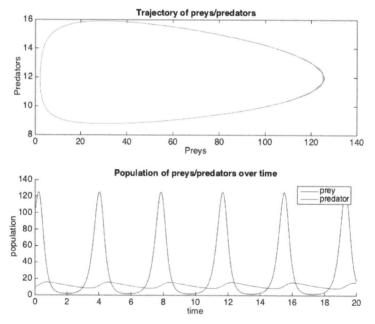

Fig. 5.3.   Trajectory and evolution of the prey and predators when $a = 0.8$ and $b = 0.85$.

How can this system be interpreted in terms of species behavior? Consider the trajectory passing through the point $(15.92, 125.92)$ in Figure 5.3. In such a case, the ratio of predators to prey is important. It implies that the population of predators drops and thus the ratio of predators to prey reduces, and so the population of prey increases. Once there are lots of prey, the numbers of predator will again start to increase. The resulting cyclic behavior is repeated over and over as shown in Figure 5.3.

5.3.2. *Our case: Without reform*

We consider a modified evolution model (prey–predator model) in order to assess the evolution of the market economy in China. Let x_t denote the size of the planned economy and y_t the size of the market economy. Note that $z_t = x_t + y_t$ can be interpreted as the realized output at time t. The evolution of the size of the planned economy before the introduction of reforms is

$$\dot{x} = (1 - x - y)x. \tag{5.5}$$

The evolution of the planned economy is given by $(1 - x - y)x$. In such a configuration, the planned economy grows at the rate $(1-x)x$. It also shows that the rate at which the planned economy replaces the market economy is given by xy. Let us consider now the evolution of the size of the market economy before any reforms take place:

$$\dot{y} = \left(\frac{b}{a} - \frac{x}{a} - y\right) y, \text{ if } y > \tilde{y}. \tag{5.6}$$

The parameter b/a represents the relative efficiency in production of the output; meanwhile, the parameter $1/a$ denotes the external effect of the market. In such a configuration, the market economy grows at the rate $\left(\frac{b}{a} - y\right) y$. It also shows that the rate at which the market economy replaces the planned economy is given by xy/a. In other words, the terms xy in (5.9) and xy/a in (5.6) represent planned and market economy interactions, respectively.

Once we have introduced the system defined by (5.5) and (5.6), our first task is to ensure the existence and possibly the multiplicity of its stationary solution. At the steady state the variables must be constant, i.e. one needs $\dot{x} = 0$ and $\dot{y} = 0$. By inspecting (5.5) and (5.6), a steady state of the reduce dynamics is thus a two-tuple $(x, y) \gg (0, 0)$ satisfying the following system of equations:

$$(1 - x - y)x = 0, (b - x - ay)y = 0. \tag{5.7}$$

Before analyzing the steady state, let us assume the following:

Assumption 1. $0 < a < b < 1$.

Such an assumption implies that $1/a$ and b/a are higher than one. Since b/a represents the relative efficiency of the market economy, the assumption 1 implies that the market economy is more efficient than the planned economy for the production of output.

The following proposition shows the multiplicity of solution of (5.7).

Proposition 5.1. *Assume that assumption 1 is satisfied. Then, there exist three corner stationary solutions and one interior stationary solution of* (5.7):

$$(x, y) = (0, 0); (x, y) = \left(0, \frac{b}{a}\right),$$

$$(x, y) = (1, 0); (x, y) = \left(\frac{b - a}{1 - a}, \frac{1 - b}{1 - a}\right).$$

There exist three corner solutions $(x, y) = (0, 0)$, $(x, y) = (0, b/a)$, and $(x, y) = (1, 0)$. When $(x, y) = (0, 0)$, both the market economy and the planned economy collapse; meanwhile, when $(x, y) = (0, b/a)$ or $(x, y) = (1, 0)$, there is only the market economy or the planned that is operating. Note that under assumption 1, it holds that the market economy is able to produce more output than the planned economy as it is relatively more efficient, i.e. $b/a > 1$.

Finally, there is a solution where both the market and planned economies coexist $(x, y) = ((b - a)/(1 - a), (1 - b)(1 - a))$. In such a configuration, the planned economy will have realized output higher (resp. lower) than the market economy if and only if b is higher (resp. lower) than $(1 + a)/2$.

After having shown the existence and the multiplicity of the stationary solution, we now turn to the analysis of the transitional dynamics of the system, i.e. we aim at appraising the stability properties of each stationary solution by studying the linearized dynamics of the economy around it. Straightforward computations show that the linearized dynamics of a system defined by (5.5) and (5.6) are generated by the following Jacobian matrix:

$$J = \begin{pmatrix} 1 - 2x - y & -x \\ -\dfrac{y}{a} & \dfrac{b}{a} - \dfrac{x}{a} - 2y \end{pmatrix}. \tag{5.8}$$

In order to analyze the local stability of system defined by (5.5) and (5.6), we follow the usual procedure consisting in studying the characteristic polynomial $P(\lambda)$ of the Jacobian matrix (5.8) and in analyzing its eigenvalues. From a direct inspection of (5.8), we establish the stability properties of the dynamic system. We will find two pictures for the local dynamics: two unstable stationary solutions and two stable stationary solutions.

Proposition 5.2. *Assume that assumption 1 is satisfied. Then, the following results generically hold:*

$\lfloor i \rfloor$ *the stationary solutions $(x, y) = (0, 0)$ and $(x, y) = \left(\frac{b-a}{1-a}, \frac{1-b}{1-a} \right)$ are unstable,*

$\lfloor ii \rfloor$ *the stationary solutions $(x, y) = \left(0, \frac{b}{a} \right)$ and $(x, y) = (1, 0)$ are stable.*

See Appendix.

Such a proposition shows that there are two stable steady states and that, depending on the initial conditions, the trajectory of the planned/market economy will converge to one of these two stationary solutions. In the following, we are considering a case where the economy converge to a planned economy.

In our numerical example, we provide a numerical example represented in Figure 5.4 when the initial conditions (x_0, y_0) are set to $(100, 10)$ and the parameters equal $a = 0.8$ and $b = 0.85$. In such a case, the external effect of the market $1/a$ is equal to 1.1, while the relative efficiency of the market economy b/a is equal to 1.056. The sizes of the planned economy and the market economy are not fluctuating; they are converging respectively to one and zero.

Consider the trajectory passing through the point $(10, 2)$ in Figure 5.4. The ratio of market economy to planned is relatively low $1/5$. The sizes of both the market and planned economies will shrink as will their ratio. It implies that the market economy will reduce even more until it disappears as shown in Figure 5.4.

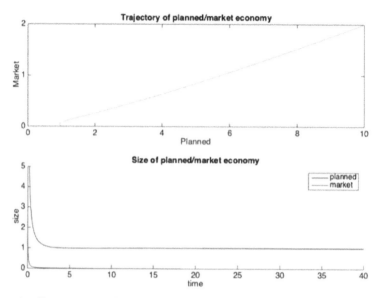

Fig. 5.4. Trajectory and evolution of the size the market and the planned economies when $a = 0.8$ and $b = 0.85$.

The goal of the following section is to show that when some reforms are introduced, they will affect the evolution of the market economy positively. In fact, it will result in only a unique outcome: an economy operating with only a market structure.

5.3.3. *Case with reforms*

In this configuration, we consider that the evolution of the planned economy as before. In other words, it is assumed that the planned economy size is not affected by the reforms:

$$\dot{x} = (1 - x - y)x. \tag{5.9}$$

Conversely, the market economy will be affected positively by the reforms as follows, when the output the market economy is sufficiently low:

$$\dot{y} = \left(\frac{b}{a} - \frac{x}{a} - y\right)y + c, \text{if } y \leq \tilde{y}. \tag{5.10}$$

The term c represents the benefit of reforms on the market economy. It has a positive effect of the output realized by the market economy. Indeed, we show that when the output of the market economy is sufficiently high, the only outcome will be a market economy due to the external effect.

Our first objective is to determine the number of stationary solutions of the system defined by (5.9) and (5.10). At the steady state, the variables must be constant, i.e. one needs $\dot{x} = 0$ and $\dot{y} = 0$. By inspecting (5.9) and (5.10), a steady state of the dynamics is thus a two-tuple $(x, y) >> (0, 0)$ satisfying the following system of equations:

$$(1 - x - y)x = 0, \quad \left(\frac{b}{a} - \frac{x}{a} - y\right) y + c = 0. \tag{5.11}$$

The unique valid steady state from an economic point view, i.e. $x, y >> 0$, is

$$(x, y) = \left(0, \frac{b}{2a}\left[1 + \sqrt{1 + 4c\left(\frac{a}{b}\right)^2}\right]\right).$$

Now, we aim at appraising the stability properties of the unique stationary solution by studying the linearized dynamics of the economy around it. Straightforward computations show that the linearized dynamics of a system defined by (5.5) and (5.6) are generated by the following Jacobian matrix:

$$J = \begin{pmatrix} 1 - 2x - y & -x \\ -\dfrac{y}{a} & \dfrac{b}{a} - \dfrac{x}{a} - 2y \end{pmatrix}. \tag{5.12}$$

Replacing the values of x and y of the unique solution in the Jacobian matrix yields

$$J = \begin{pmatrix} 1 - \dfrac{b}{2a}\left[1 + \sqrt{1 + 4c\left(\frac{a}{b}\right)^2}\right] & 0 \\ \dfrac{b}{2a^2}\left[1 + \sqrt{1 + 4c\left(\frac{a}{b}\right)^2}\right] & -\dfrac{b}{a}\sqrt{1 + 4c\left(\frac{a}{b}\right)^2} \end{pmatrix}. \tag{5.13}$$

Then, as both eigenvalues of the associated characteristic polynomial are negative the following proposition holds:

Proposition 5.3. *Assume that assumptions 1 is satisfied. Then, the unique stationary solution* $(x, y) = \left(0, \frac{b}{2a} \left[1 + \sqrt{1 + 4c \left(\frac{a}{b} \right)^2} \right] \right)$ *is stable.*

There is only one stable steady state and thus the trajectory of the planned/market economy is converging to the case where only the market economy is operating.

We provide a numerical example based on the value of the previous section. We set c to be equal to 0.1. Such a value indicates that local biased reform increases the market output by 10%. Figure 5.5 presents the trajectory of the planned/market economy and the size of the planned and market economy. We obtain totally different dynamics for the economy. In fact, as in the case without reforms, the

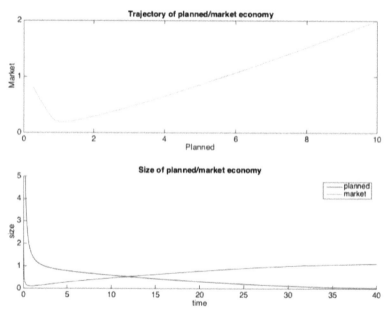

Fig. 5.5.   Trajectory and evolution of the size of the market and planned economies when $a = 0.8$, $b = 0.85$, and $c = 0.1$.

sizes of the planned economy and the market economy are not fluctuating, they are converging respectively to zero and one. In contrast to the previous case, the planned and the market economies are not dropping monotonically with time, but at a certain period of time, there exists a reverse trajectory.

Consider the trajectory passing through the point $(10, 2)$ in Figure 5.5. The ratio of market economy to planned is relatively low $1/5$. The sizes of both the market and planned economies will shrink as will their ratio. The market and planned economies will reduce. Eventually, due to the presence of c, the planned economy disappears as shown in Figure 5.5.

5.4. Conclusion

In this chapter, we consider an evolutionary model to explain how a planned economy and a market economy interact and evolve over time. We assume that the evolution of the market and planned economies affects each other by the means of two differential equations in the spirit of Lotka (1926) and Volterra (1926). We assume that the market economy is subject to more relative efficiency in production of the output and an external effect.

We analyze the impact of reforms on the existence of stationary solutions and their stability properties. We first show that in the case without reforms, there exist four stationary solutions. More specifically, the only two stable stationary are (i) a full market economy and (ii) a full planned economy. After the introduction of reforms, we are able to prove that there is only one stable stationary solution that corresponds to a full market economy. Such a result implies that reforms are an important driver of the evolution toward a market economy and thus a "take-off."

An important extension of the model could be to introduce microfoundations and optimization behavior of economic agents in order to understand how the interaction between economic agents, their incentives, and the introduction of reforms will lead to an evolution from a planned economy to a market economy.

Appendix

Proof of Proposition 5.2

If $(x, y) = (0, 0)$, one eigenvalue is 1 and the other one is b. The equilibrium is unstable. When the equilibrium is at (0,0), the addition of a small proportion of the size of the market economy and the size of the planned economy will allow both of them to take-off.

$$J = \begin{pmatrix} 1 & 0 \\ 0 & \dfrac{b}{a} \end{pmatrix}. \tag{A.5.1}$$

If $(x, y) = (0, \frac{b}{a})$, both eigenvalues are negative $((a - b)/a$ and $[b(a - 2)]/a)$. It is an asymptotically stable equilibrium.

$$J = \begin{pmatrix} -\dfrac{b}{a} & 0 \\ \dfrac{b^2}{a} & -\dfrac{b}{a} \end{pmatrix}. \tag{A.5.2}$$

If $(x, y) = (1, 0)$, both eigenvalues are negative (-1 and $b - 1$). It is an asymptotically stable equilibrium.

$$J = \begin{pmatrix} -1 & -1 \\ 0 & -\dfrac{1}{a} \end{pmatrix}. \tag{A.5.3}$$

If $(x, y) = (-\frac{b-a}{1-a}, b - 1 - \frac{1}{1-a})$, the product of the characteristic roots is negative, which means that there is a positive and a negative eigenvalues. Thus, it is a unstable equilibrium.

References

Bolton, P. (1995). "Privatization, and the Separation of Ownership and Control: Lessons from Chinese Enterprise Reform," *Economics of Transition*, 3, 1–12.

Brandt, L., T. G. Rawski, and J. Sutton (2008). "China's industrial development," In L. Brandt and T. G. Rawski (Eds.), *China's Great Economic Transformation*, New York, NY: Cambridge University Press, 569–632.

Brandt, L., J. Van Biesebroeck, and Y. Zhang (2012). "Creative Accounting or Creative Destruction? Firm-level Productivity Growth in Chinese Manufacturing," *Journal of Development Economics*, 97, 339–351.

Byrd, W. A. (1987). "The Impact of the Two-tier Plan/Market System in Chinese Industry," *Journal of Comparative Economics*, 11, 295–308.

Che, J. and Y. Qian (1998). "Institutional Environment, Community Government, and Corporate Governance: Understanding China's Township-village Enterprises," *Journal of Law, Economics, & Organization*, 14, 1–23.

Chen, Z., T. Bengtsson, and J. Helgertz (2015). "Labor supply responses to new rural social pension insurance in China: A regression discontinuity approach," *IZA Discussion Papers*, No. 9360.

Choe, C. and X. Yin (2000). "Contract Management Responsibility System and Profit Incentives in China's State-owned Enterprises," *China Economic Review*, 11, 98–112.

Chow, G. C. (2003). "Impact of Joining the WTO on China's Economic, Legal and Political Institutions," *Pacific Economic Review*, 8, 105–115.

Eggleston, K., A. Sun, and Z. Zhan (2018). "The Impact of Rural Pensions in China on Labor Migration," *The World Bank Economic Review*, 32, 64–84.

Elliott, R. and Y. Zhou (2013). "State-owned Enterprises, Exporting and Productivity in China: A Stochastic Dominance Approach," *The World Economy*, 36, 1000–1028.

Feltenstein, A. and S. M. Nsouli (2003). "'Big Bang' Versus Gradualism in Economic Reforms: An Intertemporal Analysis with an Application to China," *IMF Staff Papers*, 50, 458–480.

Gao, X. M., E. J. Wailes, and G. L. Cramer (1996). "Partial Rationing and Chinese Urban Household Food Demand Analysis," *Journal of Comparative Economics*, 22, 43–62.

Han, B., Z. Yuan, X. Liao, Y. Xiao, and Y. Hong (2010). "Follow-up Survey on the Influence of the New Rural Cooperative Medical System to the Equity of Health Service Utilization," *Chinese Journal of Social Medicine*, 27, 373–375.

Heerink, N., M. Kuiper, and X. Shi (2006). "China's New Rural Income Support Policy: Impacts on Grain Production and Rural Income Inequality," *China & World Economy*, 14, 58–69.

Huang, Y. (2012). "How Did China Take Off?" *The Journal of Economic Perspectives*, 26, 147–170.

Koo, A. Y. (1990). "The Contract Responsibility System: Transition from a Planned to a Market Economy," *Economic Development and Cultural Change*, 38, 797–820.

Li, C., Y. Hou, M. Sun, J. Lu, Y. Wang, X. Li, F. Chang, and M. Hao (2015). "An Evaluation of China's New Rural Cooperative Medical System: Achievements and Inadequacies from Policy Goals," *BMC Public Health*, 15, 1079.

Liew, L. H. (1993). "Rent-seeking and the Two-track Price System in China," *Public Choice*, 77, 359–375.

Lin, J. Y. (1992). "Rural Reforms and Agricultural Growth in China," *American Economic Review*, 34–51.

Liu, G. S. and G. Garino (2001). "Privatisation or Competition?" *Economics of Planning*, 34, 37–51.

Lotka, A. J. (1926). "Elements of Physical Biology," *Science Progress in the Twentieth Century (1919–1933)*, 21, 341–343.

Maddison, A. (1983). "A Comparison of Levels of GDP Per Capita in Developed and Developing Countries, 1700–1980," *Journal of Economic History*, XLIII.

Murdoch, W. W., C. J. Briggs, and R. M. Nisbet (2003). *Consumer-Resource Dynamics (MPB-36)*, Berlin, Germany: Princeton University Press.

Naughton, B. (1995). *Growing Out of the Plan: Chinese Economic Reform, 1978–1993*, Cambridge, MA, USA: Cambridge University Press.

Naughton, B. J. (2006). *The Chinese Economy: Transitions and Growth*, Cambridge, MA, USA: MIT Press.

Qian, Y. (2000). "The Process of China's Market Transition (1978–1998): The Evolutionary, Historical, and Comparative Perspectives," *Journal of Institutional and Theoretical Economics*, 156, 151–171.

Ran, R. and F. Jin (2007). "The Access on Health Care and Equity of the Out-of-pocket Expenditure after the Implement of New Cooperative Medical Scheme," *Chinese Health Economics*, 26, 27–31.

Riskin, C. (1987). *China's Political Economy: The Quest for Development since 1949*, Oxford, UK: Oxford University Press.

Roland, G. (2000). *Transition and Economics: Politics, Markets, and Firms*, Cambridge, MA, USA: MIT Press.

Seo, G. and D. L. DeAngelis (2011). "A Predator–prey Model with a Holling Type I Functional Response Including a Predator Mutual Interference," *Journal of Nonlinear Science*, 21, 811–833.

Taylor, J. R. (1993). "Rural Employment Trends and the Legacy of Surplus Labor, 1978–1989," in *Economic Trends in Chinese Agriculture: The Impact of Post-Mao Reforms*, pp. 273–310.

Turchin, P. (2003). *Complex Population Dynamics: A Theoretical Empirical Synthesis (MPB-35)*, Princeton, New Jersey, USA: Princeton University Press.

Volterra, V. (1926). "Variazioni e fluttuazioni del numero d'individui in specie animali conviventi," *Memoria della Reale Accademia Nazionale dei Lincei*, VI vol. 2, 31–113.

Wang, X. and Y. Shen (2014). "The Effect of China's Agricultural Tax Abolition on Rural Families' Incomes and Production," *China Economic Review*, 29, 185–199.

Wong, C. P. (1988). "Interpreting Rural Industrial Growth in the Post-Mao Period," *Modern China*, 14, 3–30.

Wu, J. and R. Zhao (1987). "The Dual Pricing System in China's Industry," *Journal of Comparative Economics*, 11, 309–318.

Yu, M. and J. Li (2014). "Imported Intermediate Inputs, Firm Productivity and Product Complexity," *Japanese Economic Review*, 65, 178–192.

Yu, W. and H. G. Jensen (2010). "China's Agricultural Policy Transition: Impacts of Recent Reforms and Future Scenarios," *Journal of Agricultural Economics*, 61, 343–368.

Zhang, C., J. Giles, and Y. Zhao (2014). "Policy Evaluation of China's New Rural Pension Program: Income, Poverty, Expenditure, Subjective Wellbeing and Labor Supply," *China Economic Quarterly*, 14, 203–230.

Zhiming, Z., Z. Xin, and C. Riming (2013). "Research on the Effects of WTO Accession on China's Economic Growth: Path Analysis and Empirical Study," *Journal of Chinese Economic and Foreign Trade Studies*, 6, 70–84.

Zhou, Z., J. Gao, Z. Zhou, X. Yang, and Q. Xue (2012). "Effects of New Rural Cooperative Medical Scheme on the Equity of Health Care Utilization," *Chinese Health Economics*, 31, 37–39.

https://doi.org/10.1142/9781800611238_0007

Chapter 6

New Evidence on the Impact of Institutions on Economic Development in China*

Linda Glawe[†,‡] **and Helmut Wagner**[†,§]

[†] *Faculty of Economics, University of Hagen, Germany*
[‡] *linda.glawe@fernuni-hagen.de*
[§] *helmut.wagner@fernuni-hagen.de*

Abstract

It is by now a well-established fact that good institutions are decisive for economic growth and development. However, only recently, the impact of this underlying growth driver has been investigated for probably the most striking economic success story of the last century: the Chinese economy. China presents a particularly interesting case study since it is often regarded as an exception by having achieved double-digit growth rates for several decades despite relatively low institutional quality. However, new empirical evidence indicates that within China, the picture is more nuanced and that institutional quality plays, in fact, an important role for the economic performance of a province. In our chapter, we add further arguments to this discussion by focusing on the government efficiency index as a proxy for institutional quality. Using 2SLS regression, we show that institutional quality has a highly significant positive impact

---

*This chapter was first presented at the 12th International Conference on the Chinese Economy organized by Mary-Françoise Renard, "A New Era for China: Growth Sustainability and Broaden International Development," CERDI, IDREC, University of Clermont Auvergne, France and CCES, Fudan University, Shanghai, China, held in Clermont-Ferrand, France, 24–25 October 2019.

on the provincial per capita income, trumping the remaining two deep determinants, integration and geography, which only have an indirect effect via institutions. Our results indicate that in order to sustain growth in the future and thus avoid a prolonged growth slowdown, policymakers should be more aware of this important growth driver which still has a large potential for generating growth in the provinces that are currently lacking behind in terms of institutional quality.

6.1.   Introduction

Why are some countries and regions so much richer than others? This is one of the central questions of growth theory. Neoclassical and endogenous growth models offer a variety of proximate factors for explaining differences in economic performance (such as factor accumulation and total factor productivity); however, even though these models provide important insights into the mechanisms of growth, the postulated growth drivers seem to rather redescribe what it means to be prosperous instead of providing an explanation for differences in prosperity (Acemoglu *et al.*, 2005, 2014). North and Thomas (1973: p. 2) put it in a nutshell: "The factors we have listed (innovation, economies of scale, education, capital accumulation, etc.) are not causes of growth; they are growth." In their view, the fundamental source for comparative economic growth and development is differences in institutions. It still took several decades until institutional quality played an increasing role in the economic development literature. The first empirical studies were conducted by Knack and Keefer (1995) and Barro (1997), followed soon by the works of Hall and Jones (1999) and Acemoglu *et al.* (2001), the latter two being the first to take into account potential endogeneity problems between economic growth and institutions. Rodrik *et al.* (2004) and Bhattacharyya (2004) finally postulated the primacy of institutions over the other potential "deep" determinants, such as integration and geography. Since these seminal works, a considerable body of literature has emerged, dealing with the causal impact of institutions on growth and potential interrelationships with other factors of the production function. Also in the field of economic history, institutions play an important role. Today, it is a well-established fact that sound institutions, such as property right protection and contract enforcement, are decisive for the economic performance of a country or region (for survey articles, see for example Easterly and Levine, 2003; Spolaore and Wacziarg, 2013). Against this background, it is surprising that relatively little research has been conducted in order to evaluate the impact of institutional quality within China, a country that has undergone one of the most remarkable economic transformations over the last century. Within only three decades, the poverty ratio fell dramatically from above 90% in 1978 to only about 10% in 2010 and per capita GDP (in constant 2010 USD) increased almost 15-fold. Still, China is said to have relatively poor institutions in international comparison. How could China succeed despite its (seemingly) weak institutional framework? This "puzzle" (also sometimes labelled as the "China paradox," cf. Rothstein, 2015) however can be partly disentangled by taking a look at the level of institutional quality at the provincial level. Figure 6.1 reveals that the average institutional quality (proxied by the government efficiency index which is scaled between −1 and 1 and captures, among others, the provision of

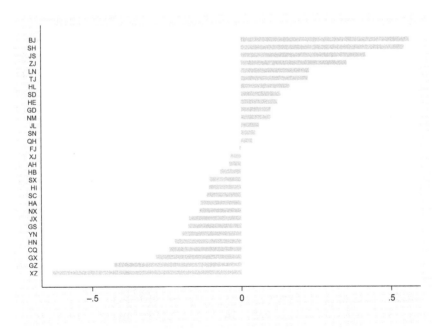

Fig. 6.1.   Mean institutional quality over 2001–2010.

Note: Institutional quality is proxied by the government efficiency index.

Source: Authors' calculations based on Tang *et al.* (2014).

public services as well as the legal environment) varies widely across regions. While some provinces, such as Beijing and Shanghai, report on average very high levels above 0.5, 17 provinces only score below 0. Interestingly, many provinces recording high levels of institutions also have a relatively high per capita GDP, and there is a strong positive correlation between these two variables with a coefficient around 0.83 (significant at the 1% level). This is a first hint that, at the provincial level, institutional quality can indeed have a decisive role for the economic performance.

Institutional quality can differ across provinces due to geographical, political, cultural, and historical reasons or a mix of them (Ji *et al.*, 2014; Glawe and Wagner, 2019). For instance, the government created a benign policy environment for coastal provinces in the wake of the get rich first policy under Deng Xiaoping. The decision to focus first on the coastal region was probably driven by the proximity to ports of these provinces, that is, their favorable geography. These factors set the basis for institutional differences at an early stage which can persist upon today. In sum, when analyzing the impact of institutions on the economic performance in China, it seems to be necessary to take a more nuanced perspective at the regional level: Even if institutions appear not to be decisive for growth in China at the national level when focusing on cross-country comparisons, they might play an important role for the economic success of a province in China. The overall below-average institutional quality is probably the result of very mixed levels of institutions at the regional level.

First empirical evidence on the positive impact of institutional quality on the provincial economic development is provided by Glawe and Wagner (2019, 2020b) and Liu *et al.* (2018), focusing on the marketization index and the governance quality index, respectively. Our chapter aims to add further arguments to this (rather novel) literature examining the impact of institutional quality for provincial development by focusing on the government efficiency index. In particular, we analyze how far the government efficiency (including the provision of public services and the legal environment) is the source of differences in prosperity among Chinese provinces by using OLS and 2SLS regression analyzes. In addition, we investigate whether within China, institutions trump geography and integration, that is, the other two main underlying factors of economic development suggested by the deep determinants literature (cf. Rodrik *et al.* (2004)). Moreover, we investigate how the deep determinants influence each other. Finally, we briefly discuss the implications for China's future growth strategy. In sum, our chapter tries to bridge a gap between the Acemoglu–North–Rodrik general (cross-country) institutional literature as well as the literature that aims at investigating the growth drivers at the regional level in China.

The reminder of this chapter is structured as follows: Section 6.2 presents our data and provides some summary statistics. Our estimation strategy and the main results regarding the impact of institutions on income are discussed in Section 6.3. Section 6.4 then sheds more light on the interrelationships between institutional quality and the other two deep determinants, namely, geography and integration. Section 6.5 offers some additional robustness checks. Final remarks as well as some policy implication are provided in Section 6.6.

6.2. Data Description and Summary Statistics

In this section, we first briefly describe our data and present some summary statistics. We employ a cross-sectional dataset covering 31 provinces, autonomous regions, and municipalities.[1] Most of our time-varying variables are of the year 2010 (otherwise indicated in the following). Table 6.1 provides descriptive statistics of our key variables, and Table 6.2 presents a correlation matrix.

Income is our dependent variable, and it is defined as the logarithm of per capita income in constant 2005 Yuan. Integration is proxied by trade, in particular, the logarithm of the trade share (defined as import plus exports) in GDP.[2] Both variables are calculated using NBS data. The government efficiency index is our measure of institutions and is provided by Tang *et al.* (2014). It is a standardized index varying between -1 (weak government efficiency) and $+1$ (strong government efficiency) and consists of four indicators, namely "government public services," "public infrastructure," "government size," and "welfare of residents" as well as various sub-indicators and 47 indexes (cf. Tang *et al.* (2014),

---

[1]We exclude Hong Kong, Taiwan, and Macao due to missing data.

[2]It would also be very interesting to distinguish between different dimensions of trade, for instance, between inter-industry and intra-industry trade or also regarding the trade partner. This is, however, beyond the scope of our chapter and left for future research.

Table 6.1.   Summary statistics.

Variable (short description)	Obs.	Mean	S.D.	Source
Income (logarithm of GDP p.c. in constant 2005 Yuan)	31	10.29	0.46	NBS.
Institutional quality (government efficiency index)	31	−0.01	0.30	Tang *et al.* (2014)
Trade (logarithm of the trade share in GDP)	31	2.89	1.01	NBS.
Latitude (distance to the equator)	31	0.37	0.08	—
Distance (distance to Beijing or Shanghai, whichever is less)	31	975.25	703.48	—
Coast (coastal dummy)	31	0.35	0.49	Google maps
Investment (logarithm of the investment share in GDP)	31	4.07	0.26	NBS.

Table 6.2.   Correlation matrix.

		1	2	3	4	5	6	7
Income	1	1						
Institutions	2	0.8279*	1					
Trade	3	0.7486*	0.6196*	1				
Latitude	4	0.3046	0.3594*	−0.0707	1			
Distance	5	−0.7070*	−0.7721*	−0.4130*	−0.2693	1		
Coastal	6	0.6834*	0.5663*	0.8225*	−0.2186	−0.3920*	1	
Investment	7	−0.4119*	−0.4985*	−0.6262*	0.1959	0.4582*	−0.4059*	1

Note: * indicates statistical significance at the 5% level.

p. 146). It is important to be aware that all indicators that measure institutional quality are only proxies that depict a certain aspect of the "true" set of institutions (which is far more complex and cannot be fully captured). The government efficiency index focuses, among others, on the provision of comprehensive legal systems and public services (cf. Tang *et al.* (2014), p. 142).

Especially, the latter aspect distinguishes it from other indices such as Fan *et al.* (2009) marketization index studied in Glawe and Wagner (2019) and the Business-Friendly Environment index which can be calculated using data from the World Bank report, *Doing Business in China 2008. Geography* is captured by latitude, that is, the distance to the equator. Latitude is used as a proxy for geography (in particular, climate) by many cross-country deep determinants studies (e.g. Acemoglu *et al.*, 2001; Rodrik *et al.*, 2004). Finally, we use investment ratios as an additional control variable in the robustness check section.

As mentioned above, we use instrumental variable estimation techniques in order to control for the problem of endogeneity. Our choice of instruments is based on the study of Glawe and Wagner (2019). In particular, we use the distance to Beijing or Shanghai, whichever is less, calculated with the Great Circle Distance formula as instrument for institutional quality and a coastal dummy as an instrument for integration (i.e. the trade share). More information on the reasoning of the instruments is provided in Section 6.3.2.

6.3. Institutions, Integration, and Geography

In this section, we analyze the impact of institution on economic performance within China. We are particularly interested in whether institutions "trump" integration and geography. In Section 6.3.1, we use simple OLS regression, while in Section 6.3.2, we take into account the potential endogeneity problem by employing 2SLS estimations.

6.3.1. *OLS estimation*

Our regression model to estimate the effect of institutional quality (proxied by the government efficiency index) on the provincial per capita income is given as follows:

$$y_i = \alpha_1 + \alpha_2 \text{INS}_i + \alpha_3 \text{INT}_i + \alpha_4 \text{GEO}_i + \varepsilon_i, \qquad (6.1)$$

where y_i denotes the logarithm of per capita GDP of province i in 2010 (in constant 2005 Yuan). INS_i is our main variable of interest, namely the provincial level of institutional quality in 2010.

In robustness checks discussed in Section 6.5, we also use the average government efficiency over the period 2001–2010 as an alternative institutional measure since this specification is also used by some empirical studies. INT_i captures integration, that is, the logarithm of the trade share in GDP in 2010, and GEO_i stands for our geography measure, namely latitude. Our choice of explanatory variables follows the seminal chapters of Acemoglu *et al.* (2001) and Rodrik *et al.* (2004). The corresponding theoretical explanation is provided, among others, by Sachs and Warner (1997), North and Thomas (1973), and Bhattacharyya (2004). In a nutshell, they argue that the proximate factors, such as factor accumulation, are themselves functions of institutions, integration, and geography, the so-called three "deep determinants." However, in some robustness checks, we additionally include provincial investment ratios. To eyeball the data, Figure 6.2(a) presents a scatter plot of the log per capita income and institutional quality in 2010. There is a strong positive correlation between these two variables.[3]

The corresponding OLS estimates are presented in panel A of Table 6.3. As displayed in column (1), institutional quality has a positive and highly significant impact on per capita income with a coefficient of 0.38. Column (2) shows that integration is also positively signed and has a reasonable high coefficient of around 0.35 (significant at the 1% level). These findings stay robust when adding geography (cf. columns 3 and 4) and also when simultaneously including institutional quality and integration (cf. columns 5 and 6). Both coefficients are still highly significant; however, they are slightly reduced in their magnitude. Geography (that is, latitude) has a moderate positive impact with a coefficient of 0.17 (see column 4); however, it turns insignificant as soon as we control for institutions.[4] In sum, institutions slightly trump integration regarding the magnitudes of their effects on per capita income (Since we use standardized measures, we can directly compare the coefficients of the different regressors).

---

[3]Figure 6.2(b) reveals that this positive visual correlation remains valid when using instead the average provincial institutional quality over the period 2001–2010. We will later present the respective regression results in the robustness check section.

[4]If we only include geography, it is positively signed and significant at the 10% level, however, the R-squared is relatively small.

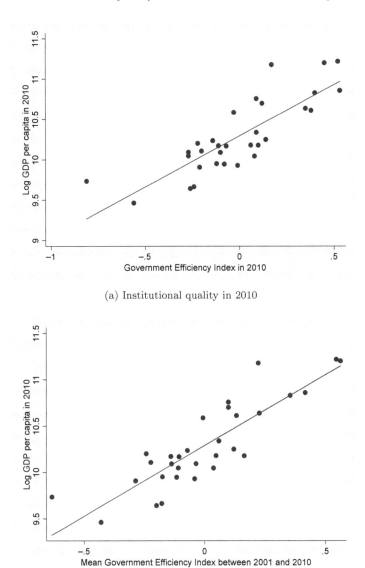

(a) Institutional quality in 2010

(b) Mean institutional quality (2001–2010)

Fig. 6.2. Relationship between institutional quality and percent GDP.
Source: Government efficiency index: Tang *et al.* (2014). Real GDP per capita in 2010 (in constant 2005 Yuan): NBS, own calculations.

Table 6.3. Correlation matrix.

	(1)	(2)	(3)	(4)	(5)	(6)
Panel A: OLS estimates						
Institutions	0.3825***		0.3812***		0.2730***	0.2237***
(GE-Index)	(0.0553)		(0.0588)		(0.0572)	(0.0549)
Integration		0.3459***		0.3576***	0.1767***	0.2126***
(Trade)		(0.0585)		(0.0444)	(0.0615)	(0.0595)
Geography			0.0038	0.1660***		0.0754
(Latitude)			(0.0478)	(0.0567)		(0.0509)
R-squared	0.6854	0.5604	0.6855	0.6889	0.7755	0.7950
Observations	31	31	31	31	31	31
Panel B: 2SLS estimates						
Institutions	0.4231***		0.4276***		0.3446***	0.3127***
(GE-Index)	(0.0850)		(0.0924)		(0.0921)	(0.1047)
Integration		0.3839***		0.4294***	0.1466**	0.1795*
(Trade)		(0.0607)		(0.0417)	(0.0737)	(0.0923)
Geography			−0.0129	0.1711***		0.0411
(Latitude)			(0.0464)	(0.0571)		(0.0542)
R-squared	0.6777	0.5536	0.6767	0.6649	0.7598	0.7754
Panel C1: First stage (institutions)						
Distance	−0.7721***		−0.7281***		−0.6500***	−0.5181***
	(0.1268)		(0.1313)		(0.1270)	(0.1210)
Coast					0.6405***	0.8880***
					(0.2058)	(0.1790)
Latitude			0.1632			0.3151***
			(0.0989)			(0.0794)
F-statistic	37.08		30.74		21.39	22.37
R-squared part.	0.5961		0.5646		0.6782	0.7216
Panel C2: First stage (integration)						
Distance					−0.1070	−0.0699
					(0.1347)	(0.1390)
Coast		1.6911***		1.7426***	1.6049***	1.6746***
		(0.2469)		(0.2421)	(0.2706)	(0.2790)
Latitude				0.1146		0.0885
				(0.1171)		(0.1279)
F-statistic		46.93		51.83	25.92	26.72
R-squared part.		0.6765		0.6875	0.6862	0.6910

Note: Dependent variable: log per capita GDP in constant 2005 Yuan. The independent variables are all scaled in the sense that they present deviations from the mean divided by the standard deviation. Robust standard errors are in parentheses. Significance at the 10%, 5%, and 1% levels are denoted by *, **, and ***, respectively. "R-squared part." denotes the partial R-squared of excluded instruments.

6.3.2. *TSLS estimation*

While our OLS regression results reveal a positive and statistical significant correlation between institutions and per capita income, it does not allow us to make any statements about the causality of this relationship. For instance, we do not know whether institutions positively affect per capita GDP or whether a higher per capita income enables institutional improvements. The reality probably lies somewhere between these two extremes. In order to deal with endogeneity problems, such as reverse causality and omitted variable biases, we can make use of instrumental variable estimation techniques. As suggested by Glawe and Wagner (2019), the distance to Beijing or Shanghai, whichever is less, is an adequate instrument for institutional quality at the provincial level in China. In their study, they use the marketization index as a proxy for institutions; however, as they write, it can be also used for various other institutional indicators, including the government efficiency index.

The reasoning for the choice of the institutional instrument is the following: Glawe and Wagner (2019, p. 6) argue that being far from Beijing or Shanghai, that is, the centers of the political and financial power, has an adverse impact on institutional quality. They list three main arguments for this negative relationship. First, increasingly remote provinces are under less control of the central government to provide a good institutional environment (such as the provision of property rights that are captured in our index of institutional quality). Second, the local politicians might be more likely to be captured by local interest groups, which may also have a negative effect on the quality of institutions in the respective provinces. Third, it is common to use geographical variables as instruments for contemporary endogenous regressors such as institutional quality (cf. Easterly, 2007; Becker and Woessmann, 2009; Becker and Woessmann, 2010; Naritomi *et al.*, 2012). In addition, many of these studies use the distance to a city or a country as an instrument. Finally, Glawe and Wagner (2019) show that their distance measure passes all possible tests regarding the validity of the exclusion restriction. It has to be noted however that the exclusion restriction can never be really fully tested. This is a limitation that applies to all studies that use instrumental variable estimations. While we cannot overcome this weakness, we still think that our choice of instrument for institutions is reasonable. We also follow Glawe and Wagner (2019) and control for the potential endogeneity of integration by using a coastal dummy variable as instrument for the trade share in GDP. Therefore, the first stages are given by Eqs. (6.2) and (6.3):

$$INS_i = \beta_1 + \beta_2 DIST_i + \beta_3 COAST_i + \beta_4 GEO_i + \varepsilon_{INS_i}, \quad (6.2)$$

$$INT_i = \gamma_1 + \gamma_2 DIST_i + \gamma_3 COAST_i + \gamma_4 GEO_i + \varepsilon_{INT_i}, \quad (6.3)$$

where $DIST_i$ and $COAST_i$ are the instruments of the institutional and integration variables, respectively. $DIST_i$ is the distance to Beijing or Shanghai, whichever is less, and $COAST_i$ is a coastal dummy indicating whether a province is located at the coastline or not.

As shown in Figure 6.3(a), there is indeed a strong negative relationship between the distance to Beijing/Shanghai and the government efficiency index. Also, if we use the mean institutional quality between 2001 and 2010, this relationship does not change (cf. also the robustness checks in Section 6.5).

Panel B of Table 6.3 presents the 2SLS estimation results; the corresponding first stages of institutions and integration are displayed in panels C1 and C2, respectively. In all columns, the institutional quality measure is highly significant with coefficients ranging from 0.31 to 0.43. Also, integration stays significant at the 1% level in columns (2) and (4); however, as soon as we simultaneously control for institutional quality in columns (5) and (6), the coefficient of the trade share is much reduced, so does its significance level. In column (6), that is, our main specification which comprises all three deep determinants, integration is only marginally significant. As before, latitude is insignificant as long as we control for institutions. Regarding the first stage relationships, there is a clear significant correlation between the respective endogenous variable and the corresponding instrument (that is, between institutions and the distance measure and between integration and the coastal dummy). Moreover, the coastal dummy also has a significant positive impact on institutions, while there is no such positive relationship between the distance measure and the trade share in GDP (cf. columns 5 and 6 of panels C1 and C2). When simultaneously including all regressors, latitude is positively and significantly correlated with institutions but not with the trade share. In all columns, the F-statistic of the

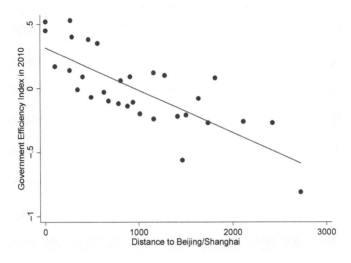

(a) Institutional quality in 2010

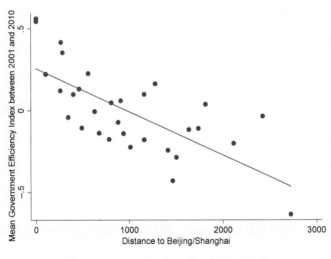

(b) Mean institutional quality (2001–2010)

Fig. 6.3.   Relationship between institutional quality and distance to Beijing/Shanghai.

Source: Government efficiency index: Tang *et al.* (2014). Distance to Beijing or Shanghai, whichever is less: own calculations based on the great circle distance formula.

excluded instrument varies between 21 and 37 for institutions (cf. panel C1) and between 26 and 52 for integration (cf. panel C2) and thus, in both cases, far exceeds the critical threshold of 10 suggested by Staiger and Stock (1997). Moreover, the partial R-squared values are reasonable high. In sum, our findings clearly support the primacy of institutions over integration (and geography). In this respect, our results are similar to those reported in the study of Glawe and Wagner (2019) using the marketization index. However, in contrast to their findings, latitude is insignificant in the OLS and 2SLS regressions; however, it has a strong first stage impact on institutions.

6.4. Interrelationships between Institutions and Integration

In Section 6.3, we derived the conclusion that institutional quality is decisive for the economic development of a province in China. Moreover, as soon as we control for institutional quality (and for potential endogeneity problems), integration and geography turn insignificant at the 5% level and their coefficients are reduced in their magnitude. However, this does not mean that trade and geography are negligible for the economic performance of a province since they can have a positive impact by influencing institutional quality (this is already indicated by the positive and significant first stage relationships between latitude and institutions and the coastal dummy and institutions). Therefore, in this section, we examine the interrelationships between the deep determinants.

Table A.6.1 reveals that institutions and integration have a strong positive effect on each other. Moreover, latitude has a positive significant impact on institutional quality while its coefficient is negative and statistically insignificant at the 5% level for integration. In combination with the results obtained in Table 6.3, panel B, column (6), we can calculate the total impacts of each determinant: The total impact of institutional quality on per capita income amounts to 0.43, consisting of a direct effect of 0.31 and an indirect effect via integration of 0.12.[5] The total impact of integration also amounts to 0.43,

---

[5]The total effect of institutions on per capita income is calculated as follows: $0.3127 + 0.1795 * 0.6489 = 0.3127 + 0.1165 = 0.4292 \approx 0.43$.

consisting of a direct impact of 0.18 and an indirect effect through institutions of 0.25.[6] However, if we only consider the statistically significant coefficients (at the 5% or 1% level), the total impact of institutions comes solely from the direct effect and is reduced to 0.31, whereas the total impact of integration stems only of the indirect effect via institutional quality and thus only amounts to 0.25. Moreover, the indirect effect of latitude via institutional quality amounts to 0.13 (the direct effect is insignificant, cf. column 6 of Table 6.3, panel B). In sum, also when taking into account the indirect effects, institutional quality trumps integration and geography.

If we compare our findings to the study of Glawe and Wagner (2019), some differences emerge: First, latitude has a positive and highly significant impact on the government efficiency index (with a coefficient of 0.42), while there is no such positive relationship between the marketization index and latitude. Instead, latitude directly affects per capita income, while there is no such positive direct effect when controlling for the government efficiency index. Second, trade has a slightly stronger indirect impact via institutions when using the marketization index (0.28 vs. 0.25),[7] whereas the direct effect of trade is somewhat smaller (0.14 vs. 0.18).[8] compared to when using the government efficiency index as institutional measure. Overall, while the positive impact of institutions on development remains mostly unchanged independent of which institutional indicator is used, the interrelationships with other factors can differ.

6.5.   Robustness Checks

In this section, we perform various robustness checks. We start by using the mean institutional quality between 2001 and 2010 as an

---

[6]The total effect of integration on per capita income is calculated as follows: $0.1795 + 0.3127 * 0.7991 = 0.1795 + 0.2499 = 0.4294 \approx 0.43$.

[7]Cf. Glawe and Wagner, 2019, column (1), panel B of Table A.6.1 and column (6), panel A of Table 6.3 as well as this chapter, column (1), panel B of Table A.6.1 and column (6), panel B of Table 6.3.

[8]Cf. Glawe and Wagner, 2019, column (6), panel A of Table 6.3 as well as this chapter, column (6), panel B of Table 6.3.

alternative proxy for institutional quality.[9] Table A.6.2 shows the corresponding OLS and 2SLS regression results. Overall, our main results do not change. In fact, they support the primacy of institutions hypothesis even more since trade is not even significant at the 10% level once controlling for institutional quality (and endogeneity, cf. panel B of Table A.6.2, columns 3 and 4). Also, the coefficient of institutional quality slightly increases, ranging from 0.40 to 0.48 for the 2SLS estimates.

As a further robustness check, we additionally include provincial investment ratios to our set of covariates. The estimation results are reported in Table A.6.3. Panel A displays the OLS estimates (columns 1–2) and 2SLS estimates (columns 3–4), respectively. The first stages of the 2SLS estimates are reported in panel B. Again, our main finding regarding the primacy of institutions remains unchanged. The coefficient of the investment ratios itself is positive and marginally significant in some specifications (ranging from 0.08 to 0.11). These findings are also confirmed when using the mean institutional quality instead (only the investment ratios report an increase in their significance and their coefficients slightly increase).

Finally, we modify our instrument for institutional quality. In particular, we employ the distance to Beijing, Shanghai, or Hong Kong (whichever is less) as an instrument for the government efficiency measure. Hong Kong is often argued to be China's financial center (even though its role might diminish in the future, and Shanghai is nowadays also an important financial hub). Hong Kong is one of the freest economies worldwide and has strong institutions, which might induce positive spillover effects to nearby regions in China. This is already visible for the Shenzhen Special Economic Zone which learns from Hong Kong in institutional reform and transition (cf. Tao and Lu, 2018). As shown in Figure A.6.1, there is also a strong negative correlation between the distance measure (extended by Hong Kong) and the government efficiency index in 2010.

Further, our econometric results support this view (cf. Table A.6.4). In particular, the positive impact of institutions on per capita income remains largely unchanged. Also, the first stage reveals that our instruments are significantly correlated with the

---

[9]In addition, our results remain mostly valid when using the difference of institutional quality between 2001 and 2010.

institutional variable, and also, the *F*-statistics are sufficiently large (even though somewhat smaller compared to those in Table 6.3).

6.6.   Conclusion

We have examined the role of the deep determinants—institutions, integration, and geography—for the economic performance of a province in China by using OLS and 2SLS regression analyzes. Our findings indicate that institutional quality, proxied by the government efficiency index, has a strong positive impact on provincial per capita income, trumping integration and geography, which only have an indirect impact by influencing institutions. While our main result (primacy of institutions) confirms the results of other studies using alternative institutional indices, some difference regarding the interrelationships between the deep determinants become apparent: Integration has a slightly weaker (positive) impact on the government efficiency index compared to the marketization index, which focuses also on the organization of markets and the government–market relations (cf. the study of Glawe and Wagner, 2019). In contrast, geography has a positive impact on the government efficiency but not on the marketization index. Against this background, it is important to take into account that different institutional indicators measure different aspects of the true set of institutions. Investigating the differences between the various aspects of institutional quality in China is an interesting topic for future research.

In international comparison, China's overall institutional quality is still relatively low. Figure 6.4 depicts the development of the government effectiveness in China compared to two advanced economies (US and Germany) and the East European post-communist New EU Member States (NMS) country group. The government effectiveness indicator is one of the six Worldwide Governance Indicators (WGIs) devised by Kaufmann *et al.* (2010), which is probably most closely related to our provincial institutional indicator. It ranges between -2.5 and 2.5, a higher value indicating stronger institutions. China reports the lowest level of government effectiveness in our sample, and between 2007 and 2013, there was even a diverging trend. Only since 2014, China shows a catching-up tendency.

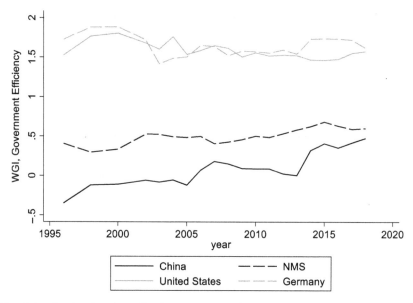

Fig. 6.4.   Institutional quality in international comparison.

Note: The NMS group comprises seven countries representing the majority of the post-communist countries in the EU (Bulgaria, Czech Republic, Hungary, Lithuania, Poland, and Romania).

Source: Kaufmann *et al.* (2010).

Our findings also have some important policy implications: China might have only been able to achieve such an immense growth at the national level because some provinces (mostly located in the east) have much better institutions than others, resulting in a higher per capita income in these provinces which consequently positively contributes to the nationwide GDP per capita. However, it is questionable how long China can still rely on the growth performance of only some provinces, especially when their growth will naturally slow down in the course of the neoclassical convergence process. In order to avoid becoming a victim of a prolonged growth slowdown at the middle-income range (the so-called phenomenon of the "middle-income trap," cf. Glawe and Wagner, 2016, 2020a), China has to exploit the growth potential of the inland provinces by improving the institutional quality in these regions. The increasing institutional quality trend at the national level depicted in Figure 6.4 is probably the first indication that China may succeed in this ambitious task.

Appendix

Table A.6.1. OLS and 2SLS estimates, interrelationships between institutions and integration.

	(1)	(2)
Panel A: OLS estimates		
Dependent variable	Institutions	Integration
Integration	0.1952***	
(Trade)	(0.0345)	
Institutions		0.7512***
(GE-Index)		(0.1831)
Geography	0.1220***	−0.3417**
(Latitude)	(0.0321)	(0.1488)
R-squared	0.5473	0.4828
Observations	31	31
Panel B: 2SLS estimates		
Dependent variable	Institutions	Integration
Integration	0.7991***	
(Trade)	(0.1340)	
Institutions		0.6489***
(GE-Index)		(0.2506)
Geography	0.4159***	−0.3049*
(Latitude)	(0.1087)	(0.1591)
R-squared	0.5247	0.4739
Panel C1: First stage institutions		
Dependent variable	Institutions	Integration
Distance		−0.7281***
		(0.1313)
Coast	1.7426***	
	(0.2421)	
Latitude	0.1146	0.1632
	(0.1171)	(0.0989)
F-statistic	51.83	30.74
R-squared part.	0.6875	0.5646

Note: Dependent variable: institutional quality (column 1) and integration (column 2). The independent variables are all scaled in the sense that they present deviations from the mean divided by the standard deviation. Robust standard errors are in parentheses. Significance at the 10%, 5%, and 1% levels are denoted by *, **, and ***, respectively. "*R*-squared part." denotes the partial *R*-squared of excluded instruments.

Table A.6.2.   OLS and 2SLS estimates, mean institutional quality between 2001 and 2010.

	(1)	(2)	(3)	(4)
Panel A: OLS estimates				
Institutions	0.3997***	0.4085***	0.3096***	0.2704***
(GE-Index)	(0.0446)	(0.0475)	(0.0660)	(0.0750)
Integration			0.1279*	0.1586**
(Trade)			(0.0672)	(0.0767)
Geography		−0.0222		0.0441
(Latitude)		(0.0458)		(0.0580)
R-squared	0.7483	0.7502	0.7869	0.7923
Observations	31	31	31	31
Panel B: 2SLS estimates				
Institutions	0.4608***	0.4801***	0.3968***	0.4118**
(GE-Index)	(0.0834)	(0.0956)	(0.1075)	(0.1624)
Integration			0.1099	0.0951
(Trade)			(0.0797)	(0.1283)
Geography		−0.0507		−0.0168
(Latitude)		(0.0475)		(0.0779)
R-squared	0.7601	0.7286	0.6925	0.7564
Panel C1: First stage institutions				
Distance	−0.7088***	−0.6484***	−0.5744***	−0.4078***
	(0.1561)	(0.1580)	(0.1537)	(0.1366)
Coast			0.7048***	1.0177***
			(0.2387)	(0.2236)
Latitude		0.2242***		0.3972***
		(0.1294)		(0.0982)
F-statistic	20.62	16.84	14.63	18.64
R-squared part.	0.5024	0.4637	0.6018	0.6772
Panel C2: First stage integration				
Distance			−0.1070	−0.0699
			(0.1347)	(0.1390)
Coast			1.6045***	1.6746***
			(0.2706)	(0.2790)
Latitude				0.0885
				(0.1279)
F-statistic			25.92	26.72
R-squared part.			0.6862	0.6910

Note: Dependent variable: log per capita GDP in constant 2005 Yuan. The independent variables are all scaled in the sense that they present deviations from the mean divided by the standard deviation. Robust standard errors are in parentheses. Significance at the 10%, 5%, and 1% levels are denoted by *, **, and ***, respectively. "R-squared part." denotes the partial R-squared of excluded instruments.

Table A.6.3.   OLS and 2SLS, adding investment ratios.

	(1)	(2)	(3)	(4)
	Panel A: OLS and 2SLS estimates			
	OLS estimates		2SLS estimates	
Institutions	0.2902***	0.2526***	0.4029***	0.4227***
(GE-Index)	(0.0493)	(0.0499)	(0.0804)	(0.1067)
Integration	0.2261***	0.2407***	0.1617**	0.1432*
(Trade)	(0.0641)	(0.0614)	(0.0741)	(0.0854)
Physical capital	0.0960*	0.0761	0.1118*	0.1147*
(Invest. ratio)	(0.0530)	(0.0549)	(0.0637)	(0.0681)
Geography		0.0521		−0.0235
(Latitude)		(0.0491)		(0.0513)
R-squared	0.8009	0.8091	0.7653	0.7537
Observations	31	31	31	31

Panel B: First stages of institutions and integration

Dep. variable	Institutions	Integration	Institutions	Integration
Column	(3)	(3)	(4)	(4)
Instrument INS	−0.6140***	0.0190	−0.4125***	0.1315
(Distance)	(0.1183)	(0.1188)	(0.0954)	(0.0959)
Instrument INT	0.5845**	1.4087***	0.8164***	1.5382***
(Coastal dummy)	(0.2276)	(0.2198)	(0.1683)	(0.2100)
Physical capital	−0.1017	−0.3568***	−0.2225**	−0.4242***
(Invest. ratio)	(0.1128)	(0.1256)	(0.0902)	(0.1131)
Geography			0.3787***	0.2114**
(Latitude)			(0.0728)	(0.0892)
F-statistic	17.20	21.39	17.78	27.15
R-squared part.	0.5819	0.6366	0.6076	0.6888

Note: Dependent variable: log per capita GDP in constant 2005 Yuan. The independent variables are all scaled in the sense that they present deviations from the mean divided by the standard deviation. Robust standard errors are in parentheses. Significance at the 10%, 5%, and 1% levels are denoted by *, **, and ***, respectively. "R-squared part." denotes the partial R-squared of excluded instruments.

Table A.6.4.   OLS and 2SLS estimates, institutional quality in 2010, alternative instrument.

	(1)	(2)	(3)	(4)
Panel A: 2SLS estimates				
Institutions	0.4312***	0.4300***	0.3055**	0.3029**
(GE-Index)	(0.1115)	(0.1065)	(0.1220)	(0.1244)
Integration			0.1738*	0.1874*
(Trade)			(0.0963)	(0.1063)
Geography		−0.0136		0.0451
(Latitude)		(0.0471)		(0.0537)
R-squared	0.6740	0.6759	0.6770	0.7225
Observations	31	31	31	31
Panel B1: First stage institutions				
Distance	−0.6499***	−0.6964***	−0.4850**	−0.4751***
	(0.1505)	(0.1192)	(0.1791)	(0.1323)
Coast			0.6130*	0.8492***
			(0.3415)	(0.2288)
Latitude		0.4340***		0.5006***
		(0.0870)		(0.0897)
F-statistic	18.63	34.10	10.10	19.62
R-squared part.	0.4223	0.6085	0.4840	0.6814
Panel B2: First stage integration				
Distance			−0.0263	−0.0241
			(0.1301)	(0.1270)
Coast			1.6612***	1.7151***
			(0.2770)	(0.2771)
Latitude				0.1142
				(0.1197)
F-statistic			23.08	25.40
R-squared part.			0.6770	0.6879

Note: Dependent variable: log per capita GDP in constant 2005 Yuan. The independent variables are all scaled in the sense that they present deviations from the mean divided by the standard deviation. Robust standard errors are in parentheses. Significance at the 10%, 5%, and 1% levels are denoted by *, **, and ***, respectively. "R-squared part." denotes the partial R-squared of excluded instruments.

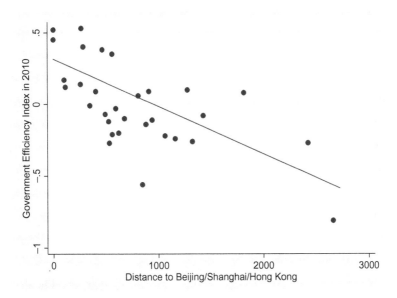

Fig. A.6.1. Relationship between institutional quality and the extended distance measure.

References

Acemoglu, D., F. Gallego, and J. A. Robinson (2001). "The Colonial Origins of Comparative Development: An Empirical Investigation," *American Economic Review*, 91, 1369–1401.

Acemoglu, D., F. Gallego, and J. A. Robinson (2005). "Institutions as a Fundamental Cause of Long-Run Growth," In: Aghion, P. and S. N. Durlauf (Eds.), *Handbook of Economic Growth*, Volume 1A, 386–472, Amsterdam: Elsevier.

Acemoglu, D., F. Gallego, and J. A. Robinson (2014). "Institutions, Human Capital and Development," *Annual Review of Economics*, 6, 875–912.

Barro, R. J. (1997). *The Determinants of Economic Growth: A Cross-Country Empirical Study*, Cambridge: MIT Press.

Becker, S. O., F. C. and L. Woessmann (2010). "The Trade-off between Fertility and Education: Evidence from before the Demographic Transition," *Journal of Economic Growth*, 15, 177–204.

Becker, S. O. and L. Woessmann (2009). "Was Weber wrong? A Human Capital Theory of Protestant Economic History," *The Quarterly Journal of Economics*, 124, 531–596.

Bhattacharyya, S. (2004). "Deep Determinants of Economic Growth," *Applied Economics Letters*, 11, 587–590.

Easterly, W. (2007). "Inequality Does Cause Underdevelopment: Insights from a New Instrument," *Journal of Development Economics*, 11, 755–776.

Easterly, W. and R. Levine (2003). "Tropics, Germs, and Crops: How Endowments Influence Economic Development," *Journal of Monetary Economics*, 50, 3–39.

Fan, G., X. Wang, and H. Zhu (2009). *NERI INDEX of Marketization of China's Provinces 2009 Report* (in Chinese), Beijing: Economics Science Press.

Glawe, L. and H. Wagner (2016). "The Middle-income Trap: Definitions, Theories and Countries Concerned—A Literature Survey," *Comparative Economic Studies*, 58, 507–538.

Glawe, L. and H. Wagner (2019). "The Deep Determinants of Economic Development in China—A Provincial Perspective," *Journal of the Asia Pacific Economy*, 24, 484–514.

Glawe, L. and H. Wagner (2020a). "China in the Middle-income Trap?" *China Economic Review*, 60, 101264.

Glawe, L. and H. Wagner (2020b). "The Role of Institutional Quality and Human Capital for Economic Growth Across Chinese Provinces—A Dynamic Panel Data Approach," *Journal of Chinese Economic and Business Studies*, 18, 209–227.

Hall, R. E. and C. I. Jones (1999). "Why Do Some Countries Produce So Much More Output Per Worker Than Others?" *Quarterly Journal of Economics*, 114, 83–116.

Ji, K., J. R. Magnus, and W. Wang (2014). "Natural Resources, Institutional Quality, and Economic Growth in China," *Environmental and Resource Economics*, 57, 323–343.

Kaufmann, D., A. Kraay, and M. Mastruzzi (2010). "The Worldwide Governance Indicators: A Summary of Methodology, Data and Analytical Issues," *World Bank Policy Research Working Paper No. 5430*. Washington, DC: The World Bank.

Knack, S. and P. Keefer (1995). "Institutions and Economic Performance: Cross-country Tests Using Alternative Measures," *Economics and Politics*, 7, 207–227.

Liu, J., B. Tang, and Z. Liang (2018). "The Effect of Governance Quality in Economic Growth: Based on China's Provincial Panel Data," *Economies*, 6, 1–23.

Naritomi, J., R. R. Soares, and J. J. Assunção (2012). "Institutional Development and Colonial Heritage within Brazil," *The Journal of Economic History*, 72, 393–422.

North, D. C. and R. P. Thomas (1973). *The Rise of the Western World: A New Economic History*, Cambridge and New York: Cambridge University Press.

Rodrik, D., A. Subramanian, and F. Trebbi (2004). "Institutions Rule: The Primacy of Institutions Over Geography and Integration in Economic Development," *Journal of Economic Growth*, 9, 131–165.

Rothstein, B. (2015). "The Chinese Paradox of High Growth and Low Quality of Government: The Cadre Organization Meets Max Weber," *Governance—An International Journal of Policy, Administration, and Institutions*, 28, 533–548.

Sachs, J. and A. Warner (1997). "Fundamental Sources of Long-run Growth," *American Economic Review*, 87, 184–188.

Spolaore, E. and R. Wacziarg (2013). "How Deep are the Roots of Economic Development?" *Journal of Economic Literature*, 51, 325–369.

Staiger, D. and J. H. Stock (1997). "Instrumental Variables Regression with Weak Instruments," *Econometrica*, 65, 557–586.

Tang, R., T. Tang, and Z. Lee (2014). "The Efficiency of Provincial Governments in China from 2001 to 2010: Measurement and Analysis," *Journal of Public Affairs*, 14, 142–153.

Tao, Y. and Z. Lu (2018). *Special Economic Zones and China's Development Path. Research Series on the Chinese Dream and China's Development Path*, Singapore: Springer.

Chapter 7

Rise of Capitalism and Chinese Women's Internal and Cross-Border Migrations 1980–2020: A Gender Study

Beatrice Zani

Department of East Asian Studies, McGill University,
688 Sherbrooke W., Montreal, QC, Canada
beatrice.zani92@gmail.com

Abstract

In this chapter, Beatrice Zani draws the contours of a gender approach to migrations in China. In China, women's labor migrations from the countryside to the city and marriage migrations to Taiwan have been complexifying and pluralizing over the last 40 years. A crossed analysis of two generations of migrant women's mobility experiences, professional paths, and economic practices helps to identify lines of continuity and of discontinuity in rural-to-urban and cross-border migratory patterns and to pinpoint broader social and economic transformations characterizing contemporary Chinese capitalism. This chapter provides an innovative gender approach to apprehend how women's internal and cross-border migrations are framed into the large-scale historical restructuring of Chinese capitalism, society, and labor market. It combines a micro-sociological analysis of migrants' biographical, professional, social, and economic careers with a gender perspective to project mobility experiences and practices into the larger scale of macro social and economic transformations. Both the first and second generations of Mainland Chinese rural women have been engaged in a double-step migration: from the countryside to the city in Mainland China and from the Mainland to Taiwan. By focusing on the changes in terms of marriage practices, as well as social and economic experiences in Chinese and Taiwanese societies, and labor markets, the author looks at the extent to which globalization and modernity contributed to the transformation of migratory paths as well as actors' biographical and professional careers. These are nowadays increasingly oriented toward the achievement of urbanity, economic independence, and social mobility by young migrants. These prove their ability to mobilize innovative and inventive tools to achieve their projects, which digital labor and e-commerce are illustrative of.

7.1.   Introduction

Within China, rural-to-urban migration of peasants who leave their rural areas in inner provinces for employment in the cities does not represent a recent phenomenon (Solinger, 1999; Li, 2013; Roulleau-Berger, 2013). Since the 1980s, flows of rural migrants (*nonmingong* 农民工) have left their villages of origin and migrated to the cities to integrate into the local labor market (Pun, 1999). Women represent an important component of the labor employed in the cities from the 1980s to the present (Pun, 2005; Yan, 2008). These women (*dagong mei* 打工妹) leave the countryside to work in the large coastal cities, especially in the industrial sector of local and multinational companies. If rural-to-urban migration has become an established praxis, the analysis of its reproduction and transformation over time catches my attention. Since the 1980s, migrations have not stopped growing and women's migratory paths have complexified and pluralized, in terms of mobility and professional experiences as well as of the spaces invested by such movements. Scholars (Li, 2003, 2013 amongst others) have distinguished between two generations of migrant workers, whose migratory and circulatory paths have varied. In this sense, contemporary migrations are composed of a multiplication of movements and of circulations among different provinces and cities as well as the pluralization of the labor experiences. As a result, women's contemporary biographical and migratory *careers* (Becker, 1963; Roulleau-Berger, 2014) can be apprehended in terms of times, spaces, and identities (Tarrius, 2002), which vary over time, following the opportunity and constraint structure (Aldrich and Waldinger, 1990) of Chinese society and the transformation of its labor market as well as the mutable rhythms of globalization and modernity.

In the early 1980s, a first generation of rural migrant workers (*di yidai nonmingong* 第一代农民工) left rural areas to temporarily work in the city. This generation was born during 1960s and had experienced misery during childhood. The end of the Cultural Revolution and Maoism made rural-to-urban migration an imperative for a rapid economic development (Gallagher, 2005). The first generation of migrant workers abandoned the rural areas without any ambition of long-term settlement and installation in the city. It was a matter of temporary work, aimed at increasing individuals' revenues (Shen, 2006) and improving an adverse economic condition (Oi, 1999; Pun, 1999).

China's progressive penetration by transnational markets and globalization has gradually influenced migrant workers' mobility patterns, labor experiences, and migratory projects. Over the years, in accordance with the urban and professional opportunities and constrains of the labor market, a second generation of migrant workers (*xin shengdai nonmingong* 新生代农民工), born after 1980 (*baling hou* 80 后) has emerged, partially following the paths set down by the first generation. However, their biographical and professional careers were now constructed towards a long-term urban integration, aimed at settling down in the city. In this sense, the current generation of migrant workers has developed a new "capacity to aspire" (Appadurai, 1999), i.e. the projection towards a globalized and modern horizon of ambition and of social status transformation. Nowadays, migrant women leave the countryside to work in the city, seeking upward social mobility, a metropolitan positioning as well as a modern status.

Simultaneously, since the 1980s, both the first and second generations of migrant women have developed a second-step mobility from the Mainland to Taiwan. This means that both generations initially left the countryside for the city, and later, some of them remigrated to Taiwan through marriage. Over the past decades, cross-border migration from the Mainland to Taiwan has been a significant phenomenon, which however, has remained quantitatively constant. For some Mainland women, migration has become the main channel for long-term settlement in Taiwan. Until December 2017, a total of 10,567 female migrant spouses from the Mainland had adopted Taiwan as their home after marrying to Taiwanese men (MoI, 2017). In December 2010, 11,900 marriage migrants from the Mainland were residing in Taiwan (MoI, 2010), while in 1992, this number was approximatively 9,000 (MoI, 1993).

For both generations, marriage is the necessary condition to enter Taiwanese territory and settle down there (Friedman, 2010; Cheng, 2013). Migrations both within China and from the Mainland to Taiwan are constructed by coping with social hierarchies and economic inequalities. Local migratory policies and political economies inhibit rural migrants to earn a decent income and to durably settle down in the city (Pun, 2005; Li, 2013). In fact, the attribution of social rights is inegalitarian between those born in rural areas and in the urban space. In light of social disqualification and economic marginalization migrant workers face in Chinese cities (Solinger, 1999; Siu, 2007; Roulleau-Berger, 2013), the rapid increase in the number of marriages between Taiwanese men and Chinese women (Tsay, 2004) is attributed to the potential for hypergamy (Constable, 2003), i.e. the upward social mobility that marriage migration to Taiwan can provide.

Despite this apparent similarity, a combined scrutiny of first- and second-generation migrant women internal and cross-border migratory paths gives reason to assume that these have diversified over time, in terms of social, economic, and migratory experiences and practices. The multiplication of the urban and labor experiences as well as the transformation of the channels through which marriage migration to Taiwan is negotiated suggest the heterogeneity of the two generations' experiences, which not only derive from important changes of the migratory practices, but also, and crucially, from fundamental transitions of the Chinese society and labor market. To quote Shen Yuan's expression, if "migrations echo the multiple shifts of Chinese society" (2006, p. 9), their production, reproduction, and changes might inform us of large-scale social and economic transformations of Chinese society and economics.

Over the last 30 years, migration and migrants' circulations in internal China have been abundantly investigated by Chinese and international scholarship. Migratory issues were inscribed in the framework of China's "compressed modernity" (Chang, 1999) since the Reform era, thus in the context of an accelerated urban development, where flows of rural migrants moved from the countryside of inner rural areas to work in the industrial sector of the large coastal cities where their labor was exploited. Scholars have focused on the inegalitarian urban apparatus, which produces social and institutional inequalities and economic hierarchies, resulting in migrant workers being treated as "second class citizens" (Li and Tian, 2010) in the city. Empirically, much attention has been paid to migrant workers' networks and social relations developed during migratory paths and to the situations of exploitation in the urban factories (Pun, 2005, 2016). Scholarship has thus focused on the familiar and social bonds which sustain the negotiation of opportunities in the city, especially in terms of access to employment. Social resources in terms of familiar ties, social networks, and migratory knowledge capitalized by the different generations of rural migrants play an important role in the process of settlement in the city and bring about diversified labor experiences. Accordingly, if rural-to-urban migration is not a recent phenomenon in China, it has developed and transformed over time. Two generations of migrant workers have progressively left rural areas and migrated to the city, where they faced similar social and economic obstacles to integration. Nevertheless, the repertories of savoir-faire and competences they employed are not the same and have followed not only the social and economic, but also spatial and temporal, opportunities and barriers existing in the cities.

Concurrently, researches have examined migrations from Mainland China to Taiwan. These also began in the early 1980s and were characterized by a highly gendered dimension, since marriage is the *conditio sine qua non* for Chinese women to legally enter the Taiwanese territory. The 1992 Act Governing Relations between the People of the Taiwan Area and the Mainland Area (*taiwan diqu yu dalu diqu renmin guanxi tiaoli* 台湾地区与大陆地区人民关系条例) and its progressive amendments have so far elucidated Mainland women's status and rights in Taiwan. Until 2009, women from the Mainland were not allowed to work until they acquired residence status. Their right to work was thus linked to their right to residency. Residence could only be obtained two years after the first entry to Taiwan, which meant that the first stages of their stay were qualified as "visitation" and, later, "family reunification." The reform of 2009 abolished these temporary stages, and Mainland spouses' ingress was granted upon the permission of residing, hence of working. However, despite this legislative effort, Chinese women in Taiwan still face situations of social (Lan, 2008), gender (Cheng, 2013), and economic (Zani, 2018) inequalities in Taiwan.

This panorama on women's internal migration from the countryside to the city in Mainland China and cross-border marriage migration from the Mainland to Taiwan signals a multiplication of the spatialities and temporalities of rural-to-urban and cross-border migrations. Undoubtedly, the Chinese global city (Sassen, 1995) produces social hierarchies and economic inequalities towards female migrant workers which have persisted over the years. Informative as studies on migration within Mainland China and on cross-Strait migration may be, they nevertheless fail to focus on the social, spatial and temporal continuities and discontinuities of women's two-step migrations and on the ways biographical, social, marital, and professional experiences vary over time among the different generations of migrants. In fact, even though the numbers of Mainland migrant women in Taiwan since the 1990s appear fairly constant, mobility paths seem to have complexified according to the temporalities of migrations as well as the biographical, social, and professional changes among the different generations of migrant workers. The statistical stability of migrant women's migrations is tricky. Variations and dissonances cannot be investigated only through numbers. A close investigation of the mutations of migratory, marital, social, and economic experiences and practices leads me to decipher and explain the complexification of mobilities and their alteration over time.

On the basis thereof, I hereby wish to propose a contribution which simultaneously considers the heterogeneous spatialities and temporalities of mobilities and a feminization of labor and migrations. This novel approach might help us to simultaneously apprehend both the variations of migrations and mobilities as well as the broader social and economic changes of Chinese society and its labor market. In this respect, a cliometric approach in economic sociology to mobilities sustains a fresh understanding of the ways biographies and mobility patterns are entangled with macro-social and large-scale economic transformations, and how these two levels mutually inform each other. Considering the variations in terms of biographical, social, and professional careers of women who undertake rural-to-urban migration first and cross-border marriage migration later, in this chapter, I look at the generational continuum and discontinuum of women's migratory practices and at the ways the transformation of Chinese society, labor market, global capitalism, and globalization mutually influence each other and produce changes in the mobility experiences. Comprehensively, this contribution draws on an innovative methodology to capture and conceptualize the ways Chinese migrant women's internal and cross-border migrations are framed into the large-scale historical restructuring of Chinese capitalism, society, and labor market. It should be emphasized that the traditional qualitative techniques of micro-sociological inquiry—*in situ* observations, ethnographic work, and biographical interviews—can be creatively mobilized for a heuristic view of the macro-scale social and economic reorganization inside which migrant women's mobility patterns are inscribed. Let me elucidate such an approach. Considering that ethnography aims at pursuing "thick description" (Geertz, 1973) as a field grounded method for "understanding how people make sense of their lives, make the experience of the world and produce social change (Glaser and Strauss, 1967, p. 23), a conundrum arises. To what extent can ethnographic work contribute to an understanding of the macro-social and economic transformations that the micro-social biographical, migratory, and professional experiences of the actors investigated inform of? The qualitative methodological tools I employ to diachronically frame the variation of women's mobility paths in internal China and from the Mainland to Taiwan suggest that an ethnographic analysis of the migratory patterns, of migrants social, professional, and marital experiences is not incompatible with a cliometric perspective, more attentive to the historical mutations of the economic models and the structure of the labor market. On the contrary, based on the empirical evidence of actors' biographies, social and professional experiences, economic activities, and migratory practices, the qualitative techniques I have employed for a micro-sociological analysis of migrations coherently complete the cliometric arsenal. Thus, micro-social situations, experiences, and practices remain the point of departure of ethnographic work, albeit these are projected into a larger-scale frame of macro-social and economic change. Clearly, from this angle it is possible to assemble two only apparently separated pieces of the puzzle: the temporal and spatial variations of women's migrations and mobilities follow the rhythm of the social and historical transformations of Chinese capitalism.

Drawing on this theoretical conceptualization, in this chapter, I aim at answering the following research questions: (i) In internal China first and from the Mainland to Taiwan later, how are migratory and professional careers of rural migrant women constructed over time? (ii) What are the main changes in terms of social status, marriage and mobility paths, professional experiences, and economic practices between the first and the second generation of Mainland migrant women within this two-step mobility? (iii) How do such continuities and discontinuities inform of larger-scale change of Chinese society and its labor market?

Addressing these puzzles, to examine and compare the making of biographical, migratory, social, and economic careers of these two generations of women, this chapter is guided by the hypothesis that the careers of Chinese women in internal China and from the Mainland to Taiwan exhibit social, economic, and moral continuities and discontinuities which are punctuated by the penetration of globalization and modernity in the Chinese society. From the 1980s onward, two generations of rural women migrated in internal China, seeking employment in the urban areas and faced multi-situated social inequalities and economic hierarchies. After few years of temporary work in the city, some women, through marriage, remigrate further on to Taiwan. Different from the first generation, the second generation of Chinese migrant women's careers are constructed through a stronger "capacity to aspire" (Appadurai, 1999) which sustains the mobilization of innovative repertories of social and economic resources to claim a place in the Chinese and Taiwanese societies and labor markets. Creative social experiences and digital economic practices are produced to "contest" (Steiner, 2005) the inequalities and hierarchies faced by women during migration. New opportunities are negotiated inside the novel scales, spatialities, and temporalities of transnational migration. Thereby, a crossed study enables me to investigate the similarities and differences in the construction of migratory careers, together with the social experiences, and the economic practices between two generations of migrant women, i.e. those born after 1960 and those born after 1980, which inform of the social and economic transformations occurring in contemporary Chinese society.

7.2. Research Methodology and Field Sites

Aiming to contextualize the making of migratory careers by two generation Chinese women rather than achieve statistical representation, this chapter presents findings of a multi-sited ethnographic work (Marcus, 1995) and 151 biographical interviews carried out in Mainland China and Taiwan between 2016 and 2018. Fieldwork was conducted for a doctoral dissertation about women's mobilities and translocal economies between Mainland China and Taiwan (Zani, 2021).

A sociological approach to migratory and mobility paths in term of career (Becker, 1963; Roulleau-Berger, 2014) sustains a diachronic understanding of migrations, which is compatible with a cliometric understanding of the migratory paths between the two generations of Chinese women.

By declining migratory paths on such a diachronic and diatopic dimension (Becker, 1963), the notion of *career* facilitates the concurrent study of the spatial and temporal level of mobilities. I have conducted *in situ* (Glaser and Strauss, 1967) observations of women's daily lives and professional activities both in their rural village of origin, in the cities, and in the factories both on the Mainland and in Taiwan. Through informal conversations and in-depth interviews, I have reconstructed the biographical, migratory, and professional careers of 40 women belonging to the first generation of migrants, i.e. born between 1960 and 1980, and of 111 women belonging to the second generation of migrants, i.e. born after 1980. Both generations were engaged in rural-to-urban migration in internal China first and in cross-border marriage migration to Taiwan later.

The "story narrative" technique (Ossman, 2013) has been particularly helpful to look at the objective and subjective dimension of the career making process (Becker, 1963). This leads us to an analysis where the effects of social structures are considered, together with the mobilization of social, economic, and moral resources by the actors as well as the capitalization of repertories individual skills and competences.

At the very same time, the scale of the sample collected permits comparison and sustains the identification of variations over time and spaces in terms of migratory paths, social and professional experiences between the two generations of migrants. First generation women were born during 1960s in Chinese inner provinces' rural areas. They all spent their childhood in the villages and migrated during 1980s to the cities to temporarily work in the local factories. Between 1980 and 1990, they engaged in cross-border marriage migration and settled down in Taiwan. Women from the second generation were born after 1980. They are also from rural areas and migrated between the end of 1990 and the beginning of 2000 to large coastal cities and later to Taiwan through marriage. The crossed analysis of the biographical and mobility patterns of these two generations helps to apprehend the lines of continuity and of discontinuity between internal and cross-border migration as well as in terms of mobility projects between the two different generations.

Diatopically and diachronically speaking, the field sites correspond to women's rural villages of origin in the inner provinces of Mainland China (mainly Jiangxi, Shandong, Guanxi, Anhui, Henan, Hunan, Hubei...), the large coastal cities where women were employed in local factories (mainly Shenzhen, Dongguan, Guangzhou, Foshan, Zhuhai, Zhongshan in Guangdong province) and could meet their future Taiwanese husbands, as well as the cities where they settled down after marriage migration to Taiwan, mainly Taipei, Hsinchu, Taoyuan, and Hukou.

However, *in situ* observations at these sites and biographical, migratory, social, and professional careers' reconstruction have not been sufficient to comprehend the complexity of these two-step mobilities and their generational variations. Aimed at elucidating how "modernity at large" (Appadurai, 1999) and the reconfiguration of the spatialities and temporalities within a globalized context contribute to the transformations of migratory careers, I realized that the second generation of Mainland migrant women in Taiwan partially constructs its life patterns and its social and economic experiences within novel spaces for inter-action. Situations, practices, and experiences are being increasingly produced inside the novel virtual spaces of digital platforms (Urry, 2007; Hine, 2015). Therefore, virtual ethnography (Hine, 2015) has become an imperative for "physical" ethnography, to better investigate not only the migratory careers, but especially, the economic practices that young "connected migrants" (Diminescu, 2008) of the second generation generate to face economic inequalities and hierarchies after cross-border marriage migration and settlement in Taiwan. The digital platform *WeChat* (*weixin* 微信) has become a space for ethnography and *in situ* observations. This led to the examination of online conversations, situations, and economic practices occurring inside the chat groups set by Mainland migrant women in Taiwan. From my smartphone, I joined a few of these groups. These included, for example, "the Group of Mutual Help among the Chinese Sisters in Hsinchu county" (*xinzhu jiemei huxiang qun* 新竹姐妹互相群), with 221 participants; "Mainland Sisters–Hometown Group" (*dalu jiemei jiaxiang qun* 大陆姐妹家乡群), which includes 500 women; "the Community of Mainland Sisters in Taiwan" (*dalu jiemei zai taiwan-shetuan qun* 大陆姐妹在台湾-社团群), composed of 428 members.

7.3. Genealogy and Transformations of Rural-to-Urban Migrations

"Setting China on the track of globalization" (*yu quanqiu jiegui* 与全球接轨) has been the slogan promoted by the Chinese government, allied to the translocal market since the late 1970s. Reforms were perceived as necessary to break the socialist tradition of collectivism (Oi, 1999). It was imperative to support the penetration of the increasingly visible hands of transnational markets, which at the crossroad between global trade and local migrations, could draw new "geographies of extraction" (Sassen, 2014) of migrants' labor in the cities.

Post-reform China underwent three major, unprecedented, and accelerated transitions (Liu, 2008; Roulleau-Berger, 2014): from a centralized planned economy to a market economy; from a mainly agricultural to an industrial society; from almost exclusive rurality to strong and growing urbanization.

Reforms began in the countryside, where the Maoist commune system of collective economy was progressively dismantled and replaced by the policy of "contracting production to households" (Oi, 1999), namely the "Household responsibility system" (*hukou zhidu* 户口制度), aimed at increasing the commodification of the means of production, agricultural produce, and overall marketization (Li, 2013). In the 1980s the State introduced a series of policy measures that consolidated the household contracted production responsibility system and stabilized land contract relationships in the countryside (Solinger, 1999).

However, despite an initial rapid improvement in rural production, the fundamental weakness of the small peasant economy soon became apparent as the pattern of the market economy guided by the penetration of global capitals took shape, proving to be unproductive and uncompetitive in the market (Gallagher, 2005). The small peasant production mode of individual household farming led to low levels of agricultural industrialization (Lee, 1998; Pun, 1999), and the countryside was drawn deeper into the great tide of marketization. Peasants' livelihoods became strongly dependent on the market and cash incomes (Li and Tian, 2010). Moreover, having lost their collective economy as their foundation, it was no longer possible to provide for the welfare and social security previously enjoyed under the collective system (Li, 2013).

Therefore, it became hard to continue living in the petty peasant economy. Reforms have thus been implemented in the contradictory frame of "Chinese compressed modernity" (Chang, 1999): a "telescoping" where "pre-modern, modern, and post-modern regimes" (Roulleau-Berger, 2018) mix and merge, oscillating between socialism and *sui generis* capitalism (Aglietta and Bai, 2012). Thereby, rural people were forced to abandon their land and move to the cities to seek other means of living. This was the origin of the "migrant worker tide" (Lee, 1998) and the creation of "new laboring subjects" (Pun, 2005, 2016), who enabled China's rise to "the factory of the world." This vast rural population represented a crucial, strategic resource for China's industrialization and urbanization.

Meanwhile, reforms were also carried out in the urban spaces. In the 1980s, the establishment of Special Economic Zones (SEZs) signified the opening of China's urban economy to export-industrial development. Southern provinces, in primis Guangdong province, the Pearl river delta area (*zhu san jiao* 珠三角), and the city of Shenzhen were the major centers of industrial zones, factory compounds, and workers' dormitories. In 2001, China's entry into the World Trade Organization (WTO) represented a complete incorporation of the Chinese economy into the arena of global markets. Simultaneously, this rapid and targeted development of coastal areas' (*yanhai chengshi* 沿海城市) economies—Jiangsu, Zhejiang, Fujian, and Guangdong provinces—was accompanied by a massive harnessing of young rural workers, in particular unmarried women (Lee, 1998; Pun, 1999, 2005; Yan, 2008).

The Chinese government actively coordinated the transfer of rural surplus labor (*nongcun shengyu laodong zhuanli* 农村剩余劳动专利) to the booming cities, to support local and global extraction logics. Sun Liping's (2003) insightful expression "the factory mirrors contemporary society" reflects this historical paradox. It elucidates the societal magnitude and the impact of the transformation of the socialist redistribution system into a flexible market system. This led to an increased segmentation of the labor market (Li, 2013), together with the multiplication of floating labor experiences (Roulleau-Berger, 2014), especially for low-qualified rural workers. Therefore, the deployment of precise migratory and labor policies contributed to orient and channel this rural surplus of labor toward the industrial urban apparatus. The above mentioned "Household registration system" (hukou) has served as an important tool for the national government to control the flows of population (Li, 2013). Everyone was assigned a residence permit that entitles the holder to certain benefits, such as welfare rights, social protection, medical care, insurance, and education (Li and Tian, 2010; Roulleau-Berger, 2013), in a specific place, either a rural or urban location. Hence, to administer services and welfare protection, it officially divided the population into holders of "rural" and "urban" residence (Solinger, 1999) and quickly turned into a real metaphor of discrimination through which "the oppositions between town and country could be expressed" (Siu, 2007, p. 330). In this manner, the inegalitarian attribution of rights and social protection between the rural and urban populations is not without an impact on migratory and labor paths of rural migrant workers and their transformations. But let me proceed by order.

Women's rural-to-urban migrations have varied over time. A first generation of rural migrant women left the countryside and moved to the cities beginning in the 1980s. Since the dismantlement of the Maoist peasant economy in the rural areas of inner provinces, women associated migration to an "inevitable process" (Li, 2003) aimed at ameliorating a poor economic condition. For instance, Xiang was born in 1963 in rural Hunan, and she currently resides in Hukou (Taiwan) with her second husband. She got married at the age of eighteen and had three children. In 1981, she was living with her family in the countryside, where she helped her father with agricultural work in the rice paddies. Xiang's family had been cultivating rice for a long time, mainly for local demand. When the market was liberalized after the reforms, Xiang's family realized that the rapidly increasing price for the agricultural products provided a very little added value. When trade in agriculture was liberalized, local rural production proved to be insufficient for the daily survival of her family. Xiang soon saw her co-villagers and family members leaving their villages and moving to the cites looking for an urban employment. Hence, as she explained, she did the same and migrated to the developing city of Shenzhen, in Guangdong province, where the newly established multinational companies and transnational enterprises provided jobs to the rural surplus of labor:

> "I did not want to leave my village, I felt scared. I did not want to move to the city, but I had no choice [...] we had no money at home, and I needed money for myself and for my parents, who were getting old. That is why we left. I arrived in Shenzhen and I felt awkward and scared. Everything was so huge! I did not want to live there, I wanted to go back to my village as soon as possible [...] The environment of Shenzhen was unfriendly [...] Work was horrible, but I had no choice. Local people maltreated me, I could not understand what they said since my mandarin was poor [...] I worked 15, 16, 17 hours per day for very little money [...]."

Xiang, 57 years old, Hunan native, Hukou, 12.02.2017

Xiang's words illustrate her attachment to her village of origin: a place that she did not want to leave. Like her, the first generation of rural migrant women moved to the cities to earn a little income through factory work before remigrating back home. Few years after her urban mobility, a friend introduced Xiang to her future Taiwanese husband, and she currently resides in Hukou (Taiwan). Scared of the urban world, inexperienced and low-qualified, Xiang's urban and labor experiences in the Mainland were limited to a couple of textile factories in Shenzhen:

> "I did not want to change my job. I did not say that I liked my job, actually I could not stand that. But I had no

choice [...] there were so many people in the city, all the factories were overloaded, people were everywhere, and it was hard to find another job. So, I stayed in the same factory, I needed money. I thought that if I left, I could not find anything else [...]"

The progressive spread of market economy and modernity in China strengthened rural-to-urban mobilities and imposed to the first generation of rural migrants' urban labor experiences as an inevitable means of survival. As Xiang explained, the massive and sudden flows of migrants from rural-to-urban areas made it difficult for them to find a job in the developing cities. The ratio between labor's offer and demand was by that time still unbalanced (Pun, 2005). Labor and urban experiences being time-limited, for the first generation of rural migrants it was a matter of "making the most money possible in the shortest period," as Xiang explained. This led them to accept dehumanizing and inegalitarian labor conditions in the industrial sector, performing whatever job they could find in the city (Yan, 2008).

The situation seems to be rather different for the second generation of migrant women's labor and migratory experiences. "Modernity at large" (Appadurai, 1999) has abundantly influenced the construction of the "urban imaginaries" (Miller, 2010) amongst young migrant workers, i.e. those born after 1980. This is the case for Ding Ding, 30 years old, Anhui native, who currently lives in Taipei. At the age of sixteen, she voluntarily abandoned school, since she was fascinated by the narrations of the city she could hear from her fellow villagers who worked in Cantonese factories. She migrated to Kunshan (Jiangsu province), where she worked for a few years before remigrating to Taiwan through marriage:

"At that time, I was young and naïve. I did not know much about the real world, but I wanted to leave my village like my fellow villagers did before to see the world [...] I felt stupid and bored at home as I did not have much to do, I helped my grandmother in the fields and to cook, nothing more [...] My co-villagers were all away working, and I wanted to join them. The countryside was backyard and underdeveloped (*tu* 土), people were rude (*meiyou suzhi* 没有素质) and dirty [...] I also wanted to live in the city [...] I was so excited when I packed my luggage:

Kunshan was a good opportunity for me to improve myself and to be independent [...] My parents were in Guangdong province, the sky is high, the emperor is faraway (*tiangao huangdi yuan* 天高皇帝远) [she laughs], I thought I could finally do what I wanted [...]."

Ding Ding, 30 years old, Anhui native, Nanshijiao (Taipei), 28.12.2016

Ding Ding's words are emblematic of the strong rejection of life and professional perspectives in the rural communities characterizing the second generation of migrant workers. Different from their parents, for the younger generation it was a matter of achieving modernity, consumerism, and autonomy through migration. The urban landscape and the city, as promised lands, were socially and emotionally constructed as spaces for long-term integration. Dissimilar from older Xiang, Ding Ding's labor and urban experiences pluralized. She first moved to Kunshan (Jiangsu province), and later to Fuzhou (Fujian province), to Shenzhen, to Canton, and to Dongguan (Guangdong province), alternating jobs within several factories. This reinforced the experiences of social exclusion and economic discrimination at work, but it also enabled Ding Ding to improve her skills and knowledge of the structure of the labor market as well as to capitalize social and economic resources through the multiplication of the professional positions.

From this perspective, the strategically negative image of rural villages and the countryside spread by modernity, global capitalism, and the State's discourse (Pun, 2005) of which Ding Ding's words are figurative, strengthened the desire of migrating, of abandoning the village, and moving toward global cities among the young generation of rural girls. Migrations are socially and emotionally constructed towards modern subjectivity making processes, seeking an urban, independent and autonomous status, unobtainable in rural areas, considered, to quote Ding Ding's opinion, "backyard" (*tu* 土) and "miserable" (*qiong* 穷).

The abrupt advent of the capitalist apparatus in regulating not only the economic but also the social and cultural life generated and supported a doubled-edged biopolitical modern project, which indirectly invested individuals' lives and existences (Pun, 2005) to orient their movements towards the urban factories where their cheap labor could be exploited. Juan's description of her community of origin and of local people point out the extent to which a precise discourse of modernity had penetrated rural areas, promoting a disqualified representation of the countryside and of peasants. Individuals' understanding of their social, economic, and moral positioning inside their rural communities of origin are influenced by this retrograde and backward representation, aimed at sustaining their movements toward the city:

> "I had three wishes when I went working in Shanghai: buying a nice mobile phone, buying some new clothes, and buying a computer. I wanted to learn how to use it [...] I wanted to leave my village, there was nothing there. The city was my future. It was modern and developed. I wanted to live there, I wanted to leave Fuyang, get a job and become rich."

Juan, 32 years old, Anhui native, Taipei, 27.12.2016

Juan's words show the progressive construction by rural women of a precise, idyllic and idealized image of the city: a place where upward social mobility is possible. With this in mind, in the formulation of the migratory project, the political economies of imaginaries cannot be overlooked while comparing the mobility patterns of the first and second generations of migrant workers. The city impregnates such imaginaries and projections (Miller, 2010). It is a socially, economically, and emotionally constructed space, and "modernity at large" (Appadurai, 1999) seems to contribute to forging such an imaginary. Women's words emphasize how the urban telos appropriates the rural (Yan, 2008). The rhetorical opposition between the rural and urban developmental projects produce very precise social imaginaries strengthening the desire to move.

This relationship of necessary co-determination of the individual, as a subject, to the social is questionable and requires further discussion. It cannot be denied that at the crossroad between labor surplus, global economy, and national political economy, new *dagong* 打工 ("temporary work") subjects have been strategically constructed by the state and the market to increase productivity and rural labor exploitation (Pun, 1999; Yan, 2008). The meaning of the word dagong elucidates this critical process and embodies the logics

of extraction of labor on which current economics are built. Dagong
signifies "working for a boss," "selling labor" connoting the marketization and commodification of the labor exchange. It embodies a
deskilled work (Pun, 1999) exchanged in any informal environment
based on temporary contracts (Harvey, 2007, p. 285). In contrast to
the term *gongren* 工人 (worker), largely employed during the Maoist
era (Pun, 2005), this new word dagong implies a lower status in a
context shaped by the rise of market factors in labor relations and
hierarchies (Shen, 2006; Shen and Wen, 2014). Young female peasant-
workers are usually called *dagong mei* 打工妹 ("laboring girls"), that
is to say a new gendered labor subject (Pun, 1999), produced at
a specific socio-historical moment when the private global market
penetrated China.

7.4.   Praxis of Migration and Migrants' Generations

The temporary, transient nature of the urban experience is in confor-
mity with the first generation of migrants' projects, oriented towards
a return to the village. Yet, it collides with young women's imaginaries, aspirations, and ambitions of upward social mobility and
long-term urban status's attainment. Despite the persistence of inegalitarian treatments of low-skilled migrant workers in the urban
labor market as well social as exclusion and institutional discrimination, individuals' imaginaries have undeniably varied over time. Since
the 1980s, rural-to-urban migrations have progressively imposed as a
praxis in the rural areas. Entire households and families abandoned
the villages to temporarily work in the cities. Nevertheless, a crossed
examination of a mother and of her daughters' mobility patterns
helps to shed light on this divergence. To solve this puzzle, let me
look at the following snapshot.

*February 2018. Liaobu district, Dongguan city, Guangdong
province.*

*While living at Xiao Hui's lodgings in Dongguan city, we received
a visit from her mother, who moved from Sichuan to Guangdong
province to receive better medical treatment, thanks to the economic
support of her daughter. Xiao Hui, her mother, her son, and I went*

to the Taiwanese hospital in Dongguan, considered to be not only cheaper but also of better quality than Chinese hospitals. When we entered, Xiao Hui and her son went queuing, while I waited with her mother. Looking around the hospital, she looked surprised and she suddenly projected herself 30 years before, while she was also temporary working (dagong) in the city of Shenzhen, saying:

> "Thirty years ago, there were no hospitals like this! This is a very-well developed hospital, I am happy I can come here! [...] I think that in Europe you have hospitals like this."

Then, she took my hand and started reading it. She described some characteristics of my personality, which to my surprise I found very accurate. I asked her how she could know these things about me, and she answered:

> "Twenty years of dagong work (*dale ershi nian de gong, zenme buhui zhidao* 打了二十年的工，怎么不会知道) taught me a lot; my daughter does not have the same knowledge. She has abandoned the village too early and there are many things she does not know [...] When I left the village, my only dream was to come back, but my daughter is different. When she left, her main dream was not to come back [...] and she succeeded. She has married a rich man, who can support my medical fees. You should also marry a rich man, so that your mother does not have to worry about you. But looking at your hand's lines, this is not likely to happen [...]."

Xiao Hui's mother, Liaobu (Dongguan), 02.02.2018

This explanation elucidates the intergenerational variation in terms of migratory ambitions and projects, which re-define and re-orient mobility paths and biographical trajectories. This generational gap reveals fresh processes of construction of subjectivity amongst the new generation of migrant workers, which follow the social transformation of the Chinese countryside, of the urban reforms and labor market's changes. The desire of long-term urban integration, modernity, autonomy, and consumerism digs a trench which is synchronic-generational and diachronic-temporal.

Xiao Hui's mother left the village during her adulthood, after being socialized in the countryside. Hence, she perceived the urban labor experience as a reversible phase of her life, aimed at temporarily improving her economic situation but oriented toward a return to the community of origin.

The progressive emptying of rural villages during the last three decades was emblematic of migrations dictated by urgent economic necessity. For her generation, migration was, to quote Li Lulu (2003), an "inevitable process" (*nizhuan guocheng* 逆转过程), aimed at survival (*wei fazhan chulai* 为发展出来). Building a new house in the village to replace the old one, supporting children's education or marriage, and earning money for old age were the main reasons for temporary migration. In contrast, for Xiao Hui's generation, migration corresponds to an individual, autonomous choice. As she claimed, she "migrated by herself and for herself" (*wei ziji chulai* 为自己出来). The oppositions in terms of life ambitions between Xiao Hui and her mother draws a chronotope (Bakhtin, 2008) of the rural–urban dichotomy, whereby living and residing in the countryside and being a peasant implies being left behind temporally in the drive toward progress and development.

Since the beginning of her migratory career, Xiao Hui has demonstrated how migration corresponds to a new relation to the selves inside a novel urban, modern, and consumerist world. She has constructed her path in the Chinese city first and in Taiwan later by following an ambition of long-term settlement and upward social mobility through geographical and professional displacements. In this vein, by analyzing the first generation of migrant workers during the 1980s, Chinese sociologist Fei Xiao Tong (1968) has coined the following expression to describe the transient, temporary, and return-oriented dimension of migration: "leaving the fields without leaving the village" (*litu bu lixiang* 离土不离乡), "entering the factory without entering the city" (*jinchang bu jincheng* 近厂不近城). To restate Sayad's expression (1999), while migration was characterized by "a sentiment of provisional" (Sayad, 1999, p. 111) for the first generation, for the contemporary generation of migrant workers it is a matter of "a sentiment of durable provisional, which leads to a new repertory of practices, influencing the perception of the social world" (1999, p. 112). Let me look at Aju's narration:

"I could not find a decent job [...] they preferred to hire local people, Cantonese, they thought that migrants had to stay in the factory [...] in China it is like this: when you want a job and you come from the countryside, you need guanxi, you need to know someone, or you pay. But I did not know many people in that field [...] I was finally employed in a beauty salon... as a cleaner. I cleaned the floors, the toilet and the kitchen, basically. It was extremely frustrating [...] And I did not earn much money; the problem was that when I worked in the factory, I was provided with a bed in the [...] My mother wanted me to go back to the village and get married, but I did not want to, I wanted to marry in the city and become a rich woman [...]."

Aju, 33 years old, Hubei native, Taipei, 06.04.2017

Aju's experience is characterized by feelings of strong frustration, dissatisfaction, and disappointment against the unfairness which is common in the urban labor market in China. The first jobs she performed supported the emergence of new ambitions and aspirations, which lead Aju not to give up. In the disqualifying segments of the labor market women have access to, jobs are unstable, poorly paid, and do not offer any form of career mobility. The low wages cannot support the high cost of urban living, negating the possibility to save money to invest in a future urban life, increasingly perceived as an unachievable horizon:

"After I left my home village, I did not want to go back, I wanted to remain in the city. But gradually I was realising that I had no chance. I wanted to change my destiny (*gai ziji de mingyun* 改自己的命运), but I had nothing (*yiwu suoyou* 一无所有). I could only count on myself (*wo zhi neng kao ziji* 我只能靠自己), but often relying on oneself is not enough (*dan kao ziji ye bugoule* 但靠自己也不够了). Opportunities and money were for local people. Guangdong province did not want us, people from rural inner provinces (*waidi ren* 外地人)... we are not recognised, we are just invisible labour [...] We were excluded (*paiwai* 排外), people looked down on us (*kan buqi* 看不起) [...] Life in the village was not what I dreamed of, but I did not want to spend the rest of my life around the assembly line either [...] When you are born dagong mei, you remain a dagong mei forever (*dagong chushengde na jiu yizhi yongyuande shi ge zai dagong de dagongmei* 打工出生的那就一直永远的是个在打工的打工妹).”

Xiao Mei, 30 years old, Anhui native, Taipei 23.01.2017

Xiao Mei's statement "when you are born dagong mei, you remain a dagong mei" illuminates her reflexive understanding of urban hierarchies and social inequalities, which also characterizes the narrations of first-generation migrant women. For instance, Xiao Mei was aware of the difficulties of long-term integration in the city and social mobility perspectives. At the very same time, and differently from older migrants, her words illustrate that she was not willing to move back to her rural community of origin. Xiao Mei wanted to remain in the city to settle-down. As a matter of fact, dagong life and labor experiences are supposed to be temporary. After a few years of urban work, women are expected to move back to the countryside to get married (Tong, 2012).

However, it seems that this perspective does not match with young women's ambitions and expectations. Urban life and work contributed to strengthen women's aspirations for independence and autonomy. A rural marriage could, in this sense, jeopardize the making of their autonomy project, framed inside a modern and urban horizon. The more complex, numerous, and pluralized the circulations and the professional experiences are, the more undesirable it is for women to return to the village to marry a local man:

> "I had been working in Shenzhen for almost three years and I enjoyed the city a lot. You cannot imagine how many jobs I had performed at that time, that was crazy, I kept on changing! I worked in several factories, in restaurants, in some shops, but later I found a job in a hairdressing salon owned by a co-villager, a friend of my dad. It was better than the factory even if my co-villager was controlling me a lot, and reporting my attitude to my father [...] At that time, I was dating a poor dagong man from Anhui: he was very nice to me, but he had no money [...] He had also spent a long time in Guangdong and was open minded like me (*kaifang* 开放) [...] My co-villager told that to my dad,

who got very upset [...] One day, he suddenly took the train with my brother and arrived in Shenzhen, to bring me back home to get married with a co-villager [...] I cried. I told him I did not want to go back and get married, it was too early, I was only twenty. I still wanted to stay in the city and have fun for few years [...] I did not want to think about marriage, at that time, I was still living day by day (*zou yitian, suan yitian* 走一天, 算一天)."

Chunchun, 30 years old, Hubei native, Taipei, 16.03.2017

7.5. Continuity and Change in Cross-Border Marriage Practices

After few years of temporary work in the cities, since the 1980s, some Chinese female migrants of both first and second generations have later engaged since in cross-border marriage migration to Taiwan. Nevertheless, translocal marriages and marriage-migratory patterns have varied over time. Once again, as a mirror of the transformations investing Chinese society and economy, a crossed analysis of such variations simultaneously points out the changes of urban society, of the labor market, and of the related practices of marriage. To identify the continuum and discontinuum in terms of practices, let me look at two different cases. Beibei is 58 years old, and she currently lives and works in Zhudong, Taiwan. She works at a local street market and she resides with her Taiwanese husband and her parents-in-law. At the age of 14, she left her home village in Shandong province and migrated to Shanghai first and to Shenzhen later, where she worked in several electronic and textile factories for five years. At the age of 19, she was called back by her parents, and through a match-making agency, a marriage with a Taiwanese native was arranged. The man lived in rural Zhudong and worked as a taxi driver. Both Beibei and her family considered marriage to a Taiwanese as an opportunity to improve Beibei's social status and to achieve economic independence. Marriage was thus commercially arranged (*maimai hunyin* 买卖婚姻) as a brokered practice (*xiangqin* 相亲) and represented a strategy of hypergamy (Constable, 2003; Tsai and Hsiao, 2006). Beibei and her husband did not know each other, and they first met a few days before the wedding, when the Taiwanese men moved to the Mainland for the ceremony. Both the way this marriage was organized and Beibei's husband identikit—a rural taxi driver—suggest that when cross-border marriages in Taiwan gained demographic significance in the mid-1980s, the earlier bridegrooms were from socially disadvantaged, lowly educated backgrounds (Lu, 2005). Thereby, Beibei explained:

> "I had to get married, this is a duty for a woman [...] I was introduced to my husband by my aunt who had a friend in Taiwan [...] My husband paid some money to my family, but that was hard for him since he did not have much money [...] His job was unstable, but he needed to get married [...] We all thought that moving to Taiwan would have been a great opportunity for me, I could not work in the city all my life long and in the village there were not much opportunities for a decent life [...]"

Beibei, 57 years old, Shandong native, Zhubei, 13.12.2016

Like Beibei's husband, during the 1980s, Taiwanese men who looked for brides in the Mainland had difficulties to marry local women (Momesso, 2016). Marrying a woman from the Mainland is an option for Taiwanese men who are deemed to be disadvantaged in the local marriage market and thus have trouble finding a Taiwanese wife. Such a "marriage squeeze" (Akers, 1967) is believed to be the result of the socioeconomic transformation that has taken place in Taiwan in the wake of industrialization and urbanization. Consequently, over the past several decades Taiwanese women have achieved higher educational standards and greater participation in the labor market and have elevated themselves out of the range of social contact by these disadvantaged men (Tsay, 2004).

The proximity in terms of language, culture, and ethnic background influenced the propensity of Chinese women for Taiwanese men (Lu, 2005). Since the late 1980s, the number of Chinese brides has gradually been increasing. As the demand for foreign spouses was not high at the early stage, Taiwanese men and their families looked for wives abroad via their contacts in Mainland China, like Beibei's aunt. For the first generation of Chinese migrant women, cross-border marriages were thus highly mediated through brokerage practices (*xiangqin* 相亲) or agencies (*zhongjie* 中介), acting as intermediaries and constituting a marriage-migration industry (Lan, 2008; Xiang *et al.*, 2012; Hsia, 2015; Yeoh, 2016). Given the restrictive immigration policies in Taiwan, Taiwanese men often needed to travel to meet women. They joined them in their rural villages of origin, from which cross-border migration started. The travel, the introduction, the ensuing arrangements of marriage registration, and the wedding as well as the negotiation of the bride price and dowry needed to be facilitated: the mediators were therefore fundamental.

Nonetheless, the design of contemporary encounters turns out to be rather different from the past. Since the beginning of the 1990s, the opening of the Chinese economy to transnational investments and global markets has not only intensified rural-to-urban migrations but also transnational capitals' movement and foreign entrepreneurs and managerial class' mobility (Sassen, 1998; Tseng, 2008). To control their overseas investments and to facilitate technology transfers, transnational firms sent managers or technical workers to their overseas sites, for instance Mainland China. If this migration was intended as a relatively short-term assignment (Tseng, 2014), it also progressively became long term for "transnational business owners"—foreign personnel, managers, and businessmen (Hsiao and Wang, 2002; Tseng, 2008; Chen, 2015). As such, during the past 30 years, this capital-linked migration included the huge movement of Taiwanese[1] (Sellami, 2013), Hongkonguese, Japanese, and Korean capital-owners (Hsiao, 2018), professionals, and technical workers to the economically strategic Chinese provinces of Jiangsu, Zhejiang, Fujian, and Guangdong, where the economic opportunities for investment were particularly abundant (Schubert and Shu, 2010; Tseng and Wu, 2011).

The attractiveness of China's enormous market, together with the implementation of State's business programs to encourage foreign investments (Lee, 1998; Solinger, 1999; Sellami, 2013) and the availability of cheap labor, has thus facilitated capital accumulation and the creation of employment opportunities for foreign entrepreneurs

---

[1] According to the Taiwanese Ministry of Foreign Affairs, between 1990 and 1996, the number of Taiwanese out-migrants increased more than fourfold, from 25.5 thousand to 119.1 thousand, the majority of which were middle-class businesspersons, investors, and professionals (Wang and Hsiao, 2009).

and professionals, who massively migrated to China. Concurrently, since the beginning of the 1990s, Taiwan has turned into an important sending-capital site (Hsiao and Wang, 2002; Hsiao, 2018), especially to the Mainland (Yang, 2006), where a growing number of Taiwanese entrepreneurs—*taishang* 台商—nourished diaspora communities, benefiting from local profitable business programs, foreign direct investment, economic incentives, and advantages in terms of social protection and welfare (Hsiao, 2018). The word taishang, literally "Taiwanese merchant," describes those who migrate to open and operate their overseas business. In this respect, since the 1990s emigration from Taiwan has been dominated by the middle and upper-middle classes (Tseng, 2008). It was pulled by the global economy (Tseng, 2014), which encouraged the dislocation of Taiwanese companies in Southern China, where labor was cheaper.

The case of Xiao Hui, Sichuan native, 28 years old, living in Taipei, illustrates such a social and economic transition of the Chinese labor market, where Taiwanese investments pluralized, accompanied by the displacement of Taiwanese managers and high-skilled workers. This is a main point to keep in mind for understanding the transformation of cross-border encounters leading to marriage migration. Crucially, and differently from the previous marital practices arranged in the countryside, contemporary encounters followed the rhythms of the penetration of translocal firms and capitals in Southern China. Xiao Hui met her future husband Kinge—42 years old, Tainan native entrepreneur—in 2009, when he was in Dongguan to take care of his electronic enterprise established there. By that time, young Xiao Hui had left Sichuan province and moved to Dongguan (Guangdong province). There, she had been initially employed in a few electronic and textile factories, where salaries were poor and working hours extremely long. Later, she worked in a restaurant where she got in touch with the Taiwanese reality for the first time. Serving the tables, she met a middle-age Taiwanese businessman, and she was touched by his generosity and paternalistic attitude:

> "Work was long and hard (*youku youlei* 又苦又累), I worked around fifteen hours per day, washing the dishes, and cleaning the floor. I earned 600 Yuan (*yuan* 元), and my family desperately needed money, so I had to send back all the money I earned. One month, when I got my period, I did not even have money to buy pads and I had to borrow

some from a friend [...] I left that place as the owner mal-treated me and he refused to pay me in the end [...] Later, I found another job at a luxurious hotel, I had to serve the tables. There were many foreigners there, I had never seen foreigners before: they were so classy and educated! (*hen you limao* 很有礼貌) [...] One day, a client started asking me questions. He asked me where I came from, how much money I earned, what the conditions of my family were [...] He was Taiwanese and he was very kind [...] He had a factory and he suggested that I went working there, I told him that I could not do much, but he insisted and I accepted [...]."

This positive encounter with the Taiwanese businessman sup-ported the construction of a positive social and emotional represen-tation of Taiwan, which later sustained Xiao Hui's choice of life and marriage. After a few weeks, Xiao Hui found a new employment in a Taiwanese enterprise, owned by Kinge, her current husband, with whom she started a love affair:

"He was very nice to me. I was young at that time and I did not know much about men. My friends were all jealous that I was dating a Taiwanese. They said, money can give you the sense of security you need (*youqian caiyou anquan gan* 有钱才有安全感). But for me, it was not only a matter of money, you know. Dongguan was a dangerous and messy place; I was so tired of factory work. I felt so exhausted. I tasted so much bitterness (*ku chi de tai duole* 苦吃得太多了), I just wanted a secured life in the city [...] Every time he came back to Taiwan, he brought expensive presents for me. I felt embarrassed. I did not want to accept luxurious rings and cosmetics [...] He gave very expensive things to me, that I had never used before. Once he brought me a perfume and I did not even know what that was. It was too sophisticated for me! [...]."

One day in 2012, while working in Dongguan and dating Kinge, Xiao Hui was suddenly called back by her family to her home vil-lage. Her parents were arranging a marriage for her since the time had come. She obeyed and returned to Sichuan. There, she had an appointment with a local matchmaker (*meipo* 媒婆). Xiao Hui acknowledged having complained to the meipo about the rural man she was supposed to "match" with:

"You know what she told me? She said that I was smug and pretentious, that I had spent too much time in the city: "little girl, what are such high criteria? You are so skinny, what kind of men do you expect? (*zheme name shoule, you shenme yaoqiune?* 这么那么瘦了，有什么要求呢?)" I was shocked. It was such a backward, narrow-minded thinking. I refused to marry that ugly man and I just desired returning to Dongguan as soon as possible [...]."

Xiao Hui, Taipei, 02.02.2017

Xiao Hui's experience demonstrates that since migrant workers are denied access to social recognition and economic exclusion from decent, stable, and fair employment opportunities in the city, migration through marriage with a Taiwanese native offers an option that women can contemplate in order not only to achieve hypergamy (Constable, 2003; Lu, 2005) but also to reach a place where status transformation can be negotiated. In this respect, differently from Beibei's case, the second generation of migrant women tends to develop their marital career individually and independently. Accordingly, encounters are not arranged in the rural areas by families or local matchmakers but autonomously constructed with Taiwanese natives that young factory girls can meet in the cities and the companies they are employed in. Therefore, in the new global cities (Sassen, 1995), the Taiwanese factories in Southern China become the sites for new interactions between translocal entrepreneurs and local workers, of which Kinge and Xiao Hui's case is emblematic.

Hence, the comparison between Beibei and Xiao Hui's marriage-mobility patterns and the ways these two women negotiated translocal encounters suggests that in the context of globalized global labor regimes, internal migration of rural workers and transnational translocal mobilities of businessmen and entrepreneurs frame new paths and sites for contacts and meetings. Implicitly, arranged marriages and brokerage practices become rare. Let me look at the following snapshot, which helps to understand the functioning and the social, economic transformation of a brokerage agency's activities in Taiwan.

January 31st 2017. Taoyuan (Taiwan).

In Taoyuan (Taiwan) I met 34-year-old, Anhui native Zi Yu, who works for a local brokerage agency (zhongjie 中介). While working as dagong in Jiangsu province, Zi Yu met her husband in a Taiwanese electronic factory in Kunshan, a city where many Taiwanese-owned industrial compounds were present. Once in Taiwan, facing obstacles in entering the Taiwanese labor market, Zi Yu was mobilized by the owner of the brokerage agency to help in mediating marriages between Taiwanese men and Chinese women. In the agency, one Vietnamese, one Cambodian, and one Indonesian woman were also employed. Zi Yu's migratory experiences in China have been numerous and her social capital is important: it constituted a resource for the agency to find and communicate with Chinese local partners in arranging marriages.

Brokerage being forbidden by law since 2008, the agency is hidden in an old building and located on the third floor.

At the main entrance, there is no doorbell: to open the door, I had to ring at number "999." Zi Yun came downstairs to meet me, and to make sure that I was alone and that nobody had followed me. We went upstairs. The interior of the agency looked rather austere: few sofas, two little tables, and some posters with wedding pictures. Zi Yu patiently showed me the catalogues of Chinese brides, illustrated with pictures and listing the bride price and the dowry, the sum of money to be included in the "red packet" (hong bao 红包)—the red envelope—as a gift to the family, together with the agency's fees. The potential bridegroom contacts the agency and explains his preferences in terms of country and ethnic origin.

However, Zi Yun explained that since 2012 when she had started collaborating with the agency, she has observed a progressive decrease of the number of brokered marriages between Chinese women and Taiwanese men. With a sarcastic but realistic tone, she explained:

> "Chinese girls look for their husbands by themselves and I am losing my job! Less and less girls accept their families matching them with men, and I succeed arranging less and less marriages during the last years [...] The fact is, Vietnamese and Indonesian girls are cheaper, and in Taiwan there is a strong economic crisis; Taiwanese men have no money for Chinese women [...] and they want a virgin! But where can you find a virgin today in China?! [...]."

Zi Yun, 34 years old, Anhui native, Taoyuan, 31.01.2017

Despite her irony and cold humor, Zi Yun's words indicate how nowadays young migrant women autonomously negotiate encounters with Taiwanese men inside the working place of the factories in Southern China. To illustrate this generational transformation, drawing on the 151 empirical cases collected, I scratch here a brief cartography of the ways through which women negotiated the encounter with a Taiwanese native which led, for a second time, to cross-border marriage migration from the Mainland to Taiwan. This elucidates the intimate link between the global and cosmopolitan dimensions of the Chinese city and its labor market and the possibility for translocal encounters.

Out of the 111 women belonging to the current generation of migrants, 100 met their future Taiwanese husbands autonomously at the factory they were working in (100/111). Only one met her husband autonomously in a nightclub in Kunshan city, Jiangsu province (1/111). Few of them used means of marriage intermediation, through brokerage (4/111) or online applications for matching and encounters (6/151).

Further, let me may observe the professions of the husbands who got married to this young generation of Chinese migrant women. Two elements deserve attention. First, it should be noted that there is a relation between the way women met their Taiwanese husband and his profession. What stands out is the fact that if women did not employ any marriage-intermediation practice (101/111), in most cases there is an evident link between women's and husbands' professions. The transnational couples studied who met without any form of intermediation, 100/101 derived from encounters inside Taiwanese delocalized factories in Southern China. Among them, 19/100 Taiwanese grooms were managers (*taishang* 台商), and 81/100 were high-skilled workers (*taigan* 台干).

In contrast, when looking at the 40 cases collected among older women belonging to the first generation of migrants, the situation appears to be different. Out of these 40 women, 38 have used brokerage practices to meet their future Taiwanese husband, and only 2 out of 40 women met him autonomously in the city they were working. Among the 38 cases of brokerage, 34 out of 38 used the intermediation of an agency (like the one Zi Yun worked for in Taoyuan), and 4 out of 38 were introduced to their future husband by a friend who, in turn, married to a Taiwanese man. The encounters did not take place in the Chinese global cities, but the future grooms temporarily travelled from Taiwan to the Mainland to get married in women's rural villages of origin before moving to Taiwan together. As suggested supra, most of first-generation women's husbands were from lower social classes: 32 out of 40 were local workers in Taiwan, 6 were taxi drivers, and 6 were unemployed.

In summary, the crossed examination of first and second generations women's cross-border marriage-migratory paths enables to identify three important comparative elements. First, the social inequalities and economic hierarchies which characterize migrant workers' mobility and labor experiences in the Chinese city have not varied over time. Both the first and the second generations of women experienced flexible, precarious, and unstable urban jobs. Thus, in their choice of marriage migration to Taiwan, they took into account the potential for hypergamy represented by marriage, which sustains the achievement of upward social mobility and economic independence and an urban status. However, the construction of cross-border mobilities has radically varied over time. This has followed the rhythms of globalization, of labor mobility, and of the economic transformations of the Chinese labor market, where Taiwanese enterprises have proliferated during the last 30 years. Therefore, the first generation of marriage-migrant women called on a precise marriage industry, and marriage was arranged by rural families. In contrast, for the young generation of Chinese migrants, the negotiation of the encounter and of marriage itself represents a form of individual affirmation and independence. Encounters and cross-border marriages are produced through the mobilization of individuals' social resources within the framework of the opportunity structure represented by the globalized dimension of the Chinese cities and companies.

In fine, lines of continuity between internal and cross-border mobilities emerge among the experiences of both generations of women. The making of rural-to-urban migratory paths as well as marriage migration to Taiwan only appear to be separated. The achievement of social, economic, and emotional repositionings are inscribed with similar motivations and need to be considered as a continuous experience. The urban living experience and the hardship of the industrial labor regimes in the factory might have lessened women's ambitions and aspirations because of the multiplication of moral conflicts among the labor regimes, the lack of opportunities of social and professional mobility, individuals' desires, and ambitions of upward social mobility. However, this is true only to a certain degree. As clearly stated by Xiao Hui, "modernity at large" (Appadurai, 1999) persists as a project of transformation which orients the future making of the careers, which are shaped through marital opportunities and cross-border mobilities to Taiwan.

7.6. Experiences of Cross-Border Migration to Taiwan: From Unpaid Reproductive Labor to Digital Entrepreneurship

Whether arranged by their rural families and agencies or negotiated independently from the social experience of factory work, marriage with a Taiwanese native represents the *conditio sine qua non* for migration for both first and second generations of women. Marriage is the institutional tool to enter Taiwanese territory legally, and it reveals how the dialectic between mobility and location are major concerns for biopolitics and governmentality. Undoubtedly, this becomes visible from the change in terms of status imposed on women from the Mainland by the Taiwanese legislation (Tsai and Hsiao, 2006; Lan, 2008; Cheng, 2013). Migrants newly position themselves as "spouses" (*peiou* 配偶) in the Taiwanese society and in its institutional system. By the same token, the ready equation between movement and freedom is highly challenged: cross-border mobility as a reaction and a response to social and economic injustices in Mainland China can generate new forms of precarity in Taiwan. New social, economic, and moral constraints are produced by the marriage-migratory industry (Hsia, 2015) and the mobility restrictions in terms of rights' attribution. This provokes new economic barriers and social obstacles to women's positioning, which challenge their settlement and installation patterns in Taiwan. When looking at Lilli's experience of arriving in Taiwan, the control exerted by the "mobility regime" (Glick Schiller and Salazar, 2013) on women's movements becomes discernible. At the airport, women undergo an interview, aimed at verifying the authenticity of the just-contracted marriage, as Lilli's case clarifies:

> "When I was on the flight, before take-off I had a double feeling of excitement and anxiety. I did not know where I was going, and I told myself whether I go further, or I go

back, but stepping into the plane I realised I had nothing to lose [...] But then, I started feeling confused [...] I was asked many questions by the police, and the same happened to my husband, but we were separated [...] they asked me about many documents [...] Suddenly I had the impression that they did not want me to stay in Taiwan [...] the Police was unfriendly [...]."

Lilli, 30 years old, Hunan native, Taipei, 07.02.2017

When flying to Taiwan, Lilli wished to succeed in hiding, or perhaps, even deleting her rural identity. Through marriage migration, she did not merely want to achieve her hypergamy objective. She aspired to reach a modern, independent, and urban status at the new place she was heading to. However, the imposition of the status of "spouse" to women points out the extent to which the "politics of imposed identity" (Ong, 1999) enforce a rigid definition of women's rights and roles. These are highly dependent on the marital regime which frames their movement. In practice, this means that the rights to residency and to work are obtained via the mediation of complex legal rules (Cheng, 2013), which render women legally dependent on their husbands.

The above-mentioned 1992 Act Governing Relations between the People of Taiwan and the Mainland Area (*taiwan diqu yu dalu diqu renmin guanxi tiaoli* 台湾地区与大陆地区人民关系条例) and its progressive amendments (1996, 2002, 2009) have so far regulated and directed Mainland spouses' status and rights in Taiwan. Taiwan's administration has reservations about the entry and settlement of Chinese spouses. Until 2009, Chinese women were not allowed to work until they had acquired residency status (*juliu* 居留). Their right to work (*gongzuo quan* 工作权) was linked to their right to reside. Residence could be obtained two years after the first entry to Taiwan, which meant that the first stages of their stay were qualified as "visitation" (*tingliu* 停留), and later, "family reunification" (*jiating tuanju* 家庭团聚). The reforms of 2002 and of 2009 abolished these temporary stages, and Chinese spouses' ingress was granted upon the permission of residing, hence of working.

If institutional changes occur, what requires investigation is the way these have shaped and contributed to re-framing women's positioning and the making of their social and professional careers in

Taiwan. Unavoidably, over the years, the access to the Taiwanese familiar order and to the society as well as the economic integration in the labor market have been following the formal changes of such migratory policies. In this light, how did social, biographical, and professional careers and experiences change? Once again, a crossed examination of the continuities and variations between two generations of women might elucidate the imbrication among the social and economic opportunities and constraints' structure and the practices of the actors, which lead to the transformation of situations.

Mi Xiang, 58 years old, rural Guanxi native, has been living in Taiwan since 1998. She belongs to the first generation of migrant women since she was born in 1961. After a few years of pluri-migration and labor experiences in different cities of Guangdong and Fujian provinces on the Mainland, a friend arranged a marriage with a Taiwanese man and she arrived in Taipei, where she is currently residing and working. Pregnant at her arrival, she immediately went to live with her husband's parents, where she performed domestic work, taking care of the house, of her husband's younger brother as well as her parents-in-law. Initially deprived of the working permission, Mi Xiang was excluded from the formal sector of the labor market:

> "When I arrived here, my husband told me that I didn't need to work, that I just had to take care of his parents and his daughter (he had previously divorced). This is not what I planned to do in Taiwan [...], this was not what I imagined for my future life when I left the Mainland [...] It was horrible; I spent the first three years taking care of his mother who was sick and who was not even able to wash her ass. I had to help my husband's younger brother to cook lunch and dinner, I had to wash his clothes and clean his shoes... I was pregnant and tired, yet I had to wake up early, I prepared breakfast, then I went to the street market to help the sister of my husband to sell tofu, then I went back home to prepare lunch, then back to the market until night. Then, back home to cook dinner. After that, I had to take care of my husband who came back home late at night after work and who wanted to make love. Whereas I didn't want to. I felt like a slave [...] Do you know how many times I cried alone in the toilets late at night? [...]

> My husband's parents have passed away and... I feel a bit
> relieved [...] I am still not independent, I have never worked
> here in Taiwan [...] When I arrived, I did not have the right
> to work... today... I do not know... but I think that things
> will not change; I will remain at home in the future [...]."

Mi Xiang, 58 years old, Guanxi native, Taipei, 22.12.2016

This narration convincingly illustrates how, as a foreign spouse, as
a mother, and as a daughter-in-law, Mi Xiang was required to provide
reproductive labor, i.e. biological reproduction as well as the work
necessary for the reproduction of the family (Wang and Hsiao, 2009;
Parreñas, 2011). Deprived of a working permission, she was confined
to her home, cleaning her parents-in-law's lodgings, preparing food,
and caring for children and elders.

Institutionally speaking, most of second-generation women who
migrated to Taiwan before the Reform of 2009 have also experienced
denial of access to jobs. However, the making of their social and
professional careers within the familiar order and the labor market
seems to be rather different compared to the ones of the older generation. Heqin, 32 years old, Chongqing native, arrived in Taiwan in
2007. Being low-skilled and provided with only weak social resources,
in terms of social networks, as well as knowledge of the employment
opportunities in Taipei, she started walking around the city, stopping
by restaurants, little shops or beauty centers, looking for a position.
Her status did not enable her to work, so she faced several refusals,
which became a source of stress, anxiety, and frustration. Stopping
by a street-corner restaurant, she begged the Taiwanese owner to give
her a chance. She was asked for the working card (*gongzuo zheng* 工
作证) that she did not have. The restaurant tenant suggested that
she stay hidden in the kitchen to wash dishes and clean the floor.
Through a tacit and fragile agreement, the boss gave her some money
at the end of every week:

> "I did not really have clear tasks to do, I did everything
> that was necessary [...] I washed the dishes, I cleaned the
> floor, if some food was missing, I went shopping for it [...]
> I stayed at the restaurant, inside the kitchen from six in
> the morning until late at night, even if I was not always
> busy with stuff [...] sometimes, I just stood there waiting

for the boss to tell me what to do [...] we did not really
fix a salary [...] at the end of each week, or every ten days
for example, the boss gave me something [...] He told me
to stay in the kitchen since police controls were frequent
at that time: if the police came and saw me without the
working card, I risked expulsion and the boss risked a huge
fine and serious problems [...]."

Heqin, 32 years old, Chongqing native, Taipei, 09.01.2017

These two examples convincingly demonstrate that the impact of
the lack of working right ripples through from the public sphere of
the workplace to the marital intimacy of the private home. On these
occasions, work as a right does not just impart the implications of
equality and sameness but also constitutes a social relation whereby
inclusion and exclusion can be experienced by a migrant. Notwithstanding, the significance attributed to work and to the making of a
professional career diverges between the two generations of Mainland
spouses. Different from Mi Xiang, who internalized her wifely and
motherly duties and accepted her role by staying at home, younger
Heqin contested (Steiner, 2005) the formal legal ban which inhibited her to work and "negotiated with illegality" (Ambrosini, 2008),
seeking a job in the "grey" zones of the local labor market, where
restrictions are porous and less likely to occur.

Heqin's negotiations demonstrate how the younger generation of Chinese migrants deploys a stronger "capacity to aspire"
(Appadurai, 1999). The multiplication of labor experiences in internal China during pluri-migrations, leading to the capitalization of
broader repertories of social and moral resources, tacit knowledge and
skills sustains the identification of novel channels towards employment. Crucially, as during the previous factory labor experiences, the
younger generation of migrants from the Mainland associates work
and employment with autonomy and economic independence. Marriage migration as means towards hypergamy has therefore varied not
only in terms of individual significance but also of social and professional practices. In contrast to the older generation, the very process
of negotiation of cross-border mobility by younger Mainland migrants
sustains the mobilization of "reflexive competences" (Beck, 2003;
Roulleau-Berger, 2014). These are composed of a specific knowledge
and understating of situations, savoir-faire, and moral competences,

which during settlement in Taiwan, support the identification of novel strategies for the making of upward social mobility and an autonomous, modern status. In this regard, the younger generation has capitalized larger repertories of social and economic competences during labor migration on the Mainland, which implemented the social and moral resources that can be rekindled after remigration to Taiwan to identify strategies to cope with inequalities. As for the older generation, a more limited number of migratory and labor experiences before marriage and settlement in Taiwan reduced the scope of the repertories of resources to mobilize and limited the possibility to negotiate with the inequalities and hierarchies characterizing Taiwanese society, familiar and institutional orders as well as the labor market.

Such opportunities are likely to be arranged mainly within the metropolitan space of the city of Taipei. In this respect, if looking at women's spatial relocation after remigration to Taiwan, an interesting element catches my attention. In Taiwan, the first generation of Mainland spouses mainly resides in rural areas (38 out of 40 informants), while most of the younger generation of women (102 over 111 migrants) live in the capital city of Taipei. This spatial and generational gap might be explainable by the above-mentioned divergence of women husbands' professions and social status. Younger generation women's husbands were from lower-income social classes and resided in the countryside, where the real estate prices are lower. On the contrary, married to managers and businessmen, the younger generation of Mainland spouses can enjoy the city life of Taipei, where their husbands predominantly live. Presumably, in the capital city of Taipei, job opportunities are more numerous and more easily negotiable despite the social and economic exclusion Chinese women endure.

The policy revision of 2009 provided women with immediate access to the right to work after their arrival in Taiwan. Nevertheless, despite the removal of legal barriers, the labor market still presents difficulties of access and integration for low-qualified migrants from the Mainland. Previously, working as factory girls in Mainland China, women are equipped with poor education level and weak qualification since their previous working experiences, despite their multiplicity, are reduced to industrial production activities. Although they do have legal access to the formal job market, there are still, and yet again, relegated to disqualifying employments in economic segments where precarity, flexibility, and instability are strong. They mainly work, part time or full time, in manufacturing (43/151), catering (37/151), or care (16/151); they also follow gendered professions in the field of cosmetics, hairdressing and make-up (35/151), or massage (21/151). Digging into these numbers, it becomes clear that women who are employed in the field of manufacturing and in the care sector are mainly from the first generation and reside in rural areas (Zhudong, Hukou, Taoyuan, etc.): 38 out of 43 in manufacturing and 13 over 16 in care work. In contrast, most women who perform jobs in the field of cosmetics or catering are from the second generation and live and work in the urban areas, principally in the city of Taipei. The structure of the market, the labor offer and demand as well as the possibility to negotiate opportunities are thus different between rural and urban areas and lead to the development of diverse professional patterns and economic activities.

For instance, second-generation Xiao Ping, 32 years old, Hubei native, has been working in the field of cosmetics for three years since her arrival. While narrating her professional experiences, she often mentioned differences in terms of remuneration, of tasks she was asked to perform, or even of working hours compared to her Taiwanese colleagues. She was even asked to buy lunch for her boss and colleagues every day or to go shopping for her boss' wife. I met her in February 2017 and again in April 2018. Within a year, she had changed seven employments. Every time, she wished to find a better working environment or a higher salary, but she often faced similar obstacles:

> "I am now working near the train station, I arrived here a couple of months ago [...] since you were gone, I had changed many times because I was upset [...] Today, same problems as usual, I am so sick of this country! We are five women working there and I am the only Chinese. The shop is small, we are not numerous, so we are very busy [...] This new boss looked nice to me at the beginning, that is why I decided to work there [...] But she keeps me working overtime, she says that I am lazy, and it is because I am lazy during the day that I have to work more. I think I will leave again, but, you know, this keep on changing job process is exhausting [...] and this place is quite far from

my children's school [...] I told the boss that this is unfair, but she said that it was not true [...] Taiwanese employees get 30 000 NTD per month, but I get only 20,000 [...] she says it is because they work more and that if I am not happy with this job, I can leave and look for another one."

Xiao Ping, 32 years old, Hubei native, Taipei, 03.05.2018

When the access, the entrance, or the permanence in the diverse segments of the local labor market are inhibited, difficult, or limited, the younger generation of women proves its capacity to identify alternative possibilities by exploring new and different markets, increasingly overstepping local and physical boundaries. Hence, inner frontiers built to exclude migrants from employment can be challenged, contested, and transgressed through the mobilization of a plurality of resources and competences. Economic precarity and unfair treatment at work concurrently represent a factor of anxiety, stress, and preoccupation for Mainland migrants, but these obstacles can also become the basis for inventing new, creative, alternative employments. These migrants exit the formal segments of the labor market and enter novel worlds where hierarchies and inequalities are less likely to occur. Therefore, previously capitalized repertories of knowledge and competences can be rekindled while seeking a "decent place" (Margalit, 1996) in the market. Together with newly capitalized social resources, these can lead to innovative labor experiences and employment opportunities. Let's look at how 22-year-old, Chongqing native Wenfeng invented a new job. This is produced and performed at the crossroad among social networks, economic exclusion, and an ingenious use of the digital application *WeChat*.

Inside her little kitchen in Luzhou, in the suburbs of Taipei, Wenfeng prepared all the ingredients to cook some juefen 厥粉 *(spicy Sichuanese noodles). Wenfeng looked skilful. She cut carrots and peppers quickly, even though she was not a professional cook. Before migrating to Taiwan, she had worked at a textile factory in the south of China (Guangdong province). Sick of the repetitive food in the canteen of the factory, she used to go eating at her uncle's restaurant nearby: she observed the preparation of dishes, she tasted food and memorized the recipes. While washing soya beans, Wenfeng opened her smartphone and posted some pictures of the dishes she had just prepared to the WeChat group "The Sisters from Chongqing" with the caption*:

> Wenfeng: "Who would like to order some food today? (*jintian you ren yao ding bu?* 今天有人要定不?)"; "for dinner, I will cook some spicy noodles for you. But if there are few people and if it rains, I will not go out. (*wo jintian wanshang chao xiao juefen qing dajia chi weidao o. ren shao xiayu de hua wo keneng bu hui qu o.* 我今天晚上炒小厥粉请大家吃味道哦。人少下雨的话我可能不会去哦。)"

Immediately, the WeChat group's participants animated and, progressively, every woman ordered a portion:

> Heqin: "Wenfeng, a portion of juefen, please. (*Wenfeng, yi fen juefen xiexie.* 文风，一份厥粉谢谢。)"

> Miao Miao: "Are juefen very spicy? Can I have some not too spicy? (*juefen hui la ma? keyi bu la ma?* 厥粉会辣吗?可以不辣吗?)"

Wenfeng reacted quickly and she typed on the keyboard: "that is possible (keyi a 可以啊)."

Fujin, member of the group, simultaneously ordered food and made advertisement for her newly arrived bras:

> "Wenfeng, dear, please, I also want some juefen, very spicy if possible. Oh! I have not eaten anything today, I am so busy. (*Wenfeng, qinai de, mafan ni zai lai yi fen juefen. aya! jintian shenme dou meiyou chi, wo chaoji mang.* 文风，亲爱的，麻烦你再来一份厥粉。啊呀! 今天什么都没有吃，我超级忙。)"

In the meanwhile, food was ready and Wenfeng could add some spicy sauce, typical from her native province, Sichuan.

Wenfeng claimed that the spicy sauce was the key ingredient since it produced a specific taste. When she migrated to Taiwan, Wenfeng brought with her previously capitalized knowledge and savoir-faire, here represented by the culinary traditions of her hometown, that she cleverly uses to survive as she cannot find a job in Taipei. Hence, the food she cooked was to be sold to several Mainland fellow migrants residing in Taipei.

After having properly seasoned her noodles, Wenfeng charged the food on her little scooter and got ready for distribution among the Chinese sisters living in her neighborhood who ordered their dinner on WeChat.

Wenfeng explained in the following way the rationale of her activity:

> "I kept on being fired at work, and I felt very depressed [...] When I was not maltreated by my colleagues, then it was my husband who did not want me to work. His mother wanted me to get pregnant, but I still do not want to, I am too young [...] My husband works all day long and I feel so lonely at home, do not know what to do. I have no money to go shopping or to study, so I stay at home, but the more I stay at home, the more I feel depressed [...] That's why I started cooking, this is the only thing I can actually do [...] I first cooked traditional food for myself, since I missed home, but later, I realised that other sisters also miss home and used to cook traditional food, but they work and do not have much time [...] So, I told myself! Let's cook for the other sisters, and let's sell food to them [...] I feel less bored and I can also earn some money [...]."

Wenfeng, Taipei, 15.02.2017

Not surprisingly, when the access to the formal labor market is obstructed, entrepreneurship turns out to be an important tool for migrants to negotiate an employment and to earn an income. This does not represent a novelty. Several studies (Tarrius, 2002; Portes, 2003; Ambrosini, 2008; Waldinger, 2008) have pointed out how auto-employment and entrepreneurship help migrants to adjust to the situations of vulnerability which characterize their professional positioning and to cope with the market's disadvantages in terms of underemployment or lack of recognition (Kloosterman and Rath, 2001; Martinelli, 2004). Yet, what seems curious is that such economic practices are produced on and performed through digital platforms, and more specifically, the online application *WeChat*. This digital social media platform is popular in the Mainland. It is broadly used as an infrastructure for communication and information exchange as well as a social network to chat and keep in touch. Notwithstanding, in Taiwan, the social use of this platform is extended by migrant women to the sphere of business and commerce, since it frames novel economic activities. The young generation of Mainland migrants make good use of the information and communication technologies (ITC) to negotiate their social and professional positioning in the unfair context of life and work in Taiwan. Both the first and the second generations of migrant women are provided with the cultural resources to handle and operate the digital *WeChat*. They had formerly learnt its use in the Mainland, where this application is commonly mobilized, and they daily operate on it to keep in touch with family and friends in loco. Still, only the younger generation reveals the ability to negotiate a novel scope for this digital platform, turning it into a space for business practices. This is what Wenfeng and her Mainland fellows did within the supra presented chat group.

Wenfeng's case decisively demonstrates that entrepreneurship can also be placed on the digital level of the virtual world, where a new market is constructed. Social resources, knowledge, and digital competences are thereby creatively mobilized by a young "connected migrant" (Diminescu, 2008) seeking a stable income and a decent employment, aspiring to the recognition of her skills and her social status, and fighting against feelings of loneliness, solitude, and nostalgia. Among the 111 second-generation women I identified in Taiwan, 108/111 were part of a few *WeChat* groups and were in conversation with other Mainland migrants residing in Taiwan. Interestingly, 104 out of these 108 had used this application for heterogeneous economic transactions, which include selling or buying goods and commodities at least once. To the very contrary, among the 40 women belonging to the first generation, only three had made use of a digital application for business purposes. They claimed that they broadly felt less familiar with such a technological device and the opportunities it generates in terms for sociality and potential commerce. Older women did not seem to know much about the potential for economic transactions and money transfer provided by *WeChat*, which sustains commercial practices. The two payment functions, the "Red packet" (*hongbao* 红包) and "Transfer" (*zhuanzhang* 转账), permit a simultaneous online money transfer. Thus, when Wenfeng's clients placed an order inside a chat group, they could immediately and simultaneously pay the corresponding amount of money to her.

Astutely, the application *WeChat* is transformed into a tool for business by the young generation of migrants who is endowed with the social and cultural resources to handle e-commerce. This is made possible through a simultaneous translation of skills and competences previously capitalized in the Mainland during pluri-migration and multiple professional experiences, which the older generation is not equipped with. Wenfeng was a factory girl, employed in several urban factories in the Mainland. Nevertheless, despite her young age and her poor educational level, her professional experiences multiplied. She had also been working in small shops or restaurants in Shenzhen or Canton, where she could acquire repertories of savoir-faire, which later proved to be crucial for her survival in Taiwan. It is thus thanks to a previous labor experience in a restaurant of Canton that she could learn how to cook the traditional food that she now sells online in Taiwan. Hence, such skills were rekindled in Taiwan on a physical but also digital level of novel economic practices and were performed on a new digitalized scale for action. Through her business, Wenfeng proved her capacity to mix her former knowledge and individual resources with the new social resources she could capitalize via her networks of fellow Mainland Chinese in Taiwan. This became fundamental for the success of her business, which shifted from the physical to the digital dimension, the two being highly entangled.

In view of this, Wenfeng's e-commerce synthesizes a juxtaposition among inequalities in the labor market, a novel use of digital platforms and economic processes. It elucidates a crucial transformation in terms of economic practices developed by the younger generation of migrant women to overcome the long-lasting presence of inequalities and hierarchies in the Taiwanese labor market. This shows the extent to which the multiplication of mobility patterns and professional experiences in the Mainland brings about the capitalization of important repertories of social, economic, and cultural resources, knowledge, and competences which can be rekindled and remodeled after remigration to Taiwan to cope with a condition of precarity and of social and professional disqualification. Comparatively speaking, the older generation of migrant women is less equipped with such repertories of resources and savoir-faire and thus less inclined to contest an inegalitarian economic order through the exploration of alternative professional and business paths toward recognition and financial independence. By the same token, online business and virtual entrepreneurship constitute a means to gain autonomy and self-esteem for women through fair work, decent employment, and economic gain. It contributes to the negotiation of a novel social positioning in Taiwan by the young generation of "connected" migrants who show an increased capacity to aspire.

7.7. Conclusion

It has been suggested that it is possible to identify lines of continuity and of discontinuity in rural-to-urban and cross-border migratory patterns through a crossed-analysis of two generations of Mainland Chinese women's mobility experiences and economic practices. Such a crossed-perspective on the first-and-second generation women's migrations enables me to pinpoint broader social and economic transformations characterizing contemporary China. Such changes do not become visible through statistical examinations and quantitative data analysis. Yet, they do exist and represent a fundamental component of the contemporary mutations of migration patterns. In this light, the proposed qualitative scrutiny of internal and cross-border mobilities, through the study of migrants' biographical, social, and professional careers helps to identify the continuum and discontinuum occurring in their migratory paths over the last decades.

The temporal, spatial, and scalar variations in terms of social and professional practices observable through women's mobility careers are embedded in, and in turn, sustain larger-scale social and economic transformations of Chinese society and its labor market since the 1980s. This chapter presented such an examination from the life experiences of the first and the second generations of Mainland Chinese rural migrant women, engaged in a double-step migration: from the countryside to the city in Mainland China and from the Mainland to Taiwan. By focusing on the changes that have occurred regarding marriage practices, as well as social and economic experiences in the Chinese and the Taiwanese labor market, this chapter showed the extent to which globalization and modernity have contributed to the transformation of migratory paths as well as of actors' biographical and professional careers. These are nowadays increasingly oriented towards the achievement of urbanity, economic independence, and upward social mobility by young migrants. They show their ability to mobilize innovative and inventive tools to achieve their projects, like digital technologies and online applications.

To answer the questions put forward at the beginning of this chapter, I found that instead of being an "inevitable process" (Li, 2003), as it was the case for the first generation of migrants, contemporary migratory and marital patterns are increasingly constructed on an individual's "capacity to aspire" (Appadurai, 1999). After several years of temporary labor in Chinese large coastal cities, young migrant women remigrate to Taiwan through marriage, seeking an autonomous, modern, and independent status.

Therefore, different from the first generation of migrant workers, young women's urban and labor experiences in internal China multiply. Far from being a familiar imposition (Tong, 2012), cross-border marriage migration is, at present, autonomously and independently negotiated by women who identify the opportunity for transnational encounters in the global city (Sassen, 1995). Despite the reproduction of social inequalities and economic hierarchies from the Mainland Chinese to the Taiwanese society and their labor markets, the pluralization of mobility experiences and the capitalization of repertories of knowledge and savoir-faire enable the current generation of women to negotiate with social and economic barriers in order to achieve the autonomy project. Accordingly, the strategies of negotiation with the economic marginalization characterizing the Taiwanese labor market were addressed in this study. The examination of entrepreneurship and e-commerce produced by young migrants is representative of the tactics designed to claim a decent place in an inegalitarian labor market and to reposition themselves in the society of arrival. This implies a "contestation" (Steiner, 2005) of an inegalitarian social and economic order and the use of digital tools available in the contemporary social world.

The mutually constitutive dimension of migrations and socioeconomic transformations illustrates the fact that the relationship between individual experiences and generational shifts is not linear but rather discursive. The continuum and discontinuum of the two generations of migrants' experiences cannot be dispelled without a holistic understanding, simultaneously grounded on the actors' subjectivity and practices, as well as on larger-scale social and economic transformations of contemporary Chinese society. Yet, a crossed analysis of the generational variations and transformations of migrations offered a viewpoint from which to understand the transition of Chinese society toward a globalized horizon, the transformation of its labor market, of the urban landscape and, broadly, of capitalism.

References

Aglietta, M. and G. Bai (2012). *China's Development. Capitalism and Empire*, Routledge. London.

Akers, D. S. (1967). "On Measuring the Marriage Squeeze," *Demography*, 4, 907–924.

Aldrich, H. E. and R. Waldinger (1990). "Ethnicity and Entrepreneurship," *Annual Review of Sociology*, 16, 111–135.

Ambrosini, M. (2008). *Un'altra globalizzazione. Le sfide delle migrazioni transnazionali*, Il Mulino. Bologna.

Appadurai, Q. (1999). *Modernity at Large. The Cultural Consequences of Globalisation*, Cambridge: Polity Press.

Bakhtin, M. M. (2008). *The Dialogic Imagination*, Michael Holquist (Ed.), Austin and London: University of Texas Press.

Beck, U. (2003). *The Cosmopolitan Vision*, Cambridge: Polity Press.

Becker, H. (1963). "Outsiders," *Studies in the Sociology of Deviance*. New York: Free Press of Glencoe.

Chang, K.-S. (1999). "Compressed Modernity and Its Discontents: South Korean Society in Transition," *Economy and Society*, 28, 30–55.

Chen, C.-J. J. (2015). "Taiwanese business in China: Encountering and coping with risks," アジア研究 *(Asian Studies)*, 60, 31–47.

Cheng, I. (2013). "Making Foreign Women the Mother of Our Nation: The Exclusion and Assimilation of Immigrant Women in Taiwan," *Asian Ethnicity*, 14, 157–169.

Constable, N. (2003). *Romance on a Global Stage. Pen Pals, Virtual Ethnography and 'Mail-Order' Marriages*, Berkeley: University of California Press.

Diminescu, D. (2008). "The Connected Migrant: An Epistemological Manifesto," *Social Science Information*, 47, 565–579.

Friedman, S. L. (2010). "Marital Immigration and Graduated Citizenship: Post Naturalization Reflections on Mainland Spouses in Taiwan," *Pacific Affairs*, 83, 73–93.

Gallagher, M. E. (2005). *Contagious Capitalism. Globalisation and the Politics of Labour in China*, Princeton: Princeton University Press.

Geertz, C. (1973). *The Interpretation of Cultures: Selected Essays*, New York: Basic Books.

Glaser, B. G. and A. L. Strauss (1967). *The Discovery of Grounded Theory. Strategies for Qualitative Research*, New Brunswick and London: Aldine Transaction.

Harvey, D. (2007). *A Brief History of Neoliberalism*, Oxford: Oxford University Press.

Hine, C. (2015). *Ethnography for the Internet. Embedded, Embodied and Every Day*, London: Bloomsbury.

Hsia, H.-C. (2015). "Reproduction Crisis, Illegality and Migrant Women Under Capitalist Globalisation: The Case of Taiwan," S. L. Friedman and P. Mardhavi (Eds.). *Migrant Encounters. Intimate Labour, the State, and Mobility Across Asia.* Philadelphia: University of Pennsylvania Press, pp. 160–183.

Hsiao, H.-H. M. (2018). "Taishang in China and Southeast Asia: Culture and Politics of Taiwanese Transnational Capital," *Asia Review*, 72, 163–180.

Hsiao, H.-H. M. and H.-Z. H-Z. Wang (2002). "Social Capital or Human Capital? Professionals in Overseas Taiwanese Firms," *Journal of Contemporary Asia*, 32, 346–362.

Kloosterman, R. and J. Rath (2001). "Immigrant Entrepreneurs in Advanced Economies: Mixed Embeddedness Further Explored," *Journal of Ethnic and Migratory Studies*, 27, 189–201.

Lan, P. C. (2008). "Migrant Women's Bodies as Boundary Makers: Reproductive Crisis and Sexual Control in the Ethnic Frontiers of Taiwan," *Signs*, 33, 833–861.

Lee, K. (1998). *Gender and the South China Miracle. Two Worlds of Factory Women*, Berkley: University of California Press.

Li, L. (2003). "'向城市移民: 一个不可逆转的过程' (Migrations Towards the Cities: An Inevitable Process)," In P. Li (Ed.). 农民工:中国进程农民工的经济社会分析 (*Social and Economic Analysis of Migrants' Arrival in the Cities*), 社会科学文献出版社. Beijing: Social Science Literature Press, pp. 65–76.

Li, P. (2013). "The World's Largest Labour Force Migration," In L. Roulleau-Berger and P. Li (Eds.), *China's Internal and International Migration.* London and New York: Routledge, pp. 20–25.

Li, P. and F. Tian (2010). "Influence of Human Capital of the Socioeconomic Status in the Chinese Labour Markets," *Chinese Journal of Sociology*, 30, 69–87.

Liu, S. (2008). "Structure des droits de propriété et mécanisme du changement dans les entreprises de bourg et de village chinois," In L. Roulleau-Berger, Y. Guo, P. Li, S. Liu (Eds.), *La Nouvelle Sociologie Chinoise.* CNRS Editions, pp. 183–215.

Lu, M. C. W. (2005). "Commercially Arranged Marriage Migration: Case Studies of Cross-border Marriages in Taiwan," *Indian Journal of Gender Studies*, 12(2–3), 275–303. DOI: 10.1177/097152150501200206.

Marcus, G. E. (1995). "Ethnography in/of the World System: The Emergence of Multi-sited Ethnography," *Annual Review of Anthropology*, 24, 95–117.

Margalit, A. (1996). *The Decent Society*, Cambridge, MA and London: Harvard University Press.

Martinelli, A. (2004). "The Context of Entrepreneurship: The Case of Ethnic Entrepreneurs," *The Tocqueville Review*, 25, 81–108.

Miller, D. (2010). *Stuff*, Cambridge: Polity Press.

MoI (1993). "Ministry of the Interior of the People Republic of China (Taiwan). Numbers of Foreign Spouses and Mainland Spouses (including those from Hong Kong and Macao) by Immigration Status (外籍配偶人大(含港澳)配偶人件分 (in Chinese)) (Migrations Towards the Cities: An Inevitable Process)."

MoI (2010). "Ministry of the Interior of the People Republic of China (Taiwan). Numbers of Foreign Spouses and Mainland Spouses (including those from Hong Kong and Macao) by Immigration Status (外籍配偶人大(含港澳)配偶人件分 (in Chinese)) (Migrations Towards the Cities: An Inevitable Process)."

MoI (2017). "Ministry of the Interior of the People Republic of China (Taiwan). Numbers of Foreign Spouses and Mainland Spouses (including those from Hong Kong and Macao) by Immigration Status (外籍配偶人大(含港澳)配偶人件分 (in Chinese)) (Migrations Towards the Cities: An Inevitable Process)."

Momesso, L. (2016). "From someone, to no-one, to a new-one: A subjective view of Taiwan's immigration policies in the context of multiculturalism," In J. Damm and I. Cheng (Eds.), *Berliner China-Hefte— Chinese History and Society*. Special Issue, Taiwan: Self Versus Other, 48, 24–36.

Oi, J. C. (1999). *Rural China Takes Off. Institutional Foundations of Economic Reform*, Berkeley: University of California Press.

Ong, A. (1999). *Flexible Citizenship*, Cambridge: Polity Press.

Ossman, S. (2013). *Moving Matters: Paths of Serial Migration*, Stanford: Stanford University Press.

Parreñas, R. (2011). *Servants of Globalisation. Women, Migration and Domestic Work*, Stanford: Stanford University Press.

Portes, A. (2003). "Theoretical Convergences and Empirical Evidence in the Study of Immigrant Transnationalism," *International Migration Review*, 37, 814–892.

Pun, N. (1999). "Becoming Dagongmei. The Politics of Identity and Difference in Reform China," *The China Journal*, 42, 1–19.

Pun, N. (2005). *Made in China: Women Factory Workers in a Global Workplace*, London: Duke University Press.

Pun, N. (2016). *Migrant Labour in China: Post-Socialist Transformations*, Cambridge and Malden: Polity Press.

Roulleau-Berger, L. (2013). "Migrations, Plural Economies and New Stratifications in Europe and in China," In L. Roulleau-Berger and P. Li (Eds.), *China's Internal and International Migrations*. London and New York: Routledge, pp. 259–274.

Roulleau-Berger, L. (2014). "New Internal Boundaries, Intermediate Spaces and Cosmopolitism in Chinese Cities," In N. Aveline-Dubach, S. C. Jou and H-H. M. Hsiao (Eds.), *Globalisation and New Intra-Urban Dynamics in Asian Cities*. Taipei: National Taiwan University Press, pp. 353–377.

Roulleau-Berger, L. (2018). "Temporalités, espaces et individu compressé en Chine," In L. Roulleau-Berger Et N. Liu (Eds.), *Numéro Spécial "Compressed Modernity et Temporalités Chinoises."* Temporalités.

Sassen, S. (1995). *The Global City: New York, London and Tokyo*, Princeton: Princeton University Press.

Sassen, S. (1998). *Globalisation and Its Discontents*, New York: New Press.

Sassen, S. (2014). *Expulsions—Brutality and Complexity of the Global Economy*, Harvard: Harvard University Press.

Schubert, G. and K. Shu (2010). "Taishang as a Factor Shaping Taiwan's Domestic Policies," In S. Tsang (Ed.), *The Vitality of Taiwan*. Basingstoke: Palgrave Macmillan, pp. 139–163.

Sellami, H. (2013). *Les Taïwanais en Chine*, France: Presses Universitaires De Rennes. Rennes.

Shen, Y. (2006). "'社会转型与工人阶层的再形成' (Social Transition and the Reconstruction of the Working Class)," *Sociological research*, 2, 7–24.

Shen, Y. and X. Wen (2014). "Recherches sociologiques sur les transformations des marchés du travail Chinois: Théories et méthodes," In L. Roulleau-Berger Et S. Liu (Eds.), *Sociologies Economiques Française et Chinoise: Regards Croisés*. Lyon: ENS Editions, p. 143.

Siu, H. F. (2007). "Grounding Displacement: Uncivil Urban Spaces in Post-Reform South China," *American Ethnologist*, 34, 329–350.

Solinger, D. (1999). *Contesting Citizenship in Urban China. Peasant Migrants, the State and the Logic of the Market*, Berkeley: University of California Press.

Steiner, P. (2005). "The Market According to Economic Sociology," *Revue Européenne Des Sciences Sociales*. XLIII-132, 31–64. DOI: 10.4000/ress.326.

Sun, L. (2003). "失衡: 断裂社会的运作逻辑 (Imbalance: The Operational Logic of a Ruptured Society)." Beijing: 社会科学文献出版社 (Social Science Documentation Press).

Tarrius, A. (2002). *La mondialisation par le bas: Les nouveaux nomades de l'économie souterraine*, Paris: Ballard.

Tong, X. (2012). "Three Decades of Chinese Women. State, Family, Women: Comments on the Last Two Decades of Women or Gender Related Sociological Studies," In L. Roulleau-Berger and P. Li (Eds.), *European and Chinese Sociology: A New Dialogue*. Leiden: Brill, pp. 309–317.

Tsai, Y.-H. and H.-H. M. Hsiao (2006). "The Non-governmental Organisations for Foreign Workers and Foreign Spouses in Taiwan: A Portrayal," *Yatai Yanjiu Luntan Di Sanshisan Qi* 洲研究 第三十三期, 1–31.

Tsay, C.-L. (2004). "Marriage Migration of Women from China and Southeast Asia to Taiwan," In G. W. Jones and K. Ramdas (Eds.), *Untying the Knot: Ideal and Reality in Asian Marriage*. Singapore: Asia Research Institute, National University of Singapore, pp. 173–191.

Tseng, Y.-F. (2008). "Marriage Migration to East Asia. Current Issues and Propositions in Making Comparisons," In M. Lu and W. S. Yang (Eds.), *Asian Cross-Border Marriage Migration. Demographic Patterns and Social Issues*. Amsterdam: Amsterdam University Press, pp. 31–45.

Tseng, Y.-F. (2014). "How Do Identities Matter? Taiwanese Cultural Workers in China," In J. Wang (Ed.), *Border Crossing in Greater China: Production, Commodity and Identity*. New York: Routledge, pp. 189–201.

Tseng, Y.-F. and J. Wu (2011). "Reconfiguring Citizenship and Nationality: Dual Citizenship of Taiwanese Migrants in China," *Citizenship Studies*, 15, 265–282.

Urry, J. (2007). *Mobilities*, Cambridge: Polity Press.

Waldinger, R. (2008). "Between 'Here' and 'There': Immigrants Cross-Border Activities and Loyalties," *International Migration Review*, 42, 3–29.

Wang, H.-Z. and H.-H. M. Hsiao (2009). *Cross-Border Marriages with Asian Characteristics*, Taipei: Academia Sinica.

Xiang, B., B. S. A. Yeoh, and M. Toyota (2012). *Return: Nationalizing transnational mobility in Asia*, Durham: Duke University Press.

Yan, H. (2008). *New Masters, New Servants: Migration, Development and Women Workers in China*, London: Duke University Press.

Yang, C. (2006). "Divergent Hybrid Capitalisms in China: Hong-Kong and Taiwanese Electronic Clusters in Dongguan," *Economic Geography*, 83, 395–420.

Yeoh, B. S. (2016). "Migration and Gender Politics in Southeast Asia," *Migration, Mobility and Displacement*, 2(1), 74–88. DOI: 10.18357/mmd21201615022.

Zani, B. (2018). "Gendered Transnational Ties and Multipolar Economies. Chinese Migrant Women Wechat Commerce in Taiwan," *International Migration*, In Cheng and L. Momesso (2019). Special issue. Rethinking transnationalism in the global world: Contested state, borders, society and the people in between, *International Migration*, p. 57.

Zani, B. (2021). *Women Migrants in Southern China and in Taiwan. Mobilities, Digital Economies and Emotions*. Routledge: Abingdon and New York.

Part III
China's Financial Institutions and Financial Integration

Chapter 8

Chinese Presence in Africa: A Panel Smooth Threshold Regression Approach*

Ibrahim Nana

*Université Clermont Auvergne, CNRS, IRD, CERDI,
F-63000, Clermont-Ferrand, France*
ibrahim.nana@etu.uca.fr

Abstract

Considering China's growing but criticized presence in Africa over the last decades, this chapter investigates the effect of the presence of China in Africa (through value-added trade and foreign direct investments) on the level of technological sophistication of African countries' exports independently of the determinants of this presence. Using a panel smooth threshold regression model on 49 African countries from 1995 to 2015, we attempted to identify whether interactions between China and African countries through global value chains have led to technology transfer. Technology transfer was split into direct and indirect technology transfer. The results highlighted the absence of direct technology transfer from China to African countries except for those that are highly endowed with human capital and strong institutions. In addition, evidence existed of indirect technology transfer through imports of intermediate goods

---

*This chapter was first presented at the 12th International Conference on the Chinese Economy organized by Mary-Françoise Renard, "A New Era for China: Growth Sustainability and Broaden International Development," CERDI, IDREC, University of Clermont Auvergne, France and CCES, Fudan University, Shanghai, China, held in Clermont-Ferrand, France, 24–25 October 2019.

by African countries from China. Compared with relevant literature, we used the export sophistication index following the methodology of Maurer (2017) and investigated technology transfer resulting from value addition created in China and exported to African countries; this prevented us from capturing technology transfer that resulted from China in addition to its trade partners.

8.1.   Introduction

International cooperation between countries has long been characterized by profit maximization as well as political and geopolitical interests. The last decades have been distinguished by the increasing presence of China on the international economic stage and its increasing presence in Africa. This is marked by the presence of Chinese-owned firms in Africa, the increasing volume of trade between the two parties (China has become the first trade partner of African countries overall Chen *et al.*, 2018), and Chinese loans to these countries. The presence of China in Africa has long been debated by policy makers in Africa and abroad. Some analysts think that China's increasing interest in Africa is only guided by its need for natural resources to meet energy needs (Cai, 1999; Chen *et al.*, 2018). Former US presidential candidate Hillary Clinton warned against "new colonialism" in Africa. However, despite this negative conception of the Chinese presence in Africa, other analysts consider the interaction between China and Africa to be a way for African countries to upgrade and to foster their growth (Dollar, 2016); this is in line with what China's President Xi Jinping declared during the 2018 Beijing summit of the Forum on China–Africa Cooperation: "China does not invest in vanity projects in Africa and is helping the continent build its infrastructure." Therefore, two theories exist regarding the presence of China in Africa. Proponents of the Chinese presence usually argue in favor of its spillover effects on African countries growth (i.e. the resulting learning effects from Chinese experience). Indeed, trade and foreign direct investments (FDIs) through global value chains (GVCs) have become effective channels through which developing economies can upgrade their industrialization process and avoid following the same path that developed countries used to achieve their development. With changes in the production process and international fragmentation, countries have become more connected with each other. Such a connection (i.e. openness through GVCs) may be a good opportunity for developing countries to learn from advanced countries and upgrade their technology. This is why some policy makers believe that, regardless of the objective behind China's presence in Africa, the relevant question is whether this interaction have been beneficial for African countries.

Since its accession to the World Trade Organization in 2001, China has been one of the best examples in Asia as well as globally in terms of technology upgrading, economic development, and GVC integration. The country's success in trade is partly because of its success in taking advantage of FDIs. However, since the 2008 financial crisis, which lowered the demand for Chinese goods, China has been planning to change its economic model. In addition, the minimum wage is increasing in China, and the resulting higher labor costs are encouraging Chinese firms to relocate overseas, providing opportunities for less developed countries in Africa and Asia (Chen *et al.*, 2015). The presence of multinational enterprises (MNEs) in China was partly because of the low labor costs; the fact these costs are increasing raises the issue of the location of these MNEs and Chinese state-owned enterprises (because of competitiveness concerns). Fan *et al.* (2018) showed that the increase in the minimum wage can explain approximately 32.3% of the growth in outward investment from China during 2001–2012. Therefore, China is offshoring some firms to countries in Asia and Africa. Thanks to lower transportation and coordination costs, MNEs are now able to maximize their profits even with offshore firms. China's shift from an industrial product-assembling country to a producer of high-tech intermediate goods demonstrates its ability to take advantage from international cooperation (Maurer, 2017).

The aim of this chapter is to investigate whether the presence of China in Africa during the past 20 years has led to technology transfer. Through applying a panel smooth threshold regression (PSTR) approach on 49 African countries from 1995 to 2015, this chapter determines the empirical effects of Chinese exports to Africa as well as Chinese FDIs on the level of African countries' export sophistication. The results hold evidence of the absence of direct technology transfer with the existence of a threshold of absorptive capacity (human capital and quality of institutions) above which direct technology transfer starts to be effective. This study is a contribution to a large body of extant literature on the spillover effects of FDIs. The remainder of the chapter is organized as follows. Section 8.2 presents a literature review on the presence of China, FDIs, imports and the international cooperation—technology transfer nexus. Section 8.3 presents a historical approach to Sino-African relations, while Section 8.4 describes the methodology used for our study. Section 8.5 presents the results of our estimations, and Section 8.6 concludes the chapter.

8.2. Literature Review

The literature review will cover all the aspects of the international cooperation—technology transfer nexus. We will first question the literature on the channel through which FDIs and trade can lead to technology transfer and then focus on the key findings of the literature about China's presence in Africa.

The effect of interactions between countries (in the context of GVCs) on technology transfer is an old debate that has taken many forms: it has been presented through the spillover effects of FDIs and imports as well as directly through the advantages of integrating GVCs. Technology transfer can occur through licensing and FDIs as well as more indirectly through imports of intermediate goods and/or machinery, transport equipment, and demand effects. Licensing is a way for developing countries to benefit from high technology. However, licensing is said to be risky for the developed country (or lead firm) that provides the license if the receiving country does not have a strong rule of law or strong contract enforcement systems (Stone *et al.*, 2015). FDIs are the second way in which interactions in GVCs can lead to direct technology transfer. The literature on technology transfer through FDIs is highly rich and varied. Indeed, this is embodied in the literature on FDIs' spillover effects, from which two types can be distinguished: horizontal and vertical spillover effects. Horizontal spillover effects rely on firms acting in the same sectors; studies have found evidence of negative effects caused by foreign competition that capture market shares to the detriment of domestic firms (Aitken and Harrison, 1999; Stone *et al.*, 2015). Vertical spillover effects are the more probable and represented by the case of a lead firm deciding to improve the efficiency of the value chain to which it belongs, which it achieves through giving technology to its suppliers and taking advantage of a comparative advantage owned by the supplier in a specific task. In addition, once the lead firm's demand pattern changes and becomes more technology intensive, the suppliers must follow that evolution and upgrade in technology to meet the demand (Stone *et al.*, 2015; Havranek and Irvosa, 2011). The literature on trade spillover effects shows that capital and the movement of intermediate goods as well as the knowledge they embody can lead to technology transfer. First, imports of capital goods are likely to lead to technology transfer because capital goods mainly comprise machinery transport equipment, which contains high-tech components. Therefore, for developing countries, importing capital goods from developed countries can lead to a technological upgrade (Stone *et al.*, 2015; Eaton and Kortum, 2001). This positive effect can be explained through the diffusion of knowledge from the use of machinery imported by a firm. In addition, workers can export that knowledge to competitors and spread it through the country. Moreover, firms can use their engineering skills to deconstruct and understand how technology works and attempt to use it in their own production process or make a reproduction of the given capital good. Second, having access to the world market of intermediate goods helps countries obtain access to high-tech inputs that they would not have been able to produce. Thus, countries obtain access to sophisticated inputs, which increase their own productivity and development of new products (Amiti and Konings, 2007; Goldberg *et al.*, 2010). Another indirect method of technology transfer is demand effects, which pass through demand. When developing countries produce to meet local demand, they tend to be less concerned with quality and standards. However, in the case of GVCs, some countries are integrated in global markets and have to supply developed countries' domestic demand. In that case, they will attempt to follow international standards, which will lead to technology upgrade (Bastos and Silva, 2010; Manova and Zhang, 2012; Atkin *et al.*, 2014).

The literature on the Chinese presence in Africa is well furnished but composed of divergent findings. A growing body of literature considers the presence of China in Africa as a grace because the approach of China differs from those of Western countries, which have a bad reputation in Africa because of their role in the continent's colonial past. Some recent studies have found evidence of positive effects of the presence of China in Africa (Kalver and Trebilock, 2011; Otchere *et al.*, 2019; Donou-Adonsou and Lim, 2018). However, some less optimistic studies have highlighted the absence of positive spillover effects of China's presence in Africa (Ademola *et al.*, 2009; Kalver and Trebilock, 2011; Osabutey and Jackson, 2019). Osabutey and Jackson (2019) investigated the effect of Chinese MNEs' presence in Africa, mainly in Ghana. Their findings suggested the absence of specific technology and knowledge transfer policies and strategies in Sino-African relations. Kalver and Trebilock (2011) analyzed Chinese investment in Africa and identified seven ways Chinese investment contribute to African growth (commodity prices, capacity to extract, infrastructure, manufacturing, employment, market access, and consumers' access to cheap products). Their findings also highlighted the existence of negative effects because Chinese FDIs may deindustrialize Africa by outcompeting African firms given that African manufacturing is weak and suffers from many ills. Without econometric analyzes, Ademola *et al.* (2009) conclude on the existence of both negative and positive effects, but the negative effects may outweigh the positive ones for many African countries. Alfaro *et al.* (2004), investigate the existence of a channel through which Chinese FDIs may have positive spillover effects focusing on physical or human capital. They find no evidence of physical or human capital as the main channels through which countries benefit from FDIs. However, earlier in in the 1990s, Borensztein *et al.* (1998) highlighted that FDIs positive effects are highly dependent on the level of educated workforce. In a more recent literature, Alfaro *et al.* (2004) used both theoretical and empirical approaches to examine the different links between FDIs, financial markets, and growth. The model shows that increased foreign investment increases output in the investment sector (foreign production) and in the domestic sector (domestic production). Their empirical results indicate that investment contributes to economic growth owing to the development of the local financial market. Using human development index and real GDP per capita as measures of poverty and following approximately the same method, Gohou and Soumaré (2012) examined the effect of FDIs on poverty reduction in Africa. Their results indicated a significant positive relationship between the two variables. In a different approach (i.e. using poverty headcount to measure poverty), Fowowe and Shuaibu (2014) and Fauzel *et al.* (2015) confirmed the positive relationship between

FDIs and poverty reduction. Additional studies have investigated the effects of FDIs on growth. Otchere *et al.* (2019), in a study of the direction of the causality between FDIs and financial market development, find that FDIs has a positive and significant effect on economic growth in Africa. This result is corroborated by Soumaré (2015), when investigating foreign investment and economic development in Northern Africa. Donou-Adonsou and Lim (2018) used fixed effects and instrumental variable to investigate the effects of Chinese presence. Their results indicate that Chinese investment improves income in Africa. However, they found a more pronounced impact for US and German investments. Most research on direct and indirect technology transfers has been in the form of firm-level-based studies, and the level of technological sophistication is often captured by productivity. Few country-level studies have been conducted on this topic, and those that have tried have focused on the spillover effects of FDIs on productivity, growth, and poverty. The aim of this chapter is to study country-level technology transfer using the export sophistication index.

8.3. History of Sino-African Relations and Stylized Facts

8.3.1. *China–Africa: A historical perspective of the Chinese presence in Africa*

China and Africa have made contact throughout history, and up to 1949, these interactions were more the result of international trade with common trade partners and merchant civilizations (Arabs, Persians, and Turks). Such contact with African countries would later move from passive indirect contact to more involved relationships. The post-1949 relations between China and African countries have been easier because of their common past under Western imperialism.

Historically, Chinese interactions with African countries are not recent and started with indirect trade relations. In fact, while not as well documented as Africa's links with Europe, trade relations between China and Africa date back to the first Han emperors of the 2nd century BCE (Renard, 2011; Jinyuan, 1984). Indeed, according to Alden and Alves (2008), Chinese interaction with African countries started during the reign of Emperor Wuti (140–87 BCE) through an expedition sent west in search of allies. This expedition is said to have reached Alexandria (Egypt), which may have resulted in contact with African civilizations. The major economic achievement of the Han Dynasty (206 BCE–220 CE) was probably the opening of the Silk Road, the routes of which stretched from China through India, Asia Minor, up throughout Mesopotamia, to Egypt, Greece, Rome, and Britain. Africa was a part of this Silk Road trade between different civilizations, and Africa and China may have made contact even indirectly through the Silk Road. This indirect contact via trade was made possible by intermediates that were common trade partners to both parties. Chinese products where imported by African countries through Arabs, Turks, and Persian merchants that used to trade with Chinese. These civilizations where in contact with both parties and were trading with them. At the same time, they were selling African products to Chinese. Contacts between China and Africa also occurred during the Tang Dynasty (618–907) and were characterized by trade with Arab merchants. In addition, under the Song Dynasty (960–1279), indirect contact (via common trade partners as previously described) was made and instances became more frequent. This historical fact was evidenced by archaeological discoveries in eastern Africa and Chinese written records provide further proof (Alden and Alves, 2008). Chinese knowledge of Africa increased during the Yuan Dynasty (1279–1368) due to Chinese contact with the Arabs, Persians, and Turks. The climax of relations between China and Africa was reached during the Ming Dynasty (1368–1644), when China was at the height of shipping technology, leading to a series of expeditions that reached East Africa under the command of Admiral Zheng He (Alden and Alves, 2008). History states that Admiral Zheng He's fleet visited the eastern coast of Africa (Somalia and Kenya) two or three times and made contact with local kings, who reciprocated by sending official delegations to China. This growing friendship was however relatively short because of internal issues, conducing the Ming Dynasty to forbid any overseas contact, simultaneously paving the way for the Europeans' incursions in Africa. This was also the starting point of Western countries presence in Asia. Different from their previous contact and beyond their indirect trade relations, contacts between China and Africa occurred in the early 20th century when European powers used Chinese labor to work in their African colonies. During this period, both China and Africa were victims of colonialism, a situation that would later reinforce the relations between the two. After these periods of contact, it was only with the establishment of the People's Republic of China in 1949 that the Chinese again raised their interest in other developing countries, mainly after the Bandung Conference.[1] However, the presence of China in other developing countries has not been limited to the economic and commercial domains. China has supported the independence process of various less developed countries (Burma, Malaysia, and Vietnam) and it has provided economic assistance to some of them (Mongolia and North Korea). In the post-colonial period, China positioned itself, for the least developed countries, as an alternative to the former colonialists' power. The need for the Chinese to extend their influence in developing countries made them adopt a strategic plan consisting of sharing a common anti-imperialist doctrine with the least developed countries and proposing alternative solutions that were, or appeared, better.

Later, after the establishment of the People's Republic of China in 1949 and the waves of African countries' political independence movements, China found natural allies in these newly independent countries and a potential solution to its legitimacy problems (reinforced by their common colonial links). This was important because China was not a member state of the United Nations (UN) or recognized by the United States (US), which maintained diplomatic relations with the Republic of China on the island of Taiwan, supporting it as the legitimate government of China. At the beginning, China's involvement in Africa was driven by its close relations with the Soviet Union. Its direct involvement was soon confirmed with the Afro–Asian Peoples' Solidarity Organization, created in 1957. The foreign policy of China toward Africa was focused on three main axes: the export of the "Chinese model," the struggle against the superpowers, and China's third world policy (Yu, 1977, 1988).

---

[1]Bandung Conference: In April 1955, representatives from 29 governments of Asian and African nations gathered in Bandung, Indonesia to discuss peace and the role of the Third World in the Cold War, economic development, and decolonization.

During the first Cold War, several African countries recognized the People's Republic of China as the legitimate government of China, namely Morocco and Algeria in 1958 and Sudan and Guinea in 1959. The following two decades turned out to be much more fertile in terms of international recognition with 14 African countries establishing diplomatic ties with China during the 1960s and 22 during the 1970s (Alden and Alves, 2008). This was the result of the independence movements of African states in the southern Sahara. The official ties of African countries with China consisted of four main categories:

- friendship treaties based on the "Five Principles of Peaceful Coexistence";
- cultural pacts;
- trade and payment agreements intended to promote commercial relations;
- economic aid and technical assistance agreements.

However, these prominent, growing relationships between China and Africa did not last long because of the Cultural Revolution in 1966, which saw an end to overt Chinese political activism on the continent. Furthermore, African countries made strategic rapprochements with the US in response to the increasing "Soviet menace" in the 1960s and 70s, as evidenced by Sino-Soviet border clashes in 1969 and the Brezhnev doctrine,[2] which was accompanied by the Soviet invasion of Czechoslovakia in 1968, making the Soviet Union China's primary enemy.

The evolution of Sino-African diplomatic relations during the Cold War was marked by many diplomatic achievements, which are represented by the following specific cases:

- **1956:** Egypt was the first African country to establish official diplomatic relations with China. China currently maintains diplomatic relations with 54 African states, with Sao Tome and Principe (2016) and South Sudan (2011) being the most recent.

---

[2]The Brezhnev doctrine allows Moscow to interfere in any socialist country.

- **1971:** China secured a permanent seat on the UN Security Council with support of 26 African states (34% of the General Assembly votes).
- **1970–1975:** The most celebrated Chinese development assistance project in Africa was the Tazara Railway, requested by the previous Zambian president Kenneth Kuanda and his Tanzanian counterpart, Julius Nyerere.

In recent years, China has continually trumpeted its 50-year-old involvement in Africa as positive, progressive, and grounded in the eternal and principled truths of non-interference (Strauss, 2009). However, rigorous analysis of available data must be undertaken to estimate the effect of China's presence in Africa before concluding to any positive effect.

8.3.2. Stylized facts: Trade and investment between China and Africa

8.3.2.1. African countries' trade: Change in trade partners

The configuration of African countries' trade partners has evolved over time. Before 1995, African countries' exports were mostly routed to France, which was the first export partner of African countries overall (African countries' total exports). After 1995, the US was the largest importer of African products, followed by France—positions they would retain until 2012. Data highlight an increasing presence of China as an important trade partner (importer) of African countries over the years. In 2009, China became the second largest importer of African products, and in 2012, African countries' exports to China reached USD 64 billion, conferring to China the position of the largest importer of African products, replacing the US until 2016 (Figure 8.1).

From 1990 to 2006, France was the largest exporter to African countries overall (African countries' gross imports), followed by the US and Germany. In 2006, the US and Germany lost their places to China, which became the primary exporter to African countries until 2017 (Figure 8.2). Between 2006 and 2017, African countries' imports from China increased at an annual average growth rate of 10%, going from approximately USD 20 billion in 2006 to USD 65 billion in 2017,

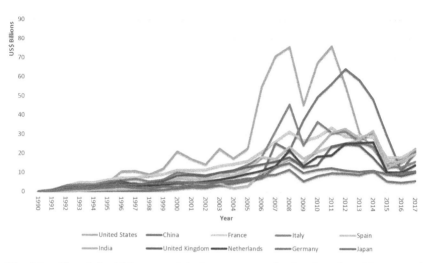

Fig. 8.1.   Trends in African countries' gross export destinations (top 10 partners) from 1990 to 2017.

Source: Authors' calculation based on UN-COMTRADE data.

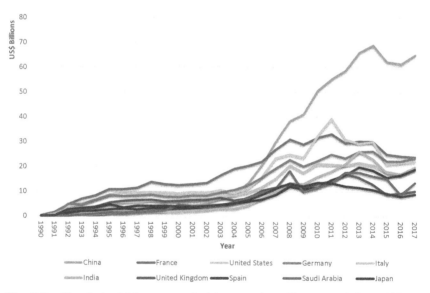

Fig. 8.2.   Trends in African countries' imports (top 10 partners) from 1990 to 2017.

Source: Authors' calculation based on UN-COMTRADE data.

reaching its highest value in 2014 (USD 69 billion). This trend of African countries' gross imports shows that China started being a major actor in African countries' economies in 2006, and it is now a major trade partner if not the top. This is why it is necessary to investigate the increasing and deep presence of China in Africa.

The composition of African countries' imports from China by product[3] type is necessary to include when investigating the reasons for as well as the effects of the Chinese presence in Africa. Since the 1990s, African countries' imports from China have mainly comprised manufactured goods, machinery and transport equipment, and miscellaneous manufactured articles. In 2001, 2009, and 2015, the top product types imported by African countries from China were machinery and transport equipment, followed by manufactured goods and miscellaneous manufactured articles. The common property of these products is the technology they embody (Figure 8.3).

However, the structure of African countries' exports to China is different, which mainly comprise mineral fuel and lubricants followed by crude materials, except food and fuel, and manufactured goods (2009–2015). In contrast to imports from China, these exports are more resource based (Figure 8.4). This highlights the objective and

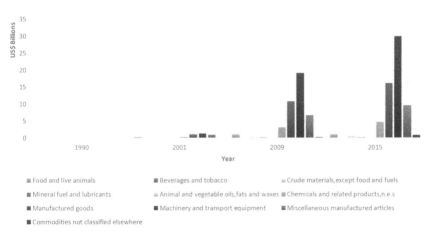

Fig. 8.3.   African countries' imports from China by product types.
Source: Authors' calculation based on UN-COMTRADE data.

---

[3]The nomenclature used is: SITC Revision 3.

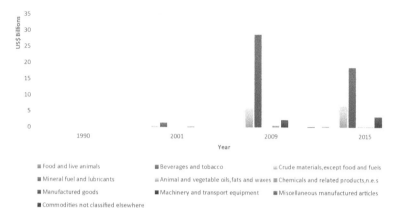

Fig. 8.4.   African countries' exports to China by product types.
Source: Authors' calculation based on UN-COMTRADE data.

the potential gain of China in its trade relations with African countries, namely obtaining market opportunities for their products and
natural resources to meet their energy concerns. Therefore, it will be
difficult for African countries to take advantage of their exports to
China in terms of technology upgrade.

8.3.2.2.   *Foreign direct investments*

Relevant data on Chinese FDIs to African countries are recent and
date back to 2003. Analyzing these data by income group provides an
idea about which income group receives the most FDIs from China.
Indeed, from 2003 to 2015, Chinese FDIs were directed more to
lower-middle-income countries, except in 2008 where approximately
90% of Chinese FDIs in Africa were located in upper-middle-income
countries. Low-income countries have also received FDIs from China,
starting from 16% in 2003 and increasing to 27% in 2015 with minor
fluctuations in the trend. Although we claim that FDIs are located
more in lower-middle-income countries, the reparation by income
groups tends to be equal with small differences (except in high-
income countries) and according to the considered period. In fact, the
mean percentages (2003–2015) of Chinese FDIs by income group are
as follows: lower-middle-income countries (40%), followed by upper-
middle-income countries (35%), low-income countries (24%), and
high-income countries (1%) (Figure 8.5).

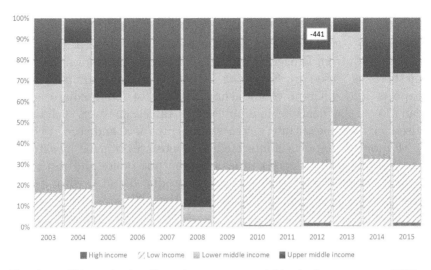

Fig. 8.5.   Chinese foreign direct investments to Africa by income group (2003–2015).

Note: In 2012, net FDI inflow to upper-middle-income countries was negative (USD 441 million), meaning that FDI outflows from Africa upper-middle-income countries into China was higher than FDI inflows from China.

Source: Authors' calculation based on Chinese official reports.

8.4.   Empirical Methodology

8.4.1.   *Variables and data sources*

The dataset includes annual data from 1995 to 2015 for 49 African countries. Our variable of interest is the technological sophistication index, which is computed following Maurer (2017). The explicative variables are mainly trade in intermediate goods, computed using input–output tables, and Chinese FDIs registered in Chinese official reports as overseas FDIs (OFDI) and obtained from the China Statistical Yearbook, which reports data on FDIs to African countries from 2003 to 2015 in USD. The control variables are labor (employed population), which is obtained from the World Bank (World Development Indicators' data); private capital stock, which comes from the IMF Investment and Capital Stock Dataset (2017); and human capital, measured using the ratio of gross enrollment in tertiary education, which comes from the World Bank.

8.4.2.   *Imports of intermediate goods from China*

We compute imports of intermediate goods from China using input–output data from Lenzen *et al.* (2013). The process follows the same methodology used by Koopman *et al.* (2014) to decompose gross exports into different components. Exports of intermediate goods can directly be identified in input–output tables; however, such tables also include domestic intermediate goods produced and used at home.

Exports or imports of intermediate goods are obtained by extracting all intermediate goods from input–output tables and setting to zero (0) domestic intermediate goods produced and used at home. The general formula is as follows:

$$M_{k,i} = \sum_{j=2i-1 \ k\neq i}^{2i+n-2} (a_{j,2k-1} + a_{j,2k+n-2}), \qquad (8.1)$$

where $M_{k,i}$ is the imports of country k from country i, and n is the number of sectors.

Reminder: $a_{1,3}$ represents exports of intermediate goods from country 1 (sector 1) and used (imported) by country 2 in its sector 1.

Following the general example of Table 8.1, we can attempt to compute imports of intermediate goods of country 2 from country 1.

The general formula of imports of intermediate goods of country 2 from country 1 is presented as follows:

$$M_{2,1} = \sum_{j=1}^{2} (a_{j,3} + a_{j,4}) = (a_{1,3} + a_{1,4}) + (a_{2,3} + a_{2,4}). \qquad (8.2)$$

Table 8.1.   First part of the input–output table: Intermediate goods.

		Country 1		Country 2		Country 3	
		Sector 1	Sector 2	Sector 1	Sector 2	Sector 1	Sector 2
Country 1	Sector 1	a_{11}	a_{12}	a_{13}	a_{14}	a_{15}	a_{16}
	Sector 2	a_{21}	a_{22}	a_{23}	a_{24}	$\cdots$	a_{26}
Country 2	Sector 1	a_{31}	$\vdots$	$\ddots$			$\vdots$
	Sector 2	a_{41}	$\vdots$		$\ddots$		a_{46}
Country 3	Sector 1	a_{51}	a_{52}			$\ddots$	
	Sector 2	a_{61}	a_{62}	$\cdots$	a_{64}	$\cdots$	a_{66}

8.4.3. *Methodology*

In this study, we draw a distinction between two types of technology transfer: direct technology transfer through licensing and FDIs and indirect technology transfer through imports of intermediate goods or/and machinery and transport equipment and demands effects.

The analysis follows a PSTR approach to model the effects of Chinese presence in Africa in terms of technology transfer. Following the literature, we make the assumption that the capacity of African countries to take advantage of their interaction with China depends on their absorptive capacity (human capital and governance). Absorptive capacity can be defined as the ability of an organization or a region to take advantages from its interactions between other entities by identifying, assimilating, and exploiting knowledge from the environment (Cohen and Levin, 1989). The literature on technology transfer has continuously highlighted the role of countries' absorptive capacity in capturing technology embodied in FDIs and imported products (Stone *et al.*, 2015; Fu, 2008).

Technology transfer between countries is supposed to help the recipient country upgrade, thereby increasing its productivity and leading to sustainable and inclusive development. However, the recipient country should have a strong absorptive capacity to capture technology from its partner (Figure 8.6). Given this condition for absorbing technology, the effect of the Chinese presence in Africa seems not to be linear and conditioned by African countries' capacities. Therefore, we should choose an appropriate model to take into account this nonlinear effect, which is why we use a PSTR model.

8.4.4. *Presentation of the PSTR model*

As a reminder, threshold regression models draw a jumping character, a structural break in the interaction (relation) between two variables. These models consider that individual observations can be split into classes based on the value of an observed variable (Hansen, 1999) and are developed for non-dynamic panels with individual fixed effects. Threshold regression models are therefore a type of regime-switching model that are characterized by a changing slope parameter according to the regime. Indeed, the first panel threshold regression (PTR) model developed by Hansen (1999) assumes

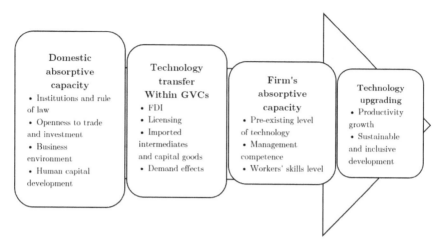

Fig. 8.6.   From technology diffusion to national upgrading—the role of absorptive capacity.

Source: Illustrative figure obtained from Stone *et al.* (2015).

a brutal transition between regimes, which is not really realistic. Rather than being brutal, the transition between regimes should be smooth if we want the model to be closest to reality. The PSTR method proposed by González *et al.* (2004), in contrast to the PTR model, assumes a gradual transition between regimes. Thus, the transition function, instead of being an indicator, will be a continuous function. The PSTR model is presented in the following form:

$$Y_{it} = \alpha_i + \beta_0 X_{it} + \beta_1 X_{it} g(q_{i,t}; \gamma; c) + \theta_3 W_{i,t} + \epsilon_{it}, \qquad (8.3)$$

where α_i represents the individual fixed effects; ϵ_{it} is the error term, which is independent and identically distributed; Y_{it} is the explained variable represented here by the logarithm of the technological sophistication index; X_{it} represents the explicative variables; q is the transition variable, which is represented here by two types of variables, namely human capital and government effectiveness (GE; e.g. political stability, rule of law, and control of corruption), representative of the absorptive capacity; and W_{it} is a vector of control variables composed of labor and capital. We follow Granger *et al.* (1993) and González *et al.* (2004) by supposing that the transition function is a logistic function with a single threshold:

$$g(q_{i,t}; \gamma; c) = \left(1 + \exp\left(-\gamma \prod_{j=1}^{m}(q_{it} - c_j)\right)\right)^{-1},$$

$$\text{with } \gamma > 0, c_1 \leq \cdots \leq c_m, \tag{8.4}$$

where $c = (c_1 \leq \cdots \leq c_m)$, which represents a vector (dimension m) of location parameters (threshold parameters), and γ is the slope of the transition function.

According to the values taken by the slope parameter and location parameters, several cases exist:

First case: With $m = 1$ and $\gamma \to \infty$, Eqs. (8.3) and (8.4) represent the two-regime PTR (Hansen, 1999). Second case: With $m > 1$ and $\gamma \to \infty$, the number of identical regimes is two, and the function switches between zero and one at $c_1, \ldots, c_m$. Third case: With $\gamma \to 0$, the transition function (Eq. (8.4)) is constant, and the model is the standard linear fixed-effect model.

The marginal effect is given by the following equation:

$$\frac{dY_{it}}{dX_{it}} = \beta_{it} = \beta_0 + \beta_1 g(q_{it}; \gamma; c) \quad \text{with } \beta_0 \leq \beta_{it} \leq \beta_0 + \beta_1. \tag{8.5}$$

In this case, we have two extreme values: β_0, which is the effect of FDIs or imports of intermediates from China on the level of technological sophistication if $g(q_{it}; \gamma; c)$, and $\beta_0 + \beta_1$, which represents the effect if $g(q_{it}; \gamma; c) = 1$. However, if the transition function takes any value between 0 and 1 (if $g \in]0, 1[$), the effect is given by $\beta_{it} = \beta_0 + \beta_1 g(q_{it}; \gamma; c)$. This PSTR model can be generalized to $r+1$ extreme regimes. Therefore, the model becomes

$$Y_{it} = \alpha_i + \beta_0 X_{it} + \sum_{j=1}^{r} \beta_j X_{it} g(q_{i,t}; \gamma; c) + \theta_3 W_{i,t} + \epsilon_{it}, \tag{8.6}$$

with $g(q_{i,t}; \gamma; c)$ given in (8.4).

The estimation of the parameters of the PSTR model consists of using the fixed effect estimator and nonlinear least squares on the previously transformed model (González *et al.*, 2004; Colletaz and Hurlin, 2006). Before estimating the PSTR model, following

González *et al.* (2004), we use a testing procedure to first test the linearity against the PSTR model and then to determine the number "*r*" of transition functions. The tests consist of testing the linearity of the model first without introducing the transition function. Hypotheses are presented as follows:

- H0: $r = 0$, linear model without introducing the transition function (linearity).

- H1: $r = 1$, model with threshold effects with a minimum of a transition function.

If it is rejected, then this means that no linearity exists, and we have at least one transition function in the model. Then, three statistics are computed: the Wald tests (LM), Fisher tests (LM$_F$), and pseudo-LRT statistics:

$$LM = \left[\frac{TN(SSR_0 - SSR_1)}{SSR_0}\right], \tag{8.7}$$

$$LM_F = \left[\frac{(SSR_0 - SSR_1)mK}{SSR_0(TN - N - mK)}\right], \tag{8.8}$$

$$LRT = \log(SSR_0) - \log(SSR_1), \tag{8.9}$$

where K is the number of explanatory variables; SSR_0 is the panel sum of squared residuals under H0 (linearity); SSR_1 is the panel sum of squared residuals under H1; N is the number of countries; and T is time. The LM and pseudo-LRT statistics have an $\chi^2(mK)$ distribution under a null hypothesis, whereas the F-statistic (LM$_F$) has an approximate $F(mK; TN - N - mK)$ distribution under a null hypothesis.

Once the test confirms the absence of linearity, the next step is to change the hypothesis by increasing the number of values that "*r*" can take to find the number of transition functions that should be admitted in the model. In other words, this involves testing the number of possible significant transition functions in an iterative manner, ranging from two (when $r = 1$) to "*r*+1" possible transition functions:

- H0: $r = j$, model with threshold effects with a minimum of j transition functions ($j \geq 2$).

- H1: $r = j + 1$, model with threshold effects with a minimum of $j + 1$ transition functions ($j \geq 2$).

As in the previous cases, we use the LM, LM_F, and pseudo-LRT statistics computed according to the same definitions. The procedure ends when the null hypothesis H0 is accepted, and the conclusion is that there are j transition functions. However, if the null hypothesis of linearity is rejected and the null hypothesis of "H0: $r = 2$" is also rejected, we have a situation of nonlinearity with one transition function.

8.5.   Results of the PSTR

In the past, international trade was driven by developed countries (North–North flows). However, in the last two decades, North–South and South–South trade flows have risen considerably. By 2014, the value of South–South trade had reached almost USD 5.5 trillion, a magnitude close to that of trade between developed countries (North–North) (UNCTAD 2019; Autor *et al.*, 2013). In 2018, goods worth USD 6.9 trillion (36%) were exchanged between developed economies (North–North trade), whereas merchandise trade among developing and transition economies (South–South trade) amounted to USD 5.4 trillion (28%). Exports from developed to developing economies and vice-versa (North–South, and South–North trade) totaled USD 6.9 trillion (36%). This chapter investigates technology transfer in South–South trade and investment relations and relies on comparative advantages theory.

The interpretation of the empirical results relies on theoretical foundations, namely the well-known Heckscher–Olin (H–O) model. According to the H–O theory of comparative advantages, countries should specialize according to their production factors' endowment, enabling countries with more skilled labor to specialize in the production of high-tech products, while countries with a higher share of unskilled labor specialize in low-tech products. However, this model no longer expresses the reality of trade because countries specialize in tasks instead of the production of a whole product. Therefore, a country can export high-tech products, but it might not be certain whether this country is richly endowed with skilled labor and technology. The best example is China at the beginning of 2002. It started exporting high-tech products, but this was partly because of its role in the production of low-tech components embodied in imported high-tech goods that were re-exported. This can also be explained by the role of China in assembling high-tech products produced abroad and then re-exporting them, which gave the impression that China was producing high-tech products. This comparative advantages theory is the foundation of our econometric results interpretation, but it is important to note that it has evolved overtime. It has recently experienced very strong renewed interest from a theoretical as well as an empirical point of view. Matsuyama (2013), Costinot (2009), and Costinot *et al.* (2015) have reviewed the well-known comparative advantages theory extending it in their studies. Costinot *et al.* (2015) investigated the comparative advantages implications for how nations should conduct their trade policy. Their findings suggested that countries have more room to manipulate prices in their comparative-advantage sectors.

In this chapter, the export sophistication index is computed using the Balassa index of revealed comparative advantages (Balassa, 1965) on the basis of gross exports. Given the link between the explained variable and the revealed comparative advantage index, if the export sophistication index reflects an increase in technology due to foreign value addition embodied in gross exports, it should be negatively correlated with factors (labor and capital); however, if it reflects an increase in technology created domestically by African countries and embodied in exports, then it should be correlated positively with factors (labor and capital). In addition to providing an interpretation of the coefficient associated with Chinese FDIs, coefficients associated with factors (labor and capital in regime 1 will help confirm the presence or absence of technology transfer.

The PSTR model draws a structural break in the interaction (relation) between two variables, allowing a smooth transition between regimes. Threshold variables used in this study comprise a set of variables that capture the absorptive capacity of African countries. These variables are as follows: human capital measured by the gross enrollment ratio in tertiary education, GE, political stability, rule of law, and control of corruption. Missing human capital is completed using linear interpolation. Before proceeding with estimations, we should ensure that the model is nonlinear and can be estimated using PSTR. The results show that there is at least one transition function. Therefore, the model is nonlinear, and we can search for threshold effects (Table 8.2).

Table 8.2.   Linearity tests.

H0: Linear Model and H1: PSTR model with at least one threshold variable
($r = 1$)

Threshold variables	Human capital	Government effectiveness	Political stability	Rule of law	Control of corruption
Wald Tests (LM)	47.437***	19.077***	13.616**	16.035***	12.066**
Fisher Tests (LMF)	10.601***	3.722***	2.145**	3.082**	2.275**
LRT Tests (LRT)	52.674***	19.951***	14.054**	16.646***	12.408**

Note: *$p < 0.1$, **$p < 0.05$, ***$p < 0.01$.

The second step consists of identifying the number of regimes. The linearity test is repeated with increasing values of "r" (H0: $r = j$ and H1: $r = j+1$, with $j \geq 2$) until the null hypothesis is accepted. Tables in Appendix (Tables A.8.1–A.8.3) present the results of LM, LM$_F$, and pseudo-LRT statistics tests. All the tests conclude in nonlinearity with a single threshold (i.e. "$r = 1$") except when the threshold variable is "Rule of Law," where the number of thresholds equals 2. Once the nonlinearity of the model is confirmed and the number of regimes is defined, the estimations provide the results detailed in the following sections.

8.5.1.   *Human capital as the threshold variable*

When considering the level of human capital as the threshold variable, in regime 1 (below the threshold), FDIs have a negative effect on the level of technological sophistication, while in regime 2 (above the threshold) they have a positive effect (Table A.8.4 and Figure A.8.5). Indeed, FDIs received by African countries from China have a negative effect on technological sophistication when the level of human capital is below the threshold. This negative effect can be explained by two factors, with the first being the nature of FDIs received by African countries from China. These FDIs are mostly located in extractive industries and are mostly natural resource based. Indeed, FDIs' composition varies from one country to another and they are more diversified in some countries than in others (Chen *et al.*, 2015). The main determinants of FDIs are as follows: the importance of the host country's market size (Morisset, 2000; Jaumotte, 2004), natural resources (Asiedu, 2006), and a low cost of labor (Wheeler and Mody,

1992; Mody and Srinivasan, 1998). Findings on FDIs' spillover effects highlighted that FDIs' determinants affect their impact (Chen *et al.*, 2015). This means that FDIs that have been attracted by skilled labor, for example, will have stronger effects than FDIs attracted by unskilled cheap labor. This can explain the negative effects of Chinese FDIs in Africa because most are located in extractive sectors[4] and come with a crucial role of their own workers at the expense of the local labor force. Second, this negative effect is explained by the low level of human capital because benefiting from foreign firms' technology requires the presence of a high level of human capital to learn, understand, and copy this technology. In addition, countries with low human capital attract FDIs that are unskilled-labor-intensive, which does not encourage increases in human capital and the level of technological sophistication. When unskilled-labor-intensive companies enter a country, the need for unskilled workers will increase their average wage and decrease the average wage of highly skilled workers. The direct consequence will be a decrease in people willing to learn and become qualified since the preference for unskilled labor in the country is high. This will have negative effects on the level of human capital and therefore on the level of technological sophistication of the country. This result highlights that when African countries reach a certain level of gross enrollment ratio in tertiary education,[5] FDIs from China start to have positive spillover effects on the level of technological sophistication of the host country.

Focusing now on imports of intermediate goods, the results are different from FDIs. Indeed, imports of intermediate goods from China have a positive effect on technological sophistication (Table A.8.4). Intermediate goods are imported to be used in the production of final or other intermediate goods that will be exported or used domestically. Over the years, China increased its production of high-tech intermediate goods; therefore, imports of intermediate goods by African countries from China help them to increase the

---

[4]When looking at country level, some countries have more diversified FDIs.

[5]This threshold of gross enrollment ratio in tertiary school is 3.72% that seem to be very low. However, this threshold has been obtained using a sample of countries with low gross enrollment ratio. Therefore, the value of 3.72 is not so important. The importance is the presence of the threshold and the change sign between the two regimes.

level of technological sophistication of their exports through learning effects.

8.5.2. *Quality of institutions as the threshold variable*

The quality of institutions is measured through the GE index, with political stability, rule of law, and control of corruption. The interaction between China and African countries through GVCs led to a technological transfer after a certain threshold of GE (Table A.8.5 and Figure A.8.3). In the literature on technology transfer, the level of institutional quality is said to be a key determinant of technological transfer. Indeed, in regime 1, FDIs and imports of intermediates from China have negative and significant effects on the level of technological sophistication of African countries; however, after a certain threshold of GE, FDIs from China and imports of intermediates have positive effects on the level of technological sophistication. The results of this estimation show that no direct and indirect technological transfer exist in the interaction between China and Africa until the level of GE of African countries reaches a certain level.[6] Above that threshold, interactions between China and Africa through FDIs and imports of intermediates start leading to an increase in the level of technological sophistication of exports (a positive and significant effect). Indeed, the greater the GE, the higher the spillover effects of Chinese FDIs and their exports of intermediates to Africa. Therefore, governments should create a better environment to take advantage of foreign technology. Political stability can also be a proxy of African countries institutional strength, and it is a part of absorptive capacity. The stability of a state is a prerequisite for its technological and economic upgrading. The results of the PSTR indicate the existence of a threshold of political stability (PS),[7] below which (regime 1) Chinese FDIs have a negative impact on African countries' level of technological sophistication. However, this PS is not always necessary for taking advantage of foreign technology embodied in intermediate goods. In regime 2, the coefficient in front of Chinese

---

[6]With the threshold of government effectiveness $= -0.71$ and $GE \in [-2.45, 2.44]$ for all the countries.

[7]Threshold of political stability $= -0.24$ and $PS \in [-3.31, 1.96]$ for all the countries.

FDIs is positive and non-significant, whereas the coefficient in front of imports of intermediates is positive and significant (Table A.8.6 and Figure A.8.2). Using rule of law as threshold variable provides the same results. Chinese FDIs in both regimes 1 and 2[8] are non-significant, whereas the import of intermediate goods is significant and positive in regime 2 (Table A.8.7 and Figure A.8.1). Control of corruption is also a key variable that measures the quality of institutions; therefore, it can also be considered a proxy of absorptive capacity. Using control of corruption as a threshold variable, regime 1 shows a negative and significant effect of both FDIs and imports of intermediates on the level of technological sophistication. The effect becomes positive and significant in regime 2 above the threshold (Table A.8.8 and Figure A.8.4).[9] These results as well as the previous one reconcile both parties of literature and demonstrate that the existence of both negative and positive effects depends on the level of the host country's absorptive capacity.

8.6. Conclusion

This chapter investigated the question of the Chinese presence in Africa over the past 20 years, focusing on its effect on the level of technological sophistication of African countries' exports (technology transfer from China to African countries). The relations between China and African countries, historically characterized by indirect contact and relations through intermediaries (e.g. Arabs, Persians, and Europeans), have increased in recent years. These increasing relations have essentially been through Chinese FDIs and trade relations. Empirical findings highlighted that the relations between China and African countries have not had a positive impact on the level of technological sophistication of African countries. However, things are different for African countries that are well endowed with human capital and strong institutions. Depth analysis using the PSTR model revealed the existence of a threshold of absorptive capacity of African countries (human capital level and institutional concerns), above which direct technology transfer (FDIs) through GVCs is effective.

---

[8]Threshold of rule of law $= -0.80$ $RL \in [-2.06, 2, 10]$ for all the countries.
[9]Threshold of control of corruption $= -0.91$ with $CC \in [-1.868714, 2.469991]$ for all the countries.

Moreover, the results revealed a positive effect of imports of intermediate goods from China (indirect technology transfer) that becomes negative above a certain threshold of human capital.

In terms of policy, the results presented in this chapter provide proof that African countries should first redefine their cooperation with China to attract more diversified FDIs from China. Second, they should work to improve their absorptive capacity because it matters from the beginning to the end of the process of international relations. Indeed, good institutions will ensure upstream that FDIs are growth- and development-friendly and will favor efficient contract enforcement. Moreover, the level of human capital is crucial for technology upgrading through GVCs; therefore, policy makers should try to invest more in tertiary education by offering a wide range of education and training programs if they want to take advantage in terms of technology upgrading from future FDI inflows. Regardless of the relations between China and African countries, the following question remains to be answered: Can the competition in capturing market shares between China and Western countries help African countries improve their level of export sophistication?

Appendix

Table A.8.1.   Wald tests (LM).

Hypothesis on the number of thresholds using Wald tests (LM)	Threshold variables				
	Human capital	Government effectiveness	Political stability	Rule of law	Control of corruption
H0: $r = 0$ vs. H1: $r = 1$	47.437***	19.077***	13.616**	6.035***	12.066**
H0: $r = 1$ vs. H1: $r = 2$	2.807	4.219	6.228	11.897**	1.758
H0: $r = 2$ vs. H1: $r = 3$	NA	NA	NA	NA	NA

Note: *$p < 0.1$, **$p < 0.05$, ***$p < 0.01$.

Table A.8.2. Fisher tests (LMF).

Hypothesis on the number of thresholds using F-tests (LMF)	Threshold variables				
	Human capital	Government effectiveness	Political stability	Rule of law	Control of corruption
H0: $r = 0$ vs. H1: $r = 1$	10.601***	3.722***	2.145**	3.082**	2.275**
H0: $r = 1$ vs. H1: $r = 2$	0.49	0.728	0.889	2.128*	0.3
H0: $r = 2$ vs. H1: $r = 3$	NA	NA	NA	NA	NA

Note: *$p < 0.1$, **$p < 0.05$, ***$p < 0.01$.

Table A.8.3. Pseudo-LRT.

Hypothesis on the number of thresholds using LRT tests (LRT)	Threshold variables				
	Human capital	Government effectiveness	Political stability	Rule of law	Control of corruption
H0: $r = 0$ vs. H1: $r = 1$	52.674***	19.951***	14.054**	16.646***	12.408**
H0: $r = 1$ vs. H1: $r = 2$	2.823	4.260	6.318	12.229**	1.765
H0: $r = 2$ vs. H1: $r = 3$	NA	NA	NA	NA	NA

Note: *$p < 0.1$, **$p < 0.05$, ***$p < 0.01$.

Table A.8.4.   PSTR results: Threshold variable is human capital.

Threshold variable: log of human capital

| | Coefficient estimate | |
	Régime 1	Régime 2
FDIs	−0.0023***	0.0022***
	−0.0005	−0.0005
log Imports of intermediates	0.1168***	−0.1540***
	−0.0337	−0.026
Labor	−0.0128**	0.0147***
	−0.006	−0.0025
Capital	0.0519	0.2024***
	−0.0891	−0.0381
log Exports of intermediates	0.0197*	−0.0268**
	−0.0125	−0.0128

Transition functions

	Estimated transition parameter
Slope parameters (γ)	6.8940
Threshold (c)	1.3133

Note: *$p < 0.1$, **$p < 0.05$, ***$p < 0.01$.

Table A.8.5.   PSTR results: Threshold variable is government
effectiveness index.

Threshold variable: Government effectiveness index

	Coefficient estimate	
	Régime 1	Régime 2
log FDIs	−0.0027***	0.0025**
	−0.0011	−0.0011
log Imports of intermediates	−0.0573*	0.1455***
	−0.0374	−0.0287
Labor	0.0100**	−0.0154***
	−0.0057	−0.0025
Capital	0.2621***	−0.1331***
	−0.1026	−0.0711
log Exports of intermediates	0.0006	−0.0031
	−0.0063	−0.0075

Transition functions

	Estimated transition parameter
Slope parameters (γ)	10.7052
Threshold (c)	−0.7129

Note: $^*p < 0.1$, $^{**}p < 0.05$, $^{***}p < 0.01$.

Table A.8.6. PSTR results: Threshold variable is political stability and absence of violence.

Threshold variable: Political stability and absence of violence

	Coefficient estimate	
	Régime 1	Régime 2
log FDIs	−0.0004	0.0002
	−0.0003	−0.0004
log Imports of intermediates	0.0273	0.1950***
	−0.0349	−0.0416
Labor	0.0094*	−0.0131***
	−0.006	−0.0031
Capital	0.4207***	−0.3447***
	−0.1012	−0.0637
log Exports of intermediates	0.0016	−0.002
	−0.0064	−0.0085

Transition functions

	Estimated transition parameter
Slope parameters (γ)	29.1382
Threshold (c)	−0.2445

Note: $^*p < 0.1$, $^{**}p < 0.05$, $^{***}p < 0.01$.

Table A.8.7. PSTR results: Threshold variable is rule of law.

Threshold variable: Rule of law		
	Coefficient estimate	
	Régime 1	Régime 2
log FDIs	−0.000	−0.0004
	−0.0006	−0.0007
log Imports of intermediates	−0.0342	0.0948***
	−0.034	−0.0236
Labor	0.0079*	−0.0066***
	−0.006	−0.0018
Capital	0.2554***	−0.1451***
	−0.0861	−0.0446
log Exports of intermediates	−0.0053	0.0086
	−0.0072	−0.0088

Transition functions	
	Estimated transition parameter
Slope parameters (γ)	1.1693e+03
Threshold (c)	−0.7956

Note: $*p < 0.1$, $**p < 0.05$, $***p < 0.01$.

Table A.8.8. PSTR results: Threshold variable is control of corruption.

Threshold variable: Control of corruption		
	Coefficient estimate	
	Régime 1	Régime 2
log FDIs	−0.0028**	0.0026**
	−0.0014	−0.0014
log Imports of intermediates	−0.1190**	0.2192***
	−0.0687	−0.0765
Labor	0.0235***	−0.0266***
	−0.0098	−0.0088
Capital	0.1559	−0.103
	−0.125	−0.1449
log Exports of intermediates	−0.0011	−0.0043
	−0.0076	−0.0105

Transition functions	
	Estimated transition parameter
Slope parameters (γ)	5.0221
Threshold (c)	−0.9071

Note: *$p < 0.1$, **$p < 0.05$, ***$p < 0.01$.

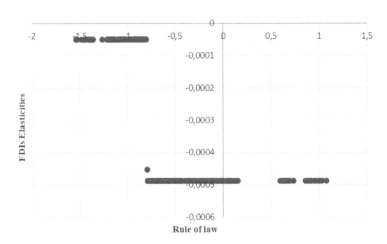

Fig. A.8.1. Transition function when the threshold variable is rule of law.

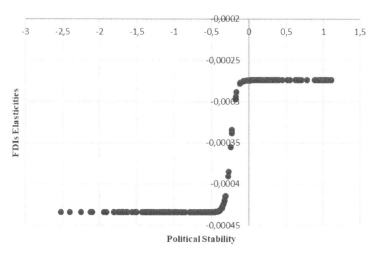

Fig. A.8.2.   Transition function when the threshold variable is political stability.

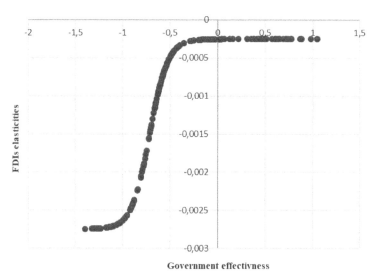

Fig. A.8.3.   Transition function when the threshold variable is government effectiveness.

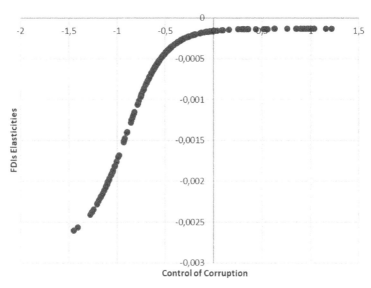

Fig. A.8.4. Transition function when the threshold variable is control of corruption.

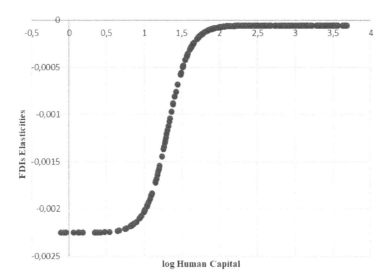

Fig. A.8.5. Transition function when the threshold variable is human capital.

References

Ademola, O. T., A. S. Bankole, and A. O. Adewuyi (2009). "China-Africa Trade Relations: Insights from AERC Scoping Studies," *European Journal of Development Research*, 21, 485–505.

Aitken, B. J. and A. E. Harrison (1999). "Do Domestic Firms Benefit from Direct Foreign Investment? Evidence from Venezuela," *American Economic Review*, 89, 605–618.

Alden, C. and C. Alves (2008). "History and Identity in the Construction of China's Africa Policy," *Review of African Political Economy*, 35, 43–58.

Alfaro, L., A. Chanda, S. Kalemli-Ozcan, and S. Sayek (2004). "FDI and Economic Growth: The Role of Local Financial Markets," *Journal of International Economics*, 64, 89–112.

Amiti, M. and J. Konings (2007). "Trade Liberalization, Intermediate Inputs, and Productivity: Evidence from Indonesia," *American Economic Review*, 97, 1611–1638.

Asiedu, E. (2006). "Foreign Direct Investment in Africa: The Role of Natural Resources, Market Size, Government Policy, Institutions and Political Instability," *The World Economy*, 29, 63–77.

Atkin, D., A. K. Khandelwal, and A. Osman (2014). "Exporting and Firm Performance: Evidence from a Randomized Trial," *Working Paper 20690. National Bureau of Economic Research*.

Autor, D., D. Dorn, and G. Hanson (2013). "The China Syndrome: Local Labor Market Effects of Import Competition in the United States," *American Economic Review*, 103, 2121–2168.

Balassa, B. (1965). "Tariff Protection in Industrial Countries: An Evaluation," *Journal of Political Economy*, 73, 573–594.

Bastos, P. and J. Silva (2010). "The Quality of a Firm's Exports: Where You Export to Matters," *Journal of International Economics*, 82, 99–111.

Borensztein, E., J. De Gregorio, and J. W. Lee (1998). "How Does Foreign Direct Investment Affect Economic Growth?" *Journal of International Economics*, 45, 115–135.

Cai, K. G. (1999). "Outward Foreign Direct Investment: A Novel Dimension of China's Integration into the Regional and Global Economy," *The China Quarterly*, 160, 856–880.

Chen, G., M. Geiger, and M. Fu (2015). "Manufacturing FDI in Sub-Saharan Africa: Trends, determinants, and impact," *Working Paper, World Bank Group*.

Chen, W., D. Dollar, and H. Tang (2018). "Why is China Investing in Africa? Evidence from the Firm Level," *The World Bank Economic Review*, 32, 610–632.

Cohen, W. M. and R. C. Levin (1989). "Empirical studies of innovation and market structure," In R. Schamalensee and R. D. Wiilig (Eds.), *Handbook of Industrial Organization*, 2, 1059–1107.

Colletaz, G. and C. Hurlin (2006). "Threshold effects of the public capital productivity: An international panel smooth transition approach," *Document de Recherche du Laboratoire d'Economie d'Orléans. Working Paper No.* 2006-01, 1–42.

Costinot, A. (2009). "An Elementary Theory of Comparative Advantage," *Econometrica*, 105, 1165–1192.

Costinot, A., D. Donaldson, J. Vogel, and I. Werning (2015). "Comparative Advantage and Optimal Trade Policy," *Quarterly Journal of Economics*, 130, 659–702.

Dollar, D. (2016). "China's Engagement with Africa: From Natural Resources to Human Resources."

Donou-Adonsou, F. and S. Lim (2018). "On the Importance of Chinese Investment in Africa," *Review of Development Finance*, 8, 63–73.

Eaton, J. and S. Kortum (2001). "Trade in Capital Goods," *European Economic Review*, 45, 1195–1235.

Fan, H., F. Lin, and L. Tang (2018). "Minimum Wage and Outward FDI from China," *Journal of Development Economics*, 135, 1–19.

Fauzel, S., B. Seetanah, and R. V. Sannassee (2015). "Foreign Direct Investment and Welfare Nexus in Sub Saharan Africa," *Journal of Development Area*, 49, 271–283.

Fowowe, B. and M. I. Shuaibu (2014). "Is Foreign Direct Investment Good for the Poor? New Evidence from African Countries," *Economic Change and Restructuring*, 47, 321–339.

Fu, X. (2008). "Foreign Direct Investment, Absorptive Capacity and Regional Innovation Capabilities: Evidence from China," *Oxford Development Studies*, 36, 89–110.

Gohou, G. and I. Soumaré (2012). "Does Foreign Direct Investment Reduce Poverty in Africa and Are There Regional Differences?" *World Development*, 40, 75–95.

Goldberg, P. K., A. Khandelwal, N. Pavcnik, and P. Topalova (2010). "Imported Intermediate Inputs and Domestic Product Growth: Evidence from India," *The Quarterly Journal of Economics*, 125, 1727–1767.

Gonzalez, A., T. Terasvirta, and D. van Dick (2005). "Panel smooth transition regression models." SSE/EFI Working Paper series in economics and finance No. 604, 1–33.

Granger, C. W., T. Terasvirta, and H. M. Anderson (1993). "Modelling nonlinearity over the business cycle." In J. H. Stock and M. W. Watson (Eds.), *Business Cycles, Indicators and Forecasting*, Chicago: The University of Chicago Press, pp. 311–325.

Hansen, B. E. (1999). "Threshold Effects in Non-dynamic Panels: Estimation, Testing, and Inference," *Journal of Econometrics*, 93, 345–368.

Havranek, T. and Z. Irvosa (2011). "Estimating Vertical Spillovers from FDI: Why Results Vary and What the True Effect Is," *Journal of International Economics*, 85, 234–244.

Jaumotte, F. (2004). "Foreign direct investment and regional trade agreements: The market size effect revisited," *International Monetary Fund*, 2004(206), 1–32.

Jinyuan, G. (1984). "China and Africa: The Development of Relations Over Many Centuries," *African Affairs*, 83, 241–250.

Kalver, M. and M. Trebilock (2011). "Chinese Investment in Africa," *Law and Development Review*, 4, 168–217.

Koopman, R., Z. Wang, and S.-J. Wei (2014). "Tracing Value-added and Double Counting in Gross Exports," *American Economic Review*, 104, 459–494.

Lenzen, M., D. Moran, K. Kanemoto, and A. Geschke (2013). "Building Eora: A Global Multi-region Input–Output Database at High Country and Sector Resolution," *Economic Systems Research*, 25, 20–49.

Manova, K. and Z. Zhang (2012). "Export Prices Across Firms and Destinations," *Quarterly Journal of Economics*, 127, 379–436.

Matsuyama, K. (2013). "Endogenous Ranking and Equilibrium Lorenz Curve Across (ex-ante) Identical Countries," *Econometrics*, 81, 2009–2031.

Maurer, M. (2017). "Supply Chain Trade and Technological Transfer in the ASEAN + 3 Region," *China Economic Review*, 46, 277–289.

Mody, A. and K. Srinivasan (1998). "Japanese and U.S. Firms as Foreign Investors: Do They March to the Same Tune?" *Canadian Journal of Economics*, 31, 778–799.

Morisset, J. (2000). "Foreign Direct Investment in Africa: Policies Also Matter," *Transnational Corporations*, 9, 107–125.

Osabutey, E. L. C. and T. Jackson (2019). "The Impact on Development of Technology and Knowledge Transfer in Chinese MNEs in Sub-Saharan Africa: The Ghanaian Case," *Technological Forecasting and Social Change*, 148, 119725.

Otchere, I., I. Soumaré, and P. Yourougou (2019). "FDI and Financial Market Development in Africa," *The World Economy*, 39, 651–678.

Renard, M.-F. (2011). "China's Trade and FDI in Africa," *African Development Bank Group, Working Paper No. 126*.

Soumaré, I. (2015). "Does FDI Improve Economic Development in North Africa Countries?" *Applied Economics*, 47, 5510–5553.

Stone, S., M. Mikic, M. Agyeben, W. Anukoonwattaka, A. Duval, Yabd Heal, S. Kim, M. Prokscg, R. Ratna, A. Saggu, F. Huang, M. Scagliusi, B. Shepherd, C. Utoktham, L. Parisotto, and M. Tomova

(2015). "Asia-Pacific Trade and Investment Report 2015: Supporting Participation in Value Chains," *The United Nations ESCAP Asia-Pacific Trade and Investment Report 2015*.

Strauss, J. C. (2009). "The Past in the Present: Historical and Rhetorical Lineages in China's Relations with Africa," *The China Quarterly*, 199, 777–795.

Wheeler, D. and A. Mody (1992). "International Investment Location Decisions: The Case of U.S. Firms," *Journal of International Economics*, 33, 57–76.

Yu, G. T. (1977). "China's Role in Africa," *Annals of the American Academy of Political and Social Science*, 432, 96–109.

Yu, G. T. (1988). "Africa in Chinese Foreign Policy," *Asian Survey*, 28, 849–862.

Chapter 9

Did Financial Reforms Improve Shanghai and Shenzhen Stock Markets Performance?[*]

Marie-Eliette Dury[†,§] and **Bing Xiao**[‡,¶]

†*Université Clermont Auvergne, CNRS, IRD, CERDI*
F-63000, Clermont-Ferrand, France
‡*Université Clermont Auvergne, IUT Aurillac*
CLERMA EA 38 49, France
§*m-eliette.dury@uca.fr*
¶*bing.xiao@uca.fr*

Abstract

The Chinese equity market is one of the emerging equity markets which offers an opportunity for international diversification. Since the 1990s, the Chinese equity market has changed substantially in two ways: both the size of listed companies and the size of the market itself have increased, in addition the institutional and individual investors have become more mature. The reforms in regulations as well as in the attitudes of regulators have rendered the stock market more efficient. In addition, it would be a question of promoting sustainable development in China. In such cases, we expect an alteration in anomalies in the Chinese stock market. In this chapter, we examine the daily data from the Shenzhen A-share market and the Shanghai A-share market

---

[*]This chapter was first presented at the 12th International Conference on the Chinese Economy organized by Mary-Françoise Renard, "A New Era for China: Growth Sustainability and Broaden International Development," CERDI, IDREC, University of Clermont Auvergne, France and CCES, Fudan University, Shanghai, China, held in Clermont-Ferrand, France, 24–25 October 2019.

over the 1995–2019 period. Despite the disappearance of some seasonal effects, we find a strong Chinese New Year effect and a negative Thursday effect in Shenzhen and Shanghai stock markets. However, we observe that Chinese stock markets become more efficient and more market-oriented, especially after the reform of October 2011. Both the upward and downward adjustments have increased the return.

9.1.   Introduction

9.1.1.   *The reforms improve the efficiency in the Chinese stock market*

Stock price is a suitable indicator of a company's financial performance, and the stock market represents a major channel for investment and financing for Chinese companies (Wen *et al.*, 2018). China's stock market is a relatively new stock market. It was characterized by a high level of information asymmetry, low quantity and quality of information disclosed by listed companies, and low governance transparency. Chinese investors are described in the academic literature as shortsighted and speculative and very oriented to the short run and to heavy trading.

In efficient markets, stock prices are the discounted values of fundamentals; however, speculation may weaken the link between prices and fundamentals. Beltratti *et al.* (2009) studied the effect of state-owned enterprises (SOE) reform on the Chinese stock markets, and they indicated that the Chinese investors did not properly react to corporate measures. According to them, speculation was strongly associated with abnormal returns, and most of the cross-section of average returns was explained by volume, a variable linked with speculation. At the same time, a relationship exists between the average returns and various fundamentals (price-to-earnings Ratio, size, bid–ask spread), nevertheless the relationship is not robust.

To render the stock market more efficient, the Chinese government had enhanced the legislative and regulatory framework and revised Chinese accounting standards several times in an attempt to improve the poor information environment. Ambitious reforms to build a modern financial system and reduce the role of the state in the economy accelerated China's move toward deregulation. We can distinguish these reforms in four aspects.

9.1.1.1. *Early reforms in the Chinese stock market*

Historically, the Chinese stock market has been described as having a "low" information environment. According to the semi-strong efficient markets hypothesis (EMH), informationally-efficient market returns cannot be predicted on the basis of any publicly available information, including returns in other markets. Groenewold *et al.* (2004) examined the inter-relationships between the stock markets of the Chinese mainland—Shanghai and Shenzhen—and those of Hong Kong and Taiwan, before and after the Asian crisis of 1997–1998. They found that mainland markets are isolated from the other two markets considered. In fact, the Hong Kong stock market had weak predictive power for returns on the Shanghai and Shenzhen stock markets but the reverse was not true. However, since the 1990s, the reforms in regulations as well as in the attitudes of regulators have rendered the stock market more efficient.

1. *Reforms in deregulating bank lending and deposit rates*: In 1993, the State Council issued a decision on financial system reforms that incorporated a strategy for interest rate liberalization. The objective was to encourage banks to lend to small- and medium-sized enterprises, which tended to receive fewer loans than larger firms that were seen to be more creditworthy. In the early 2000s, the authorities began a process of gradually liberalizing interest rates on loans that culminated in the removal of nearly all such restrictions in 2013.

2. *Reforms against the speculators*: One of the most important reforms was price limit reform in 1996. The variation range of stock price during a business day was limited to be no more than 10%. After the reform, the stock prices were no longer easily driven up by the institutional investors. The China Securities Regulatory Commission (CSRC), enhanced the supervision of and increased the penalty for speculators from 2001 onwards. Liu *et al.* (2010) showed that the Shenzhen stock market was more efficient after the price-limited reform.

In order to help stabilize the stock markets and strengthen corporate governance, the government made a strategic decision in year 2000 to develop securities mutual funds as institutional investors in tradable shares. The presence of institutional investors has been noticeable since 1998, with an especially large increase in the number and width of mutual fund companies since 2001. Finally, both the size of listed companies and the size of the market itself increased very fast since 2001, making it presumably harder and harder to corner the markets.

3. *Reforms of governance*: Realizing the problems with the split-share structure, the Chinese government began to reduce the proportion of state ownership by selling state-owned shares in the market in June 2001. To help solve the fundamental governance problems, the Chinese government initiated a split-share structure reform program in April 2005 (SOE reform). The aim of the reform is to convert non-tradable shares into tradable shares. The non-tradable shareholders gain from the reform as their shares become tradable. This increases liquidity and enables controlling shareholders to sell at market prices. Chong *et al.* (2005) found that significant positive profits are most common in the pre-SOE reform period but not in the post-reform period, which suggests that the SOE reform played an important role in improving efficiency in both stock exchanges.

4. *Reforms of information disclosure*: Administrative Measures on Information Disclosure (AMID) by Listed Companies were introduced in 2007. The reforms were expected to have implications for the information environment of the Chinese A-share market.

According to the EMH, the observed price reflects at all times all the information available; however, the existence of costs for the acquisition and processing of information has very strong consequences on efficiency. The empirical evidence suggests that the increase in the level of information disclosure of the Chinese A-share sample can be attributed to the 2007 AMID reforms. Gong and Marsden (2014) suggested that AMID reforms have resulted in an increase in the level of information disclosure by Chinese listed A-shares to the market. This greater level of information disclosure should improve market fairness for all investors and reduce any information asymmetry between informed and uninformed investors. In this context, we can expect that Chinese individual investors and institutional investors may be better informed, and they can adopt more mature behavior, and more relevant anticipation. Their rational anticipation can render Chinese stock markets more efficient. In this case, we expect a reduction in seasonal anomalies in the Chinese stock market due to increasing maturity of the market.

9.1.2. *Reform of CSRC in October 2011*

In October 2011, the CSRC which is the Chinese market regulator, announced measures to reform the Chinese stock market. The reform project would first of all allow the country's financial markets to mature. The stock market in China is barely 20 years old. Many companies, including banks, have entered after 2005.

The next step would be to liberalize the Chinese stock market, effectively mobilize Chinese savings, restructure and modernize Chinese industries, and develop innovation.

Last, it would be a question of promoting sustainable development.

9.1.2.1. *Lower transaction costs*

First, the CSRC decided to reduce transaction fees of the Shanghai and Shenzhen stock exchanges. The fees would amount to 0.0087% of the trading volume in the two stock markets compared to 0.011% previously for the Shanghai Stock Exchange and 0.0122% for the Shenzhen Stock Exchange.

9.1.2.2. *Initial Public Offering (IPO) system*

China's IPO system is built in such a way that prices are constantly overvalued, serving the interests of newly introduced companies and their underwriters and damaging the interests of investors who end up suffering losses after a few days of transactions. In order to avoid such situations, the regulator asks Chinese companies to provide additional financial information when their price-to-earnings (PE) ratio is 25% higher than the industry average.

9.1.2.3. *Withdrawal of the rating*

The CSRC has also announced measures to strengthen the exit rules. The regulations in force had been found to be too lax and encouraging speculative behavior. To be withdrawn, the company had to record three consecutive years of net losses.

Between 2001 and 2011, only 40 companies withdrew. Some companies accounted for non-recurring items in net income and used public institutions to post profits and avoid going out.

The reform, which aims to delete the "garbage equities," would consider eight new conditions to strengthen the requirements for delisting, including three consecutive years of operating income below 10 million Yuan. Companies with net negative assets will no longer be able to remain listed.

9.1.2.4.   *Encouragement of incoming and outgoing flows*

Another measure taken by the stock exchange authority was to increase Qualified Domestic Institutional Investor (QDII) quotas, licenses allowing domestic actors to invest abroad and Qualified Foreign Institutional Investor (QFII) quotas, licenses allowing foreign investors to buy shares listed on the domestic market. QFII quotas were extended to USD 80 billion, compared with USD 30 billion after the reform, distributed among 158 investors with institutions like the Korea Investment Corp or the Kuwait Investment Authority.

Beyond the expansion of quotas, the CSRC would seek to ease the conditions for obtaining a license to allow foreign investors to buy securities in the country. The current rules require that an actor has at least USD 5 billion assets under management and has been in business for at least five years. The thresholds imposed on banks and brokerage firms are higher.

9.1.2.5.   *Accelerating financial innovation*

Eleven proposals were made by the regulator to address the lack of differentiation between products perceived as an obstacle to the rise of the financial industry in China.

Other developments were proposed such as the following: encouraging mergers and acquisitions between securities companies; promoting investor participation in the over-the-counter (OTC) market; adjustment of risk management systems, distribution of dividends, in particular by public companies; the possibility for pension funds to invest in the stock market.

9.1.2.6.   *Opening of the capital of brokerage firms to foreign operators*

China has agreed to raise the threshold for foreign investors to hold the equity stake in domestic brokerage companies from 33% to 49%.

This new rule should not really change the profile of the industry dominated by more than 100 local companies, and the interference with policy interests is important. However, it would be a significant step forward.

The reforms previously discussed in this chapter must render the market efficient. We expect an alteration in seasonal anomalies in the Chinese stock market. According to Li and Lin (2015), the implementation of the new pricing reform may potentially have affected the uncertainty of the Chinese stock market, particularly in relation to energy-intensive sectors. Peng (2019) shows that the structural reforms have facilitated business formation and led to a higher aggregate output.

9.1.3. *Seasonal effects on financial markets*

In developed stock markets, anomalies are a well-documented stylized fact. The cross-sectional stock returns are among the most robust findings. There are two sorts of anomalies: the cross-sectional stock anomalies, for example the size effect, book-to-market anomaly, and so on, and the seasonal effect, for example the January effect, the week effect. The issue of anomalies generates a large amount of interest in academic circles. The major reason is theoretical: if it were possible to show that investment strategy based on anomalies is capable of systematically beating the market, the efficient market theory would be faulty. The regulations and the attitudes of regulators have rendered the stock market more efficient.

In finance, seasonality refers to the differences that exist in the mean returns of an asset (Gultekin and Gultekin, 1983), which can be related to anomalies. Schwert (2003) defined an anomaly as an inconsistency. There exist different types of anomalies that had been studied through the years, such as the day-of-the-week effect, the week-of-the-month effect, the holiday effect, the month-of-the-year effect, the turn-of-the-month effect.

Seasonalities in returns are among the most robust findings. There are two sorts of seasonalities: high frequency seasonality, for example the day of the week effect and the turn of the month effect. A day of the week effect was detected in the US market by Cross (1973), French (1980), Gibbons and Hess (1981), and Rogalski (1984). These studies document a negative mean return for Mondays and a positive mean return for Fridays. French (1980) hypothesized that the standard deviation for Monday returns should be the highest because a greater number of shocks can manifest themselves over the weekend break.

The month-of-the-year effect was found by Roll (1983) and Ritter (1988). They found a positive January effect and a negative December effect. Keim (1983) and Reinganum (1983) showed that much of the abnormal returns of small firms, measured by the capital asset pricing model (CAPM), occur during the first two weeks in January. Cooper *et al.* (2006) report US evidence that returns in January have predictive power for returns over the subsequent 11 months. Chen and Chien (2011) explained that there will be a January effect when the whole market had positive performance in the preceding year.

The seasonal effect also poses a problem with regards to the validity of the CAPM, validity according to which the expected yield of securities depends on the systematic risk level, the "Beta." According to behavioral finance researchers, seasonal anomaly is proof of the irrationality of individuals. On the other hand, researchers who support the concept of rationality suggest that seasonal effect can be attributed to risk factors other than the market.

The seasonal effect is one of the anomalies of the financial market. For example, if there is a negative day-of-the-week effect, the rational arbitrageurs could sell stocks short in the morning of that day and buy them back the next day. Such trading activity would eventually result in the disappearance of the effect. French (1980) finds that expected returns contain risk premiums that move inversely with business conditions. Kim and Burnie (2002) advanced the hypothesis according to which size effect might be driven by the economic cycle. L'Her (2002) also pointed out that risk premiums vary according to economic conditions. DeStefano (2004) found that stock returns decrease throughout economic expansions and become negative during the first half of recession.

Among the emerging equity markets, the Chinese equity market is one that offers an opportunity for international diversification. Since the 1990s, the reforms in regulations as well as in the attitudes of regulators have rendered the stock market more efficient. However, it would seem that in the Chinese stock market, the seasonal anomalies persist. The evidence regarding day-of-the-week effects is rather mixed as conclusions from various studies seem to depend heavily on the particular choice of sample period. Using daily returns, Mookerjee and Yu (1999) found that the seasonal patterns of the Chinese stock markets are at odds with the majority of findings for other stock exchanges around the world. They found positive Thursday returns. In contrast with this study, Mitchell and Ong (2006) found the evidence of negative Tuesday returns in the Chinese stock market. Bouman and Jacobsen (2002) document the "Sell in May and go away" puzzle, which means that stocks have higher returns in the November–April period than the May–October period. Girardin and Liu (2005) and Jacobsen and Zhang (2012) found a Red-May effect in which returns would be higher after the Labor Day holidays than at any other time of the year. Girardin and Liu (2005) found a positive June effect and a negative December effect in China's stock market. Guo *et al.* (2014) confirm that the "Sell in May" effect exists in the Chinese stock market.

Some anomalies seem to disappear after they are documented in the finance literature: the rational arbitrageur's trading activity would eventually result in the disappearance of the effect. Does their disappearance reflect sample selection bias, so that there was never an anomaly in the first place? The contributions of our chapter to this literature concern the investigation of the seasonality of Chinese stock markets using long-term data. We analyze the evolution of the daily data from the Shenzhen A-share market and the Shanghai A-share market over the 1995–2019 period. Now, to the best of our knowledge, this has never been done on Chinese stock markets before. Furthermore, a lot of event studies on seasonality uses the cross-sectional analysis. In this chapter we work on time series; we use three different methods: descriptive statistics method, ARMAX–GARCH model and unobserved components time series model (UCM). Thus, our chapter contributes to the existing finance literature by investigating the seasonal anomalies during the long period.

We organize the chapter as follows. Section 9.2 focuses on the database and methodology, while Section 9.3 discusses the results. Section 9.4 concludes the chapter.

9.2.   Methodology

9.2.1.   *Data*

The Chinese stock market has a relatively short history, there are two stock exchanges operating independently in China, the Shenzhen Stock Exchange (SZSE) and Shanghai Stock Exchange (SSE). Chinese stock markets separate foreign investors from domestic investors through dual classes of stocks. Individual shares are divided into two classes of shares: A-shares and B-shares. A-shares are available for domestic investors and B-shares are available for foreign investors. The Shenzhen Stock Exchange was established on April 11, 1991. On August 11, 2019, there were already 2175 listed companies in the Shenzhen Stock Exchange (www.szse.cn). The Shenzhen Composite (SZC) Index is a market-capitalization weighted index of stocks in the SZSE which tracks the daily price movements of all the shares in the exchange. The index began on April 3, 1991, with a base price of 100. The current SSE was re-established on November 26, 1990. On August 11, 2019, there were 1514 listed companies in the Shanghai Stock Exchange (www.sse.com.cn). It is the world's fourth largest stock market by market capitalization at USD 5.5 trillion as of April 2018.

Figure 9.1 shows the price series for the Shenzhen index, the requisite data is obtained from the Factset database (see also in

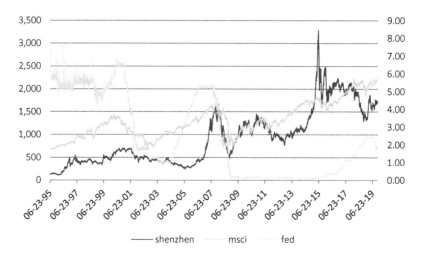

Fig. 9.1.   Prices for Shenzhen A-share index 1995–2019.

Appendix Figures A.9.5 and A.9.6 including the prices series for the Shanghai index). The stylized facts of the financial series are noted, we can see the price can be difficult to model directly. The trend is far from stationary since its mean level is not constant and rises over time.

A standard procedure models the logarithmic price return rather than prices themselves. The logarithm of the gross return R_t is given by

$$R_t = \ln\left(\frac{P_t}{P_{t-1}}\right), \tag{9.1}$$

where R_t is the rate of return at time t, P_t is the price at time t, and P_{t-1} is the price just prior to the time t.

9.2.2. *Methods*

The seasonal effect is one of the anomalies of the financial market. For example, if there is a negative day-of-the-week effect, the rational arbitragers could sell stocks short in the morning of that day and buy them back the next day. Such trading activity would eventually result in the disappearance of the effect. A considerable body of literature has been produced that documents anomalies in stock returns. A day-of-the-week effect was detected in the US market by Cross (1973), French (1980), Gibbons and Hess (1981), and Rogalski (1984); these studies document a negative mean return for Monday and a positive mean return for Friday. The month-of-the-year effect was found by Geske and Roll (1983). They found a positive January effect and a negative December effect.

Girardin *et al.* claim that one of the seasonal anomalies in the Chinese A-share stock markets so called "Red-May" can be explained by bank credit (Girardin and Liu (2005); Guo *et al.* (2014)). Xiao and Coulibaly (2015) find evidence for fixed seasonality with a positive and significant February and May effects for the Shenzhen A-share market index.

The higher returns on a particular weekday are due to the higher risk assumed on that day: a higher standard deviation is associated with higher daily mean returns except Monday. French (1980) hypothesized that the standard deviation for Monday returns should be the highest because a greater number of shocks can manifest themselves over the weekend break. The basic model to estimate the day of the week effect is given by the following equation (Mookerjee and Yu, 1999):

$$R_t = a_0 + a_1 d_{1,t} + a_2 d_{2,t} + a_3 d_{3,t} + a_{4,t} d_{4,t} + e_t, \qquad (9.2)$$

where R_t is the return on day t and $d_{i,t}$ is a dummy variable that takes the value of one for a given day of the week and is zero otherwise.

9.2.2.1. ARMAX–GARCH model

To control the time varying volatility of returns, a lot of authors use the GARCH$(1, 1)$ models, in addition to the OLS regression model, to examine calendar effects (Gregoriou $et\ al.$, 2004; Khan and Rabbani, 2019). The model is given by

$$R_t = a_0 + a_1 \text{Monday} + a_2 \text{Tuesday} + a_3 \text{Wednesday}$$
$$+ a_{4,t} \text{Thursday} + a_5 \text{Friday} + \delta_{before} D_t + \delta_{after}(1 - D_t) + e_t, \qquad (9.3)$$

where D_t is a dummy variable that takes the value of one after the reform and zero otherwise.

Another way to stabilize the variance error by using autoregressive models is employing an ARMAX–GARCH-based structure augmented by several interaction terms (Wen $et\ al.$, 2018; Mobarek and Fiorante, 2014). The ARMAX(p, q) model is given by

$$R_t = a_0 + \sum_{j=1}^{p} b_j R_{t-j} + \sum_{i=1}^{q} c_i \varepsilon_{t-q} + a_1 \text{Int}_{t-1} + a_2 R_{\text{world},t-1} + a_3 \text{Day}_t$$
$$+ \delta_1 D_{\text{up},t}(1 - D_t) + \delta_2 D_{\text{down},t}(1 - D_t)$$
$$+ \delta_3 D_{\text{up},t}(D_t) + \delta_4 D_{\text{down},t}(D_t) + e_t, \qquad (9.4)$$

where R_t is the daily return on stock price series on day t and D_t is a dummy variable that takes the value of one after the reform and zero otherwise; R_{t-1} is the lagged daily return on each stock price series; ε_{t-1} is the lagged residuals; $\ln t_{t=1}$ is the change of interest rates on day $t - 1$; $R_{\text{world},t-1}$ is the lagged daily return on the world stock market index; Day_t is a vector of dummy variables such that the first element is 1 if Day_t is Monday and 0 if otherwise.

The GARCH model is a generalized ARCH model developed by Bollerslev (1986) and Taylor (1986) independently. They introduced a moving average term in the ARCH estimation. A fixed lag structure is imposed. The GARCH(p, q) model (where p is the order of the GARCH terms and q is the order of the ARCH terms ε^2. Ramasamy and Munisamy (2012) and Dury and Xiao (2018) found that the GARCH models are able to predict the volatility of return on assets better.

$$\sigma_t^2 = w + a_1\varepsilon_{t-1}^2 + \cdots + a_q\varepsilon_{t-q}^2 + \beta_1\sigma_{t-1}^2 + \cdots + \beta_p\sigma_{t-p}^2$$

$$= w + \sum_{i=1}^{q} a_i\varepsilon_{t-1}^2 + \sum_{i=1}^{p} \beta_i\sigma_{t-i}^2. \tag{9.5}$$

The form of GARCH(1,1) is given in the following, Eq. (9.6) provides the conditional variance equation, σ_t^2 is the one period forecast variance based on past information, σ_t^2 is determined by a_0, ε_{t-1}^2, and σ_{t-1}^2. The term ε_{t-1}^i provides the information about volatility from the previous period, measured as the lag of the squared residual from Eq. (9.5), and σ_{t-1}^2 is used to be considered as the last period forecasted variance:

$$\sigma_t^2 = a_0 + a\varepsilon_{t-1}^2 + \beta\sigma_{t-1}^2. \tag{9.6}$$

Engle (1982) indicated that the coefficient ($\alpha + \beta$) measures the volatility shock, when ($\alpha + \beta$) is close to one, the volatility shocks are persistent, this means that the volatility may take a long time to return to a stable phase.

9.2.2.2. *Unobserved components time series model (UCM)*

We approach our series of prices by using an unobserved components time series model (UCM), first introduced by (Harvey, 1989). The model allows us to decompose the index I_t between three components given by

$$I_t = \mu_t + \gamma_t + \varphi_t + \varepsilon_t, \quad \varepsilon_t \sim NID\left(0, \sigma_\varepsilon^2\right), \tag{9.7}$$

where μ_t, γ_t, and ε_t represent trend, seasonal, and irregular components, respectively. The trend and seasonal components are modeled by linear dynamic stochastic processes which depend on disturbances. They are formulated in a flexible way and can change over time rather than being deterministic. The term φ_t corresponds to a set of explanatory and dummy variables.

The trend component is simply modeled as a random walk process according to the structure of our data:

$$\mu_{t+1} = \mu_t + \eta_t, \quad \omega_t \sim NID\left(0, \sigma_\eta^2\right), \tag{9.8}$$

where $NID\left(0, \sigma_\eta^2\right)$ refers to a normally independently distributed series with zero mean and variance σ_η^2.

For the seasonal component, we want to study if, for a given month, deviations from trend tend to be of the same sign from one year to the next. Let there be s seasons during the year; in our case $s = 12$. We use a stochastic dummy variable seasonal model for the effect γ_t at time t:

$$\sum_{i=0}^{s-1} \gamma_{t-i} = \omega_t, \quad \omega_t \sim NID\left(0, \sigma_\omega^2\right). \tag{9.9}$$

In this model, the sum of the seasonal effect has a zero mean although their stochastic nature allows them to evolve either slowly over time, when σ_ω^2 is small, or quickly over time, when σ_ω^2 is large. All disturbances are supposed to be mutually uncorrelated. If the variance is equal to zero, the seasonal effects are fixed and do not vary over time in contrast to the precedent specification (9.3). All models are estimated using maximum likelihood.

9.3. Results

9.3.1. *The seasonal anomalies*

To analyze the seasonal anomalies in the Chinese stock markets, we use the market index of the Shenzhen and Shanghai stock exchanges, which is common in the literature. We study daily effects and monthly effects over time, and if the efficient market hypothesis was true, we expect that daily effects and monthly effects to no longer exist after the reforms.

9.3.1.1. *The day of the week effect*

Table 9.1 reports the mean and standard deviation of daily stock returns for the Shenzhen stock market and the Shanghai stock market. For the whole period, returns have been positive. The lowest

Table 9.1. Mean and standard deviation (S.D.) of daily percentage return: Day of the week during the whole period.

Whole period (June 1995–November 2019)	Observations	Mean	S.D.
Shenzhen index	6,136	0.05873	0.018247
Monday	1,156	0.14414	0.021471
Tuesday	1,257	0.041	0.0181854
Wednesday	1,260	0.1607	0.0167734
Thursday	1,234	−0.11923	0.0175252
Friday	1,229	0.07067	0.0170216

Whole period (April 2003–November 2019)	Observations	Mean	S.D.
Shanghai index	4,180	0.03391	0.0165816
Monday	784	0.129808	0.019502
Tuesday	856	0.00904	0.0164715
Wednesday	861	0.0010658	0.0156919
Thursday	842	−0.13296	0.0157147
Friday	837	0.06329	0.0153721

daily returns were found on Thursday (negative). Returns gradually build up to a peak on Monday and then dip slightly on Friday. Tables 9.1 and 9.2 also report the standard deviation in daily returns, which would be a source of insight into whether higher returns on a particular weekday are due to the higher risk assumed by an investor on that day. But we do not find that a higher standard deviation is associated with higher daily returns in our patterns.

Traditionally, the pre-weekend effect, in which stock returns are higher on the day preceding a weekend, has been confirmed in the US market and in the European markets. The Monday effect is a well-known effect around the world: the stock returns on Monday are statistically significantly lower than for the rest of the days of the week. The existence of day-of-the-week effect is inconsistent with the weak-form efficient market hypothesis, which puts forward that capital markets are unpredictable. If the calendar effects exist, investors can use the day-of-the-week effects information to avoid and reduce the risk. Table 9.2 reports the mean return by day of week during the reforms period by using our database. The overall pattern is

Table 9.2. Mean and standard deviation (S.D.) of daily percentage return: Day of the week during the sub-periods.

	Before IPO system reform (June 1995–July 2001)	Before SOE reform (July 2001–May 2005)	Before AMID reform (May 2005–July 2007)	Before 2011 reform (July 2007–October 2011)	After 2011 reform (October 2011–October 2019)
Monday	0.26232 (292) [0.0232448]	−0.24936 (179) [0.0159193]	0.55067 (79) [0.0171993]	0.30061 (222) [0.0259761]	0.06395 (382) [0.020016]
Tuesday	−0.1292 (317) [0.0194232]	0.19545 (192) [0.0142792]	0.35594 (90) [0.0156157]	−0.23014 (241) [0.0223454]	0.188 (417) [0.0163151]
Wednesday	0.25246 (315) [0.0178576]	−0.02011 (192) [0.0142584]	0.18874 (92) [0.0163406]	0.33619 (242) [0.0206689]	0.0584 (418) [0.0142495]
Thursday	−0.05687 (309) [0.0197789]	−0.16406 (188) [0.0153809]	−0.11773 (89) [0.0141067]	−0.05941 (237) [0.0207216]	−0.18245 (410) [0.0152126]
Friday	0.27931 (307) [0.0197067]	−0.12566 (188) [0.0124063]	0.08637 (90) [0.0137739]	−0.02852 (234) [0.0202551]	0.05764 (410) [0.0151116]
Monday		−0.17953 (99) [0.0142663]	0.47368 (79) [0.0162242]	0.29385 (222) [0.0255717]	0.04272 (382) [0.0169942]
Tuesday		0.06798 (108) [0.0107172]	0.29196 (90) [0.0149942]	−0.28638 (241) [0.0215123]	0.10344 (417) [0.0143253]
Wednesday		0.08079 (109) [0.0134435]	0.12303 (92) [0.0157431]	0.26747 (242) [0.0207525]	0.01654 (418) [0.0124777]
Thursday		−0.18704 (105) [0.0124945]	−0.1493 (89) [0.0136557]	−0.07582 (237) [0.0202433]	−0.15001 (410) [0.0138251]
Friday		−0.11888 (103) [0.0119112]	0.10731 (90) [0.0133905]	0.00694 (234) [0.0191665]	0.13156 (410) [0.0140642]

Note: In each case, the first row is the mean, in parenthesis is the number of observations and in brackets is the standard deviation.

Table 9.3.   Estimated variances for the unobserved components model.

	Shenzhen index			Shanghai index		
	Coef.	Std. Err.	Prob.	Coef.	Std. Err.	Prob.
C	0.0005798	0.0004328	0.206	0.000511	0.0005054	0.312
Ar(1)	0.0679493	0.0116464	0.000***	0.0386682	0.0137943	0.005***
Monday	0.0006952	0.0005502	0.676	0.0005164	0.0007499	0.426
Thursday	−0.0002672	0.0006401	0.676	−0.0006479	0.0007499	0.388
Wednesday	0.0000485	0.0006137	0.939	−0.0000294	0.0007486	0.969
Thursday	−0.0015934	0.0006137	0.009***	−0.0017679	0.0007194	0.014***
Friday						
Variance						
C	0.0002262	3.15e-06	0.000***	0.0002088	3.49e-06	0.000***
ARCH	0.3356804	0.016185	0.000***	0.2565734	0.0173862	0.000***
Log likelihood		16209			11518.13	

Note: *, **, and *** indicate statistical significance at the 10%, 5% and 1% levels, respectively.

similar to that observed for the whole period (see Tables 9.1 and 9.3); the Monday returns have been positive on average. We find a strong negative Thursday effect. Mookerjee and Yu (1999) found a positive Thursday effect in Shenzhen and Shanghai stock markets. Chen *et al.* (2001) found a higher return on Friday in the Chinese stock markets. However, Hui (2005) and Chia *et al.* (2011) found no significant Monday and Friday effects on the Chinese stocks markets.

One of the explanations for the day-of-the-week effect might be speculation; in fact, the Chinese stock investors embezzle business funds for private trading (Gao and Kling, 2005). Consequently, the speculators have to pay the embezzled funds back before weekends (year ends and Chinese New Year). The short-time trading before the weekend can explain the profits before the weekends. This explanation is contradictory to our result during the period from 1995 to 2019. We found the lowest mean returns (negative) were on Tuesday; this result can be confirmed by the studies of Jaffe and Westerfield (1985), Solnik and Bousquet (1990), and Barone (1990). By using 2011–2016 daily data, Perez (2018) indicated that there was no statistically significant Monday effect but a possible Thursday effect in the Chinese stock market.

We use a UCM model to analyze the day-of-the-week effect on the two markets. Friday has been deleted due to collinearity; the day-of-the-week effect can be studied by using the reference day. The results confirm the negative Thursday effect.

We did not find a Monday effect, however we have detected a negative Thursday effect, with the downward trend in market prices closing on Thursday compared to the day before (Wednesday). According to behavioral finance, the effect on Monday is caused by unfavorable factors that accompany each new work week. Others believe that it is linked to the fact that companies often publish negative information on Friday evenings, just after the close of the market. This would be supported by the hypothesis that investors tend to sell all of their stocks on Friday afternoons to avoid possible slippage on weekends. We believe that one possible explanation for the negative Thursday effect is that Chinese investors are anticipating this accumulation of news on Friday, trying to settle their position on Thursday. As a result, stock prices fall on Thursday, return on Thursday is negative, and prices increase on Friday, so Friday's and Monday's returns are generally positive. Nevertheless, a more detailed study would be necessary to understand precisely this phenomenon.

9.3.1.2. *Chinese New Year effect*

The pre-holiday effect is one of the calendar effects, and according to this effect, the stock returns are higher on the day preceding a holiday. As with the day-of-the-week effect, the pre-holiday effect has been confirmed by Cadsby and Ratner (1992) and Chong *et al.* (2005). Using 2000–2012 database, Pu (2012) tested the pre-holiday effect in Chinese stock markets; the author found a pre-holiday effect statistically significant: "Both the returns and the frequency of days with positive returns in pre-holiday days are higher than those of normal days." Pu indicated that the pre-holiday effect has not diminished during the 2000–2012 period, and he concluded that the efficiency of China's market is not enough.

In general, the Chinese year end is in February, we studied the observations a week before the Chinese New Year; we created binary variables to capture the pre-New-Year effect. Here, dummy variable equals to 1 if date is a pre-New-Year day and equal to 0 otherwise. Table 9.4 indicates the performance of the two indices during different sub-periods. Indeed, we found that the abnormal positive return in pre-holiday is higher than normal days (post-holiday). By using

Table 9.4. Mean and standard deviation (S.D.) of daily percentage return: Chinese New Year effect during the whole period.

	Whole period (1995–2019)	Before IPO system reform (1995–July 2001)	Before SOE reform (July 2001–May 2005)	Before AMID reform (May 2005–July 2007)	Before 2011 reform (July 2007–October 2011)	After 2011 reform (October 2011–October 2019)
Shenzhen index	0.05873 (6136) [0.018247]	0.11475 (1510)[0.020539]	−0.07279 (919)[0.0146053]	0.20584 (435)[0.0156032]	0.04219 (1151)[0.0221403]	0.02923 (1997)[0.016316]
New year Shenzhen	0.44315 (120) [0.0131995]	0.33534 (30)[0.0074304]	0.07297 (20)[0.0108584]	0.13096 (5)[0.001783]	0.93253 (25)[0.019214]	0.44224 (40)[0.0134567]
Shanghai index	0.03391 (4180) [0.0165816]		−0.06775 (514)[0.0126698]	0.16284 (435)[0.0149697]	0.01805 (1151)[0.021599]	0.02354 (1997)[0.0144372]
New year Shanghai	0.46856 (80) [0.0139765]		0.13157 (10)[0.009504]	0.10988 (5)[0.0026619]	0.95284 (25)[0.0189707]	0.29496 (40)[0.0114003]

our database, during 1995–2019, we found a strong pre-New-Year effect (pre-holiday effect) in both Shenzhen and Shanghai stock markets, and this effect has not diminished after the different reforms. In Table 9.4, after the 2011 reform, the average daily yield during the New Year period is 0.44 against only 0.029 for the rest of the year on the Shenzhen stock market. In the same way, on the Shanghai Stock Market, the New Year yield is around 0.29 compared to 0.02 for an ordinary day.

According to Gao and Kling (2005), the Chinese stock market exhibits significantly higher monthly returns in February and November. The result of our study shows that the Chinese February effect can be explained in part by the pre-New-Year effect: the Chinese year-end is in February or at the end of January. Haugen and Jorion (1996) suggested that calendar effects should not be long lasting, as market participants can learn from experience. If investors, based on experience, are aware of pre-New-Year effect and can use trading strategies, then the pre-New-Year effect should disappear over time. The persistence of effect means lack of market efficiency. Next, we will study the monthly effect; we aim to figure out whether the monthly effect persists after the reforms.

9.3.1.3.   *The monthly effect*

Tables 9.5 and 9.6 report the mean daily return by month. By using Shenzhen index returns for the whole period, we find a negative December effect and a positive January effect. Girardin and Liu (2005) explain that the speculators accumulate their holdings of stocks in the first two months of the year, during March and April; speculators would try to corner the market and bid up the price. From the end of April, speculators would try to reduce their holdings when the price is still high. After the middle of June, they would get money back from the sale of their stocks plus speculative profit, in order to pay back what they borrowed, over a half-year period, at the beginning of the year. This practice may also explain the bad performance in June returns.

By using Shanghai index returns for the whole period, we do not find a negative December; the December returns do better than the January returns. We find negative mean returns for June and October. Both the Shenzhen market and the Shanghai market exhibit strong higher daily returns in February: 0.24433% per day for the

Table 9.5. Daily percentage average return of monthly effect in Shenzhen index.

Whole period (1995–2019)	Observations	Mean	S.D.
Shenzhen index	6,136	0.05873	0.018247
January	489	0.03428	0.0198541
February	461	0.24433	0.0173789
March	522	0.16252	0.0157868
April	498	0.14477	0.0180603
May	509	0.10289	0.0192078
June	516	−0.02732	0.0207035
July	529	0.06833	0.020069
August	554	−0.05811	0.0184137
September	505	−0.00886	0.0175369
October	554	0.06229	0.0166748
November	494	0.07245	0.0167768
December	505	−0.06734	0.017746

Table 9.6. Daily percentage average return of monthly effect in Shanghai index.

Whole period (2003–2019)	Observations	Mean	S.D.
Shanghai index	4,180	0.03391	0.0165816
January	323	0.03078	0.018807
February	307	0.21126	0.0167696
March	350	0.04377	0.0150404
April	351	0.11993	0.0164617
May	360	0.01868	0.015679
June	363	−0.20099	0.0187815
July	359	0.08456	0.017884
August	377	−0.0922	0.0177274
September	347	0.0425	0.0156861
October	375	−0.02071	0.0142894
November	331	0.08404	0.0164896
December	337	0.13459	0.0146737

Shenzhen stock market and 0.21126% for the Shanghai stock market. The results confirm our findings in the previous section: the pre-New-Year (pre-holiday) effect contributed to the stock market performance in February in Chinese stock markets.

Tables 9.7 and 9.8 report the results obtained by analyzing the sub-periods, the results confirm our findings—the December returns do better than the January returns after the 2007 AMID reform. We find a strong February effect and negative mean returns for January and June. The February effect can be explained by the fact that the Chinese year end is in February or at the end of January. Rozeff and Kinney (1976) considered the January and year end effects are related to tax-loss selling strategies. The explanation of the higher returns in January is the strategy to realize losses in December to reduce the taxable speculation gains. To avoid reporting to many losers in their portfolios at the year-end, institutional investors sell losers in December (Gao and Kling, 2005). In China, capital gains are free of taxes, so the tax motivated selling strategy should not be observed on the Shenzhen and Shanghai stock markets. These peculiarities explain the absence of the January effect and the end-of-year effect in the Chinese stock markets.

The results obtained on the Shanghai market are similar to those obtained on the Shenzhen market; February and December show significantly positive returns compared to other months, and the February effect can be explained by the Chinese year end. We observe that the average returns decline form March/April to November/December. To confirm a positive year-end effect and a February effect, we will use a UCM model on our database.

In Tables 9.9 and 9.10, we report results of the estimated variances of the different components of our unobserved components model. Column "month" presents estimations for the seasonality in the recession cycle. In column "month*dummy," we introduce the effect of expansion. We find a significant and positive February effect. After the year end, at the end of January or February, average returns are higher compared to other months. However, we cannot confirm a positive year end effect for Shenzhen and Shanghai stock markets. The Chinese New Year effect might be shifted to February due to the Chinese calendar. Over the period of 25 years considered in this study, the Chinese New Year takes place 16 times in February and 9 times in January. For 5 times, it is in late January, between January 28 and 31. Therefore, in reality the New-Year effect during this 25 years period is actually a February effect.

Table 9.7. Monthly effect during sub-periods for Shenzhen stock market.

	Before IPO system reform (1995–July 2001)	Before SOE reform (July 2001–May 2005)	Before AMID reform (May 2005–July 2007)	Before 2011 reform (July 2007–October 2011)	After 2011 reform (October 2011–October 2019)
January	0.16503 (124) [0.0167929]	−0.01398 (82) [0.0206851]	0.70056 (40) [0.0226208]	−0.1543 (80) [0.0231549]	−0.11186 (163) [0.0189326]
February	0.03513 (116) [0.0178078]	0.31773 (76) [0.0130561]	0.1469 (19) [0.0109914]	0.40856 (95) [0.0228178]	0.27377 (154) [0.0138908]
March	0.31925 (131) [0.0147553]	0.02951 (86) [0.01339]	0.10844 (23) [0.0086555]	0.07569 (110) [0.0189854]	0.17243 (172) [0.0161861]
April	0.41696 (124) [0.0200399]	−0.18743 (85) [0.0134053]	0.48625 (19) [0.0112103]	0.20582 (104) [0.0246513]	0.03423 (166) [0.0135834]
May	0.1354 (127) [0.0250605]	−0.07254 (63) [0.0127363]	0.23299 (42) [0.0177481]	0.01077 (104) [0.0200346]	0.16767 (172) [0.015956]
June	0.33247 (133) [0.0204716]	−0.10849 (62) [0.0183436]	0.10818 (44) [0.0211878]	−0.30428 (108) [0.024987]	−0.13899 (169) [0.0182429]
July	0.06121 (148) [0.0240445]	−0.09829 (65) [0.0103643]	−0.21449 (40) [0.017873]	0.51778 (106) [0.0205592]	−0.07548 (170) [0.0189933]
August	−0.13625 (132) [0.0197112]	−0.15258 (87) [0.0098988]	0.30177 (46) [0.0143346]	−0.21019 (110) [0.0240734]	−0.02732 (178) [0.0173715]
September	−0.06178 (123) [0.0197361]	−0.1298 (77) [0.0149944]	0.12188 (41) [0.0118129]	−0.07381 (103) [0.0209884]	0.09768 (161) [0.0156995]
October	0.39443 (133) [0.0194681]	−0.20378 (90) [0.0171338]	−0.08466 (43) [0.0105612]	−0.09148 (89) [0.018859]	0.06147 (198) [0.0141086]
November	0.02672 (122) [0.0144168]	0.01584 (81) [0.0155003]	0.26928 (42) [0.0122792]	0.14121 (81) [0.0256342]	0.0506 (168) [0.0145552]
December	−0.35283 (127) [0.0238545]	−0.20042 (85) [0.011004]	0.36918 (41) [0.0130335]	0.23212 (86) [0.0187623]	−0.04373 (166) [0.0150526]

Table 9.8.   Monthly effect during sub-periods for Shanghai stock market.

	Before SOE reform (July 2001– May 2005)	Before AMID reform (May 2005– July 2007)	Before 2011 reform (July 2007– October 2011)	After 2011 reform (October 2011– October 2019)
January	0.044	0.66515	−0.11568	−0.05627
	(40) [0.0118678]	(40) [0.0218564]	(80) [0.0226775]	(163) [0.0170757]
February	0.38312	0.05087	0.28554	0.14126
	(38) [0.0152094]	(19) [0.0104909]	(95) [0.0220485]	(154) [0.0138908]
March	−0.17921	−0.05133	0.08952	0.08557
	(45) [0.0113476]	(23) [0.0090394]	(110) [0.019001]	(172) [0.0136442]
April	−0.17407	0.42374	0.27779	0.09606
	(62) [0.0155849]	(19) [0.0112917]	(104) [0.0232767]	(166) [0.0112639]
May	0.03048	0.16756	−0.07377	0.03552
	(41) [0.0116154]	(42) [0.017028]	(104) [0.019155]	(172) [0.0138895]
June	−0.4318	0.08379	−0.26489	−0.17694
	(42) [0.011546]	(44) [0.02026]	(108) [0.0236835]	(169) [0.0162534]
July	−0.0166	−0.20686	0.43296	−0.03852
	(43) [0.0111418]	(40) [0.0172182]	(106) [0.0200129]	(170) [0.0178328]
August	−0.18915	0.15144	−0.23942	−0.04076
	(43) [0.0085317]	(46) [0.0130594]	(110) [0.0230661]	(178) [0.016611]
September	0.02364	0.12564	−0.03735	0.07733
	(42) [0.0161201]	(41) [0.0111378]	(103) [0.0211331]	(161) [0.0122091]
October	−0.18108	−0.08466	−0.09025	0.06568
	(44) [0.0116514]	(43) [0.01057]	(89) [0.0209083]	(198) [0.0117129]
November	0.1275	0.23213	0.01717	0.06892
	(40) [0.0137324]	(42) [0.0106949]	(81) [0.0255512]	(168) [0.0123125]
December	−0.07643	0.4243	0.17679	0.09711
	(44) [0.0099755]	(41) [0.0132208]	(86) [0.0175802]	(166) [0.0144027]

So, we should not expect a January effect (Gao and Kling, 2005). The February effect is weak evidence for the efficiency hypothesis of the Chinese stock markets.

We did not find any significant January effect in our database; this result is consistent with the studies of Mookerjee and Yu (1999), Kling and Gao (2004), and Hsieh (2016). According to tax-loss selling hypothesis, individual investors and institutional investors may tend to sell their losers in December, and then buy back the same stocks after the reporting period in January in order to re-establish their desired portfolio; such actions are the most used explanation for the January effect before 1986. However, after 1986, this explanation was weakened by tax reform. Most developed countries impose a tax on capital gains in their stock markets. To compare with the January effect in financial markets in developed countries, tax-loss

Table 9.9. Estimated variances for the unobserved components and ARCH (1) model for Shenzhen.

Shenzhen index	Month			Month * Dummy		
	Coef.	Std. Err.	Prob.	Coef.	Std. Err.	Prob.
C	0.0024316	0.0010463	0.020**			
January	−0.007376	0.001218	0.000***	0.0084802	0.0012239	0.000***
February				0.0003319	0.0013739	0.809
March	−0.0025035	0.0015441	0.105	0.0029853	0.0015409	0.053*
April	−0.003172	0.0014538	0.029**	0.0033541	0.0015331	0.029**
May	−0.0032121	0.0015964	0.044**	0.0040021	0.0014448	0.006***
June	−0.0044651	0.0013056	0.001***	0.0045809	0.0013408	0.001***
July	−0.0033608	0.0014316	0.019**	0.0033355	0.0012911	0.01***
August	−0.0033289	0.001396	0.017**	0.0020779	0.0014135	0.142
September	−0.0041893	0.0013108	0.001***	0.0021734	0.0014161	0.266
October	−0.0030169	0.0013367	0.024**	0.0017267	0.0015536	0.182
November	−0.0033866	0.0014533	0.02**	0.0020596	0.001544	0.017**
December	−0.0042008	0.0015805	0.008***	0.004051	0.0017039	0.02**
AR(1)	0.0490083	0.0115242	0.000***			
C	0.0002206	3.15e-06	0.000***			
ARCH (1)	0.3530485	0.0170986	0.000***			

Note: *, **, and *** indicate statistical significance at the 10%, 5% and 1% levels, respectively.

selling pressure should not be observable in the Chinese stock markets in December because there are no taxes on capital gains in the Shanghai and the Shenzhen stock markets.

Market efficiency theory assumes that share prices reflect all available information. In theory, this should make buying and selling overvalued stocks impossible, since any stock would always be traded at a fair price. But in practice, it is difficult to create efficient markets and even more difficult to maintain them. The anomalies prove that the theory of market efficiency is not always reliable because all the relevant information is not directly reflected. In contrast to the theory of market efficiency, behavioral finance highlights situations where markets are not rational and will try to explain the causes by investor psychology. Behavioral finance considers that the investor is not always rational and that his/her feelings are subject to its own judgment. The decision-making in situations of uncertainty is prone to cognitive bias as investors can be subjected to emotional factors, such as fear or overconfidence, which interfere during this decision. A mathematical approach is based on the study of the Hurst index

Table 9.10. Estimated variances for the unobserved components and ARCH (1) model for Shanghai.

Shanghai index	Month			Month * Dummy		
	Coef.	Std. Err.	Prob.	Coef.	Std. Err.	Prob.
C	−0.0044597	0.0006595	0.000***			
January				0.0063796	0.0012583	0.000***
February	0.007079	0.0011517	0.000***	−0.0012752	0.0013215	0.335
March	0.0029348	0.0015122	0.052*	0.0038267	0.001774	0.031**
April	0.0033902	0.0012057	0.005***	0.0033255	0.0016243	0.041**
May	0.0033814	0.0015505	0.029**	0.0018407	0.0017284	0.287
June	0.0014776	0.0011421	0.196	0.003211	0.0015271	0.035**
July	0.0043897	0.0013545	0.001***	0.0020131	0.001546	0.193
August	0.0028878	0.0011307	0.011**	0.001929	0.0014392	0.180
September	0.0034451	0.0012053	0.004***	0.0023163	0.0016915	0.164
October	0.0030534	0.0013408	0.023**	0.0016024	0.0018007	0.2
November	0.0036777	0.0012491	0.003***	0.006359	0.0015059	0.287
December	0.0033612	0.0016442	0.041**	−0.0044597	0.001931	0.001***
AR(1)	0.023922	0.013887	0.085*			
C	0.002026	3.72^e-06	0.000***			
ARCH (1)	0.2790479	0.0190543	0.000***			

Note: *, **, and *** indicate statistical significance at the 10%, 5% and 1% levels, respectively.

$H(t) \in]0, 1[$, where the market efficiency corresponds to $H(t) = 1/2$. We aim at developing in other works in the near future.

One difficulty is to find a rational justification for anomalies such as the holiday effect or the day-of-the-week effect for instance. As a rule, such deviations represent investment opportunities, which are, once known to the public, seized by investors until they are exhausted. The market is then said to be "repaired." How can we hence explain the repeated presence of such calendar anomalies, despite the fact that they are known to investors?

One explanation is the self-fulfilling prophecy: the initially unfounded belief that the Chinese New Year period is profitable. This belief can prompt investors to invest their assets at that time, causing a general rise in yields and thus confirming their "prophecy."

Another explanation is the capacity to incorporate news. In fact, during the holiday season, an unnoticed phenomenon would limit the ability of the financial markets to incorporate news as quickly as in normal time.

It is also plausible that the euphoria present among investors on the eve of holidays, and especially for the Chinese New Year, would have the effect of increasing their optimism with regard to the markets, causing a general rise in stock prices. Taking the example of the gold market, Qi and Wang (2013) found that in months such as February, April, August, and November, gold returns were higher than in other months. These months occur before the Golden Week, a seven-day holiday in China.

The monthly effect and the day-of-the-week effect are puzzling; during the 1995–2019 period, they do not disappear in the Chinese stock market. The year-end effect is shifted to February due to the Chinese New Year; hence, February plays the same role as December for US and European markets. However, we find that some calendar effects flattened after the 2011 reform. In the following section, we study the impact of the 2011 reform on the Chinese stock markets.

9.3.2. *Impact of CSRC 2011 effect on the Chinese stock markets*

Tables 9.11–9.13 report the mean and standard deviation of daily stock returns for the Shenzhen stock market and the Shanghai stock market. For the whole period, returns have been positive. The lowest daily returns were found on Thursday. Tables 9.2 and 9.3 report the mean return by day of week during the sub-period: before reform and after reform. The overall pattern is similar to that observed for the whole period; the Monday returns have been positive in each period. However, we do not find a Friday effect. Overall, the results are consistent with findings for other markets, except for the Friday

Table 9.11. Daily percentage return for Shenzhen stock market and Shanghai stock market.

	Whole period Oct. 2006–June 2019	Before reform Oct. 2006– Oct. 2011	After reform Oct. 2011–June 2019
Shenzhen A-Share	0.0005385	0.0008598	0.0003312
	(3311) [0.0183579]	(1299) [0.0213315]	(2011) [0.0161563]
Shanghai A-Share	0.0004342	0.0006827	0.0002739
	(3311) [0.0173038]	(1299) [0.0210908]	(2011) [0.0143443]

Note: In each case, the first row is the mean, in parenthesis is the number of observations and in brackets is the standard deviation.

Table 9.12. Mean and standard deviation (S.D.) of daily percentage return Shenzhen stock market: Day of the week during the whole period and sub-periods.

Shenzhen A-Share	Whole period Oct. 2006–June 2019	Before reform Oct. 2006–Oct. 2011	After reform Oct. 2011–June 2019
Monday	0.0016151	0.0029366	0.0007604
	(0.0007126) [0.023]	(0.0013192) [0.026]	(0.0008043) [0.345]
Tuesday	0.0004358	−0.001466	0.0016628
	(0.000712) [0.541]	(0.0013192) [0.267]	(0.0008033) [0.039]
Wednesday	0.00163156	0.0031841	0.0006274
	(0.0016315) [0.022]	(0.0013192) [0.016]	(0.0008043) [0.435]
Thursday	−0.0014717	−0.0007176	−0.0019594
	(0.0007126) [0.039]	(0.0013192) [0.587]	(0.0008043) [0.015]
Friday	0.000482	0.0003586	0.0005617
	(0.0007126) [0.499]	(0.0013192) [0.786]	(0.0008043) [0.485]

Note: In each case, the first row is the mean, in parenthesis is the standard deviation and in brackets is the p-value.

effect. Tables 9.11 and 9.12 also report the standard deviation in daily returns, which would be a source of insight into whether higher returns on a particular weekday are due to the higher risk assumed by an investor on that day. But we do not find that a higher standard deviation is associated with higher daily returns in our patterns.

Tables 9.12 and 9.13 show the descriptive statistics of the returns on the Shanghai and Shenzhen markets. Overall, we find a positive effect on Mondays over the whole period. However, this effect is significant before the reforms and attenuated afterwards.

Similarly, we observe a positive effect on Wednesdays, especially during the period before the reforms. We find that after the reforms, the returns on Wednesdays are not significantly different from zero for both markets. Regarding the negative effect on Thursdays, it is significant over the entire period and also significant in both sub-periods.

According to these descriptive statistics, the day-of-the-week effect is attenuated in both markets after the reforms. Despite the persistence of the effect on Thursdays, markets seem to have become more efficient after the reforms.

In Tables 9.14 and 9.15, we report results of the estimated coefficients of the different components of our unobserved components

Table 9.13. Mean and standard deviation (S.D.) of daily percentage return Shanghai stock market: Day of the week during the whole period and sub-periods.

Shanghai A-Share	Whole period Oct. 2006–June 2019	Before reform Oct. 2006–Oct. 2011	After reform Oct. 2011–June 2019
Monday	0.0014812	0.0031709	0.0003883
	(0.0006718) [0.028]	(0.0013039) [0.015]	(0.0007142) [0.587]
Tuesday	−0.000073	−0.0019341	0.0011277
	(0.00006713) [0.913]	(0.0013039) [0.138]	(0.0007133) [0.114]
Wednesday	0.0011799	0.0026333	0.0002399
	(0.0006718) [0.056]	(0.0013039) [0.044]	(0.0007142) [0.737]
Thursday	−0.0012839	−0.0006759	−0.0016771
	(0.0006718) [0.056]	(0.0013039) [0.604]	(0.0007142) [0.019]
Friday	0.0008676	0.0002165	0.0012887
	(0.0006718) [0.197]	(0.0013039) [0.868]	(0.0007142) [0.071]

Note: In each case, the first row is the mean, in parenthesis is the standard deviation and in brackets is the p-value.

model. Column "Stochastic Trend" presents estimations for the basic stochastic component model. We find a significant Thursday effect by using the UCM model.

For the Shenzhen market, we find that a Monday effect is significant. However, this effect is significant at 5% before the reforms, with a 0.029 p-value, against only 10% after the reforms with a 0.071 p-value. Overall, we do not see a global influence of the Wednesday effect over the entire period, despite the presence of this effect in both sub-periods. As for the negative effect on Thursdays, we did have a negative effect over the whole period. This confirms our descriptive statistic that there is a negative effect on Thursdays.

In the Shanghai market, the UCM model does not detect an effect on Mondays, regardless of the entire period taken into account or the sub-periods. As in the Shenzhen market, we detect an overall negative effect for Thursdays, although this effect is not significant over the sub-periods. For both stock markets, the regression results show that stochastic components and autoregressive components are significant which confirms the quality of our model.

An efficient market corresponds to rational investor and rational governors. The seasonality means the return series are not efficient.

Table 9.14. Estimated coefficients for the unobserved components model Shenzhen stock market.

Shenzhen A-Share	Whole period Oct. 2006–June 2019	Before reform Oct. 2006–Oct. 2011	After reform Oct. 2011–June 2019
Monday		4.353253	3.744837
		(0.029)	(0.071)
Tuesday	−0.3012976		6.064087
	(0.839)		(0.003)
Wednesday	0.1779017	4.480039	3.948071
	(0.904)	(0.025)	(0.057)
Thursday	−3.75051	0.5959548	
	(0.011)	(0.765)	
Friday	−1.421548	1.864696	3.013853
	(0.337)	(0.349)	(0.146)
Stochastic Trend	−0.0201068	−0.0163247	−0.0220602
	(0.000)	(0.041)	(0.000)
C	4.729348	3.797283	1.170102
	(0.005)	(0.166)	(0.644)
AR(1)	1.017609	1.011019	1.01929
	(0.000)	(0.000)	(0.000)

Note: Omitted values because of collinearity; in parenthesis is the *p*-value.

The plotted autocorrelation and partial autocorrelation of the price of the Shanghai stock index indicates that the series is non-stationary (in Appendix, Figure A.9.1); this suggests that it cannot be used to model volatility. The autocorrelation indicates the return series is stationary (in Appendix, Figure A.9.2). The ADF-test as well as the PP-test is used to get confirmation regarding whether the return series is stationary or not. The values of the ADF test statistic, −57.38, is less than its test critical value, −2.86, at 5%, a level of significance which implies that the Shanghai index return series is stationary. The findings of the PP test also confirm that the returns series is stationary, since the values of the PP test statistic is less than its test critical value (in Appendix, Tables A.9.1 and A.9.2).

The plotted autocorrelation and partial autocorrelation of squared returns indicate dependence and hence imply time-varying volatility (in Appendix, Figure A.9.3). In order to model the volatility of the returns, we need to determine their mean equation. Table A.9.3 in Appendix indicates the coefficients of the AR(1) and the ARMA(1,1) models. The return for today will depend on returns in

Table 9.15. Estimated coefficients for the unobserved components model Shanghai stock market.

Shanghai A-Share	Whole period Oct. 2006–June 2019	Before reform Oct. 2006–Oct. 2011	After reform Oct. 2011–June 2019
Monday	0.2543936	0.2324647	0.1034498
	(0.487)	(0.722)	(0.810)
Tuesday	−0.2264845	−1.44866	0.3982914
	(0.536)	(0.027)	(0.355)
Wednesday	0.1007897		
	(0.783)		
Thursday	−0.7116555	−0.9788643	−0.7040518
	(0.052)	(0.134)	(0.102)
Friday		−0.7143252	0.2974653
		(0.274)	(0.490)
Stochastic Trend	−0.0152587	−0.0145036	−0.0161635
	(0.003)	(0.080)	(0.011)
C	1.610027	2.429097	1.243403
	(0.003)	(0.007)	(0.059)
AR(1)	1.011293	1.009372	1.012902
	(0.000)	(0.000)	(0.000)

Note: Omitted values because of collinearity; in parenthesis is the *p*-value.

previous periods (autoregressive component) and the surprise terms in previous periods (moving order component). The second-order dependence in the squared residuals of the mean equation is detected; this indicates the presence of conditional heteroscedasticity in the returns (in Appendix, Figure A.9.4). The ARCH-Lagrange multiplier (LM) test confirms the presence of ARCH effects and the need to model this conditional heteroscedasticity using the ARCH family models (in Appendix, Table A.9.4).

The coefficients of the ARMAX–GARCH are presented in Tables 9.16 and 9.17. Several of the ARMAX structure coefficients are statistically significant. By using GARCH models, the coefficients of the changes in interest rates are negative, indicating that changes in interest rates are inversely related to stock market returns. The coefficients on movements in world stock prices are significantly positive in all cases. This finding means that Chinese stock market indices are influenced by price movements in the global stock market. The day-of-the-week effects are not significant in all the models. Thursday is significantly negative. This finding contradicts Wen *et al.* (2018); they found a Tuesday significantly negative.

Regarding the conditional variances, most of the ARCH and GARCH parameters are statistically significant, implying the strong GARCH effects in the Chinese stock returns. Then, we focus on the interaction terms of dummy variables. Specifically, if upward, respectively downward, adjustments before the reform of October 2011 have induced a significant increase, respectively decrease, in the return; the interaction terms will have positive, resp. negative, values (Wen *et al.*, 2018). If upward, respectively downward, adjustments after the reform of October 2011 have induced a significant increase, resp. decrease, in the return; the interaction terms will have positive, resp. negative, values.

Results from Table 9.17 indicate that the reform of October 2011 has increased the return of the Shanghai index: after the reform, both the upward and downward adjustments have increased the return. In contrast, before the reform, downward adjustments have decreased the return, but not significantly, and upward adjustments increased the return. Table 9.17 indicates the same results by using Shenzhen index.

9.4.   Conclusion

Fairly regularly, the Chinese stock markets show daily and monthly calendar effects that differ from findings obtained on other stock markets.

In our study, we find a strong February effect in Shenzhen and Shanghai stock markets. One explanation for the higher returns in February is that the Chinese New Year is on this period most often in February.

We also note a significant negative Thursday effect in Shenzhen and Shanghai stock markets, while the Monday effect and the Friday effect seem to have disappeared. The result is consistent with the studies of Mitchell and Ong (2006) and Wang *et al.* (2013) as they found a negative Thursday effect and a positive Monday effect in Chinese stock markets. Zhang and Li (2006) indicated that the Friday effect is particularly dependent on samples. Even if Mookerjee and Yu (1999) found a positive Thursday effect, the period

Table 9.16. Estimation result and the effect of the reform on Shanghai stock market returns.

	ARCH	ARCH	GARCH	GARCH
		Mean equation		
C		−0.0028465 (0.010)		−0012668 (0.28)
Shibor(−1)	0.0015982 (0.944)	0.0015972 (0.944)	−0.0041885 (0.840)	−0.0041878 (0.84)
World(−1)	0.2915695 (0.000)	0.2915694 (0.000)	0.2374203 (0.000)	0.237419 (0.000)
Monday	0.0007992 (0.345)	0.0005745 (0.467)	0.000317 (0.635)	0.0001317 (0.829)
Tuesday	−0.0006453 (0.453)	−0.00087 (0.309)	0.0006624 (0.334)	0.000477 (0.455)
Wednesday		−0.0002248 (0.803)		−0.0001854 (0.792)
Thursday	−0.001725 (0.062)	−0.0019497 (0.032)	−0.001394 (0.052)	−0.0012668 (0.280)
Friday	0.0002247 (0.803)		0.0001853 (0.792)	
$\delta 1$	0.0021952 (0.017)	0.0052663 (0.000)	0.0017173 (0.057)	0.0031694 (0.001)
$\delta 2$	−0.0030712 (0.008)		−0.0014521 (0.246)	
$\delta 3$	0.001566 (0.233)	0.0046379 (0.000)	0.0014139 (0.209)	0.002866 (0.000)
$\delta 4$	−0.0003491 (0.744)	0.0027221 (0.000)	0.0000339 (0.973)	0.001486 (0.033)
ar(1)	0.4406708 (0.582)	0.4406716 (0.582)		
ma(1)	−4531843 (0.566)	−0.4531834 (0.566)		
		Variance equation		
ω	0.0002234 (0.000)	0.0002234 (0.000)	4.99e-07 (0.000)	4.99e-07 (0.000)
α	0.2372449 (0.000)	0.2372448 (0.000)	0.04435 (0.000)	0.0443493 (0.000)
β			0.9557942 (0.000)	0.955795 (0.000)
Log likelihood	8899.139	8899.139	9326.794	9326.794

Table 9.17. Estimation result and the effect of the reform on Shenzhen stock market returns.

	ARCH	ARCH	GARCH	GARCH
		Mean equation		
C		−0.0026086		−0002097
		(0.042)		(0.876)
Shibor(−1)	−0.0008803	−0.0008803	−0.0133567	−0.0314874
	(0.973)	(0.973)	(0.555)	(0.170)
World(−1)	0.2371579	0.2371579	0.2091827	0.2096711
	(0.000)	(0.000)	(0.000)	(0.000)
Monday	0.0005378	0.0012401	−0.000517	0.0004962
	(0.541)	(0.134)	(0.948)	(0.527)
Tuesday	−0.0010438	−0.0003415	−0.0001004	0.0004436
	(0.269)	(0.723)	(0.904)	(0.590)
Wednesday		0.0007023		0.0005463
		(0.465)		(0.527)
Thursday	−0.0023488	−0.0016465	−0.0026504	−0.0021009
	(0.012)	(0.079)	(0.002)	(0.015)
Friday	−0.0007023		−0.0005441	
	(0.465)		(0.529)	
$\delta 1$	0.0028582	0.0047645	0.0028804	0.0029697
	(0.005)	(0.000)	(0.001)	(0.003)
$\delta 2$	−0.0019063		−0.0004955	
	(0.155)		(0.718)	
$\delta 3$	0.0023362	0.0042425	0.0028793	0.0033458
	(0.118)	(0.000)	(0.020)	(0.000)
$\delta 4$	−0.0000791	0.0018272	0.0005361	0.0008763
	(0.946)	(0.028)	(0.624)	(0.294)
ar(1)	0.3707141	−0.3707142		
	(0.045)	(0.045)		
ma(1)	0.4305409	0.430541		
	(0.015)	(0.015)		
		Variance equation		
ω	0.0002465	0.0002465	2.38e-06	2.39e-06
	(0.000)	(0.000)	(0.000)	(0.000)
α	0.2522595	0.2522595	0.048024	0.0480966
	(0.000)	(0.000)	(0.000)	(0.000)
β			0.9448036	0.9446948
			(0.000)	(0.000)
Log likelihood	8699.317	8699.317	8956.361	8956.932

must be taken into account as their study relates to the period from 1991 to 1994, while our study covers the period from 1995 to 2019. The day of the week effect may have changed since the study of Mookerjee and Yu (1999); as a matter of fact, Zhang and Li (2006) indicated that the Friday effect and the turn-of-the month effect seem to have disappeared in the Chinese stock market since 1997.

Results on seasonality can depend on the type of data used, either cross-sectional data or time series data. The choice and duration of the study period also influence the result.

As discussed earlier, according to Fama and French (1989), the standard deviation for Monday returns should be the highest because a greater number of shocks can manifest themselves over the weekend break: companies often publish negative information on Friday evenings, just after the close of the market. One of the possible explanations of the negative Thursday effect is that Chinese investors are anticipating this accumulation of news on Friday, trying to settle their position on Thursday, so stock prices fall on Thursday.

The calendar effects should not be long lasting, as market investors can learn from past experience: the calendar effects should disappear due to the trading strategies.

In an efficient market, the rational arbitrageur's trading activity would result in the disappearance of the negative Thursday effect. But short selling is prohibited in Chinese stock markets, so the persistence of the negative Thursday effect can be explained by the impossibility to short stocks in Chinese stock markets.

However, regularity does not mean profitability, as long as the negative Thursday effect does not generate systematic profit, market efficiency is not called into question. It is the same principle for the monthly effect. Another important fact that we want to emphasize is that, in our study, we used time series to study the seasonal effect but not cross-sectional data which can sometimes present selection bias.

With the transition to sustainable economic development, China's stock pricing mechanism has been pushed toward a more market-oriented approach. After the reform of October 2011, both the upward and downward adjustments have increased the return; this indicates that, since the reform, Shanghai stock indices have become more sensitive to the price adjustment. In particular, upward price adjustments have imposed more significant effects on the return.

Our work contributes to the current literature by examining the effects of the 2011 reform on the Chinese stock market returns. For further analysis of seasonality in China, we think it will be interesting to lead a complementary and comparative study on the multifractional aspect of the data. We have started the work on this research axis with the determination of the Hurst index for both markets. These are subjects for further research.

Appendix

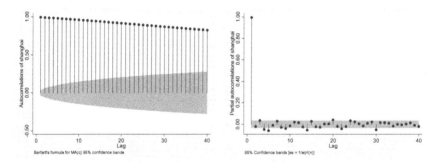

Fig. A.9.1.   AC and PAC of Shanghai index.

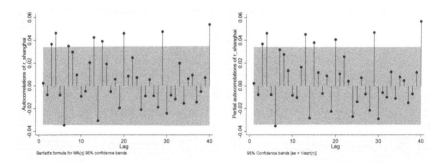

Fig. A.9.2.   AC and PAC of Shanghai index.

Table A.9.1.   Dickey–Fuller test for returns.

Test statistic	1% critical value	5% critical value	10% critical value	p-value for Z(t)
−57.38	−3.430	−2.860	−2.570	0.0000

Table A.9.2.   Phillips–Perron test for returns.

	Test statistic	1% critical value	5% critical value	10% critical value
Z(rho)	−3434.183	−20.700	−14.100	−11.300
Z(t)	−57.428	−3.430	−2.860	−2.570

Note: MacKinnon approximate p-value for Z(t) = 0.0000.

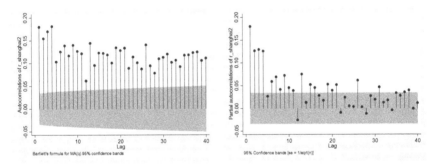

Fig. A.9.3.   AC and PAC of squared returns.

Table A.9.3.   Mean equation estimated.

	AR(1)	ARMA(1,1)
Log likelihood	8734.562	8735.445
Cons	0.000434	0.0004342
	(0.161)	(0.312)
AR	0.0023611	−0.9477329
	(0.841)	(0.000)
MA		0.9551566
		(0.000)

Note: p-values are given in parentheses.

294 Institutional Change and China Capitalism

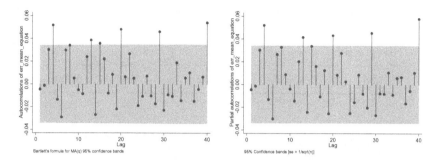

Fig. A.9.4.   AC and PAC of the squared residuals of the mean equation.

Table A.9.4.   LM test for autoregressive
conditional heteroscedasticity.

Lags(p)	Chi^2	Df	Prob. $>\text{Chi}^2$
1	105.685	1	0.0000

Note: H_0: No ARCH effects vs. ARCH(p)
disturbance.

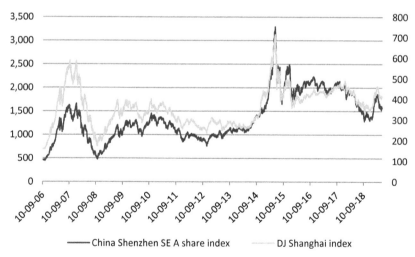

Fig. A.9.5.   Price for DJ Shanghai index and Shenzhen A-share index in USD,
2006–2019.

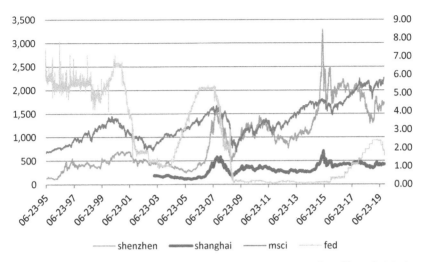

Fig. A.9.6. Prices for Shenzhen index, 1995–2019, compared to Shanghai index, 2003–2019.

References

Barone, E. (1990). "Day of the Week Effects: New Evidence form an Emerging Market," *Applied Economics Letters*, 2, 483–510.

Beltratti, A., B. Bortolotti, and M. Caccavaio (2009). "Stock Prices in a Speculative Market: The Chinese Split-Share Reform," *Paolo Baffi Centre Research Paper, No. 2009–39.*

Bollerslev, T. (1986). "Generalized Autoregressive Conditional Heteroscedasticity," *Journal of Econometrics*, 31, 483–510.

Bouman, S. and B. Jacobsen (2002). "The Halloween Indicator, 'Sell in May and GO Away': Another Puzzle," *American Economic Review*, 92, 1618–1635.

Cadsby, C. and M. Ratner (1992). "Turn-of-month and Pre-holiday Effects on Stock Returns: Some International Evidence," *Journal of Banking and Finance*, 16, 497–509.

Chen, G., C. C. Kwok, and O. M. Rui (2001). "The Day-of-the-week Regularity in the Stock Markets of China," *Journal of Multinational Financial Management*, 11, 139–163.

Chen, T.-C. and C.-C. Chien (2011). "Size Effect in January and Cultural Influences in an Emerging Stock Market: The Perspective of Behavioral Finance," *Pacific-Basin Finance Journal*, 19, 208–229.

Chia, R., V. K. Liew, and S. A. Wafa (2011). "Day-of-the-week Effects: Evidence from the Chinese Stock Markets," *Journal of International Economic Review*, 4, 51–62.

Chong, R., R. Hudson, K. Keasey, and K. Littler (2005). "Pre-holiday Effect: International Evidence on the Decline and Reversal of a Stock Market Anomaly," *Journal of International Money and Finance*, 24, 1226–1236.

Cooper, M. J., J. J. McConnell, and A. V. Ovtchinnikov (2006). "The Other January Effect," *Journal of Financial Economics*, 82, 315–341.

Cross, F. (1973). "The Behavior of Stock Prices on Fridays and Mondays," *Financial Analysts Journal*, 29, 67–69.

DeStefano, M. (2004). "Stock Returns and the Business Cycle," *The Financial Review, Eastern Finance Association*, 39(4), 527–547.

Dury, M.-E. and B. Xiao (2018). "Forecasting the Volatility of the Chinese Gold Market by ARCH Family Models and extension to Stable Models," *Working Paper*.

Engle, R. F. (1982). "Autoregressive Conditional Heteroscedasticity with Estimates of the Variance of United Kingdom Inflation," *Econometrica*, 50, 987–1007.

Fama, E. and K. French (1989). "Business Conditions and Expected Returns on Stocks and Bonds," *Journal of Financial Economics*, 25, 987–1007.

French, K. (1980). "Stock Returns and the Weekend Effect," *Journal of Financial Economics*, 8, 55–69.

Gao, L. and G. Kling (2005). "Calendar Effects in Chinese Stock Market," *Annals of Economics and Finance*, 6, 75–88.

Geske, R. and R. Roll (1983). "The Fiscal and Monetary Linkage Between Stock Returns and Inflation," *Annals of Economics and Finance*, 38, 1–33.

Gibbons, M. and P. Hess (1981). "Day of the Week Effects and Asset Returns," *Journal of Business*, 54, 576–596.

Girardin, E. and Z. Liu (2005). "Bank Credit and Seasonal Anomalies in China's Stock Markets," *China Economic Review*, 16, 465–483.

Gong, R. and A. Marsden (2014). "The Impact of the 2007 Reforms on the Level of Information Disclosure by the Chinese A-share Market," *China Economic Review*, 30, 221–234.

Gregoriou, A., A. Kontonikas, and N. Tsitsianis (2004). "Does the Day of the Week Effect Exist Once Transaction Costs have been Accounted for? Evidence from the UK," *Applied Financial Economics*, 14, 215–220.

Groenewold, N., S. H. Tang, and Y. Wu (2004). "The Dynamic Interrelationships Between the Greater China Share Markets," *China Economic Review*, 15, 45–62.

Gultekin, M. N. and N. B. Gultekin (1983). "Stock Market Seasonality: International Evidence," *Journal of Financial Economics*, 12, 45–62.

Guo, B., X. Luo, and Z. Zhang (2014). "Sell in May and Go Away: Evidence from China," *Finance Research Letters*, 11, 362–368.

Harvey, A. C. (1989). *Forecasting, Structural Time Series Models and the Kalman Filter*, Cambridge University Press, The Edinburgh Building, Cambridge CB2 8RU, UK. 573 pages.

Haugen, R. and P. Jorion (1996). "The January Effect: Still There After All These Years," *Financial Analysts Journal*, 52, 27–31.

Hsieh, C. S. (2016). "Revisiting the Monthly Effect for the Chinese Stock Markets," *Applied Economics and Finance*, 3, 73–78.

Hui, T. K. (2005). "Day-of-the-week effects in US and Asia-Pacific Stock Markets During the Asian Financial Crisis: A Non-parametric Approach," *The International Journal of Management Science*, 33, 277–282.

Jacobsen, B. and C. Zhang (2012). "The Halloween Indicator: Everywhere and All the Time," *Working Paper*. Massey University.

Jaffe, J. and R. Westerfield (1985). "Patterns in Japanese Common Stock Returns," *Journal of Financial and Quantitative Analysis*, 20, 261–272.

Keim, D. B. (1983). "Size-related Anomalies and Stock Return Seasonality: Further Empirical Evidence," *Journal of Financial Economics*, 12, 13–32.

Khan, M. S. and N. Rabbani (2019). "Market Conditions and Calendar Anomalies in Japanese Stock Returns," *Japanese Association of Financial Economics and Engineering*, 26, 187–209.

Kim, M. K. and D. A. Burnie (2002). "The Firm Size Effect and the Economic Cycle," *The Journal of Financial Research*, 25, 111–124.

Kling, G. and L. Gao (2004). "Do Chinese Institutional Investors Act like Institutional Investors," *Working Paper*.

L'Her, J.-F., T. Masmoudi, and J.-M. Suret (2002). "Effets Taille et Book-to-Market au Canada," *Revue Canadienne d'Investissement*, Été 2002.

Li, K. and B. Lin (2015). "How Does Administrative Pricing Affect Energy Consumption and CO2 Emissions in China?" *Renewable and Sustainable Energy Reviews*, 42, 952–962.

Liu, L., Y. Wang, and J. Wan (2010). "Analysis of Efficiency for Shenzhen Stock Market: Evidence form the Source of Multifractality," *International Review of Financial Analysis*, 19, 237–241.

Mitchell J. D. and L. L. Ong (2006). "Seasonalities in China's Stock Markets: Cultural or Structural?" *IMF Working Papers*, DOI: 10.5089/9781451862645.001, https://www.researchgate.net/publication/5124806.

Mobarek, A. and A. Fiorante (2014). "The Prospects of BRIC Countries: Testing Weak-form Market Efficiency," *Research in International Business and Finance*, 30, 280–290.

Mookerjee, R. and Q. Yu (1999). "Seasonality in Returns on the Chinese Stock Markets: The Case of Shanghai and Shenzhen," *Global Finance Journal*, 10, 93–105.

Peng, Q. (2019). "Financial Frictions, Entry and Growth: A Study of China," *Review of Economic Dynamics*, 34, 267–282.

Perez, A. (2018). "Monday Effect in the Chinese Stock Market," *International Journal of Financial Research*, 9, 1–7.

Pu, Y. (2012). "Pre-holiday and Pre-weekend Effects: China's Evidence on Stock Market Anomaly," *Working Paper*.

Qi, M. and W. Wang (2013). "The Monthly Effects in the Chinese Gold Market," *International Journal of Economics and Finance*, 5(10), 141–146.

Ramasamy, R. and S. Munisamy (2012). "Predictive Accuracy of GARCH, GJR and EGARCH Models Select Exchange Rates Application," *Global Journal of Management and Business Research*, 12.

Reinganum, M. R. (1983). "The Anomalous Stock Market Behavior of Small Firms in January: Empirical Tests for Tax-loss Selling Effects," *Journal of Financial Economics*, 12, 89–104.

Ritter, J. (1988). "The Buying and Selling Behavior of Individual Investors at the Turn of the Year," *Journal of Finance*, 43, 701–717.

Rogalski, R. (1984). "New Finding Regarding Day of the Week Returns Over Trading ad Non-trading Periods: A Note," *Journal of Finance*, 34, 1603–1614.

Roll, R. (1983). "Vas Ist Das?" *The Journal of Portfolio Management*, 9, 18–28.

Rozeff, M. and W. Kinney (1976). "Capital Market Seasonality: The Case of Stock Market Returns," *Journal of Financial Economics*, 3, 376–402.

Schwert, G. W. (2003) "Chapter 15 Anomalies and Market Efficiency," In: G. M. Constantinides, M. Harris, and R. M. Stulz, (Eds.), *Handbook of the Economics of Finance*, Elsevier, Vol. 1, Part B, pp. 939–974.

Solnik, B. and L. Bousquet (1990). "Day of the Week Effect on the Paris Bourse," *Journal of Banking and Finance*, 14, 461–468.

Taylor, S. (1986). *Modeling Financial Time Series*, Chichester, UK: Wiley.

Wang, Y., L. Liu, and R. Gu (2013). "Calendar Effects of the Chinese Stock Markets," *International Journal of Business and Emerging Markets*, 5, 67–82.

Wen, X., E. Bouri, and D. Roubaud (2018). "Does Oil Product Pricing Reform Increase Returns and Uncertainty in the Chinese Stock Market?" *The Quarterly Review of Economics and Finance*, 68, 23–30.

Xiao, B. and A. Coulibaly (2015). "The Recent Evolution of the Seasonal Anomalies in Chinas Stock Market: An Empirical Analysis of the Shenzhen Stock Exchange," *10th International Conference on the Chinese Economy, 22–23 October, 2015, CERDI-IDREC. Clermont-Ferrand, France.*

Zhang, B. and X. Li (2006). "Do Calendar Effects Still Exist in the Chinese Stock Markets?" *Journal of Chinese Economic and Business Studies*, 4, 151–163.

Chapter 10

China within World Networks of Equity Markets: Not So Atypical?

Cécile Bastidon[*,†,§] **and Antoine Parent**[†,‡,¶]

[*]*LEAD, Université de Toulon, France*
[†]*CAC-IXXI, ENS Lyon, France*
[‡]*Paris 8 University, OFCE-Sciences Po, France*
[§]*bastidon@univ-tln.fr*
[¶]*antoine.parent02@univ-paris8.fr*

Abstract

We propose an original approach to the historical dynamics of the integration of Chinese equity markets to world equity markets. Our database is composed of 32 countries over the period 1960–2018 with monthly frequency, which allows us to compare between the Chinese dynamics of integration and the historical dynamics of mature economies. In addition, we implement an innovative method in the field of economic history, i.e. topological networks of assets. In particular, we extend the methodology of the minimal spanning tree from portfolio management issues to financial cliometrics. Our results confirm the main stylized fact of a low integration of Chinese equity markets to world equity markets networks with respect to contemporary standards. In addition, we find that China path length measures are broadly similar to the distribution of the world sample in the long run, with even a recent surge in second-rank connectivity.

10.1. Introduction

In the relatively narrow literature on the topic, Chinese equity markets are considered as still lowly globalized (for example, Wang and Iorio, 2007; Johansson, 2010). This result is primarily attributed to the binding regulatory features of the domestic financial systems. Thus, the upcoming regulatory shocks will affect both the position of Chinese stock markets within world networks of equity markets and the shape of world networks of equity markets themselves, that is to say the global financial system, considering the economic weight of China.

These results have to be seen within the wider context of the existing cliometric literature on financial globalization, which reveals two major features regarding the convergence of developing and emerging economies. First, the issue of global convergence remains non-consensual (O'Rourke and Williamson, 1999). Second, the convergence of developing and emerging economies is especially controversial (Obstfeld and Taylor, 2004). This finding is known as the "Lucas Paradox" (Lucas, 1990) and its extensions (Gourinchas and Jeanne, 2013) stating that developing economies of the post-colonial era would generally receive very low flows of foreign investments despite large yield differentials.

The aim of this chapter is to propose an original approach to the historical dynamics of the integration of Chinese equity markets to world equity markets. Our contribution is twofold: First, we implement a historical approach over five decades. The OECD database we use is composed of 32 countries over the period 1960–2018 with monthly frequency, which allows us to compare between the Chinese dynamics of integration to world equity markets and the historical dynamics of mature economies. Second, we implement an innovative method in the field of economic history, i.e. topological networks of assets derived from the common component of price time series (for example, Mantegna, 1999; Bonanno *et al.*, 2001; Tumminello *et al.*, 2007). In particular, we extend the methodology of the minimal spanning tree from portfolio management issues to financial cliometrics.

While the usual integration indicators in the cliometric literature are measured either country by country or at a global level, these network representations take into account the interaction effects between country-level integration dynamics. In particular, this method allows us to provide both network representations and time series of network indicators of connectivity (i.e. the structure of the network) and distances (i.e. the intensity of integration). Our results confirm the main stylized fact of a low integration of Chinese equity markets to world equity markets networks with respect to contemporary standards. However, we also find that China path length measures within the network are broadly similar to the distribution of the world sample in the long run, with even a recent surge in second-rank connectivity (i.e. not the connectivity of China itself but the connectivity of its neighborhood).

The remainder of the chapter is organized as follows. In Section 10.2, we present the reference literature. In Section 10.3, we present the sample and network methods. In Sections 10.4 and 10.5, we present and discuss the network representations and time series of network indicators. Section 10.6 concludes the chapter.

10.2. Selective Survey of the Reference Literature

10.2.1. *Developing and emerging economies in the literature on financial globalization*

There are two types of usual indicators of financial globalization in the literature: quantity and price indicators. The most commonly used quantity indicators are the foreign assets to GDP ratios, foreign liabilities to GDP ratios, gross foreign investment, net foreign investment, etc. and the so-called Feldstein–Horioka coefficient (Feldstein and Horioka, 1979; Ford and Horioka, 2017), i.e. the slope coefficient in the regression of investment shares on saving shares. Assessing the dynamics of the Feldstein–Horioka coefficient over history for 15 countries and quinquennial and decadal samples, Obstfeld and Taylor (2004) find it to be dependent on the equity home bias, reflecting the size of domestic asset markets: "countries with substantial foreign asset shares in wealth (often times, smaller countries) will have low FH coefficients, whereas countries showing more extreme portfolio home biases (US and Japan) will have large FH coefficients" (p. 67). Nonetheless, they conclude that "diversification still remains low as compared to a hypothetical complete integration optimum, as the persistent home-equity bias indicates" (p. 86) and that "developing countries appear to be playing a much smaller role in today's so-called global capital market than they did before WW1."

The most commonly used price-based criteria of financial globalization are the covered nominal interest rate parity, the real interest rate convergence, and the purchasing power parity, which are all variations of the law of the one price. It has to be noted that the topological network representations we are using in this chapter are based on the common component of price time series, which is equivalent to measuring the deviations from the law of the one price. Obstfeld and Taylor (2004) find these different indicators to corroborate the stylized fact that "global capital markets have witnessed two great phases of integration, one before 1914, and one in the contemporary period, with both separated by a long phase of disintegration during the two wars and the Great Depression" (p. 121), for what emerges as their main contribution, the detection of "a U-shaped pattern of international financial integration after the late 19th century" (p. 121).

Within the broad picture of this U-shaped pattern, the second main topic in the reference literature is the issue of convergence. According to O'Rourke and Williamson (1999), the impact of financial globalization on convergence is a crucial issue. Relying on the theoretical literature on endogenous growth, they state that the first generation growth models "implied unconditional or conditional convergence (Mankiw *et al.*, 1992; Solow, 1956) [...]. The second generation growth models qualified these predictions: divergence became theoretically possible by taking into account increasing returns, learning by doing, externalities, schooling, and skills (Arrow, 1962; Lucas Jr, 1988; Romer, 1986, 1989; Sala-i Martin and Barro, 1995)." (p. 6). The empirical research on late 20th century convergence using world panels supports the view that conditional convergence would prevail over unconditional convergence (for example, Williamson, 2007).

Since O'Rourke and Williamson (1999) test the relevancy of HOS predictions within the framework of a computable general equilibrium model, they focus on GDP per capita and real wages as a proxy of the price of the labor factor. We use equity market indices as a proxy of the price of capital and assess convergence on the basis of this sole variable. In all other respects, we are in line with O'Rourke and Williamson (1999). First, the study period is split into sub-periods in order to assess the "convergence speed per decade."

Second, our methodology is based on the computation of the "variance in convergence" (p. 14) of asset prices dynamics, since the place in the network of a given asset depends on the importance of the common component of its price dynamics with the other assets of the sample. Finally, variance in convergence is broken into global dispersion, dispersion within advanced economies, and dispersion within developing and emerging economies.

As regards the financial convergence of developing economies, finally, we depart from two main contributions in the existing literature: the Lucas Paradox (Lucas, 1990) about capital flows to advanced vs. developing economies, and the "allocation puzzle" about disparities in capital flows to developing economies. The law of diminishing returns which is studied by Lucas (1990) implies that "the marginal product of capital is higher in the less productive (in the poorer) economy. Then, if trade in capital good is free and competitive new investments will occur only in the poorer economy [...] until capital/labor ratios, and hence, wages and capital returns are equalized" (p. 92). But the author observes that: "If this model were anywhere close to being accurate and world capital markets were anywhere close to being free and complete, it is clear that, in the face of return differentials of this magnitude, investment goods would flow rapidly from wealthy countries to poor countries" (p. 92). The Lucas paradox turned out to be, for a long time, the unsurpassable horizon in the field (for example, O'Rourke and Williamson (1999), Obstfeld and Taylor (2004), Prasad *et al.* (2007), and Williamson (2007)).

Recently, in Gourinchas and Jeanne (2013) the Lucas paradox opposing advanced and developing economies has turned to an "allocation puzzle" within developing economies: "The Lucas puzzle states that the volume of capital flows to the average developing country is surprisingly small [...] The allocation puzzle is instead about the allocation of capital inflows across countries, and how this allocation is correlated with cross-country differences in productivity growth. It is the Lucas puzzle, but in first differences. A very robust and intuitive prediction of the neoclassical growth framework is that countries that have higher productivity growth over long periods of time should receive more capital inflows than countries with lower productivity growth. We find that this is not the case in the data" (p. 1497). In this almost unanimous agreement against convergence, Bekaert and Harvey (1998) and Bekaert *et al.* (2002, 2011) strike a discordant note: the study of equity markets in emerging countries would reveal a gradual financial globalization. Before the late 1980s the segmentation of domestic equity markets was widespread, whereas in the late 1990s financial globalization becomes the rule, although to different degrees. This observation that from the end of the 20th century financial globalization is growing in subgroups of developing and emerging economies at least partially refutes the paradox of Lucas and the allocation puzzles. Our assessment of the dynamics of globalization of Chinese equity markets has to be viewed in this context.

10.2.2.   *International integration of Chinese equity markets: A survey*

Contrary to the literature on financial globalization, the existing literature on the integration of the equity markets of China is relatively narrow, with a bulk of papers around 2007–2010, presumably resulting from the opening of the A-share market to qualified institutional foreign financial investors in 2002. This literature is based on different definitions of the financial integration of Chinese equity markets (see Table 10.1), among which is the integration of mainland China (Girardin and Liu, 2007; Johansson, 2010; Johnson and Soenen, 2002; Tian, 2007; Wang and Iorio, 2007) but also the integration of stock markets of greater China (Cheng and Glascock, 2005; Johansson and Ljungwall, 2009; Yu *et al.*, 2010). In all cases, the remainder of the samples is composed of Asian stock markets including Japan, the rest of the world being most of time represented by the US. Usually, what is assessed is the regional dimension of the international financial integration of stock markets, not the case of the sole China. Some papers also study the economic and regulatory causes of the low international financial integration of China and in general emerging Asian economies (Lane, 2007) or provide network representations of Chinese stock markets by industrial sector (Yang *et al.*, 2014) or within regional stock markets (Sensoy and Tabak, 2014).

   These papers show a large variety of methods, from the standard multivariate Johansen cointegration (Johansen, 1988) of stock markets returns or CAPM models (Wang and Iorio, 2007) to conditional copulas (Nelsen, 1999; Patton, 2009) in Johansson (2010) and minimal spanning trees and dynamic spanning trees in Yang *et al.*

Table 10.1.   A-shares, B-shares, H-shares: The organization of Chinese equity markets.

Chinese equity markets are composed of three segments with different trading rules.

The *A-shares market* corresponds to the domestically listed companies trading in the Chinese exchanges of Shenzhen and Shanghai, in Yuan renminbi. The A-shares are available to mainland Chinese citizens and a narrow group of "Qualified Foreign Institutional Investors" and other foreign investors under strict trading programs. After 2007, Chinese citizens are allowed to purchase H-shares (see the following) of companies listed in Shanghai, in addition to A-shares.

The *B-shares market* also corresponds to domestically listed companies that trade in the Chinese exchanges of Shenzhen and Shanghai but in foreign currency contrary to A-shares. B-shares are also more widely available to foreign investors.

Finally the *H-shares market* corresponds to companies traded in Hong Kong, but regulated by Chinese law, in Hong Kong dollar. Their annual accounts must follow Hong Kong or international accounting standards. H-shares are freely tradable by foreign investors. After 2007, Chinese investors were allowed to purchase H-shares of companies listed in Shanghai in addition to A-shares, knowing that in the case of double listings A-shares are generally traded at a premium with regards to the H-shares of the same company.

The three market segments are alternatively or conjointly used in the literature, in addition to the Morgan Stanley MSCI China and the Shanghai Composite Index.

(2014) and Sensoy and Tabak (2014). The first main result of this literature, obtained with samples from around the middle of the 1990s to the end of the 2000s, is a low integration of Chinese equity markets to world equity markets, with weak nonlinear relationships (Cheng and Glascock, 2005) and short-run spillover effects (Johansson and Ljungwall, 2009). The second main result is that integration tends to increase over time, after 1994 (Johnson and Soenen, 2002), 1996 (Girardin and Liu, 2007), 2002 (Tian, 2007), post-GFC (Johansson, 2010; Yu *et al.*, 2010), or by sub-periods (Wang and Iorio, 2007). The causes of this growing integration are macroeconomic convergence and commercial flows (Johnson and Soenen, 2002) and the evolution of the regulatory framework (exchange rates, capital account, stock markets organization) (Johansson, 2010; Lane, 2007). The integration of the B-shares market remains persistently low (Tian, 2007; Wang and Iorio, 2007).

This literature also shows that there is an asymmetry in the assets (i.e. mainly low-returns foreign reserves) and liabilities (i.e. mainly foreign direct investments with usually higher returns) of China, combined with an improvement of its external position contrary to the predictions of previously mentioned neoclassical models (Lane, 2007). Finally, network representations of Chinese equity markets exhibit a relatively standard classification of industries in the minimal spanning tree of domestic markets (Yang *et al.*, 2014) along with a peripheral position of Chinese indices in the minimal spanning tree of regional markets (Sensoy and Tabak, 2014).

10.3.   Database and Methodology

10.3.1.   *Database of benchmark national equity markets indices*

Our approach consists in assessing the dynamics of integration of Chinese equity markets to world equity markets on the basis of the position of China within topological networks of world equity markets. In Section 10.4, we propose network representations by decades for the purpose of data visualization, and in Section 10.5, we assess the dynamics of the time series of network indicators computed using sliding windows. The equity markets price data are extracted from the OECD Stats Extract database. The sample is composed of 32 countries, the data being available for all countries in the post-2000 period (2000–2018, see Figure 10.1). We therefore focus on the network representations by sub-periods of Section 10.4 on the countries for which the data are available during the full time interval. This corresponds to 16, 18, 19, 27, and 32 countries (respectively including 2, 3, 4, 7, and 11 emerging and developing economies). As regards to advanced economies, the sample includes Japan and Australia (till the beginning) and New Zealand (till the 1990s sub-period) from the Asia-Pacific region. As these countries are the environment in which the existing literature usually assess the integration of Chinese equity markets, we devote a particular attention to these countries in the discussion of results. A summary table of the descriptive statistics and the detailed composition of the sample are shown in Table 10.2 and commented later in this section.

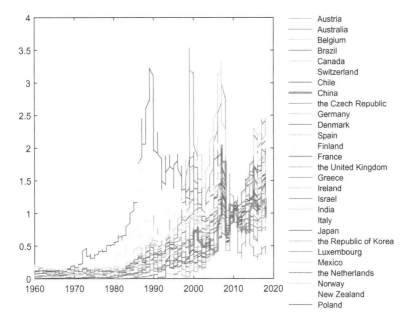

Fig. 10.1.   Time series of national stock markets indices.

Source: OECD, national benchmark equity markets indices, observations January 1950–December 2014, base 100 = 2010.

We choose to split the period of study into five sub-periods corresponding to the 1960, 1970, 1980, 1990 decades, and to the post-2000 period in order to insure comparability with the reference work of O'Rourke and Williamson (1999). Note that we performed some robustness checks by dividing the last sub-period into the pre- (2000–2007) and post- (2008–2018) Global Financial Crisis. This additional subdivision confirms the robustness of our results. The corresponding topological representations are available upon request. In addition to the comparability to the results of the existing cliometric literature, the choice of defining decadal sub-periods, rather than homogeneous periods as regards an indicator in particular also results from the fact that the integration dynamics of the countries of the sample are characterized by different break dates.

For example, Bekaert *et al.* (2002) show that in the case of emerging economies, most of the time structural breaks from segmented to integrated equity markets arise in a three-year interval around deregulation, with a high heterogeneity between countries. This result

Table 10.2.   Descriptive statistics and composition of the sample, by sub-periods.

	1960s	1970s	1980s	1990s	post-2000
Mean	1.30E+02	1.20E+02	2.94E+03	8.30E+07	1.78E+02
Median	1.16E+02	1.03E+02	1.94E+02	1.23E+02	1.37E+02
Minimum	6.81E+01	3.87E+01	3.58E+01	3.48E+01	1.02E+01
Maximum	4.17E+02	1.10E+03	1.71E+05	7.82E+09	9.69E+02
S.D.	4.44E+01	7.59E+01	1.54E+04	6.10E+08	1.42E+02

1960s	1970s	1980s	1990s	post-2000
Austria, Australia, Canada, Switzerland, Germany, Finland, France, UK, Ireland, India, Italy, Japan, NL, Sweden, US, S. Africa	Austria, Australia, Canada, Switzerland, Germany, Finland, France, UK, Ireland, India, Italy, Japan, Mexico, NL, NZ, Sweden, US, S. Africa	Austria, Australia, Canada, Switzerland, Germany, Finland, France, UK, Ireland, Israel, India, Italy, Japan, Mexico, NL, NZ, Sweden, US, S. Africa	Austria, Australia, Belgium, Brazil, Canada, Switzerland, Chile, Germany, Denmark, Spain, Finland, France, UK, Greece, Ireland, Israel, India, Italy, Japan, Korea, Mexico, NL, Norway, NZ, Sweden, US, S. Africa	Austria, Australia, Belgium, Brazil, Canada, Switzerland, Chile, China, Cz. Rep., Germany, Denmark, Spain, Finland, France, UK, Greece, Ireland, Israel, India, Italy, Japan, Korea, Lux-embourg, Mexico, NL, Norway, NZ, Poland, Russia, Sweden, US, S. Africa

Source: OECD, national benchmark equity markets indices, observations January 1950–December 2014, base 100 at the beginning of each sub-period.

means that even if regulatory shocks would occur at the same date in all countries of the sample, individual structural breaks would not. Finally, for the time series of network indicators of Section 10.5, which are computed using sliding windows, the countries are integrated to the sample as soon as the data are available and the study period is not split into sub-periods.

The descriptive statistics of the database shows that the median and minimum values are relatively stable over time. Contrariwise, the mean and especially the maximum and standard deviation are heterogeneous and characterized by largely higher values during the 1980s (mean and standard deviation) and most of all during the 1990s (mean, median, and standard deviation). The mean and median corresponding to the last sub-period (2000–2015) are close to those of the 1960s and 1970s. These distinctive features of the 1980s and 1990s are largely caused by the dynamics of the series of Mexico, Israel, Brazil, and Russia, whose maximum values, which are atypical during the whole period of study, are especially high during the corresponding decades. Finally, the distributions are highly right skewed over all sub-periods.

10.3.2. *Networks of assets methods*

As regards network methods, the chapter departs from the econophysics literature on financial networks. This literature assesses both flows networks (most often interbank markets) and price networks (most often stock markets). In the case of price networks, the structure is derived from price time series. In particular, the groundbreaking papers of Mantegna (1999), Bonanno *et al.* (2001), and Tumminello *et al.* (2010) present the standard topological graphs derived from assets prices time series, composed of nodes corresponding to the assets of a given portfolio, and edges characterized by weights or distances representing the importance of the relationship between the nodes. The minimal spanning tree (Held and Karp, 1970, 1971) and the corresponding hierarchical tree are shown to provide economically meaningful classifications. In this chapter, these graphs are used as representation of world equity markets networks in historical perspective, which is an original approach since price networks of equity markets are usually assessed with a period of study dating back to the end of the 90s or later.

In addition to network representations, our assessment of Chinese stock markets within the global network is based on the computation and analysis of the statistical properties of the time series of five network indicators (Bastidon *et al.*, 2019, 2020). We provide three indicators of distance (average distance to the nearest neighbors, average path length, eccentricity or maximal path length, which are expected to decrease when integration to world equity markets networks rises) and two indicators of connectivity (degree or number of edges of the nodes i.e. "connectivity at rank 1" and average degree of the nearest neighbors i.e. "connectivity at rank 2" (Soramäki *et al.*, 2007), which are expected to increase when integration to world equity markets networks increases). Distance measures and connectivity indicators are complementary since the former allow to assess the intensity of the integration to world equity markets itself while the later allow to display the corresponding linkages. Finally, all topological indicators can be computed at the individual (nodes) level. It is therefore possible to assess convergence (O'Rourke and Williamson, 1999) both at the global level and within emerging and developing countries ("allocation puzzle," Gourinchas and Jeanne (2013)).

We follow the minimal spanning tree method of Mantegna (1999). This methodology is usually applied to assess the dynamics of individual securities, for example the DJIA and S&P500 in the aforementioned groundbreaking paper. By contrast, we characterize the relationships within a sample of national indices, like in Kumar and Deo (2012) and Sandoval Jr (2012). For each minimal spanning tree, in a first step, we compute the Spearman's correlations matrices of log-differentiated monthly time series of assets prices:

$$\rho_{ij} = \frac{\text{Cov}(p_i, p_j)}{\sigma_{p_i} \cdot \sigma_{p_j}}, \qquad (10.1)$$

where $\text{Cov}(Y_i, Y_j)$ is the covariance of the indices of countries i and j, and σ_{Y_i} and σ_{Y_j} their standard deviations. In a second step the correlations matrix is transformed into a distance matrix:

$$d(i, j) = \sqrt{2(1 - \rho_{i,j})}. \qquad (10.2)$$

This distance measure validates the conditions of an Euclidean metric, which is required to transform the full distance matrix into the sparse minimal spanning tree matrix:

$$d\left(i,j\right) = 0 \text{ if and only if } i = j$$
$$d\left(i,j\right) = d\left(j,i\right)$$
$$d\left(i,j\right) \leq d\left(i,k\right) + d\left(k,j\right).$$

Finally, in a third and last step, we compute the corresponding unique minimal spanning tree corresponding to the distance matrix. The minimal spanning tree is connected (all nodes are connected to the network by at least one edge), cycleless, and of minimum weight among all possible spanning trees. We use the Kruskal's algorithm Kruskal (1956) and the Prim's algorithm Prim (1957) as a double-check. The hierarchical tree of identical branching is computed using the nearest neighbor method.

10.4.   Results: Topological Representations by Decades

In this section, for each decade, the topology of the sample is described on the basis of the minimal spanning tree and hierarchical tree (Figures 10.2–10.6). The two types of representations display complementary information. Minimal spanning trees provide information especially on connectivity and therefore the structure of the network branching. In the hierarchical trees the distances read on the y-axes display in a hierarchical way the distance of a given asset relative to the rest of the sample, sub-groups corresponding

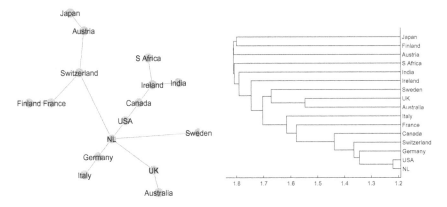

Fig. 10.2.   Minimal spanning tree, hierarchical tree, 1960s.

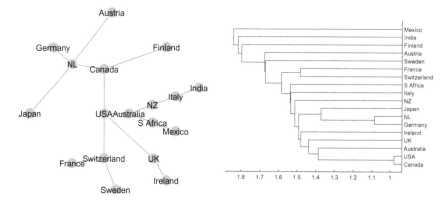

Fig. 10.3.   Minimal spanning tree, hierarchical tree, 1970s.

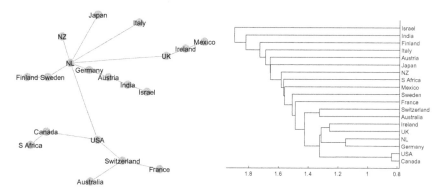

Fig. 10.4.   Minimal spanning tree, hierarchical tree, 1980s.

to selected distance thresholds enabling to characterize clusters of assets. Finally, the distribution of distances within the full distance matrices (Figures 10.7 and 10.8) and the minimal spanning trees (Figure 10.9) are used to assess the sample integration degree by subgroups and as a whole, at each sub-period. The minimal spanning tree and hierarchical tree of the complete sample are used here as benchmark results. We compare China with the remainder of the sample as a whole and by sub-groups over the decades. More precisely, in the discussion, we split the sample between advanced western economies on the one hand, non-Western economies on the other hand, which include both emerging economies and the usual Asia-Pacific sample of the literature on the integration of Chinese stock

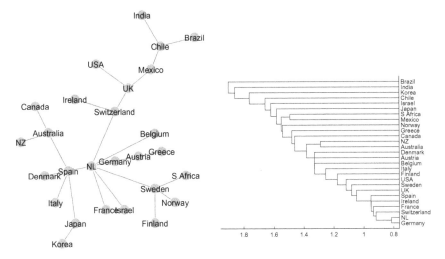

Fig. 10.5. Minimal spanning tree, hierarchical tree, 1990s.

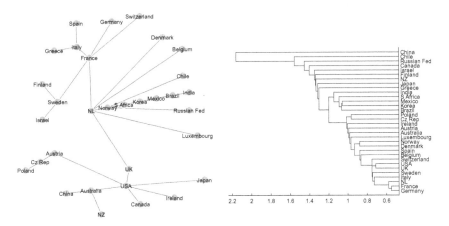

Fig. 10.6. Minimal spanning tree, hierarchical tree, post-2000.

markets. The comparison shows in particular that China does have a higher common component with the Asia-Pacific region than with the main emerging economies.

The topological representations of the 1960s (Figure 10.2) include four non-Western economies (from left to right in the minimal spanning tree: Japan, South Africa, Australia, and India). Within an overall structure organized around one highly connected hub with

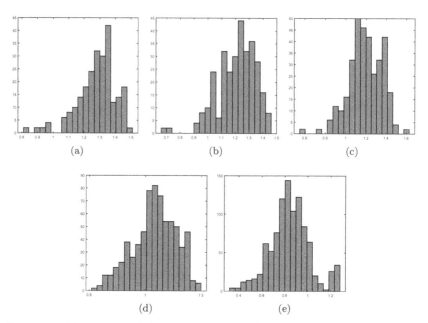

Fig. 10.7. Histograms of distances matrices: (a) 1960s, (b) 1970s, (c) 1980s, (d) 1990s, and (e) post-2000.

five nearest neighbors (NL), these non-Western economies are all located in the periphery of the minimal spanning tree, i.e. in the end of their respective branchings. Globally speaking the hierarchical tree of the 1960s shows a close similarity of the NL and US prices dynamics, but otherwise, a much weaker integration of the rest of the world. With the exception of Australia, which is in the upper-middle part of the hierarchical classification, all other non-Western economies are connected with high distances.

In the 1970s, the sample includes six non-Western economies (Figure 10.3) corresponding to the addition of NZ and Mexico to the previous sub-group. The overall structure of the minimal spanning tree has now two hubs, both connected with four edges (NL, US). As regards the position of non-Western economies within this topology, Japan is still peripheral and apart from the remainder of the sub-group. The five other countries belong to a common branching in the US sub-tree (in the middle right on the figure). In the hierarchical tree, with the exception of India and Mexico which are peripheral in the minimal spanning tree, the non-Western economies

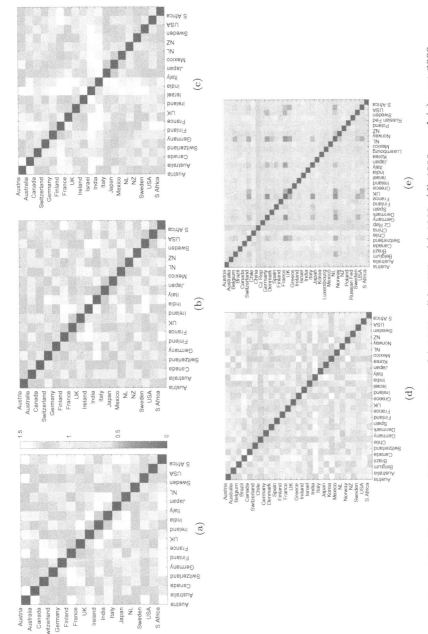

Fig. 10.8. Heatmap of distances matrices: (a) 1960s, (b) 1970s, (c) 1980s, (d) 1990s, and (e) post-2000.

are connected with middle distances. Generally speaking, they are more integrated to world equity markets networks in the 1970s than they were in the 1960s, which likely reflects the large international capital flows in this decade before the beginning of the Volcker policy and the onset of the 1982 crisis.

In the 1980s the sample includes seven non-Western economies with the addition of Israël (Figure 10.4). The minimal spanning tree remains organized around the NL and USA as the main hubs. The connectivity of the NL is enhanced with six edges and that of the US slightly reduced with three edges. All non-Western economies are peripheral, and they are split at the end of the branchings of the minimal spanning tree as in the 1960s. We also notice that the position of non-Western economies in the hierarchical tree is closest from that of the 1960s than that of the 1970s. Australia, in the middle part of the classification, is the most integrated and shows a notable difference with the remainder of the sub-group.

In the 1990s the sample includes nine non-Western economies with the addition of Brazil and Chile (Figure 10.5). The overall structure is organized around NL as the sole main hub. As in the 1970s, a specific sub-tree of non-Western economies appears. It is composed of the three Latin American economies of the sample and India. The other non-Western economies are peripheral and scattered. In the hierarchical tree, they are connected with the highest distances, with the exception of New Zealand and Australia which are in the middle part of the classification.

Finally, in the post-2000, the sample includes 12 non-Western economies, with the addition of China, Korea, and Russia (Figure 10.6). The minimal spanning tree is tripolar, with a first sub-tree of Continental European economies (upper left); a second sub-tree composed of the US, UK, Asia, and Oceania (bottom); and a third and central sub-tree around NL, including a branching of emerging economies (middle). This sub-tree of emerging economies is growing in comparison to the 1990s with seven economies. However, with the exception of Korea which is located there, all the other Asia-Pacific economies are located in the US sub-tree. This sub-tree is less central than the NL sub-tree, and once again with the exception of Australia, they are all at the end of a branching. In particular, China is connected by Australia to the US. In the hierarchical tree, the sub-tree of emerging economies corresponds to a cluster of emerging economies with medium integration (from bottom to top, Brazil to India). With the exception of Australia, the other non-Western economies of the sample show a persistently low integration.

In addition to the structure of world equity markets and hierarchical classification of national indices, the histograms of the distance matrices by sub-periods allow to visualize the distribution of distances within the complete network of which the minimal spanning tree is derived (Figure 10.7). The main finding is that the bulk of distances gradually moves from high values in the 1960s and 1970s to medium values in the 1980s and especially 1990s, and finally low values in the post-2000. This last sub-period is the sole to be characterized by the occurrence of very low distances. China seems apart from this convergence: the secondary peak located on the right side of the distribution corresponds the high distances between China and the remainder of the sample. However, these distances remain inferior to the norm of the 1960s, 1970s, and even 1980s. Even in the 1990s they would have been only slightly superior to the mode. This clearly appears on the distance matrices of Figure 10.8, where China is instantly recognizable in the post-2000, whereas with similar distances it would not have been in the previous decades. This finding is the first intuition that the position of China within world equity markets networks would be atypical only if considering a short time horizon.

The interpretation of path length matrices (Figure 10.9) does not reveal any marked specificity of Chinese equity markets. Indeed, path lengths are the result of both local distances (to the nearest neighbors) and positions within the network. Chinese equity markets are characterized, as seen in Figure 10.8, by the highest local distance measures. However, they are connected to one of the network hubs (the US) through a single intermediary (Australia). The number of steps separating them from the other nodes in the sample is therefore relatively small, which explains why the path lengths characterizing Chinese equity markets are not among the highest. In particular, Brazil or India, which are located in the end of the linear component composed of the emerging markets sub-group (Figure 10.6), have the longest path lengths, being characterized by both high local distances and the highest number of steps vis-à-vis the other countries in the sample.

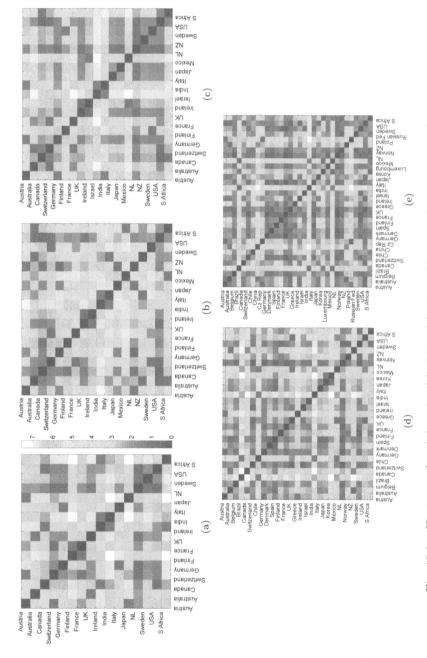

Fig. 10.9.   Heatmap of path lengths: (a) 1960s, (b) 1970s, (c) 1980s, (d) 1990s; and (e) post-2000.

10.5. Results: Time Series of Topological Indicators

10.5.1. *Time series of network indicators analysis*

In addition to these results by decade, we analyze in this section the time series of network indicators obtained by generating minimal spanning trees over 100 data points by sliding windows using the method of (Bastidon *et al.*, 2020). This analysis is a form of robustness test of the previous results as no sub-period sub-division is required here. In addition, the representations of the time series of network indicators allow a comparison of the time dynamics of the economies of the sample. The time series presented are the following: distance to nearest neighbors (Figure 10.10), average path length (Figure 10.11), eccentricity (Figure 10.12), degree of nodes (Figure 10.13), and degree of nearest neighbors (Figure 10.14).

As emphasized previously, the times series of the average distance to the nearest neighbors of China is about 25% superior to the average value at the network level. An additional finding is that it

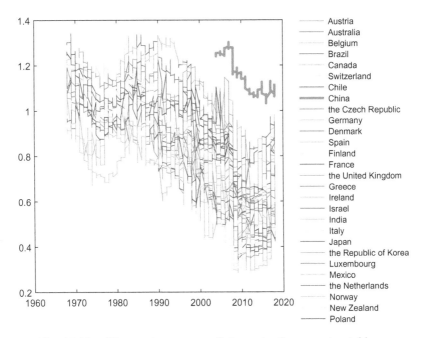

Fig. 10.10.   Time series, average distance to the nearest neighbors.

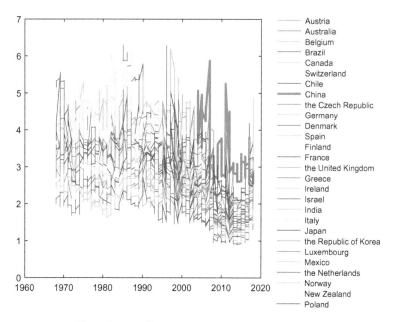

Fig. 10.11.   Time series, average path length.

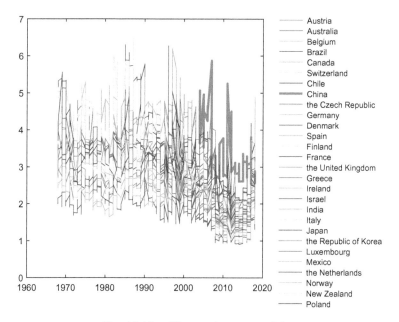

Fig. 10.12.   Time series, eccentricity.

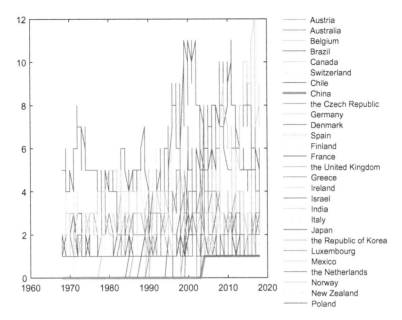

Fig. 10.13.   Time series, degree of the nodes.

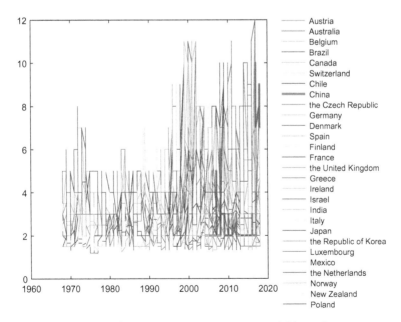

Fig. 10.14.   Time series, average nearest neighbors degree.

only shares the common trend of decrease till the Global Financial Crisis. While a majority of countries in the sample experience a sharp decrease after the beginning of the crisis and then an increase in the beginning of the 2010s, the average distance to the nearest neighbors of China remains stable. In other terms, in the case of China, local distances were relatively isolated from the crisis. However, the continuous decrease experienced previously is interrupted.

The time series of average path lengths show the same recent episode of divergence of China around the crisis (absence of clear path length reduction and increase). With the exception of the very beginning of the period when China is integrated to the sample and this episode of divergence, China is within the range of the least integrated emerging economies. This result confirms both that Chinese equity markets have been relatively isolated from the crisis, especially compared to other emerging economies, and that their global distance measures are not notably atypical. This last finding is reinforced by the study of the time series of eccentricity, i.e. for a given node, the longest possible path within the network. The eccentricity of Chinese equity markets is at the upper bound, but it is not outside the range.

The last two graphs show the time series of connectivity indicators. The degree of the nodes, i.e. the number of nearest neighbors, has the peculiarity of being always equal to one. China is the sole country within the sample in this case, meaning that it is located at the end of a branching and has always one single nearest neighbor. The average nearest neighbors degree, i.e. the average number of nearest neighbors of the nearest neighbors also shows a low connectivity to China. However, the indicator experiences two peaks: one before the Global Financial Crisis and one at the very end of the period of study, corresponding to the occurrence of a direct connection to one of the hubs of the network.

Overall, these results reinforce the results of the previous section: Chinese equity markets remain weakly integrated in terms of local distances (distance to the nearest neighbors) and connectivity at rank 1 (degree of the nodes), but their integration is increasing in terms of global distances (average path length, eccentricity) and connectivity at rank 2 (average degree of nearest neighbors). In other words, they are lowly connected to their network neighborhood, which itself gets increasingly central.

10.5.2.   *Times series indicators distributions in the long run*

Finally, we propose a comparison of the distribution of the same time series of network indicators, using box-whisker plots. This representations enable us to compare the features of Chinese equity markets to the historical features of the remainder of the sample, including advanced Western economies. The comparison reinforces the previous results on the difference between local and global indicators of distance and connectivity.

In detail, as regards local distances and local connectivity, the box-whisker plot of the average distance to the nearest neighbors shows that China is characterized by very atypical features of the distribution (Figure 10.15). In particular, the minimum value, first quartile and median value are all atypically high. The plot of the degree of the nodes confirms the highly peripheral status of China. While the difference between the main hub (the Netherlands), the secondary hubs (the US and France), and the other nodes clearly appears, in the remainder of the sample there is no other country than China whose degree is always 1. Finally, local distances and local connectivity indicate a permanently weak connection of Chinese equity markets to the network by their sole nearest neighbor, even considering historical standards.

As regards global distances and global connectivity, this conclusion has to be qualified. The box-whisker plot of average path lengths shows that China has the highest minimum value and highest first quartile, but some emerging (Chile, South Africa) and even mature economies (Finland, Italy) have higher medians. The same observation is true to a higher extent for the other features of the distribution. The plot of eccentricities also shows that China has the highest minimal value, but the other features of the distribution are within the range of the remainder of the sample. Finally the plot of the average nearest neighbors degree emphasizes that China is among the three nodes with the lowest nearest neighbors connectivity (with Brazil and the Czech Republic) but with outliers at the highest degree corresponding to the very end of the period of study. These results are important because they highlight that, considering the full period of study, the integration of Chinese equity markets characterized by distance and connectivity indicators at the network

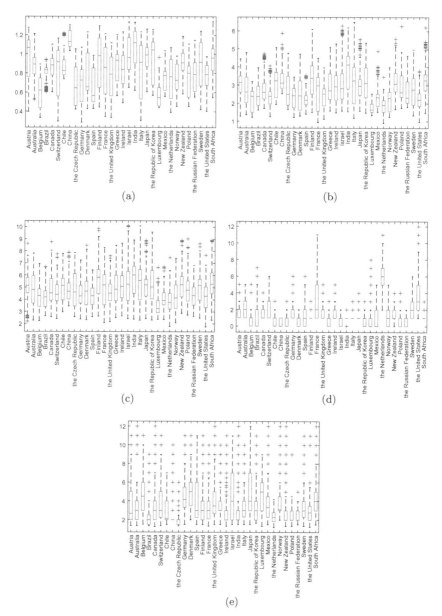

Fig. 10.15. Box-whisker plots: (a) average distance to the nearest neighbors, (b) average path length, (c) eccentricity, (d) degree of the nodes, and (e) average nearest neighbors degree.

level is comparable not only to that of emerging economies but also to that of some mature economies.

10.6. Conclusion

The main lesson of O'Rourke and Williamson (1999) for the first era of globalization is that depending on the countries of the periphery, international capital flows might prove to be either a factor in divergence or a factor in convergence. They conclude that "the failure of international capital flows to act as a systematic force of convergence is not unique to this period (1870–1910) and remains a subject of debate and controversies (for today)" (p. 277). The question we answer in this chapter relates to this context, with a focus on the dynamics of integration of China. As O'Rourke and Williamson (1999) states, "We also had a methodological goal in mind [...] the conditional convergence literature rarely goes beyond cross-country correlations and standard hypothesis testing" (p. 284). We propose a topological analysis of network effects. By exploring the notion of network periphery, we pay particular attention to the issue of the "extensive margins," focusing on one factor market, the capital market, addressed through equity market indices. Assessing notably the convergence of individual network indicators, we provide new insights.

The overall result at the sub-group level of non-Western economies, though it is not exclusively composed of developing economies, is that the Lucas paradox holds true at the global level in the early stages of the period of study, i.e. in the 1960s and 1980s in particular. At that stage all non-Western economies are located in highly peripheral locations and connected to their neighborhood with high distances exclusively. In the late stages an "allocation puzzle" appears within the sub-group. The modalities of this allocation puzzle are our first addition to the literature. Some non-Western economies are peripheral in the sense that they are located in the end of a branching, with no direct connection to the main hub, and with high local distances. Some other belong to the sub-tree which is directly connected to the main hub, with medium local distances. However, they are also peripheral in the sense that their distances to the remainder of the network are the highest since they belong to a local linear component of the network.

China is in the first case. It is integrated to world equity markets networks within the regional area: it is connected to the US by Australia, in the same neighborhood than Japan; and not with the sub-group of emerging economies directly connected to the central hub. China is characterized by atypically high local distances, even in comparison to the other emerging economies, but not with regards historical standards. Moreover, it is not connected to the remainder of the network by the longest path lengths since it is in the close neighborhood of the US. These findings shed new light on the usual results of the literature on the integration of Chinese stock markets, which usually states that they would be lowly integrated.

References

Arrow, K. (1962). "Economic welfare and the allocation of resources for invention," *NBER Chapters*, In: *The Rate and Direction of Inventive Activity: Economic and Social Factors*, pp. 609–626.

Bastidon, C., M. Bordo, A. Parent, and M. Weidenmier (2019). "Towards an Unstable Hook: The Evolution of Stock Market Integration Since 1913," *NBER Working Paper Series*, No. 26166.

Bastidon, C., A. Parent, P. Jensen, P. Abry, and P. Borgnat (2020). "Graph-based Era Segmentation of International Financial Integration," *Physica A: Statistical Mechanics and Its Applications*, 539, 122877.

Bekaert, G. and C. R. Harvey (1998). "Capital flows and the behavior of emerging market equity returns," Tech. rep., *National Bureau of Economic Research*.

Bekaert, G., C. R. Harvey, and R. L. Lumsdaine (2002). "Dating the Integration of World Equity Markets," *Journal of Financial Economics*, 65, 203–247.

Bekaert, G., C. R. Harvey, C. T. Lundblad, and S. Siegel (2011). "What Segments Equity Markets?" *Review of Financial Studies*, 24, 3841–3890.

Bonanno, G., F. Lillo, and R. N. Mantegna (2001). "High-frequency Cross-correlation in a Set of Stocks," *Quantitative Finance*, 1, 96–104.

Cheng, H. and J. L. Glascock (2005). "Dynamic Linkages Between the Greater China Economic Area Stock Markets, Mainland China, Hong-Kong, and Taiwan," *Review of Quantitative Finance and Accounting*, 24, 343–357.

Feldstein, M. S. and C. Y. Horioka (1979). "Domestic savings and international capital flows," *NBER Working Paper Series*, No. 310.

Ford, N. and C. Y. Horioka (2017). "The 'Real' Explanation of the Feldstein-Horioka Puzzle," *Applied Economics Letters*, 24, 95–97.

Girardin, E. and Z. Liu (2007). "The Financial Integration of China: New Evidence on Temporally Aggregated Data for the A-share Market," *China Economic Review*, 18, 354–371.

Gourinchas, P.-O. and O. Jeanne (2013). "Capital Flows to Developing Countries: The Allocation Puzzle," *Review of Economic Studies*, 80, 1484–1515.

Held, M. and R. M. Karp (1970). "The Traveling-salesman Problem and Minimum Spanning Trees," *Operations Research*, 18, 1138–1162.

Held, M. and R. M. Karp (1971). "The Traveling-salesman Problem and Minimum Spanning Trees: Part II," *Mathematical Programming*, 1, 6–25.

Johansen, S. (1988). "Statistical Analysis of Cointegration Vectors," *Journal of Economic Dynamics and Control*, 12, 231–254.

Johansson, A. C. (2010). "China's Financial Market Integration with the World," *Journal of Chinese Economic and Business Studies*, 8, 293–314.

Johansson, A. C. and C. Ljungwall (2009). "Spillover Effects Among the Greater China Stock Markets," *World Development*, 37, 839–851.

Johnson, R. and L. Soenen (2002). "Asian Economic Integration and Stock Market Comovement," *Journal of Financial Research*, 25, 141–157.

Kruskal, J. B. (1956). "On the Shortest Spanning Subtree of a Graph and the Traveling Salesman Problem," *Proceedings of the American Mathematical Society*, 7, 48–50.

Kumar, S. and N. Deo (2012). "Correlation and Network Analysis of Global Financial Indices," *Physical Review E*, 86, 026101.

Lane, Sergio L., P. R. S. (2007). "The International Financial Integration of China and India," *Policy Research Working Papers*, The World Bank.

Lucas, R. E. (1990). "Why Doesn't Capital Flow from Rich to Poor Countries?" *American Economic Review*, 80, 92–96.

Lucas Jr, R. E. (1988). "On the Mechanics of Economic Development," *Journal of Monetary Economics*, 22, 3–42.

Mankiw, N. G., D. Romer, and D. N. Weil (1992). "A Contribution to the Empirics of Economic Growth," *The Quarterly Journal of Economics*, 107, 407–437.

Mantegna, R. N. (1999). "Hierarchical Structure in Financial Markets," *The European Physical Journal B-Condensed Matter and Complex Systems*, 11, 193–197.

Nelsen, R. B. (1999). *An Introduction to Copulas*, Lecture Notes in Statistics. USA: Springer.

Obstfeld, M. and A. M. Taylor (2004). *Global Capital Markets: Integration, Crisis, and Growth*, Cambridge, UK: Cambridge University Press.

O'Rourke, K. H. and J. G. Williamson (1999). *Globalization and History*, Cambridge: MIT Press.

Patton, A. J. (2009). "Copula-based models for financial time series," In *Handbook of Financial Time Series*, Springer, pp. 767–785.

Prasad, E. S., R. G. Rajan, and A. Subramanian (2007). "Foreign Capital and Economic Growth," *NBER Working Paper Series*, No. 13619.

Prim, R. C. (1957). "Shortest Connection Networks and Some Generalizations," *The Bell System Technical Journal*, 36, 1389–1401.

Romer, P. M. (1986). "Increasing Returns and Long-run Growth," *Journal of Political Economy*, 94, 1002–1037.

Romer, P. M. (1989). *What Determines the Rate of Growth and Technological Change?* Vol. 279, Washington DC: World Bank Publications.

Sala-i Martin, X. X. and R. J. Barro (1995). "Technological Diffusion, Convergence, and Growth," Tech. rep., *Center Discussion Paper*.

Sandoval Jr, L. (2012). "Pruning a Minimum Spanning Tree," *Physica A: Statistical Mechanics and its Applications*, 391, 2678–2711.

Sensoy, A. and B. M. Tabak (2014). "Dynamic Spanning Trees in Stock Market Networks: The Case of Asia-Pacific," *Physica A: Statistical Mechanics and its Applications*, 414, 387–402.

Solow, R. M. (1956). "A Contribution to the Theory of Economic Growth," *Quarterly Journal of Economics*, 70, 65–94.

Soramäki, K., M. L. Bech, J. Arnold, R. J. Glass, and W. E. Beyeler (2007). "The Topology of Interbank Payment Flows," *Physica A: Statistical Mechanics and its Applications*, 379, 317–333.

Tian, G. G. (2007). "Are Chinese Stock Markets Increasing Integration with Other Markets in the Greater China Region and Other Major Markets?" *Australian Economic Papers*, 46, 240–253.

Tumminello, M., C. Coronnello, F. Lillo, S. Micciche, and R. N. Mantegna (2007). "Spanning Trees and Bootstrap Reliability Estimation in Correlation-based Networks," *International Journal of Bifurcation and Chaos*, 17, 2319–2329.

Tumminello, M., F. Lillo, and R. N. Mantegna (2010). "Correlation, Hierarchies, and Networks in Financial Markets," *Journal of Economic Behavior and Organization*, 75, 40–58.

Wang, Y. and A. D. Iorio (2007). "Are the China-related Stock Markets Segmented with Both World and Regional Stock Markets?" *Journal of International Financial Markets, Institutions and Money*, 17, 277–290.

Williamson, J. G. (2007). "Global Capital Markets in the Long Run: A Review of Maurice Obstfeld and Alan Taylor's Global Capital Markets," *Journal of Economic Literature*, 45, 400–409.

Yang, R., X. Li, and T. Zhang (2014). "Analysis of Linkage Effects Among Industry Sectors in China's Stock Market Before and After the Financial Crisis," *Physica A: Statistical Mechanics and Its Applications*, 411, 12–20.

Yu, I.-W., K.-P. Fung, and C.-S. Tam (2010). "Assessing Financial Market Integration in Asia Equity Markets," *Journal of Banking and Finance*, 34, 2874–2885.

Index